QUEST FOR EXCITEMENT

QUEST FOR EXCITEMENT

Sport and Leisure in the Civilizing Process

NORBERT ELIAS
AND ERIC DUNNING

Basil Blackwell

Copyright © Norbert Elias and Eric Dunning 1986

First published 1986

Basil Blackwell Ltd
108 Cowley Road, Oxford OX4 1JF, UK

Basil Blackwell Inc.
432 Park Avenue South, Suite 1503,
New York, NY 10016, USA

BRITISH LIBRARY CATALOGUING IN PUBLICATION DATA
Elias, Norbert
    Quest for excitement: sport and leisure in the civilizing process.
    1. Sports——Social aspects
    I. Title   II. Dunning, Eric
    306'.483   GV706.5

ISBN 0-631-14654-7

LIBRARY OF CONGRESS CATALOGING IN PUBLICATION DATA
Elias, Norbert.
    Quest for excitement.
    Bibliography: p.
    Includes index.
    1. Sports——Social aspects——Great Britain——Addresses,
essays, lectures. 2. Leisure——Social aspects——Great Britain——
Addresses, essays, lectures. 3. Soccer——Social aspects——
Great Britain——Addresses, essays, lectures.
I. Dunning, Eric.   II. Title.
GV706.5.E58 1985   306'.483 85-11199

ISBN 0-631-14654-7

Typeset by Katerprint Co. Ltd, Oxford

Printed in Great Britain

For Stephen, Barbara, Richard, Bebe, Judy,
Michael and Rachel

Contents

Acknowledgements

I should like to take this opportunity to record my great debt to Norbert Elias. Without the stimulus and encouragement I received from him – first of all as an undergraduate, later as a postgraduate and junior lecturer – I doubt whether my sociological career would have been attended by the modest success it has enjoyed. Indeed, were it not for my chance encounter with Norbert Elias when I started to read economics at the then University College, Leicester, in 1956 – I had not heard of sociology before embarking on my university studies, and did not know about Elias or the fact that he was teaching at Leicester – I doubt whether I should have embarked on a sociological career at all. The subject then was caught in a largely sterile impasse – characterized theoretically by static forms of functionalism above all, and empirically by equally static and arid forms of empiricism. It certainly would not have interested me any more than economics, a subject which I soon found not to my liking. Elias's lectures, however, and his tutorial supervisions, with their developmental, reality-orientated focus and their stress on the interdependence of theory and observation, sociology and psychology, fascinated me from the outset. I am lucky that chance led me to be taught by one of the greatest sociologists of our time and am privileged to have been able to work with him on the joint essays published in this volume. I only hope that my independent efforts included here will play a part, however small, in helping to bring about the reorientation of sociology for which Elias has been fighting for so long, a reorientation which, among other things, will make the study of sport and leisure more central as sociological concerns than they have been up to now.

I should like to record my thanks as well to a number of my present colleagues, particularly Pat Murphy, John Williams, Ivan Waddington and Tim Newburn. It is a privilege to work with such talented and committed sociologists, and I like to think that, between us, we are playing a small part in continuing and developing 'the Leicester tradition' of sociological teaching and research, the foundations of which were so successfully laid down by Elias in the 1950s and 1960s.

Finally, thanks are due to Eve Burns and Val Pheby for their unfailing charm and unflinching good humour in undertaking the laborious task of typing the present manuscript.

Eric Dunning

such as Weber,[4] the sociology of sport is fairly recent as an area of specialization. Since the early 1960s its growth has been not insubstantial, particularly in the United States, Canada and West Germany. As it exists at present, however, it is largely the creation of physical educationalists, a group of specialists whose work, because of their practical involvement in the area, sometimes lacks, firstly, the degree of detachment that is necessary for fruitful sociological analysis, and secondly, what one might call an 'organic' embeddedness in central sociological concerns. That is, much of what they have written focuses mainly on problems specific to physical education, physical culture and sport, and fails to bring out wider social connections. Moreover, it tends to be empiricist in character.[5] There are some notable exceptions.[6] However, I am sure that most sociologists would agree that much of the work so far produced in the sociology of sport is unlikely to arouse interest outside physical education or to attract the attention of 'mainstream' sociologists.

The reverse side of this coin is the fact that – with the obvious exception of football hooliganism which has attracted the attention of some deviancy theorists and Marxists[7] – few mainstream sociologists have theorized about or carried out research into any aspect of sport. This is the case even when sport appears to play an integral part in the institutions with which a particular group of sociological specialists are concerned, for instance in education.[8] It is probably symptomatic of this overall situation that, whilst the MA thesis submitted by Anthony Giddens to the London School of Economics in 1961 dealt with the sociology of sport, he has since that time – a time in which he has established a reputation as one of the foremost sociological theorists in Britain – signally failed to return to the field of sport or to regard it as a subject worthy of systematic discussion in any of the theoretical treatises which he has written. For him as for others, the values of and the opportunity structure within sociology have dictated work in more conventional areas with the result that the sociological study of sport has, for the most part, been left in the hands of non-sociologists. Again, there have been notable exceptions. Pierre Bourdieu[9] and Gregory P. Stone,[10] for example, have both made useful contributions to the field. Nevertheless, it remains true to say that few mainstream sociologists have yet engaged in systematic research into sport, theorized about or discussed it in their textbooks and other works, or integrated the study of sport into the courses that they teach.

Possible reasons for this sociological neglect of sport are not too difficult to find. David Lockwood's speculations about why 'the concept of race has not played a central role in the development of modern social theory' may provide some clues in this regard. Lockwood contends that 'it was inevitable that race could not emerge as a key concept of sociological explanation' because the development of the sociological tradition 'precluded, from the outset, biological and other forms of non-social reductionism and led instead to attention being concentrated on such basic and universal aspects of social systems as religion and the division of labour . . . '. This tendency was compounded, Lockwood argues, by the fact that 'no racial problem comparable to that of the present day presented itself in the historical situation in which the basic structure of sociological theory took shape.'[11]

Independently of whether or how far it is applicable to the sociological study of race and race relations, this speculative diagnosis does appear, at first sight, to be potentially applicable to the sociological neglect of sport. Thus, like race, sport was not – or, perhaps more properly, it was not perceived by the 'founding fathers' to be – the locus of serious social problems at the time when the basic contours of modern sociology were being formed.[12] Moreover, many would argue that it, too, forms neither a basic nor a universal property of 'social systems'. However, that is even more debatable. Thus, although the structures of such activities and their meanings to the participants vary, no human society has yet existed without some equivalent of modern sports. More significantly, many sports have partly religious roots, and Durkheim's analysis of the 'collective effervescence' generated in the religious rituals of the Australian aborigines could be transferred, *mutatis mutandis*, to the emotion and excitement generated at a modern sports event.[13] Yet, despite such ostensibly uncontentious facts, few attempts have so far been made to integrate the study of sport into the study of either religion[14] or the division of labour.[15] This suggests that the emergence of what have become the basic foci of concern in modern sociology has been a process less free from the influence of what Elias terms 'heteronomous evaluations' than Lockwood's analysis implies.[16] In short, it would appear that, despite the ostensible commitment of the majority to the ideal of 'ethical neutrality' or 'value-freedom' and to the vision of sociology as a science that deals with societies in all their aspects, present-day sociologists reveal their value-commitments among other ways through the fact that the dominant paradigms to which they adhere restrict their field of vision to a comparatively narrow range of social activities. One of the consequences of this has been the neglect of the sociology of sport. Another is the fact that there hardly exists as yet a sociology of war. Furthermore, sociology has tended to be restricted to the 'serious' and 'rational' sides of life with the result that fun, pleasure, play, the emotions and the 'irrational' and 'unconscious' tendencies of men and women are given scant attention in sociological theory and research.[17]

Sport, war and the emotions may seem to be a rag-bag of neglected topics but, if one reflects about it for a moment, one can see that there are, perhaps significant, overlaps between them. Thus, sport and war both involve forms of conflict that are subtly interwoven with forms of interdependence, co-operation, and 'we-group' and 'they-group' formation.[18] Moreover, both can arouse pleasurable as well as painful emotions, and both comprise a complex and variable admixture of rational and irrational behaviour. Also, the existence of diametrically opposed ideologies which stress, on the one hand, that sport might form a substitute for war,[19] and on the other that it is an ideal vehicle for military training in that it enhances the toughness and aggressiveness of those who take part, is further suggestive of the homologous character and perhaps of the interconnectedness of the two spheres. At a higher level of generality, of course, an implication of this discussion is that the value-orientations that inform the dominant paradigms of contemporary sociology have tended to equate 'the social system' with the contemporary nation-state and have led, correspondingly, to a neglect of international relations as a focus for theorizing and research. Let me now speculate about some of the ways in which the heteronomous values that have restricted the field of vision of sociologists may have contributed to the sociological neglect of sport.

III

Implicit in my argument so far is the idea that sociologists have neglected sport principally because few of them have yet detached themselves sufficiently from the dominant values and modes of thinking of Western societies to be able to grasp the social significance of sport, the sociological problems that it poses, or the scope that it offers for exploring areas of social structure and behaviour that are, for the most part, ignored in conventional theories. More particularly, sport appears to have been ignored as an object for sociological reflection and research because it is seen as falling on the negatively valued side of the complex of overlapping dichotomies which are conventionally perceived, such as those between 'work' and 'leisure', 'mind' and 'body', 'seriousness' and 'pleasure', 'economic' and 'non-economic' phenomena. That is, in terms of the pervasive Western tendency towards reductionist and dualistic thinking, sport is perceived to be a trivial, pleasure-oriented leisure activity which engages the body rather than the mind and is of no economic value. As a result, it is not seen as posing sociological problems of comparable significance to those associated with the 'serious' business of economic and political life. Yet, despite its comparative neglect, sport arguably forms an area of con-

siderable social significance which – at least to the extent that sociologists take seriously the claim that theirs is a *comprehensive* science of
society which deals with societies in all their aspects – requires sociological theorizing and research.

There are plenty of pointers to the social significance of sport. For
example, at least in male circles in Western industrial societies, it rivals
sex as a topic of interest and discussion. It is, moreover, nowadays
nearly ubiquitous as a leisure activity in countries all over the world.
Laurence Kitchin has even suggested of one sport, soccer, that it is
'the only global idiom apart from science',[20] and few would doubt the
international importance of events such as the Olympic Games and the
World Cup. They are ripe with opportunities for sociological research.
So, too, is the use of sporting boycotts as a weapon in international
relations. Also deserving of investigation, diachronic as well as syn-
chronic, are such areas as: sport as 'leisure' and sport as 'work';
employment patterns and social mobility patterns in and around sport;
amateurism, professionalism and 'shamateurism' in sport; the relations
between sport and industry; the economics of sport; the commercialization of sport; the role of the state in sport; politics *and* sport; the
politics *of* sport; patterns of administration, organization and control in
international, national and local sports organizations; the relations
between bodies at these different levels of organization; patterns of
control of sports organizations in 'capitalist' and 'socialist' societies,
and patterns of ownership in the former; sport in Third World countries; the mass media and sport; sport and education; sport and class;
sport and race; sport and gender; the ethics of sport; sport and violence; sports crowds and the disorderly behaviour they sometimes
engage in; and many more. Finally, sport can be used as a kind of
'natural laboratory' for the exploration of such properties of social
relations as competition and co-operation, conflict and harmony, which
seem logically and in terms of current values to be mutually exclusive
alternatives, but which, on account of the intrinsic structure of sport,
are clearly revealed in that context to be complexly interdependent.

I have now reached a point where I can summarize the principal
features of Elias's distinctive sociological theory. As will be seen, it is
centrally a theory in which the attempt has successfully been made to
break free from the yoke of heteronomous evaluations and from the
prevailing tendency towards dichotomic, dualistic thinking in order to
increase, by means of what Elias calls 'the detour via detachment', our
understanding of human beings and the societies that they form.[21]
Moreover, as the essays in this volume clearly show, it is a theory which
enables one to appreciate the social significance of sport and which,
among other things, attempts in that connection to lay the foundations

for a sociological theory of the emotions. It also lays stress on the personal and social control of violence, and on the long-term processes that can be observed in that regard. In short, it is a theory which is above all *developmental*. However, before I elaborate on these and related issues, I shall, as I said at the beginning, provide a few biographical details on Elias and locate his theory on the 'sociological map'.

IV

Norbert Elias was born in 1897 and is of German–Jewish descent. He began his sociological career in 1925 in Heidelberg as friend and collaborator of Karl Mannheim, subsequently becoming Mannheim's assistant in the Department of Sociology at the University of Frank-furt.[22] Then as now – although it shared the same building and dealt to some extent with similar problems[23] – the Frankfurt Sociology Depart-ment was separate from Adorno and Horkheimer's better known Institute for Social Research, which was the institutional base of the so-called 'Frankfurt School'. I mention this only to locate the emergence of Elias's developing synthesis in a specific place, at a specific historical-political conjuncture, and at a specific stage in the development of sociology. More particularly, Elias was beginning to develop his theory in Frankfurt just as the Nazis were coming to power. Moreover, he was embarking on this critical and fruitful stage of his sociological career at a specific conjuncture in what Germans call the *Methodenstreit* – the 'fight over method' – that is the ongoing struggle in which various schools have disputed over the years in an attempt to determine whether 'scientific' methods are appropriate for the study of human beings and the societies which they form, and which concepts and methods are most adequate in that connection.

In what follows, I shall focus solely on the sociological properties of the synthesis that Elias is developing. Before I turn to these issues, however, it is perhaps worth noting that Elias is personally a humanist who abhors violence and that his enduring interest in the relations between violence and civilization is not simply 'academic' or 'intellec-tual'. Rather, it stems at least in part from his experiences in Germany in the 1920s and early 1930s, from the fact that his mother died in Auschwitz, and from his exile, first of all in France and later in England. That is, his sociological interest in violence – in all its forms and manifestations – stems from a deep desire to further our under-standing of its social and psychological roots in the hope that such an understanding will help people to arrange their lives – their 'patterns of living together' – in ways that will enable them to avoid the sorts of violent tragedies by which humanity has recurrently been plagued. But let me turn now to a consideration of Elias's synthesis and what it entails.

In a cogent summarizing statement, Johan Goudsblom has rightly observed that Elias 'is concerned with the study of human beings "in the round", and not only with particular aspects of their lives, such as ideas, values and norms, modes of production, or instincts and sentiments and their sublimation.'[24] That is, he gives clear priority to synthesis over analysis and strives to avoid the compartmentalization of people and their societies under such categories as 'economic', 'political' and 'social' – as if 'the economy' and 'the polity' were somehow not part of 'society' – or 'biological', 'psychological' and 'sociological' – as if people could somehow exist without bodies, as if their 'minds' were somehow not physical or biological phenomena, or as if 'societies' could somehow exist independently and apart from the individual men and women who form them. However, in order to achieve his aims, an important part of Elias's work has had to consist of an attempt to resolve the dualisms which have recurrently disrupted sociology and related disciplines, and have formed principal axes of tension in the *Methodenstreit*. I am referring to the tendency conceptually to reduce the study of people and societies to one or another side in a set of partly overlapping dichotomies, a tendency that has led, time and again, to the formation of schools which fight more or less explicitly and directly over such issues as 'materialism' versus 'idealism', 'rationalism' versus 'empiricism', 'naturalism' versus 'anti-naturalism', 'agency' versus 'structure', 'voluntarism' versus 'determinism', and many others.[25] Such schools tend to become firmly committed to different but equally one- (or two-) dimensional views of the multi-dimensional social world, and it is one of Elias's contentions that resolution of the dualisms that underlie them – a task that can be fruitfully undertaken only by means of a constant cross-fertilization of theoretical reasoning and empirical research – is necessary at the present stage of sociological development in order to facilitate further growth. This growth would comprise the development of theories and models which have a better 'fit' with what can be factually observed and will help to combat the tendency towards decomposition and fragmentation into conflicting schools which has been a recurrent tendency in the development of sociology and perhaps also in the other sciences concerned with the study of human beings. The 'Eliasian' synthesis is an attempt to steer the human sciences through the maze represented by these conflicting, one- or two-dimensional – at best partial – problem-solutions. More particularly, the aim is to contribute to the development of a more object-adequate synthesis – a synthesis informed equally by theory and observation – and to a picture of people and the societies which they form which depicts them as they really are and not as they are supposed, according to the diktat of politicians, ideologists, philosophers, theologians or lay people, to be. A related aim is to contribute to the development of a method that is adequate for dealing with the human-social level of natural integration, a method that is not 'scientistic' in the sense that it erroneously imports methods just because they have proved appropriate for the study of other levels of natural integration. In order to achieve these aims, it is above all necessary, according to Elias, to develop a conceptual apparatus and a terminology that are more closely attuned to the dynamic and relational character of human beings and their societies than has so far been achieved. But let me become a little more concrete and discuss one or two aspects of Elias's emerging theory. In the space available here, I shall only be able to discuss one or two small parts of this complex and developing whole.

Take, for example, Elias's position on the 'naturalism/anti-naturalism' dichotomy.[26] Human beings and their societies, he argues, are part of 'nature'. However, 'nature' is not a seamless web but a differentiated and structured whole comprised of a series of emergent levels. These levels are interrelated yet relatively autonomous. They vary, firstly, in terms of the degrees of structuredness of the elements they comprise, and, secondly, in terms of the speed at which these elements and the patterns that they form change and evolve. There are basically three such levels: the inorganic level, the organic level, and the human-social level. They are all amenable to scientific study but the methods appropriate for one are not necessarily appropriate for the others. Thus, the human-social level emerged out of the inorganic and organic levels and, hence, continues to be influenced by processes at those levels (for instance, gravity, birth, growth and death). However, at the same time, it is relatively autonomous and has a number of emergent properties that are unique, for instance, languages, moral codes, states, strikes, kinship, marriage, economies, economic crises, wars, 'pre-sport' forms of agonistic contests, and sports.[27] According to Elias, these unique, emergent properties of the human-social level of natural integration are characterized by regularities of their own which cannot be explained reductively, i.e. in terms of methods, concepts and models derived from the study of phenomena at the inorganic and organic levels.

However, this tends not to be recognized by philosophers. Popper, for example, who is still highly regarded in some sociological circles, argues that only explanations in terms of 'general' or 'universal' laws deserve scientific status.[28] Elias subjects this view to multiple attack, showing that the concept of universal laws emerged at an early stage in the development of science, more specifically when classical physics was only just in the process of disengaging itself from theological and metaphysical conceptions.[29] Just like the latter, the concept of universal laws is, he shows, an attempt to discover something unchanging and eternal behind observable change, but it lacks object-adequacy because, in order to explain any change, reference has to be made to some prior *change* and not to some static, unchanging and eternal 'first cause'. However, recognition of this, according to Elias, is not to claim that the concept of laws lacks object-adequacy in some total sense. On the contrary, law-like explanations are relatively object-adequate regarding loosely structured, slowly evolving phenomena such as gases, but they lack object-adequacy as far as more highly structured, rapidly evolving phenomena such as organisms and societies are concerned. Here, models of structure and/or process have to take precedence over law-like generalizations. Examples are: the double-helix model of DNA; Darwin's theory of evolution; Marx's theory of the capitalist mode of production; and Elias's own theory of the relationship between the civilizing process and state-formation.[30]

According to Elias, one of the basic reasons for the lack of object-adequacy of the concept of universal laws at the human-social level is the relative speed at which the development of societies – a type of phenomenon which is highly structured – takes place. As such, the concept represents a blockage to knowledge *at that level*. A related blockage derives from certain features of language. Thus, we tend to express constant movement or constant change in ways that imply that there exists an isolated object in a state of rest and then add a verb to express the fact that this isolated object moves or changes. For example, we say 'the wind is blowing', as if the wind were actually a thing at rest which, at a given point in time, begins to blow. That is, we speak as if the wind were separate from its blowing, as if a wind could exist which did not blow.[31]

In sociology, the conceptual separation of 'structure' and 'change', 'structure' and 'process', and 'structure' and 'agency' or 'action', are examples of this tendency. Thus we say, for example, that 'the structure of sport in Britain changed between 1850 and 1950', as if this 'structure' were a 'thing' that is somehow separate from the people engaging in sport and from the changes in their modes of sporting practice. Such dichotomic and reifying forms of conceptualization imply that actionless, changeless, non-processual social structures could exist, a notion that flies in the face of what one can factually observe. Elias refers to this tendency as *Zustandsreduktion*, a German term that literally means 'state-reduction', namely the conceptual reduction of observable processes to steady states, though Mennell and Morrissey have translated it, not unreasonably, as 'process-reduction'.[32]

Closely related to this, according to Elias, is the conceptual tendency to separate the 'objects' of thought, including people, from the relationships in which they are involved.[33] Between them, these two conceptual tendencies – 'state-' or 'process-reduction' and the separation of objects from relationships – have unfortunate consequences for sociology. More particularly, they contribute to a doubly inadequate mode of conceptualization, namely to a tendency to conceptualize the 'objects' of sociological thought as on the one hand static, and on the other as separate and apart from the relationships in which they are involved. In order to contribute to a resolution of what he regards as the pervasive tendency to reify and conceptually separate individuals and societies whilst simultaneously reducing both to isolated objects in a state of rest, Elias has coined the related concepts of 'figurations'[34] and *homines aperti* or 'open human beings'.[35] The former refers to a web of interdependent people who are bonded to each other on several levels and in diverse ways. The latter refers to the open, processual, inherently 'other-directed' character of the individuals who comprise these figurations.[36] The two terms do not refer to independently existing objects but denote different though inseparable levels of the human world. Figurations, however, are not just congeries of 'other-directed' individual atoms: the actions of a plurality of interdependent people intermesh to form an interwoven structure with a number of emergent properties such as power ratios, axes of tension, class and stratification systems, sports, wars and economic crises. Since, according to Elias, power is a fundamental property of any figuration, I shall single out his discussion of that issue for special mention. I shall then briefly consider his concept of 'the immanent dynamics of figurations'.

Elias has developed a thoroughgoing relational concept of power which gets away from the pervasive tendency to reify it, to treat it as a 'thing' which some possess in an absolute sense and of which others are absolutely deprived.[37] His concept, moreover, is based on a firm recognition of the polymorphous, many-sided character of power and, as such, can serve as a corrective to the pervasive tendency to reduce it to one or another unidimensional conception, for instance, the Marxist tendency to reduce it to the ownership and control of the means of production, and the construction, on that basis, of a 'law-like' theory. 'Power', as Elias puts it,

> is a structural characteristic . . . of *all* human relationships . . . We depend on others; others depend on us. Insofar as we are more dependent on others than they are on us, they have power over us, whether we have become dependent on them by their use of naked force or by our need to be loved, our need for money, healing, status, a career, or simply for excitement.[38]

As long as one party to a relationship has a function, and hence a value, for another, he or she is not powerless, however great the discrepancy in the power ratio between them may be.

From the discussion so far, one can see that the 'figurational' and 'developmental' theory of Elias is one which rejects the more common *analytical* approach according to which societies are broken down into sets of 'factors', 'variables' or 'spheres', such as the 'political factor', the 'education variable', or the 'economic sphere', and in which the attempt is then made to assess the relative 'causal weights' of these 'factors', 'variables' or 'spheres' in the social process or some aspect of it. What is implied in this, however, is not so much a total rejection of 'factor theorizing' as a call for a shift in the balance in sociology between analysis and synthesis in favour of the latter. That means a greater concern than has been evident in many sociological theories so far for the structural location of particular 'factors' in wider figurations and for the structure of such figurations *per se*. In effect, what is being called for is greater sensitivity to and awareness of the fact that, just as the structure of the DNA molecule as worked out by Crick and Watson is a function not simply of its particular constituents and their quantities, but of their arrangement as a double helix, so the structure of human figurations – for instance their bonding as tribal, city-state or nation-state figurations – is a function not only of quantitative features such as their size or of the particularities of the individual men and women who constitute them, but also of the manner in which their individual constituents are bonded or arranged. Moreover, in social figurations, by contrast with their physico-chemical counterparts, there is a greater tendency for the qualities of constituents to vary as a function of the 'totalities' of which they form part.

It follows from this that one cannot make universal generalizations, for example about the primacy in social dynamics of the 'economic sphere' or the 'mode of production' – at least not universal generalizations of a non-tautological character that go beyond people's need to eat – because the 'economic sphere' and the 'mode of production' are manifestly not the same in all types of social figurations. They differ, for instance in their degrees of separation institutionally from the 'political' and 'religious spheres', that is to say in terms of their relative autonomy. They also differ in terms of the part played in them by express violence and force. But that is less significant for present purposes than the fact that, even though it attacks unidimensional theories, the 'Eliasian' synthesis cannot be held to constitute a form of 'vacuous interactionism', a position that asserts that, in human societies and social processes, 'everything is as important as everything else'. Nothing could be further from the truth since what the Eliasian position actually maintains is that the question of relative importance is an empirical issue and that it has to be defined structurally and relationally, for instance in terms of the strategic significance of particular institutions for controlling valued resources and handling recurrent problems. Since these resources, problems and institutions are in crucial respects developmentally specific, it is impossible to make universal generalizations about them that are meaningful; thus, the state is a strategic institution in industrial societies but in specific types of tribal societies it does not even exist. Furthermore, in industrial societies the struggle to control the state, in particular the twin monopolies of force and taxation, is a key part of the social process, yet, especially since state societies are located in an international network, the state enjoys a degree of autonomy in relation to the economy or mode of production of a society. That is, Elias is critical of the tendency, for example in Marxist theory, to treat particular societies as if they existed on their own and developed solely according to their own endogenous dynamics.[39] In particular, he has shown, taking account of inter-societal relationships leads one to see that human societies form 'attack-and-defence' or 'survival' units and that this forms one of the bases for the emergence of the state.[40]

According to Elias one can say that, together with a struggle for control over industrial, financial and educational institutions – and, in less developed state-societies, over religious institutions too – the struggle for control over the state forms one of the principal ongoing features of the dynamics of all state-societies. This struggle is channelled, as it were, by the 'figurational anatomy' of a society, that is to say, chiefly by: (1) its 'division of labour' or, in Elias's more precise, less economistic terms, the length and structure of its 'interdependency chains';[41] (2) the balance within it between 'centripetal' and 'centrifugal' pressures, namely the degree of effectiveness with which stable, state centralization has occurred; (3) the form taken by the state (whether it is, for example, 'capitalist' or 'socialist') and the degree to which it has penetrated other institutions; (4) whether the society has, for example, a barter or a money economy and, if it has the latter, whether and how far that economy is integrated into an inter-societal framework; and (5) the structurally determined balance of power between its constituent groups. This balance is fundamentally affected by the degree to which interdependency chains facilitate 'functional democratization', namely the exercise of reciprocal controls within and between groups.[42] It is also affected by the degree to which the position of groups within the overall system of interdependencies facilitates communication and organization among their members and gives them access to key institutions and their resources, including access to strategically significant knowledge.

The expression 'the immanent dynamics of figurations' refers to the ongoing process that obtains most of its momentum from such struggles. It is a process channelled by the structure of social figurations but which simultaneously transforms them. In the long term, it has a 'blind' or 'unplanned' character largely because it is the unintended outcome of the manner in which the intentional actions of innumerable unintentionally interdependent groups and individuals interweave.[43] However, though unplanned, it has a determinable structure which, in European societies since the Middle Ages, has taken the form of a 'civilizing process'. The central elements of this civilizing process have been: state-formation, that is to say increasing political and administrative centralization and pacification under state control, a process in which the monopolization by the state of the right to use force and impose taxes has been a key component; a lengthening of interdependency chains; an equalizing change in the balance of power between social classes and other groups, that is to say a process of 'functional democratization'; the elaboration and refinement of manners and social standards; a concomitant increase in the social pressure on people to exercise self-control over sexuality, aggression, over the emotions generally and in more and more fields of social relations; and, at the level of personality, an increase in the importance of conscience ('super-ego') as a regulator of behaviour. Since it has sometimes been interpreted as referring to a simple, unilinear, progressive and irreversible trend, I shall say a word or two about Elias's theory of the civilizing process before bringing this preface to a close with a discussion of the contents of the present volume.

Light is thrown onto the interpretation of Elias's theory of the civilizing process by a concept that he introduced in *What is Sociology?* as a means of determining and measuring the stage of development which a society has reached, that is the concept of what he calls 'the triad of basic controls'. More particularly, the stage of development of a society can be determined, Elias shows:

(1) by the extent of its control chances over extra-human nexuses of events, that is, over what we sometimes refer to rather loosely as 'natural events';
(2) by the extent of its control-chances over inter-human connections, that is, over what we usually refer to as 'social nexuses';
(3) by the extent to which each of its individual members has learned, from childhood onwards, to exercise self-control.[44]

Scientific and technological developments correspond to the first of
these basic controls; the development of social organization to the
second; and the civilizing process to the third. According to Elias, the
three are interdependent both in their development and in their functioning at any given stage. However, he warns against 'the mechanistic
idea that the interdependence of the three types of control is to be
understood in terms of parallel increases in all three'.[45] More particularly, the development of the three types does not occur at the same
rate, and the development of one type can contradict, impede or
threaten developments regarding the others. For example, 'it is highly
characteristic of modern societies', says Elias, 'that the extent of their
control-chances over extra-human natural nexuses is greater and grows
more quickly than that over inter-human social nexuses.'[46] Or, to put it
another way, the development of the 'natural' sciences has proceeded
farther and faster than the development of the 'social' sciences, with
the result that our ability to control extra-human nexuses is greater
than our ability to control societies. A corollary of this is the fact that
the less amenable a sphere of events is to human control, the more
emotional and fantasy-laden people's thinking about it tends to be.
And the more emotional and fantasy-laden their thinking about a
sphere of events, the less capable are they of constructing more object-
adequate models of its connections and hence of controlling it. In short,
they become trapped in a negative feed-back process, or what Elias
calls a 'double-bind figuration'.[47] Indeed, the fact that the so-called
natural sciences have developed more rapidly than the social sciences
has, by accelerating the tempo of technological and social change, and
hence adding to people's uncertainties and fears, actively contributed
to one of the principal 'double-bind figurations' in which we find
ourselves trapped today. It has also contributed to the fears and
tensions that are thus engendered by permitting the construction of
weapons – biological as well as nuclear – which have the potential for
destroying civilization as we know it, and perhaps, via a 'nuclear
winter', of completely destroying life on earth. The existence of such
weapons intensifies the mutual fears and suspicions of the antagonists
in the present-day 'cold war', in that way locking them even more
firmly into a 'double-bind figuration' of mutually escalating fears and
hostilities. And the greater the hostility and suspicion with which they
regard each other, the more they arm themselves, hence reciprocally
increasing their hostilities and suspicions, and so on in an escalating
spiral. The point, of course, is that there is no international 'monopoly
of violence' comparable to those which have had a pacifying, civilizing
effect on social relations within the more advanced nation-states, and
this means that international relations continue in many ways to be

'frozen' at a relatively low level of civilization. That is, as a result of the lack of a stable and effective violence monopoly, international relations, compared with 'domestic' social relations within the more advanced nation-states, are characterized to a far higher degree by uncontrolled tensions. And when, as happens not infrequently, these tensions break out into open warfare, 'de-civilizing' effects with wide ramifications are produced, not only on the direct combatants and their immediate victims, but, as the American experience in Vietnam showed very clearly, on people at home as well.

For present purposes, this brief and necessarily rather abstract summary of the 'figurational' and 'developmental' theory that Elias has developed must suffice. Let me turn now to the essays in the present volume as exemplifications of and additions to this distinctive approach. As will be seen, a central point that is made on several occasions relates to the contrast between the 'controlled tensions' that are to be found in sport and the uncontrolled tensions that are referred to above.

V

'The Quest for Excitement in Leisure' and 'Leisure in the Sparetime Spectrum' are exemplifications of the 'Eliasian' approach to sociological problems in two principal ways. Firstly, because they shed the limitations that are imposed on theorizing about and research into leisure by (1) the traditional 'work-leisure' dichotomy, and by (2) the prevailing tendency to perceive tensions as solely negative, as something that is entirely 'bad'. Secondly, they exemplify such an approach because, in order to lay the foundations for a more adequate theory of leisure, they attempt to escape from the constrictions imposed by the present division of academic labour, and in particular from the tendency towards the compartmentalization of the study of human beings which results from the largely separate and uncoordinated enquiries into this and related problems of sociologists, psychologists and biologists. The problem of leisure, it is argued, can only be adequately approached if such limitations are shed and the human beings involved are studied 'in the round'. That is, the distinctive characteristics and functions of leisure activities of various types can only be understood if they are seen in relation not only to occupational work but also to sparetime routines. Moreover, since their principal function appears to be the arousal of pleasurable forms of excitement, they cannot be properly understood by reference to a sociological approach which ignores their psychological and physiological dimensions. In fact, these two essays lay the foundations for a multidisciplinary – a sociological, psychological and physiological – theory of emotions. They also contribute to the theory of the civilizing process by showing some of the ways in which societies have coped with the routinization that a civilizing process engenders.

Norbert Elias's 'The Genesis of Sport as a Sociological Problem' and 'An Essay on Sport and Violence' also contribute to the theory of the civilizing process in various ways. The former looks at the game-contests of ancient Greece and shows that they were less civilized than modern sports. Given the fact that the ancient Greek city states were not characterized by such relatively firm and stable central (that is, state) control over the means of violence as modern nation-states enjoy, that is what the theory of the civilizing process would lead one to expect. In 'An Essay on Sport and Violence' this theory is subjected to further development by means of an analysis of fox-hunting, a sport which many people today might feel represents a contradiction of the theory. However, by means of a painstaking analysis of primary sources, Elias is able to show that fox-hunting, as it developed in England in the eighteenth century, grew into its then-existing form as part of a civilizing trend. He also sheds new light onto the social preconditions of this trend and onto the development of sport in England more generally. Finally, by elaborating insights originally developed in 'The Quest for Excitement in Leisure' and 'Dynamics of Sport Groups with Special Reference to Football', he sets forth the elements of a more general sociological theory of sport.

'Folk Football in Medieval and Early Modern Britain' presents a fairly comprehensive sociological account of the developmental antecedents of modern soccer and rugby. It, too, is a contribution to the theory of civilizing processes. 'Dynamics of Sport Groups with Special Reference to Football' is a contribution to that theory as well. It develops a critique of the prevailing tendency to see social processes such as co-operation and competition, harmony and conflict, as dichotomous opposites, and conceptualizes sport groups as 'groups in controlled tension' in which a 'tension-balance' has to be struck between the opposites in a 'complex of interdependent polarities'. 'The Dynamics of Modern Sport' seeks to add to this theory of sport but it is principally an attempt to construct a figurational and developmental explanation of the increasing social significance of sport in modern societies and of the increasing tendency for sport in such societies to be characterized by achievement-striving.

'Social Bonding and Violence in Sport' develops a preliminary typology of violence and proposes a figurational explanation for the long-term observable shift in sport in Western countries in the balance between 'affectual' ('expressive') and 'rational' ('instrumental') forms of violence. 'Spectator Violence at Football Matches' (written by Eric Dunning jointly with Patrick Murphy and John Williams) applies an 'Eliasian' perspective to the problem of 'football hooliganism' in Britain. It looks at the problem developmentally and proposes a figurational explanation of the sociogenesis in lower working-class communities of the 'aggressive masculine style' which, it is argued, has come to be regularly associated with soccer in this country. Finally, in 'Sport as a Male Preserve', the outlines of a figurational explanation of the changing balance of power between the sexes is developed and applied to specific observable changes in masculine identity and behaviour which, it is hypothesized, can be centrally traced to the weakening of 'patriarchy' and the growing power of women.

VI

None of the essays in this volume is intended, in any sense, to be the 'final word' on the subject with which it deals. Nor should any of them be seen as such. They all grow out of an emerging synthesis which is attempting to chart a new way forward for sociological theory and research – in general, and not just with respect to the subjects of leisure and sport. It is a manner of approaching the study of sociological problems that will, hopefully, lessen the chances of the divisive and ultimately sterile disputes that have so often characterized sociology in the past. Hopefully, too, it will at the same time increase our chances of focusing on the 'objects' of sociological research, namely human beings and the societies which they form. In that way, to the extent that it measures up to its objectives, it will help to reveal more of the complexities of the real human-social world and be less prone to the unnecessary jargon and sophistry that have all too frequently up to now tended to mar the products of some so-called sociological perspectives.

It would, of course, be absurd to claim that every aspect of Elias's emerging synthesis is new. That is not the case. Particular emphases can be seen elsewhere. Thus, elements similar to a figurational approach – although in both cases more static – can be seen in some of the works of Simmel or, more recently, in some forms of 'network analysis'. Similarly, there is a wider consensus among sociologists nowadays on the need for a synthesis of sociology and history than there was in the 1950s and 1960s when static forms of functionalism and what C. Wright Mills called 'abstracted empiricism' tended to reign supreme.[48] What is new is the *synthesis*, the systematic bringing together into a coherent body of a set of studies that are (1) guided by a central theory – the theory of the civilizing process; (2) simultaneously and equally theoretical and empirical in the sense that they transcend the traditional dichotomy between theory and research, reason and observation; and (3) both figurational and developmental; furthermore, (4), they treat human beings and their societies 'in the round', thus helping to avoid the compartmentalization and fragmentation that tend to result from the present division of academic labour. Hopefully, the essays in the present volume will help to clarify for a greater range of English-speaking sociologists than has hitherto been the case what the 'Eliasian' synthesis claims and what it actually entails. Hopefully, too, they will help to persuade more 'mainstream' sociologists that sport, leisure and their social settings and interconnections are interesting and important subjects for theorizing and research, and in that way help to bring the sociology of leisure and the sociology of sport out of the limbo in which they have tended to exist up until now.

Introduction

Norbert Elias

I

Some parts of this book, as one can see, are the products of collaboration between Eric Dunning and myself. It lasted several years. I greatly enjoyed it. Now that the fruits of that collaboration are, for the first time, collected in one volume, greatly enhanced by Eric Dunning's own work, I should like to help them on their way by explaining and elaborating on some of the central themes of this volume.[1]

When we started on this work, the sociology of sport was still in its infancy. I well remember Eric Dunning discussing with me the question of whether sport, and particularly football, would be considered by the authorities to be a respectable subject of research in the social sciences and, in particular, for an MA thesis. I think we helped a little to make it that.

Sociological enquiries into sport have the task of bringing to light aspects of sport which were not known before or which, if known, were known only vaguely. In such cases, the task is to give knowledge greater certainty. We were very conscious that knowledge about sport was knowledge about society.

Most types of sport embody an element of competition. They are contests involving bodily strength or skills of a non-military type. Rules constraining the contestants are aimed at reducing the risk of physical injury to a minimum. Thus, at the back of these studies of sport, there is always the question: what kind of society is it where more and more people use part of their leisure-time to take part in or to watch these non-violent contests of bodily skill and strength that we call 'sport'? Of course, in some sports there are always grey areas where violence is practised. But in most sport-contests, rules are designed to keep such practices under control. What kind of societies are they, one may ask, where people in great numbers and almost world-wide enjoy, as actors or spectators, physical contests between individual people or teams of people and the tensions, the excitement engendered by these contests under conditions where no blood flows, no serious harm is done to each other by the contestants?

Much research remains to be done before a non-controversial solution of a problem such as this can be discovered. But it has to be said that sociological discovery is the task. The social sciences, and sociology in particular, are in danger of disintegrating into a congeries of seemingly unconnected professional specialisms. I hope it is still possible to find understanding for the fact that the essays presented in this volume contain some modest advances, not only in the knowledge of sport, but in that of human societies as well.

The difficulty which one encounters here, it seems to me, is closely connected with an uncertainty among sociologists about the aim of scientific research. This aim, as far as I can see, is the same in all the sciences. Put simply and cursorily, the aim is to make known something previously unknown to human beings. It is to advance human knowledge, to make it more certain or better fitting and, in somewhat more technical terms, to extend the fund of human symbols to areas not covered by it before. The aim is, as I have said, *discovery*. That simple substantive aim has been greatly obscured by formalistic discussions about the 'method' of scientific research. This shift of emphasis from a discussion of the aim and function of scientific research to that of its method is, in sociological terms, symptomatic of a power struggle. Natural scientists, together with the type of philosophers of science who are deeply committed to the belief in the primacy of law-like natural sciences, have used all their intellectual strength and their social power in order to convince others that the 'method' of the natural sciences, and in particular that of classical physics, is the only legitimate method of scientific discovery. The defenders of this view, as a rule, have very little experience in social science research. Their research strategy is mostly philosophical or orientated towards a 'history of ideas' tradition. It needs to be said, therefore, clearly and unequivocally, that it is possible to advance knowledge and to make discoveries in the field of sociology with methods which can be very different from those of the natural sciences. The discovery, not the method, legitimizes research as scientific.

I will try to use one of my own experiences as an illustrative example. It may help towards a fuller understanding of one of the research results presented in this volume. An investigation lasting several years, now published under the overall title *The Civilizing Process*,[2] showed, to put it very briefly, that the social standard of conduct and sentiment, particularly in some upper-class circles, began to change fairly drastically from the sixteenth century onwards in a particular direction. The ruling of conduct and sentiment became stricter, more differentiated and all-embracing, but also more even, more temperate, banishing excesses of self-castigation as well as of self-indulgence. The change found its expression in a new term launched by Erasmus of Rotterdam and used in many other countries as a symbol of the new refinement of manners, the term 'civility', which later gave rise to the verb 'to civilize'. Further research made it probable that state-formation processes and particularly the subjection of the warrior classes to stricter control, the 'courtization' of nobles in continental countries, had something to do with the change in the code of sentiment and conduct.

As it happened, research into the development of sport showed an overall development of the code of conduct and sentiment in the same direction. If one compares the folk-games played with a ball in the late Middle Ages or even in early modern times with soccer and rugby, the two branches of English football which emerged in the nineteenth century, one can notice an increasing sensitivity with regard to violence. The same direction of change can be seen, for instance, in the development of boxing. Older forms of boxing, a popular way of settling conflicts between males, were not entirely without standardized rules. But the use of bare fists was often supplemented by the use of legs as a weapon. Though not totally unruled, the popular standard of unarmed fighting involving the fists was rather elastic. Like many other bodily contests, fighting with bare knuckles assumed the characteristics of a sport in England where it was first subjected to a tighter set of rules which, *inter alia*, totally eliminated the use of legs as a weapon. The growth of sensitivity showed itself in the introduction of gloves and, as time went on, in the padding of gloves and the introduction of various classes of boxers which ensured greater equality of chances. In fact, it was only in connection with the development of a more differentiated and in some ways tighter set of rules and the greater protection of the contestants against serious injury which followed from it, that a popular form of fighting assumed the characteristics of a 'sport'. These characteristics of boxing as a sport help to explain why the English form of boxing was adopted as a standard form in many other countries, often replacing, as it did in France, traditional indigenous forms of boxing. In the same way and largely for the same reason, other forms of physical contests with the characteristics of sports were exported from England and adopted by other countries, among them horse-racing, tennis, competitive running and some other forms of athletics. The 'sportization' of pastimes, if I may use this expression as shorthand for their transformation in English society into sports and the export of some of them on an almost global scale, is another example of a civilizing spurt.

Without a developmental approach and thus a comparative method, it is difficult to perceive and understand the distinguishing characteristics of 'sports'. To this day they are widely ignored. There is thus room for discovery. Sociologists, I believe, have to discover for themselves which methods of research are best suited to the making of discoveries in their particular field of enquiries. My own experience is that, for reasons into which I need not go here, a developmental approach is indispensable for advances in the study of human society. Philosophically-minded sociologists, or those with a 'history of ideas' approach, will find it difficult to understand that my conviction regarding the usefulness of a developmental approach has taken shape through the practical task of research itself. It is not a philosophical doctrine, not an axiom chosen as a result of personal predilection. It is a theoretical position which formed itself in and through the experience of research itself. It cannot be refuted by philosophical argument without concern for empirical evidence. It can be refuted only by showing with the help of adequate evidence, for instance that civilizing spurts, long-term directional changes in the code of human conduct and sentiment such as those indicated by me, have not taken place.

Moreover, as it happened, another investigation pointed in the same direction. I was asked to write an article about time. I started on it and was carried away by the intriguing problems which a sociological enquiry into time presented. These problems I explored for their own sake and over a considerable period without any awareness that the study of timing, and especially of the long-term development of social timing, would once more provide evidence for long-term changes in the social personality structure in the same direction as those which I had conceptualized as civilizing processes. Although, in retrospect, it seems obvious that the social requirements which give the concept of time its primary meaning have not simply changed in the haphazard manner characteristic of an historical description but have, rather, undergone (though with many ups and downs) long-term changes in a specific direction and with a clearly recognizable order of succession.

The direction of changes in the use of time as a means of orientation both at the social and the physical levels of the universe, and the direction of changes in its use as a means of regulating human conduct, supplemented and confirmed what I had said before about the nature and direction of civilizing processes.[3] To put it in a nutshell, the time-regulation required for life in a relatively undifferentiated and self-ruling community of hunters or agriculturalists comprising two hundred people at the most is different from that of a large industrial community comprising many thousands or even millions of people. All the former need are a few point-like and intermittent time-signals such as the rising of the sun in the morning, the setting of the sun in the evening, or the visible coming of the new moon. Members of the latter require for their orientation and the regulation of their conduct minutely differentiated timing devices. They miss the bus if they are two seconds late! For the life most of them lead, it is not enough to have a public time-piece at a nearby street-corner. Most of them carry a personal watch round their wrist. They live within easy reach of time-meters which regulate their conduct day and night. For them, gone is the time when it was enough for a well-regulated person to listen to hourly chimes from the clock in a nearby church tower.

I have briefly referred to three types of evidence for long-term changes in the social standards of conduct and feeling of the type and in the direction conceptualized here as civilizing processes. Some of the essays in this volume will, I hope, be better understood if one is aware of this wider context to which they belong. Thus, for instance, the essay on the genesis of sport or that on folk football may help to give a broader view on the development and characteristics of sport. But they can also be read as contributions to knowledge of changes in the social habitus of people and of the societies they form with each other. Perhaps I am going too far in suggesting that they, as some others in this volume, can stimulate reflections about the relationship between people perceived as individuals and people perceived as societies, or, in the more traditional but somewhat misleading version, between 'the individual' and 'society'.

The fact that, in the course of the twentieth century, the competitive bodily exertions of people in the highly regulated form that we call 'sport' have come to serve as symbolic representations of a non-violent, non-military form of competition between states, need not make us forget that sport has been in the first instance, and that it remains, a competitive exertion of human beings that excludes as far as possible violent actions which can seriously hurt the competitors. That the self-escalating pressure of inter-state competition in sport often induces participant athletes to do harm to themselves through over-exertion or the use of steroids is a characteristic development of the present age. It is indicative of the growing significance of achievements in sport as a status symbol of nations. But it need not concern us here, except perhaps as the symptom of a long-term trend in the course of which the swing of the pendulum, instead of remaining moderate, sometimes reaches an extreme form. In this case, the social pressure towards self-control in sports activities so as to avoid injuries to others has driven self-control to a level where it does harm to oneself.

What does deserve some discussion in this context is the question of why the civilizing of game-contests and the restraint on violence to others through social rules which require a good deal of individual self-control developed first in England. The relatively quick reception of English models of sport by other countries seems to indicate that a need for more firmly regulated, less violent, yet pleasurable, competitive physical exertions requiring a good deal of sublimatory skill, existed in other countries too. This need was evidently met by the relatively quick and easy adoption by other societies of some, though by no means all, of the various types of English sport and, in some cases, their further development there in accordance with special social conditions. There remains the question of why models of relatively non-violent physical contests developed in England first and were symbolically represented there, with an evident feeling for their novelty and distinctness, by a new, more specialized use of an older concept, the concept of 'sport'. Why did highly regulated contests requiring physical exertion and skill, and characterized in both their performer and spectator forms as 'sport', make their appearance first of all during the eighteenth century among the English upper classes, the landed aristocracy and gentry? '

For, from these early days, the term 'sport' was never confined to participant sport alone: it always included contests undertaken for the enjoyment of spectators, and the principal physical exertion could be that of animals as well as humans. A cricket match might be arranged between the retainers of two landowning gentlemen. But, on occasions, young gentlemen might also take part in the game themselves. In that period, the wealthy landowners of England, noblemen and gentlemen alike, no longer had any great fear of revolt by the agrarian lower classes. The enclosures had all but broken the back of the free English peasantry as a distinct social class. By and large, retainers and other dependants of wealthy squires knew their place. That made the relationship easier. It also explains why, in some cases, the customary rules of folk-games, modified in accordance with the needs of gentlemen, played a part in the development of sports.

In this volume can be found a brief study of one of the pastimes which assumed the characteristics of a sport during the eighteenth century among the English landowning classes: fox-hunting. It was, at the time, considered a sport, and already showed very clearly some of the structural characteristics which distinguished pastimes of the type known as sport from earlier pastimes which lacked these characteristics. As it emerged at the time, English fox-hunting was a highly regulated form of hunting closely associated with a specific code of manners. One may or may not like hunting. But, whether one does or not, fox-hunting provides a vivid picture of an early stage in the development of sport and can thus help towards a better understanding of the genesis and characteristics of sports in general. That is the task of the essay on fox-hunting included in this volume. It may not be easy, given the temper of our time, to study this type of hunting in a matter-of-fact way as a social process just like any other group sport, as a figuration in flux formed by human beings, such as, for example, the ongoing process of a football game. I am not unaware of the difficulties inherent in an approach which requires a fairly high level of detachment, of distancing oneself from one's object, which is not yet very common in sociological studies. But one may find it productive. It opens up vistas obscured by greater involvement.[4] Take, for example, a characteristic shift in the nature of participants' enjoyment which one discovers if one compares the characteristic pattern of English fox-hunting with earlier forms of hunting. In earlier forms, the pleasure of killing, perhaps in combination with that of eating the killed animal, often overshadowed all other aspects of the hunt. Fox-hunting, as I have tried to show, embodied a change in the nature of the enjoyment that was – and is – also characteristic of many other varieties of sport. Thus, if one watches a game of soccer, it is not only the climax, the victory of one's own side, which offers excitement and enjoyment. In fact, if the game itself is uninteresting, even the triumph of victory may be a little disappointing. The same is true if one team is so superior to the other that it scores one goal after another. In that case, the contest itself is too short and does not develop properly: that, too, is disappointing.

Fox-hunting showed the same pattern. The killing of the fox became, to some extent, devalued because foxes did not appear as a dish at the dinner table; although hunted, they were not eaten by human beings. The climax of the hunt, the victory over the fox, became only really enjoyable as the fulfilment of a sufficiently long anticipatory period of hunting. As in the case of soccer, without a fairly extensive and exciting period of forepleasure, the climax of victory lost something of its glamour. Although relatively inconspicuous, this greater emphasis on the enjoyable tension-excitement of the forepleasure, the human attempt to prolong the point-like pleasure of victory in the mock-battle of a sport, was symptomatic of a far-reaching change in the personality structure of human beings. This, in its turn, was closely connected with specific changes in the power structure of society at large.

II

Since the first appearance of the essay on 'The Genesis of Sport as a Sociological Problem' which draws attention to the English origin of sport, I have often been asked for further information which can help to explain this fact. I have given a brief preliminary answer to this question in the essay on fox-hunting included in this volume, and I am using the opportunity offered by this introduction to provide at least a brief outline indicating one of the central aspects of the connection between the development of pastimes with the characteristics of sports and the development of the power structure of English society. One can hardly find a better illustration of one of the main aims of this volume – the aim of showing that studies of sport which are not studies of society are studies out of context. Increasing specialization has contributed to the fact that items such as 'sport' or 'society' appear to assume an identity of their own. There are specialists in the study of sport, specialists in the study of society, specialists in the study of personality and numerous other specialists, each group working as it were in its own ivory tower. Within its own limits, each group no doubt produces important research results but there are many problems which cannot be explored within the confines of a single specialism. The connection between the development of the English power structure in the eighteenth century and the development of pastimes with the characteristics of sports is a good example.

Essentially, the emergence of sport as a form of physical combat of a relatively non-violent type was connected with a relatively rare development in society at large: cycles of violence calmed down and conflicts of interest and belief were resolved in a manner which allowed the two main contenders for governmental power to settle their differences entirely by non-violent means and in accordance with agreed rules that both sides observed.

Cycles of violence are figurations formed by two or more groups, double-bind processes which trap these groups in a position of mutual fear and distrust, each group assuming as a matter of course that its members might be harmed or even killed by another group if the latter had the opportunity and the means to do it. Such a figuration of human groups usually has a strong self-escalating impetus. It may end in a particularly virulent eruption of violence leading to the victory of one side or another. It may find its conclusion in a cumulative weakening or reciprocal destruction of all the participants.

In England, a cycle of violence started, as far as such a cycle can ever be said to have started at a specific date, in 1641, when King Charles I at the head of a group of his courtiers entered the House of Commons to arrest some Members of Parliament who were opposed to his wishes. The MPs were able to escape. But the king's attempt at using violence brought forth violence from the other side. Thus started a revolutionary process in the course of which the king was executed by the Puritans. Their leader, Cromwell, took the king's place and, although after his death the executed king's son was restored to the throne and there were some attempts to temper the hatred, fear and distrust which many members of the upper classes felt for middle- and lower-class Puritans, the cycle of violence rolled on, though in a less virulent and explosive form. The defeated Puritans were not only subjected to legal disabilities but often enough harrassed, persecuted and sometimes violently attacked. Their condition provided a very strong incentive for migration to the American colonies. Those who remained, the English 'dissenters', learned to live in the shadow of their revolutionary past. Although their power-chances had greatly diminished, many members of the landed upper classes continued to consider them as possible plotters of rebellion.

If one tries to discover why the tempering of violence in pastimes, which is one of the distinguishing characteristics of sport, made its appearance first among the English upper classes during the eighteenth century, one cannot avoid looking rather closely at the development of tensions and violence involving these classes in society at large. Once a country has gone through cycles of violence, of which revolutions are examples, it usually takes a long time for the groups involved in such an experience to be able to forget it. Many generations may pass before the antagonistic groups can trust each other sufficiently to live peacefully side by side and to allow, if they are members of one and the same state, a parliamentary regime to function properly. For such a regime makes highly specific demands on those who form it. To comply with these demands is not easy. Yet it is often assumed to be easy. All manner of societies, it is widely believed, can easily adopt and maintain democracy in the sense of a multi-party regime, whatever the level of tensions within them or the capacity of their members to bear tensions. In actual fact, special conditions are needed for such a regime to develop and to perpetuate itself. It is fragile and can only continue to function as long as these conditions exist in society at large. If social tensions approach or reach the threshold of violence, a parliamentary regime is in danger of breaking down. Its functioning, in other words, is dependent on the effectiveness of a country's monopoly of physical violence, on the stability of a society's internal pacification. That stability, however, is to some extent dependent on the personal restraint-level of the human beings who form these societies. This level, furthermore, is not the same for members of all human societies. By

and large, one can say that members of earlier societies have a lower
threshold of violence than members of later societies. But even among
the latter, one can observe considerable differences in the capacity to
tolerate tensions as an aspect of what is often called 'national character'. And since sustained tensions form an integral part of a parliamentary regime with its numerous non-violent battles according to firmly
established rules, the level of tension-tolerance as part of the social
habitus of a people has some bearing on the functioning of such a
regime.

In that respect, a parliamentary regime shows some affinity with
sport-games. This affinity is not accidental. A specific type of leisure
activities, among them hunting, boxing, racing and some ball games,
assumed the characteristics of sport and, in fact, were first called sport,
in England during the eighteenth century, that is, in the same period in
which the ancient estate assemblies, the House of Lords and the House
of Commons, representing small, privileged sections of society, formed
the principal battle-ground where it was determined who should form
the government. Among the chief requirements of a parliamentary
regime as it emerged in England in the course of the eighteenth century
was the readiness of a faction or party in government to hand over
office to its opponents without the use of violence if the rules of the
parliamentary game required it, for instance if an important vote in
Parliament or an election in society at large went against it. This basic
rule had a chance of being observed only as long as the hostility and
hatred of contending groups in the country and of their representatives
in Parliament did not approach or breach the threshold of violence. In
order to hand over peacefully to a group of rivals or enemies
the immense power resources which governmental offices put into the
hands of their occupants, one had to have great confidence in them;
one had to be quite sure that, once in office, one's opponents would not
be vindictive. One had to be absolutely certain that one's rivals or
enemies would not use the resources of government in order to
impeach the former office holders, harrass and use threats against
them, force them into exile, or imprison or kill them.

In the late seventeenth century, some prominent people, such as the
Marquis of Halifax, significantly called 'the trimmer', tried to heal the
wounds, to temper the distrust, fear and hatred left by the Puritan
revolution, especially by the execution of the king, and left also by the
repeated attempts of the Stuarts and their followers to establish in
England a despotic regime akin to that of Louis XIV in France, in
which the influence of the estate assemblies was virtually abolished.
During the early eighteenth century, the great fear and hatred engendered by the violent events of the seventeenth century were still very

much alive. Puritan dissenters were still associated with rebellion and dictatorship, the Stuart kings and their Jacobite followers with attempts at establishing an absolutist and Catholic regime. Between the two extremes stood the balk of the country's most powerful group, the landowners of the United Kingdom, which had come to dominate both Houses of Parliament. But they were divided among themselves. As one would expect in such a case, the Whigs, led by an immensely wealthy aristocracy of fairly recent descent, were more firm in their oppostion, their feelings of antipathy against the Stuart pretenders, and more inclined to be lenient towards Dissenters. The Tories, comprising a larger proportion of untitled gentry families, often much older than the great aristocratic Whig families, but with smaller estates, were more unrelenting in their hostility towards Dissenters while often preserving a sentimental attachment to the Stuart dynasty. However, even they were as fundamentally opposed to the Stuarts' leaning towards absolutism and Catholicism as were the Whigs.

Thus, the principal political division in England during the eight-eenth century was a division between factions of landowning groups, between Whigs and Tories, whose rivalry was not rooted in an antag-onism between different social classes with a different style of life, different social aims and economic interests. That fact, no doubt, played a significant part in the transformation of the traditional English estate assemblies into Houses of Parliament in the current sense of the word and thus in the development of parliamentary government. In many continental countries during the eighteenth century there were strong and open divisions between urban middle classes and the land-owning nobility. In France, an offspring of the former, a class of hereditary office-owners headed by an 'office nobility' (*noblesse de robe*) whose members legally remained commoners, interposed itself between the commercial middle classes and the landowning aristoc-racy. In England, a similar position as an intermediary group between the urban craftsmen, traders and merchants on the one hand and the landed aristocracy on the other, was taken by the gentry. It was a unique social formation, as characteristic of the development and structure of English society as the *noblesse de robe* was of French social structure and development. A class of landowners not belonging to the nobility could not have developed in France or, for that matter, in Germany, because, in those countries, the ownership of landed estates, partly in connection with the feudal tradition which linked the posses-sion of large landholdings to war services for the sovereign, was either reserved for noblemen or carried with it the right to the title and privileges of noble status. In England, that was not the case.

There is no need to account here for the whole concatenation of

circumstances which went into the making of this unique social formation, the English gentry. But without reference to it, one cannot quite
understand the nature of the process of pacification which England
underwent in the course of the eighteenth century and which was
closely bound up with the emergence in England of parliamentary
government as well as of pastimes in the form of sports. The existence
of a class of landowners who did not belong to the peerage and did not
sit in the House of Lords, but who were represented in considerable
numbers in the House of Commons, had important consequences for
the distribution of power-chances in the country. In many of the larger
continental countries, the landed interests were usually represented by
the estate assembly of the nobles, while the assembly of the commons
usually represented the interests of urban groups and sometimes of
peasants. But in England, partly owing to the existence of the gentry,
landed interests were also strongly represented in the House of Commons. Towards the end of the eighteenth century, representatives of
the gentry held two-fifths of the seats in the Commons. Another fifth
was held by the younger sons of aristocratic families or Irish peers who,
legally, had the status of commoners. Landed interests, in other words,
dominated not only the Upper House but the Lower House as well.
The complete disappearance of the English peasantry as a social class
was partly due to the fact that, after Elizabeth I, the power-chances of
the English sovereigns were never quite as great as those of their
continental counterparts. It was also due to the English monarchs'
lesser dependence on an indigenous peasantry as a recruiting ground
for their armies. Continental rulers to some extent protected their
peasantry against the attempt of nobles to appropriate their land by
means of enclosures, though there were exceptions. It is possible that,
in England, the speeding-up of the enclosure movement in the latter
part of the eighteenth century and the new method of doing it by
private Acts of Parliament were symptomatic of the common interest
which the landed classes, Whigs and Tories, noblemen and gentlemen
alike, had in relation to the groups of small landowners who, together
with their families and perhaps a small number of labourers, themselves did a good deal of the work required by the ownership of land.
Enduring manual work was the decisive characteristic which distinguished a landowning peasant from a gentleman farmer. It showed
the high power-ratio of the English landowning upper classes that they
succeeded in annihilating the free English peasantry, in curbing the
power of kings by subjecting them to the control of Parliament, in
subduing the Puritans, and in maintaining a measure of control over the
urban corporations, including those of the capital. That landed
interests, groups of gentlemen and noblemen owning landed estates,

controlled not only the House of Lords but also the House of Commons, must be regarded as a major factor in the dominant position which the landed classes held in the country during the greater part of the eighteenth and early nineteenth centuries. As it was among them that the transformation of earlier pastimes into pastimes with the characteristics of sport took place, that fact is of some relevance in this context. It can be said that the emergence of sport in England during the eighteenth century formed part and parcel of the pacification of the English upper classes.

The same can be said of the transformation of the traditional English estate assemblies,[5] which in many respects resembled traditional estate assemblies elsewhere, into a two-tier parliament in the modern sense of the word and thus into an integral part of parliamentary government as such, which, at the time, hardly had any parallels elsewhere. The growth of this form of government, too, was closely connected with the strong position of the landed classes in England. There were many divisions among them. The most obvious were the differences of rank and property. Great landowners, mostly dukes and earls, might each own more than 10,000 and perhaps as many as 20,000 acres from which they enjoyed an income larger than that of many of the smaller sovereign rulers on the continent and vastly more than that of the richest English merchants. At the other end of the scale, country squires might own 1,000 acres or less and live in genteel poverty. But they were united, not only by their common interests as independent landlords, but also by the social conventions of landed society, by a cultural tradition of their own which distinguished the landed classes, nobility and gentry alike, from other social classes whose male members were not considered, in terms of their social rank as well as their manners, to be 'gentlemen'.

This basic unity of the landed classes was certainly one of the conditions which made it possible that, in England during the eighteenth century, in spite of strong divisions within these classes of which those between Whigs and Tories were the most consequential, the high tensions of the seventeenth century characteristic of a period of revolutionary upheavals with its heritage of hatred and fear, gradually calmed down. Hostile factions united by a 'gentlemanly' code of sentiment and conduct learned to trust each other sufficiently for the emergence of a non-violent type of contest in Parliament. In the course of the eighteenth century, the two main factions of England's landowning classes changed their character as well as their function. Both Whigs and Tories contained members from the aristocracy and the gentry. It would be false to attribute this division of the landed classes into social factions simply to a division in terms of their rank and property. But it is probably right to say that, traditionally, aristocrats had a dominant position among the Whigs, while gentlemen who did not belong to the peerage, though they may have been knights or baronets, predominated among the Tories.

In the course of the eighteenth century, some of the issues which had originally divided them lost their former significance or faded from sight altogether. As time went on, it became obvious that the Stuarts would never come back. The Hanoverians had come to stay. Dissenters obviously had no chance and no intention of overthrowing the government by force. Gradually, the two principal hereditary factions of the upper classes came to legitimize and identify themselves as representatives of different political principles or philosophies, the predecessors of party programmes. In the name of these principles, the two factions competed with each other in Parliament for access to governmental office and, during election time, in the country at large. They competed with each other according to agreed rules and the demands of a gentlemanly code of sentiment and conduct which Whigs and Tories shared. At this stage, observance of the parliamentary and the gentlemanly codes were closely connected with each other.

Familiarity can obscure for the perception of later generations the fact that non-violent competitive struggle between two essentially hostile groups for the right to form a government was something rather new at the time. One encounters here a fairly common aspect of social development which is frequently misunderstood. Human beings may be driven, often by coincidental circumstances, into new institutional or organizational arrangements which, if they work well, soon appear to the participants as so obvious that they consider them to be 'natural', 'normal', or simply 'rational'. It was in this manner that the ruling groups of England during the eighteenth century were moving towards something quite novel, a parliamentary type of government, without quite noticing its novelty.

During the first quarter of the eighteenth century, up until about 1722 when Robert Walpole gained control of the government, tensions in England remained very high. The deep resentment and distrust between hostile sections of English society, the heritage of the seventeenth-century turbulence, were still very much alive. The heirs of the Puritan revolution, the Dissenters, although hardly any longer an active political force, still carried with them the stigma of their revolutionary past. Tory gentlemen firmly believed that the Dissenters were once more planning the violent overthrow of the monarchy and the government. For their part, the Tories were not quite able to live down their association with the Stuart dynasty and with plots, real or imagined, to bring a Stuart back to the throne by force. In the early eighteenth century, changes of government from Whigs to Tories or from Tories to Whigs still aroused the fear that a government in power would be grossly vindictive towards its opponents. Neither side could be sure that the other side, once in power, would not harrass them, throw them into prison or, under some pretext, put them to death. Thus, when Queen Anne appointed a Tory government, its members behaved with great vindictiveness towards their Whig predecessors. They tried to humiliate the leading Whigs as best they could. After the Queen's death, an election brought the Whigs back to power. Now they, on their part, set out to harrass and humiliate their Tory enemies. As a result, the leading Tories fled to the continent, joined the Stuart pretender and started plotting the invasion of England and the overthrow of the Whig government by force.

Robert Walpole, who came to power in 1722, began to steer the boat away from violence. He possessed in considerable measure the diplomatic and manipulating skills needed by the leader of a parliamentary government and gave a strong impetus to the development in that direction. But he was still able, on occasion, to treat a Tory opponent quite roughly. Before coming to power, he and his friends managed to drive a Tory leader into exile by accusing him of participation in a Stuart plot. Yet about half a century later, a Speaker of the House of Commons admonished the members that the object of debates should not be to stress differences but to produce agreed decisions as a guide for ministerial policy.[6] Later still, Burke justified the existence of different parties by the need for a regular opposition. He even suggested that one might organize opposition to the existing government so that there was always an alternative government in sight.

In less than one hundred years, two factions of the upper classes, Whigs and Tories, who, in a violent age, had often treated each other roughly and sometimes violently, had transformed themselves into upper-class parties relying on a relatively small electorate of privileged groups and fighting each other by means which may not have excluded the selling of votes and bribery but which were almost entirely nonviolent. It was a telling example of a civilizing spurt. The pacification of the upper classes and, in fact, of a large section of English society, played a part in it. So did the growing prosperity of the landed upper classes.

The manifestations of this spurt are easy to recognize. The peaceful handing over of government to an opponent presupposed a high level of self-restraint. So did the willingness on the part of a new government not to use its great power resources for the humiliation or destruction of hostile or oppositional predecessors. In that respect, the emergence in England during the eighteenth century of parliamentary government with a rather smooth rotation of rival groups according to agreed rules can serve as an object lesson. It was one of the rather rare examples of a cycle of violence, of a double-bind process tying two or more human groups in a condition of reciprocal fear of each other's violence, which resolved itself in a condition of compromise without absolute victors and absolute vanquished. As both sides gradually lost their distrust of each other and gave up relying on violence and the skills connected with it, they learned instead, and in fact they developed, the new skills and strategies required by a non-violent type of contest. Military skills gave way to the verbal skills of debate, of rhetoric and persuasion, all of which required greater restraint all round and identified this change very clearly as a civilizing spurt. It was this change, the greater sensitivity with regard to the use of violence which, reflected in the social habitus of individuals, also found expression in the development of their pastimes. The 'parliamentarization' of the landed classes of England had its counterpart in the 'sportization' of their pastimes.[7]

Like the latter, the former had economic aspects. Growing commercialization contributed to the prosperity of the wealthier and, more modestly, of the smaller landowners. That, too, helped to moderate factional passions among them. But it is a mistake to consider economic aspects of development in isolation. It is very doubtful whether the landowning upper classes of England could have made use of the economic opportunities which commerce offered them if the power struggle with their king had taken a different turn, if they, like their French counterparts, had become subject to the rule of absolute kings and their ministers instead of rising to a position of parity and, indeed, superiority in relation to king and court as a more or less self-ruling oligarchy. The emergence of parliamentary government, part of the state-formation process of England,[8] and, in particular, the shift in the balance of power between king and landed upper classes, played an active and not merely a dependent part in the development of English society. If one raises the question of why pastimes in the form of sports developed in England, one cannot omit to say that the development of parliamentary government, and thus of a more or less self-ruling aristocracy and gentry, played a decisive part in the development of sport.

A few words may be interposed about the task I have set myself in this part of my introduction. I have pointed to the problem posed by the English origin of sport. Neither praise nor reproach is intended by raising such a problem. Tracing the origins and development of the seemingly self-evident institutions among which one lives is an exciting and rewarding task in its own right. But it cannot be done with a short breath or a narrow horizon; that is, it cannot be done if one considers sport, in the manner of some specialists, as if it were a social institution of our age which has come into being and exists entirely on its own, independently of other aspects of the developing societies which human beings form with each other. Sport is an enterprise of human beings, and many of the human enterprises which are academically explored as different objects of study and thus as if they existed in different compartments are, in fact, enterprises of the same human beings. The same people who, as political beings, elect or sit as Members of Parliament, may also earn their livings by work as economic beings, pray together with others as religious beings, or go sailing and skiing as sportsmen and sportswomen in their leisure time. Hence, if one has ascertained that, in the course of the eighteenth century, the concept of sport came to be associated as a kind of distinguishing mark with pastimes of the English upper classes, one cannot limit one's enquiries to sport in isolation. One has to consider the fortunes, the development, and particularly the changes in personality structure, in the sensitivity with regard to violence, of the human beings who formed these classes. If one then discovers that, in England during the eighteenth century, the fortunes of the upper classes resulted in a pronounced spurt in their long process of pacification, one may well feel that one is on the right track.

However, to gain greater certainty in such matters, it is always of help if one uses comparisons. One may see the characteristics of the English development in better perspective if one looks at a comparable development in France. I have indicated elsewhere the part which the king's court played in France as a civilizing agency.[9] I have spoken, by way of abbreviation, of the pacification of the warriors. A powerful class of landowning warrior nobles, fairly independent masters of large estates, changed into a class of courtiers and military officers wholly dependent on the king, or into country nobles stripped of almost all their former military functions. This transformation played a central part in the pacification and civilization of French society. The principal civilizing agency of the French upper classes, particularly in the seventeenth century, was the king's court. It was there that the character of a civilizing process as a spurt, not simply towards greater restraint, but also towards a more differentiated, sublimatory pattern of conduct and sentiment, showed itself to the full. Learning the highly specific skills of a courtier, acquiring a courtier's social habitus, was an indispensable condition of social survival and success in the contests of court life. It demanded a characteristic patterning of the whole person, of movement no less than of outlook and sentiment, in accordance with models and standards which marked off courtiers from the people of other groups. The evidence found in the sources of that age shows very clearly in what ways and at what time the standards and thus people's feelings of, for example, shame or revulsion, changed, first in court society, and then also in a wider circle, in the direction characteristic of a civilizing spurt. In France, it was the turbulence of the sixteenth century that was followed, in the seventeenth, by a period of internal pacification. In this case, a cycle of violence was brought to an end by a series of victories which revealed the unequivocal superiority of the power resources of kings and their representatives in comparison with those of both the landed upper classes and the urban middle classes. That was the reason why, in seventeenth-century France, the king's court became a major, and perhaps the most powerful, civilizing agency.

As one may see, the contrast with the development and characteristics of the English landowning classes could hardly be greater. The consequences of these differences between the fortunes and characteristics of the highest-ranking classes of eighteenth-century England and seventeenth-century France make themselves felt to this day in differences between the French and English languages, and between the social habitus, sometimes called 'national character', of English- and French-speaking peoples.

Just as the pacifying and civilizing spurt of the seventeenth century in France was not the beginning of a process in that direction, so, in England, the comparable spurt of the eighteenth century was only one of several spurts of this kind, though perhaps the most decisive. Henry VIII's successful efforts to tame his barons were a step in that direction. The powerful court life at the time of Queen Elizabeth I and King James I had a similar function. But in the eighteenth century, the long-drawn-out struggle between, on the one hand, monarchs and their representatives, and on the other, the landed upper classes and the urban middle classes, resulted in a condition in which the landed upper classes, nobility and gentry, had gained parity if not supremacy in relation to king and court. Their dominant position in both Houses of Parliament and in every government also gave them a superior position in relation to the urban middle classes. The superiority of their power resources was not, however, great enough for them to disregard the interests of king and court or those of the urban corporations. Maintaining control of the country without the current of violent upheavals, of which many people had probably grown tired, required a careful weighing of their own interests in relation to those of other groups, and a readiness for compromise. The parliamentary regime developed during the eighteenth century in response to a balance of power of this kind, a balance of power which ensured that the kings of England, unlike those of France, would never transform their upper classes into courtiers or ride rough-shod over their interests. But the power resources of the monarch were, in the eighteenth century, still very considerable and they remained so for some time to come. Ministers had carefully to nurse the king's goodwill as well as that of persons influential at the court. On the other hand, the kings of England in the eighteenth century were no longer powerful enough to ensure that their court was the lynch-pin of the country's affairs, the centre from which the country was governed, where all decisions were taken, even in matters of good taste. Most of these functions had shifted to the palatial houses of great nobles and, above all, to Parliament. The transformation of the traditional estate assemblies of England into Houses of Parliament in the modern sense of the word denoted not only an institutional change, but also a change in the personality structure of the English upper classes. The unplanned development which enabled the landed upper classes of England to defeat all attempts to establish an autocratic regime, whether from below or from above, from Puritans or kings, offered a strong inducement to the groups who emerged from these struggles virtually as the ruling classes to defuse the cycle of violence, to temper their factional quarrels and to learn instead how to fight each other by non-violent means alone in accordance with mutually agreed rules. That was one of the great differences between the development of the French and the English upper classes. In France, the supremacy of the king, the autocratic manner of ruling, did not normally allow dissension and struggles between factions to come into the open. In England, the parliamentary regime not only allowed open contests between rival factions but made it *necessary* that they should come into the open. Social survival and most certainly social success in a parliamentary society depended on a capacity to fight, but to fight, not with dagger or sword, but with the power of argument, the skill of persuasion, the art of compromise. However strong the temptation in electioneering battles or parliamentary contests, gentlemen were supposed never to lose their temper unintentionally and never to resort to violence among equals except in the regulated form of a duel. One can see at once the affinity between parliamentary contests and sports contests. The latter, too, were competitive struggles where gentlemen refrained from using violence or, in the case of spectator sports such as horse-racing or boxing, tried to eliminate or to temper violence as far as possible.

There are other aspects of sport which one can perceive more clearly if one compares English and French developments. In France, a state-formation process which enshrined in the country's institutions the victory of kings over nobles and commoners resulted, as I have mentioned before, in a sharp division between court nobility and country nobility. The latter had a markedly lower status than the former because they lacked access to the seats of power, to the centres of refinement. In England, a different balance of power between kings and the landed classes resulted in a tradition which, already in the seventeenth century, established, at least among the wealthier sections of the aristocracy and gentry, close links between country life and court life, and, in the eighteenth century, between country life and the social life of the wealthier landed families in London when Parliament was sitting. The institution linking rural and urban life was 'the London Season'. All country families who could afford it, went during the Season to London, lived there a few months in their town houses, enjoying the pleasures of city life – the gambling, the debates and the Society gossip. In this manner, the way of life of the landed aristocracy and gentry, or at least of their wealthier sections, linked city life to country life, and thus may help to explain why, in the eighteenth century, outdoor pastimes such as cricket which joined rural customs and upper-class manners, as well as urban performer-contests such as boxing which adapted lower-class custom to upper-class pleasure, underwent the characteristic transformation into sports. This tradition persisted even when the formative influence of the landed classes on the development of sport was over and had passed into the hands of urban industrial classes.

One other aspect of what is usually called 'political development' had a bearing on the development of sport and deserves to be mentioned here. Again, it stands out more clearly if one compares English with French development. In France, as in many other autocratic monarchies, the subjects' right to form associations of their own choosing was usually restricted as a matter of course if not abolished. In England, gentlemen assembled as they liked. One of the manifestations of the right of gentlemen to assemble freely was the institution of 'clubs'. Significantly enough, that term was adopted by French revolutionaries when they, too, were able to claim the right to free association. The French tradition of autocratic rule had produced neither procedural precedent nor a specific concept for this kind of association.

In the development of sport, the formation of clubs established by people interested as spectators or performers in one or another of its varieties played a crucial part. At the pre-sport level, pastimes such as hunting and a variety of ball games were regulated in accordance with local traditions which often varied from one locality to another. Perhaps some of the older villagers, perhaps a local patron, saw to it that the traditional customs were observed by the younger generation; perhaps no one did.

One of the distinguishing characteristics of the emergent pastimes with the character of sports was that they were regulated above the local level by means of one of those free associations of gentlemen to which I have just referred, by means of clubs. The early development of cricket is a characteristic example. When it became customary to organize game-contests above the local level because cricket teams were travelling from one place to another, it was necessary to ensure uniformity of the game. Perhaps first within a county, therefore, gentlemen formed a country club whose members agreed on the unification of local traditions. Agreement on rules at this higher level of integration and, if they were found to be not wholly satisfactory, agreement on changes in them, was a major condition for the development of a traditional pastime into a sport. Agreement on a framework of rules and of the social customs associated with the game usually went hand in hand with the development of a supervisory body who saw to it that the rules were observed and who provided umpires for matches if they were required. It was the first step on the road towards a development which today is usually taken for granted, and as a result, proper concepts are lacking. The varieties of sport, one might say, began to assume a character of their own which impressed itself upon the people who played them. At the level of traditional local outdoor contests without hard and fast rules, the game and the players were still largely identical. An impromptu move, the whim of a player which pleased the others might alter the traditional pattern of the game. The higher organizational level of a regulating and supervising club endowed the game with a measure of autonomy in relation to the players. And that autonomy grew as supervisory agencies at a higher level of integration took over the effective control of the game, as when, for instance, a London club, the MCC, took over effective control of cricket from country clubs. One need not go further. It would not be difficult to show whether and when the development of an English sport reached the level of several local clubs, of a national association coordinating all local clubs, and in some cases, the development of several national associations with an international association coordinating them.

This brief glance at organizational developments may help to bring into better focus the aspect of sport to which I have just referred. Every variety of sport, one might say, has a physiognomy of its own. It attracts people with specific personality characteristics. It is able to do that because it has a relative autonomy in relation not only to the individuals who play it at a given time, but also to the society where it developed. That is the reason why some sports which first developed in England could be transferred to and adopted by other societies as their own. The recognition of this fact opens up a wide field for further investigation. Why, for instance, were some initially English varieties of sport such as Association Football and tennis taken up by many different societies all over the world while the spread of cricket was mainly confined to an exclusive circle of Commonwealth countries? Why did the rugby variety of football not spread as widely as the Association variety? Why did the USA, without abandoning the English varieties completely, develop its own variety of football?

Understanding the relative autonomy of a sport can contribute to a better understanding of the task of sociogenetic and psychogenetic observations such as these. It has been widely assumed that sociological enquiries necessarily have a reductionist character. The demonstration that some aspects of society such as science or art could be explained in terms of some others, for instance, in terms of economic aspects, seemed to exhaust the programme of sociologists. What I have briefly indicated here is a wider programme for sociology. I have tried to show the concatenation of events, or at least some of its aspects, which, in England, contributed to the making of sport. In terms of the latter, many of these events were coincidental. Hence, if one tries to give an idea of some of the reasons why sport developed in England, as I have done here, one presents the picture of a development, of a sequential order of steps in a particular direction; but, as I have said before, while one can show that the later step, in this case sport, was preceded by a succession of specific earlier steps as its necessary condition, one could hardly say that, from the succession of earlier events, the later event was *bound* to emerge.[10] Also, the connection between what are often called different spheres of social development, in this case, for instance, between a parliamentary upper-class regime and upper-class pastimes in the form of sports, does not have the character of a *causal* connection. It was simply that the same class of people who participated in the pacification and greater regularization of factional contests in Parliament were instrumental in the greater pacification and regularization of their pastimes. One can hardly say in that case that the parliamentarization of England's ancient House of Lords and House of Commons was the cause of which sport was the effect. Sport and Parliament as they emerged in the eighteenth century were both characteristic of the same change in the power structure of England and in the social habitus of that class of people which emerged from the antecedent struggles as the ruling group.

III

It has sometimes been said that sport in highly industrialized societies has a complementary function – that it provides physical exercise for a population with many sedentary occupations and hence with insufficient opportunities for physical exertion. That may be one aspect of the complementarity but there is another which has attracted less attention, even though, in terms of its function for human beings, it may not be of lesser significance. Its discovery, I believe, brings to light aspects of sport and other leisure-time occupations which have been somewhat neglected.

In the comparatively advanced societies of our age, many occupational, many private relationships and activities give satisfaction only if all the people concerned are able to maintain a fairly even and stable control over their more spontaneous libidinal, affective and emotional impulses as well as over their fluctuating moods. Social survival and success in these societies depend, in other words, to some extent on a reliable armour, not too strong and not too weak, of individual self-restraint. In such societies, there is only a comparatively limited scope for the show of strong feelings, of strong antipathies towards and dislike of people, let alone of hot anger, wild hatred or the urge to hit someone over the head. People strongly agitated, in the grip of feelings they cannot control, are cases for hospital or prison. Conditions of high excitement are regarded as abnormal in a person, as a dangerous prelude to violence in a crowd. However, to contain strong feelings, to preserve an even control of drives, affects and emotions steadily thoughout one's life is likely to raise tensions in a person.

Some people are lucky. They have the good fortune to find it easy to transform and canalize their drives and their feelings into activities that are fruitful for others as well as satisfying for themselves. In other cases, however, people find it very difficult, if not impossible, to reconcile the demands of a life together with others which requires an even and well tempered restraint and of its individual representatives, the agencies of self-restraint known by such names as 'conscience' or 'reason', with the demands for satisfaction of their instinctual, affective and emotional impulses. In such cases, these two sets of demands – or some of them – remain permanently in conflict with each other. By and large, in societies where fairly high civilizing standards all round are safeguarded and maintained by a highly effective state-internal control of physical violence, personal tensions of people resulting from conflicts of this kind, in a word, stress-tensions, are widespread.

Most human societies, as far as one can see, develop some counter-measures against stress-tensions they themselves generate. In the case of societies at a relatively late level of civilization, that is with relatively stable, even and temperate restraints all round and with strong sublimatory demands, one can usually observe a considerable variety of leisure activities with that function, of which sport is one. But in order to fulfil the function of providing release of stress tensions, these activities must conform to the comparative sensitivity to physical violence which is characteristic of people's social habitus at the later stages of a civilizing process. If one compares contemporary leisure activities with those of former ages, one can see easily enough that only those have survived which could be adapted in accordance with a normally rather strong repugnance against humans inflicting physical injuries on each other. Contests between gladiators or between human beings and wild animals, for centuries an enjoyable pastime of urban populations in the Roman Empire, and medieval amusements such as cat burning, public hangings or cock-fights would probably produce little enjoyment for contemporary audiences and might be felt by some of them as intolerably horrible.

The range of leisure activities in the more differentiated societies of our age is very wide; differences between them are great. Yet most of them have basic structural characteristics in common. And these common characteristics point to the function they fulfil as leisure activities in societies of a highly differentiated and complex type. While the routines of life in these societies, public or private, demand that people keep a fairly firm hold on their moods and drives, their affects and emotions, leisure occupations as a rule allow them to flow more freely in an imaginary setting specially created by these activities and in some ways reminiscent of non-leisure reality. While in the case of the latter the scope for manifestations of feeling is narrowed or confined to special compartments, leisure activities are designed to appeal to people's feelings directly and to arouse them, though in varying ways and degrees. While excitement is severely curbed in the pursuit of what one usually regards as the serious business of life – apart from sexual excitement which is more strictly confined to privacy – many leisure pursuits provide an imaginary setting which is meant to elicit excitement of some kind imitating that produced by real-life situations, yet without its dangers and risks. Films, dances, paintings, card-games, horse-races, operas, detective stories and football matches; these and many other leisure pursuits belong in this category.

If one asks how feelings are aroused, excitement is elicited by leisure pursuits, one discovers that it is usually done by the creation of tensions. Imaginary danger, mimetic fear and pleasure, sadness and joy are produced and perhaps resolved by the setting of pastimes. Different moods are evoked and perhaps contrasted, such as sorrow and elation, agitation and peace of mind. Thus the feelings aroused in the imaginary situation of a human leisure activity are the siblings of those aroused in real-life situations – that is what the expression 'mimetic' indicates – but the latter are linked to the never-ending risks and perils of fragile human life, while the former momentarily lift the burden of risks and threats, great or small, surrounding human existence. A tragedy enacted in a theatre, as Aristotle discovered, may evoke in an audience feelings of fear and pity closely related to those experienced by human beings who witness from nearby a real condition of others tragically caught in the snares of their lives. But the imaginary setting of the theatrical tragedy is human-made. Here, humans are the creators of their own world, masters of human destiny. The heaviness of the feeling produced by the unredeemable burden of human suffering in real life is lightened, the feeling itself is purified by the mimetic symbols of music or poetry, bodily movements or masks and by the mimetic tension experienced by those who witness human suffering and pain in the imaginary setting of a human-made tragedy. Thus a small child thrown into the air and falling safely again into the father's outstretched arms may enjoy the mimetic excitement of danger and fear knowing that the danger is imaginary and that there is safety in the father's arms. Thus spectators of a football match may savour the mimetic excitement of the battle swaying to and fro on the playing field, knowing that no harm will come to the players or to themselves. As in real life they may be torn between hopes of success and fear of defeat; and in that case too strong feelings aroused in an imaginary setting and their open manifestation in the company of many others may be all the more enjoyable and perhaps liberating because in society at large people are more isolated and have few opportunities for collective manifestations of strong feelings.

And yet, if tensions arise in the wider society, if restraints on strong feelings become weakened there and the level of hostility and hatred between different groups rises in good earnest, the dividing line separating play and non-play, mimetic and real battles may become blurred. In such cases a defeat on the playing field may evoke the bitter feeling of a defeat in real life and a call for vengeance. A mimetic victory may call for a continuation of the triumph in a battle outside the playing field.

The recognition of the fact that pastimes with the characteristics of sport grew into shape in England in connection with the calming down of a cycle of violence and its resolution into a non-violent political contest according to rules makes it easier to understand that sport changes its function and its character if, once more, the tide of tensions and violence within or between states is rising. If that happens, mimetic tensions and the controlled excitement connected with them, as well as the chance of a pleasurable resolution of tensions which are at the heart of leisure sport and of many other leisure pursuits, are apt to lose their distinguishing characteristics. They tend to shade into, or to merge with, tensions of a different kind in society at large. The achievement sport culminating today in the Olympic Games provides telling examples. There the struggle for world records has given the development of sport a different direction. In the form of achievement sport the playful mimetic tensions of leisure sport become dominated and patterned by global tensions and rivalries between different states. Sport assumes in that case a character which in some respects is markedly different from that of sport as a leisure pursuit. It is only in the latter case that mimetic tensions retain a measure of autonomy, a degree of distinctness in relation to the kind of tension characteristic of 'real life' situations. However, in one capacity achievement sport may retain, within limits, its function as a leisure pursuit: in its capacity as a spectator sport. Seen as such it can provide pleasurable mimetic excitement which may counterbalance the normally unenjoyable stress-tensions of societies and provide a form of refreshment in relation to them.

The highly differentiated and wealthy societies of our age offer as one of their standing features a greater variety of leisure pursuits than any other society one may think of. Many of these leisure activities, among them sport as performer or spectator activity, are designed so as to produce an enjoyable and controlled de-controlling of emotions. They offer pleasurable mimetic tensions often (though not always) leading up to a mounting excitement and to a climax of heightened feeling with the help of which, as in the case of one's own side winning a sport contest, the tension may be happily resolved. In that way the mimetic tensions of leisure activities and the related excitement which is free of danger or guilt can serve as antidote to the stress-tensions which an even and stable restraint all round is liable to produce as a common characteristic of individual people in complex societies.

The great variety of leisure activities in general and of sports in particular which complex societies have to offer allows individuals a wide choice. They can adopt one or another in accordance with their temperament, their bodily build, their libidinal, affective or emotional needs. Some of these leisure activities can mimetically evoke fear and sorrow as well as triumph and joy, hatred as well as affection and love. By allowing these feelings to flow freely within their symbolic setting, within the mimetic context of a play or a concert, a painting or a game, they lighten the burden of people's all-round restraint in their non-leisure life.

Few if any human societies exist without an equivalent to our leisure activities, without dances, sham-fights, acrobatic or musical performances, ceremonial invocations of spirits – in short, without social institutions which provide, as it were, emotional refreshment by counterbalancing the strains and stresses of ordinary life with its serious struggles, dangers, risks and constraints. The nature and function of these constraints, however, can be easily misunderstood. They are often seen only as a corollary of social life. Because human beings live together with others, so it appears, they have to control themselves, have to impose restraint upon the manifestations of their drives, their affects, their emotions. But human beings must also learn to bring these urges under their own control for their own sake. A person who is unable to do that is a danger not only to others but also to him- or herself. Inability to control these urges is at least as painful and disabling as the acquired need to control them too much.

Human beings possess no unlearned restraints of their powerful affects, their impetuous instinctual drives. Hence the social life of humans, their life together with each other could offer little enjoyment if members of a society followed their own affects and drives without restraint. Human beings, however, are made so curiously that the mobilization and patterning of their natural disposition for acquiring restraint through learning is as indispensable for the survival of human groups as it is for that of each of their individual members. A person who failed to acquire through learning patterns of self-control, a human being who remained unable to contain his or her elementary impulses would remain at the mercy of their prompting. Unable to control any animalic need welling up from within, any excitement stirred up by events without, such a person could not attune unsatisfied urges to the sources of their satisfaction outside, could not adjust affects to the realities of a situation and would therefore suffer greatly from the pain, the irresistible pressure of spontaneous urges from within, but directed towards targets outside. Being uncontrollable and thus unadjustable, these urges, or rather people in their grip, would miss or mistake these targets and thus fail to find satisfaction. In fact, such a person would not survive for long beyond early childhood and if surviving by chance would hardly be human.

The learning of self-control, in other words, is a human universal, a common condition of humanity. Without it people as individuals would not become human, as societies would quickly disintegrate. What can change, and what in fact have changed during the long development of humanity, are social standards of self-control and the manner in which they are made to activate and to pattern an individual's natural potential for delaying, suppressing, transforming, in short, for controlling in various ways elementary drives and other spontaneous feeling impulses. What has changed, in short, are the controlling agencies formed in the course of a child's individual learning process and now known by such names as 'reason' or 'conscience', 'ego' or 'super-ego'. Their structure and pattern, their boundaries and, altogether, their relationship with libidinal and other largely unlearned impulses are markedly different at different stages in the development of humanity and thus in the course of its civilizing process. In fact, changes of this kind form the structural core of this demonstrable process as of the shorter civilizing or de-civilizing spurts which one can observe.

There is thus in the social development of the human species no zero-point of civilization, no point of which one can say, it was here that absolute barbarity came to an end, here that civilized life among humans began. A civilizing process, in other words, is a social process without absolute beginning. A sequence of purely social changes without known biological changes of the species got underway without absolute discontinuity as a sequel to a bio-social and ultimately of a biological evolution. In contrast to the latter the civilizing process, like other social sequences of change in a particular direction, can go into reverse gear. A civilizing process may be followed, may even be accompanied by spurts in the opposite direction, by de-civilizing processes.

However, the direction of a civilizing process is often misunderstood. As sport is closely bound up with the conditions of civilization in society at large and thus with the interplay of civilizing and de-civilizing spurts, which is very noticeable today, a few introductory words about the direction of such processes may be useful. One of the ideas which easily comes to mind if one mentions the direction of a civilizing process is that of changes towards greater self-control. Though this is a gross simplification, one cannot say that it is wrong. Comparatives such as 'greater' or 'smaller', do not necessarily refer to relations of quantity but they can easily give the impression that this is their meaning. Hence if one speaks in this context of 'more self-control' or 'less self-control' one may appear to do that in the same way in which one speaks of drinking more wine or less wine at dinner. Present limitations of language make it a bit difficult to find less misleading expressions. Moreover, if one points out that the direction of a civilizing process cannot be adequately presented as a change in quantity, the only alternative which present usages of speaking and thinking offer is the assumption that it must be a change in quality. This is one of the many instances in which these usages clearly show the imprint of knowledge about physical nature. The study of nature has given firm support to the impression that reduction of quality to quantity is the only road to discovery and thus the only worthwhile scientific procedure. Even in the case of highly organized substances such as chromosomes this is no longer quite correct. Already at that level models of configuration have to supplement the symbolic representation of qualities in terms of quantities. The correct linguistic usage which represents quality as the only alternative to quantity begins to show its limitations. They show even more if one is concerned with the study of social groups. If one uses as a basic frame of reference for sociological studies the demonstrable development of humanity, as one sooner or later will have to do, if one keeps an eye on the long road humans have travelled from the time of the cave-groups, as the survival units of an earlier age, to the time of industrial nation-states, as the survival units of a later age, most certainly the change in the quantity of people forming a survival unit there and here is a relevant criterion of this development. But one does not get very far if one then looks for 'qualities' of these human groups which can be reduced to quantities. The term 'quality', which has a very precise meaning if one refers to physical substances, no longer has an equally precise meaning if one refers to human societies. The spontaneity with which 'quality' comes to mind as the only linguistically correct alternative to 'quantity' is one of many instances which show that in studying human societies one is at present the prisoner of languages whose most formative influences were experiences of a physical or metaphysical kind. Not all their idioms are well suited to the study of human beings either as individuals or as societies. If one uses the examples mentioned before, the earliest and the latest known types of human society, it is easy to recognize that what offers itself as an alternative to differences in size, in the quantity of people who formed these groups, is not so much differences in group-qualities as those in the structure of these groups, in the way people are bonded to each other, or in other words in the figurations they form with each other and with non-human nature. The term figuration in that case is designed to avoid the impression inherent in many traditional terms that individual people and societies are substantially different. The two concepts denote only differences in the perspective of an observer whose eyes may focus at one instant on the persons who form a group, at another on the group they form with each other. By perceiving human groups, small or great, as figurations which human beings form together, one fits one's concepts more closely to the observable data than the usual polarization of individual and society allows one to do. One could conceivably say that social structures are structures formed by human beings. This too would indicate that in the study of societies the alternative to a quantitative approach, to the vision of societies as a cumulation of initially isolated individuals, is not so much an attempt at coming to grips with the qualities of societies, but rather that of determining their structures, the structures or the figurations formed by human beings. One may notice that the term structure rather resists this coupling with human beings. It is easier to refer to figurations of human beings, for example to the flowing figuration formed by the two teams of players on the football ground. Figuration, however, is a new expression not widely understood. Its use requires a fair measure of

Introduction

detachment. The best one can do in this case is to refer to examples, which may serve as a more acceptable way of communication than general statements including an unfamiliar term.

Examples are at hand. One need only round off what was said before about the sociogenesis of sport, about the civilizing spurt of which sport formed part and about its distinguishing characteristics in relation to pastimes at an earlier stage of development.

One could see there that rules for non-violent combat between rival factions in Parliament and for peaceful handing over of governmental power to a victorious faction or party emerged more or less at the same time as the stricter constraint on violence, the greater demands on personal self-control and on sublimatory skill which gave leisure-contests involving muscle power and agility the characteristics of sports. Thus if one asserts that the contests of Parliament or sports required more self-control than the less strictly regulated and often more violent political contests of the preceding period, one does not refer to a change in the quantity of self-control which might be conceivably measured in isolation; nor does one refer to a change in the quality of human beings; one refers instead to human beings who form with each other figurations such as Parliament or cricket teams which were demonstrably more strictly regulated than those which preceded them and demanded from the people who formed them a stricter, more even and stable control of themselves. But in a Parliamentary contest, though verbal battles and party intrigues might provide for those not too deeply involved some pleasurable excitement, life-chances of wealth, status and power were at stake. A fox-hunt as it emerged in the eighteenth century, even though the hunters denied themselves the pleasure of killing and though it was altogether more firmly regulated than previous forms of hunting, allowed hunting gentlemen and ladies all the pleasures and the excitement of the chase, as it were, mimetically in the form of a wild play enacted with them as participant spectators by the hounds and the fox (see 'An Essay on Sport and Violence' in this volume). In that case, too, the diagnosis of a civilizing spurt was not based on a measurement of isolated quantities of self-control, but on the accession of self-control demanded by the whole setting, by the figuration formed by humans in this case together with horses, hounds and fox.

Within its specific setting sport, like other leisure pursuits, can evoke through its design a special kind of tension, a pleasurable excitement, thus allowing feelings to flow more freely. It can help to loosen, perhaps to free, stress-tensions. The setting of sport, like that of many other leisure-pursuits, is designed to move, to stir the emotions, to evoke tensions in the form of a controlled, a well-tempered excitement without the risks and tensions usually connected with excitement in other life-situations, a 'mimetic' excitement which can be enjoyed and which may have a liberating, cathartic effect, even though the emotional resonance to the imaginary design contains, as it usually does, elements of anxiety, fear – or despair.[11]

But while sport shares with many other leisure-pursuits its mimetic character, an ability to stir emotions akin to those experienced in other situations and even the possibility of catharsis, it differs from most others and especially from the arts by the central part played in all sports by struggles *in toto* between living human beings. In all kinds of sport, living human beings struggle with each other directly or indirectly. Some forms of sport whose design most closely resembles that of a real battle between hostile groups have a particularly strong propensity for stirring up emotions, for evoking excitement. Hence, they represent a particularly vivid example of one of the central problems of many sports: how to reconcile with each other through the design of a sport two contradictory functions – the pleasurable de-controlling of human feelings, the full evocation of an enjoyable excitement on the one hand and on the other the maintenance of a set of checks to keep the pleasantly de-controlled emotions under control.

The problem of sports centred on mock battles may perhaps stand out more clearly if one remembers once more that sport shares the function of controlling an enjoyable de-controlling of feelings with many other leisure pursuits of our age. A concert, too, can perform that function. But in that case, the physical movements of the performers, except perhaps those of the conductor, are not in the centre of attention. The audience has to keep its movements under very strict control so that no sound from them disturbs the sounds produced by the orchestra. In fact, over the years, the tendency to restrict the movements of the audience has markedly increased. A self-escalating civilizing spurt may be at work here. At present, the concert-goers' code of conduct confines applause to the end of a symphony or any multi-movement piece of music. Applause at the end of a movement is frowned upon if not rebuked. At the time of Haydn or Beethoven, however, applause after every movement was not only given but expected. Many movements were designed so as to elicit applause as a welcome release from the excitement-tension produced by the music. Yet today, the audience remains silent at the end of movements which have been written for, and which demand, applause.

The following description provides a vivid picture of such a situation. It also indicates that the function of producing a controlled but enjoyable emotional excitement is not confined to sport:

> The pulse quickens; the fiddler's left hand becomes a blur as the pianist's fingers race up and down the keyboard. The momentum builds to the final scale and triumphant chords: Ta tah! Tum tummmm! The violinist draws a long, intense down-bow; with the release his arm flies exultantly into the air.
>
> Then: awkward silence, a bit of coughing, some shifting in seats; the soloist looks at the floor; the bow arm drifts sheepishly down. From the pianist, a note or chord for re-tuning, as the performers wind down from the pitch of excitement they have built without the release of acknowledging a response to it.
>
> Where are we? In a major concert hall, amid a sophisticated audience. Otherwise, a few people who had been stimulated by all that action would have done the obvious, and their more knowledgeable neighbours would quickly have shushed them. And why? Why, because it's only the end of the first movement, and though the music says 'Please applaud', concert decorum in the late twentieth century says 'Please wait'.[12]

The restraint imposed upon an audience in this manner is all the greater since their emotions are stirred. And yet, as far as possible no muscle must stir. They should be moved without moving. Only at the end may an audience indicate through the strength and length of its movements, of its applause, how strongly it has been moved in silence before.[13]

In the case of a game of football, motion and emotion are intimately linked to each other, at least in the case of the players. Even the audiences have a far greater scope for conveying their feelings to each other and to the players by means of movements, including those of the tongue, lips and vocal cords. However, not only football but sport in general has the character of a controlled and non-violent mimetic battle. A phase of struggle, of battle-tension and excitement which may be demanding in terms of physical exertion and skill but which can be exhilarating in its own right as a liberation from the routines and stress-tensions of non-leisure life, is usually followed by a phase of decision and release from battle-tension either in triumph and victory or in disappointment and defeat.

Sport may be a battle between humans fought out individually or in teams. It may be a battle between horse-riding men and women behind a pack of hounds and a fast-running fox. It may take the form of a ski-run from high up in the mountains down into the valley, a form of sport which is not only a battle between humans but also a battle with the snow-covered mountain itself. So is mountaineering, where human beings can be defeated by a mountain or, after much exertion, reach the top and enjoy their victory. In all its varieties, sport is always a controlled battle in an imaginary setting, whether the opponent is a mountain or the sea, a fox or other human beings. Take soccer as an example. It is human imagination which makes man-handling a leather ball – with the feet only – the object of a heated but controlled struggle between two human groups. The problem to be solved, in this case as in that of other sport-games, is how to keep the risk of injuries to the players low, yet keep the enjoyable battle-excitement at a high level. If the framework of rules and skills which provides the imaginary setting of a sport is able, in practice, to maintain this and a number of related balances, the sport can be said to have reached maturity. The varieties of English football reached that condition after a period of growth and functional adjustment, and their design came to give players evenly, again and again, a good chance of a non-violent battle-tension lasting sufficiently long to be enjoyed, as well as a good chance of culmination and release from tension in the form of victory or defeat.[14] If too many games end in a draw, that is, without a tension-resolving victory, the rules of the game require adjustment. In the same way, a sport-game may lose its function if, in too many cases, victory is attained rather quickly. In that case, the enjoyable tension-excitement is missing or too short.[15] Like other varieties of leisure-sport, as one may see, soccer is precariously poised between two fatal dangers, between boredom and violence. The drama of a good game of football as it unfolds itself has something in common with a good theatrical play. There, too, an enjoyable mimetic tension, perhaps excitement, is built up for some time, then led to a climax and thus to a resolution of the tension. But a theatrical play is in most cases the work of a known person. Most varieties of sport have reached maturity in the course of an unplanned social development.

Some conditions of this development, some aspects of the sociogenesis of sport, have been shown here by way of introduction. One can regard it as a by-product that some light has also been thrown on the nature of social development itself. It is instructive to see that something initially quite innovatory and, in its own way, rather perfect such as cricket, football, tennis and some other varieties of sport, took shape in the course of an unintended development of long duration. The same, of course, can be said of the game of chess, of the English or the German language, or of the early forms of parliamentary government.

Much has been written about the individual origin of what is called 'ideas'. Who uttered an idea first is highly regarded as a topic of research. A favourite competitive pastime of learned men and women is the discovery that a certain 'idea' saw the light of day earlier than had previously been believed according to the consensus of the specialists. However, many aspects of human societies cannot be explained in terms of the history-of-ideas model of explanation. Who first spoke the English language is not a meaningful question. Nor is it meaningful to ask: which Englishman was the first to conceive of the idea of parliamentary government or, for that matter, of cricket or soccer? These and numerous other aspects of human society cannot be explained in terms of the ideas of individual people, not even in terms of an accumulation of such ideas. They require explanation in terms of a social development.

Elsewhere I have used a simple example in order to indicate one of the crucial aspects of the difference between the two types of explanation.[16] I have used a special type of game model in order to indicate that a move in the middle of the game – let us say the twentieth move in a game of chess – can no longer be explained only in terms of the plans and intentions of one or another of the two players. The interlocking of their plans and actions results in a pattern not intended and perhaps not foreseen by either of them. Yet, although not intended, this pattern and the game-process of which it forms part can, in retrospect, be clearly recognized as structured. That is the reason why, if one does not go further, the simple statement that intended actions can have unintended consequences is little more than a palliative of one's ignorance. Imagine the interlocking of the plans and actions, not of two, but of two thousand or two million interdependent players. The ongoing process which one encounters in this case does not take place independently of individual people whose plans and actions keep it going. Yet it has a structure and demands an explanation *sui generis*. It cannot be explained in terms of the 'ideas' or the 'actions' of individual people.

Terms such as 'social process' or 'social development' are simply conceptual symbols which reflect the singular mode of existence of this continuous interweaving of the plans and actions of human beings in groups. These concepts are designed to help in the exploration of the unique type of structure which results from this interlocking of individual actions and experiences, from the functional interdependence of individual actors in their various groupings. The popular term, 'interaction', does not do justice to the intertwining of the experiences as well as the actions of people. It is too closely associated with the traditional model of a society as a pure cumulative unit of a number of initially isolated human individuals.

The observation of an ongoing game of football can be of considerable help as an introduction to the understanding of such terms as interlocking plans and actions. Each team may have planned its strategy in accordance with the knowledge of their own and their opponents' skills and foibles. However, as the game proceeds, it often produces constellations which were not intended or foreseen by either side. In fact, the flowing pattern formed by players and ball in a football game can serve as a graphic illustration not only of the concept of 'figurations' but also of that of 'social process'. The game-process is precisely that: a flowing figuration of human beings whose actions and experiences continuously interlock, a social process in miniature. One of the most instructive aspects of the fast-changing pattern of a football game is the fact that this pattern is formed by the moving players of *both* sides. If one concentrated one's attention only on the activities of the players of one team and turned a blind eye to the activities of the other, one could not follow the game. The actions and experiences of the members of the team which one tried to observe in isolation and independently of the actions and perceptions of the other would remain incomprehensible. In an ongoing game, the two teams form with each other a single figuration. It requires a capacity for distancing oneself from the game to recognize that the actions of each side constantly interlock with those of their opponents and thus that the two opposing sides form a single figuration. So do antagonistic states. Social processes are often uncontrollable because they are fuelled by enmity. Partisanship for one side or another can easily blur that fact.

In the case of a game of football, the interdependence of the opponents, the interlocking of their activities and thus the fact that the rival groups in action form a single figuration, is perhaps not too difficult to recognize. It is, at present, probably much more difficult to recognize that in society at large, too, many groups of opponents are wholly interdependent and that, there, too, their actions and feelings in relation to each other cannot be understood if one does not perceive the opponents as a single figuration. Perhaps the most telling example in that respect is the arms race between two superpowers. It is an example of a self-perpetuating process which cannot be understood if one tries to perceive each side in isolation, that is, independently of the other. In this case, the equivalent of the game-process, the self-escalating armaments race, also has a relative autonomy in relation to the aims and intentions of the leading groups on either side. Each side may believe itself to be a free agent but both are, in fact, captives of the 'game's' process which, in that case, too, is likely to take a course not intended by either side.

The difficulty is that the depth and strength of one's personal involvement in favour of one side or another block the perception both of the changing figuration formed by the two sides and of its relatively autonomous dynamics which drive the interdependent enemies, locked in their clinch, towards conditions which neither of them intended. To perceive the changing figuration of interlocking opponents as a unitary process requires detachment at a fairly high level. That may be comparatively easy to attain if one watches a game of football. It is still much more difficult even for sociologists to aim at greater detachment and to perceive two sides as one process in the case of political opponents.

Another example of some relevance in this context is the problem of football violence. No doubt the game has roughened, but the players usually keep their violence within bounds. The penalties for breaking the rules overtly are high enough to prevent too many offences, too many breaches of the players' self-control. But even the roughening of the game cannot be explained if professional football matches are seen in isolation. The reasons, almost certainly, have to be found in the rising level of tensions in society at large. That can certainly be said of the violent acts committed fairly regularly by members of the public. I have tried to show that sport, and in particular game-contests played by professional players before amateur audiences, involve a controlled but enjoyable de-controlling of affects and emotions. Contained excitement forms an integral part of the enjoyment of sport, but what happens if conditions in society at large do not equip all sections with sufficiently strong controls for containing excitement, if tensions in society at large become strong enough to loosen individual controls against violence and, in fact, induce a de-civilizing spurt, induce sections of a population to find violence enjoyable?

It is by no means only in the context of football that questions such as these show their relevance. Parliamentary forms of government, too, function reasonably well only in societies in which a fairly stable and even self-control forms an integral part of the social habitus of the greater part of the population. If, in sections of a population, the capacity for stable self-control weakens, if, perhaps through a self-escalating cycle of violence, the conscience which makes people shrink from committing acts of violence is eroded, parliamentary government may be eroded, too. The peaceful rotation of governments according to set rules can no longer function properly if the enmity and hatred of different sections of the population rise above a certain level. Nor can such a parliamentary regime easily function in a society with a long autocratic tradition where the mass of the population has got used to being in public matters mainly restrained by external controls and has never had an opportunity for developing the individual self-constraint which is indispensable for the smooth functioning of a multi-party regime where the contest between parties and, thus, changes of government are strictly confined to the use of non-violent strategies.

Thus, the recurrent flare-up of violent strategies in the case of football audiences might, perhaps, also be seen in a wider context as a symptom of some defect in society at large rather than simply in that particular section which enjoys committing acts of violence – a defect which, in this form, has come to roost.

The question why some groups of spectators commit such acts has been extensively explored by Eric Dunning and his colleagues. They have contributed much to the understanding of the problem. One can find some of their research results in this volume. Perhaps I can add a point or two. The points I want to make are connected with an enquiry I undertook some time ago in collaboration with John Scotson. It was called *The Established and the Outsiders*.[17] An investigation into the relationship between a group of old-established families and the inhabitants of a neighbouring estate of fairly recent date revealed attitudes of contempt on the part of the old-established families in relation to the inhabitants of the estate and a strong tendency to close ranks against them, to exclude them from any social contact with the established group. That was all the more surprising since both groups of families were English and both were working class. There were no observable differences in their standards of cleanliness or morality, apart from one relatively small group of families living on the estate who belonged to what Eric Dunning and his collaborators have called the 'rougher' working classes. Their family life was less orderly, their houses less tidy than those of the other families on the estate. Their children were also rougher and less easily controllable than all the other children in the neighbourhood. A closer look at this group of children and adolescents showed their difficulty. They were treated by everyone else in the neighbourhood as outsiders. They knew very well that their parents, too, were treated with contempt by the whole neighbourhood. It is probably not easy for children to develop a stable self-esteem and some feelings of pride if they see, day by day, that their own parents are held in low esteem by everybody else. The children themselves were received with a cold stare and shooed away whenever they showed their faces. So they made a point of showing themselves with particular pleasure in those places where they were least wanted. Their preferred playgrounds were the streets where the old families lived. There, they were as noisy as possible and enjoyed the attention they received when neighbours tried to get rid of them. They went into a youth club established there and, after some desultory attempts at occupying themselves with toys and equipment, began to make a nuisance of themselves as best they could and to break as many toys and pieces of equipment as possible.

In this case, it is fairly clear that an explanation in terms of these young people's 'aggressiveness' does not go far enough. Why are they aggressive? Even a reference to unemployment would not get one very far. The example may help to indicate that, in such cases, explanations in terms of an isolated cause or even a whole bundle of isolated causes are inadequate. Explanation in such cases needs to include the human situation of the people concerned and their experience of it. In fact, without reference to the established–outsider relationship and its impact on the outsiders' personality structure, the aggressive and destructive behaviour of these people cannot be fully understood. To be sure, an explanation in terms of 'aggressiveness' may seem to make the discovery of a suitable remedy easier than an explanation in terms of an established–outsider relationship. But it does so by giving to a symptom the appearance of a cause.

Most of those involved in football violence appear to come from the lower end of the working classes. But in order to understand the connection, one has to translate status into experience. Most of them not only come from families held in low esteem in their society but are also themselves looked down upon by most people in an established position. Unemployment, no doubt, has a great deal to do with it. But it is the human experience characteristic of this social setting which has to be felt and remembered if one wants to find an explanation for the eruption into violence. In their ordinary life, these young people belong to a small group of low status. They hold a rather lowly position in their society. Whenever they come into contact with the established world, they are made to feel it. The neglect by society is probably all the more aggravating because these youngsters know themselves to belong to it. There are, they know, other outsiders of foreign origin and foreign appearance. They do not count; they can be treated with scorn. But they themselves, they feel, belong here; they know themselves to be English, or Scottish, or Welsh. And yet, they are treated as if they did not belong; they are treated as if they were outsiders. There is little excitement in their ordinary life; perhaps no sport and little zest for doing it themselves. They may be out of work, if they ever had work. Ordinarily, life is rather drab. Nothing much happens. Perhaps a girl, perhaps a film. No prospects; no aim. Thus, the matches of the local football team become the great, exciting events in an otherwise rather uneventful life. There, one can show the whole world that one belongs. And one can get one's own back on a society which does not seem to notice and does not seem to care. Already on the way to the match, at home or abroad, one is no longer alone, no longer with a small group of daily friends. There are now hundreds, even thousands, of one's own kind. That gives strength to a person. In one's ordinary life, one is powerless and attracts little attention. As part of a crowd, one is powerful. At the railway station, on the way to the match and even more at the football ground itself, one can draw attention to oneself. Each can dare another to do things that neither would probably ever do if on his own. And so, without quite knowing what one is doing, but enjoying the excitement, one gets one's own back on the establishment. One can avenge oneself for a hopeless and unfulfilled life. Vengeance is a strong motive. One rips up railway compartments; smashes tables and bottles in pubs. And then, at the football ground, there are thousands and thousands, many more than the police, the representatives of the established order. Or better still there are foreigners. One can take it out on them. Being in a mass gives courage. It makes the powerless seem powerful. And so it comes about that, people normally leading a humble and probably frustrating life, get their own back by taking the lid off. They shed the self-control which normally contains the excite-ment created by the game-battle between two football teams. They seek the excitement of a real battle under conditions where they can engage in one without excessively great risks for themselves. For a short, illusory moment, the outsiders are the masters; the downtrodden come out on top. In short, I think that football violence, whatever else its explanation may be, should also be seen as an outsider syndrome, as a form of behaviour and feeling characteristic of young outsiders when they are able to congregate and to form a huge crowd.

Le Bon, in his well-known study, *The Crowd*, took his cue from the riots of the French, perhaps mainly of the Parisian population.[18] At that time, the bread-riots of the poorest still occurred quite frequently. They outraged and frightened respectable citizens and, although the established–outsider aspect lay beyond his horizon, they enabled Le Bon to observe some aspects of riots that are still to be observed in football spectator violence. It is, perhaps, not uninteresting to reflect upon the fact that, in the more developed and organized countries, bread-riots have almost completely disappeared while football-riots persist. Some of the grievances at the root of the former type of violence, such as the danger of starvation, may have largely disap-peared in these affluent societies. Other grievances no less pressing find now expression in riots. Deprivation of bread which has been more or less remedied is now followed by deprivation of meaning. From the grey outsider areas which are formed around most of the large cities in the more developed societies people, especially young people, look through the windows of the established world. They can see that a more meaningful, more fulfilled life than theirs is possible. Whatever its intrinsic meaning, it has meaning for them and they know, they may perhaps only feel, that they are deprived of it for life. And though they often come to believe that a great wrong has been done to them, it is not always quite clear by whom. Hence, vengeance is often their battle-cry. One day the pot boils over and they try to avenge themselves on someone.

These few observations about football violence draw attention, once
again, to one of the major topics of this volume, to the complementarity of sport as a leisure occupation of performers or spectators and
the conditions of people's non-leisure life. The complementarity
between the breaches of violence-control at sport events and the ordinary social existence of young outsiders from the working classes is, in
that respect, no less revealing than the complementarity between the
more controlled pleasurable excitement provided by the firmly regulated battles of a leisure sport and the well-tempered control of emotions that becomes second nature, an almost inescapable characteristic
of the social habitus of the members of more complex societies in all
non-leisure activities. In that respect, the genesis of sport in eighteenth-
century England as part of a very pronounced pacification spurt is
highly revealing. The restraint of violence in the political arena which,
in the case of the English upper classes much more than in that of their
French or German counterparts, had the character of a *self*-pacifica-
tion, a restraint imposed, not by a prince and his ministers, but by the
members of a self-ruling oligarchy upon themselves and one another,
had its counterpart in a greater sensitivity with regard to violence even
in the pastimes of these classes. There is good reason to think that these
more highly regulated pastimes, at the time increasingly known as
sports, began to gain an increased importance because of their complementarity to the self-pacification of these classes. Leisure sport provided then, and as far as one can see it still provides today, the solution
to a human problem of particular significance in societies at a high level
of pacification and thus with a comparatively high sensitivity of their
members against violence and, indeed, against all kinds of physical
injuries inflicted by humans upon humans. The problem solved by
pastimes in the form of sports was how to experience the full joy of a
battle without hurting human beings, that is, with a minimum of
physical injuries. One may well ask why the battle which is at the heart
of every sport provides an excitement which is felt to be enjoyable.

A pleasing tension, an enjoyable excitement culminating in a
pleasurable climax and the relaxation of tension is well enough known
as the characteristic pattern of a sex act. One may be tempted to
consider the enjoyable tension and excitement of a battle culminating
in victory as a derivative of the natural forces at work in that act. This is
not unlikely. But perhaps it is not enough. I am rather inclined to
consider the enjoyable excitement generated by a contest as a fulfilment of a very basic, probably socially induced human need in its own
right, particularly if the contest requires bodily exertion, as it does in
the case of sport. What I am saying, in other words, is that a society
which does not provide its members, and particularly its younger

members, with sufficient opportunities for the enjoyable excitement of a struggle which may, but need not, involve bodily strength and skill, may be in danger of dulling the life of its members unduly; it may not provide sufficient complementary correctives for the unexciting tensions produced by the recurrent routines of social life.

This is, I hasten to add, not a philosophical statement. I have not chosen to discover that struggle and the enjoyable excitement produced by it provide an indispensable complement to the equally indispensable restraints of life. If I were free to choose my world, I would probably not have chosen a world where struggles between humans are found exciting and enjoyable. And I would certainly not have chosen to put this forward as a doctrine. I would probably have chosen to say: avoid struggle. Let us all live in peace with each other. But it so happens that, as a scientist, I cannot present the world as I would wish it to be. I am not free to present it otherwise than as I find it. And I have found that humans, as I can observe them, quite apart from the enjoyable excitement of sex, also need other forms of enjoyable excitement, that battle-excitement is one of them and that, in our society, when a fairly high level of pacification has been established, that problem has to some extent been solved by the provision of mimetic battles, battles enacted playfully in an imaginary context which can produce enjoyable battle-excitement with a minimum of injuries to human beings. It is, like squaring the circle, an almost impossible task. Yet it has been solved without planning, as it were by accident.

It is often taken for granted in the human sciences of our time that human drives and other spontaneous impulses are a part of human nature but that the control of drives is a socially acquired property of human beings and, as such, does not form part of human nature. In fact, the constraint of impulses is often considered nowadays to be contrary to human nature, to be 'unnatural'. However, no controls could possibly be acquired through learning and built into the human frame as one of its permanent features if the natural constitution of human beings did not contain, as an integral part, a biological disposition for controlling impulses, and if human drives and other elementary impulses did not possess, by their very nature, a potential for being contained, deflected and transformed in various ways. In fact, the natural disposition of human beings for impulse control must be counted among the unique properties of humans, one which has a very high survival value. Given the fact that they lack instinctive or inborn controls, a life in groups – social life as we know it – would be impossible among human beings if they did not possess a natural disposition for learning impulse-control and thus for civilizing themselves and each other. Nor, as I have indicated, could a human being survive individually without a natural disposition for controlling, delaying, transforming, in short, for patterning spontaneous impulses in a great variety of ways by means of learned counter-impulses. No person could acquire the essential characteristics of a human being if he or she remained, like a newborn baby, wholly at the mercy of uncontrollable urges. There is a research task lying ahead of us. For the mobilization and patterning of impulse-control is, as yet, not well understood. Knowledge of these processes is still in its early stages. Here, it is quite enough to set the problem straight. A propensity for learning social controls forms an integral part of the natural constitution of human beings. The natural constitution of human beings evidently links the learning of impulse-controls to a fairly firm time-schedule in the early years of a person's life.

What is more, their natural constitution has equipped human beings with specific relief-institutions and dispositions which, unlearned, activated solely here and now by specific social situations or by processes of social learning, can provide relief from the stresses and strains of the tensions which may arise if controlling agencies, temporarily or permanently, battle against impulses, impulses against controls. The discovery of biological institutions and dispositions designed to provide relief and sometimes a sense of liberation from the pressure of stress-tensions has a particular significance in this context. The enjoyable excitement aroused by the mock-battle of a sports contest is a telling example of a social institution that utilizes a specific natural institution for counteracting, and perhaps resolving, the stress-tensions which arise in connection with impulse control. There is a well-known joke about an alien who was overheard at a football match to say: 'Why not give each side a leather ball and have done with it?' Whether it is the mimetic battle of a soccer game, a baseball game, a tennis tournament, an ice-hockey match, a bicycle race, a boxing match, a ski race or any other variety of the sports contests which abound in our world, and in spite of all the excesses and distortions, one can observe, again and again, the liberating effect, the release from stress-tensions that is provided, first, by the spectacle of the mock-battle, and then by its tension-relieving climax, the victory of one side or the other. In that case, the freeing from tension through the triumph of victory has not been achieved through acts of violence, through the infliction of physical injuries or of death upon other human beings. Fulfilment of a human need for enjoyment and, in particular, for enjoyable excitement which balances the even control of feelings in non-leisure life is, I believe, one of the basic functions which human societies have to satisfy.

Sport is certainly not the only form in which a biological disposition for the release from stress-tensions can be socially activated and pat-terned. One of the most elementary and universal of these biological dispositions is the human propensity for laughter. Like smiling, laugh-ing is basically a pre-verbal form of communication which is unlearned and thus, in evolutionary terms, presumably relatively old. It is fairly malleable, that is, modifiable through experience, although not to anything like the same extent as the biological institution which forms the natural basis of verbal communication. As a biological institution, laughter, although undoubtedly derived from pre-human antecedents, is characteristic of the uniqueness of human beings. It indicates quite graphically the fact of provision by means of biological institutions of ways and means of counterbalancing the strains and stresses of impulse-control.

It may be that problems such as the ones broached here have not found the attention they deserve because the main groups of specialists in this field, biologists and psychologists, have a tendency mainly to consider as natural in human beings constitutional characteristics which humans share with other animals.[19] As a result, they are more con-cerned with those human characteristics which correspond to a concept of evolution as a straight-line process rather than with characteristics which, although genetically the result of a continuous development, have the character of an innovatory breakthrough, of novel features for which no equivalent can be found at the earlier stages of the evolution-ary process. Both the biological disposition for impulse-control, which has to be activated by learning, and the biological disposition for producing release from stress-tension, belong to this category. They are both characteristic of the evolutionary breakthrough from the pre-human to the human level.

The manner in which the quest for enjoyable excitement, counterbal-ancing the stress-tensions of people's non-leisure life, finds expression in social institutions and customs can vary greatly from society to society. Life and death struggles between gladiators or between wild animals and human beings played, in Roman society, a role compar-able to that of horse-racing, football matches or tennis tournaments in present-day societies. It is possible that a short-term perspective may focus attention only on the fact that, in some sports, the standard of restraint with regard to violence has become lower. It may make us forget that, seen from a long-term perspective, the standard of restraint to be witnessed in the pastimes of today is very high. And so is the sublimatory transformation, the level of skill required from a profess-ional performer in one of the numerous leisure-time pursuits.

It is possible that the rise of professionalism in sport has diverted attention away from leisure-sport. Sports activities performed by nonprofessionals inevitably show a lower level of skill than that of sports activities pursued by professionals. On the other hand, sport pursued for professional ends may be rather joyless for the performers; it may be subject to the same kinds of constraints as other professional activities. And yet, it may result in a level of perfection which can hardly ever be matched by people who engage in sports activities in their leisure-time and for the sake of their enjoyment only.

And yet leisure-sport, whether in the form of performer or of spectator sport, is very widely practised in the more affluent societies of our time. Compared with professional and high achievement-sport, it may draw less attention as a social institution. Yet, like other leisure occupations, its importance may well increase if working time continues to decrease. I have tried to clarify a little what its social and personal functions are. A game of tennis in a suburban garden, a long ski-run down the Parsenne, or a game of cricket on the village green on a sunny summer's day – each of these can be quite a delightful experience. It is all the more enjoyable if one's own side wins. And yet, if the game was a good one, quite enjoyable for its own sake, it can still be enjoyable even if one loses.

1

The Quest for Excitement in Leisure

Norbert Elias and Eric Dunning

I

The excitement which people seek in their leisure differs in certain respects from other types of excitement.[1] It is, by and large, a pleasurable excitement. Though it has certain basic characteristics in common with the excitement which people experience in seriously critical situations, it has distinct characteristics of its own.

Seriously critical situations which generate a tendency among people to act in a highly excited manner have become, as far as one can see, less frequent in the most advanced industrial societies compared with less developed societies. It is merely another aspect of the same development that people's ability to act in such a manner in public has become more restricted. In the course of such a development, social control and self-control of strong excitement in public increase. Within each of the more advanced industrial societies, though not in their relations with each other, many of the more elementary crisis situations of mankind such as famine, floods, epidemics, violence by socially superior persons or by strangers, have been brought under stricter control than ever before. And so have people's passions. Uncontrolled and uncontrollable outbreaks of strong communal excitement have become less frequent. Individual people who openly act in a highly excited manner are liable to be taken to hospital or to prison. The social and the personal organization for excitement control, for containing passionate excitement in public and even in private, has become stronger and more effective. Not strong and effective, but stronger and more effective. The comparative is significant. Even in the most highly developed contemporary societies, standards of excitement control, as of restraint in general, may still appear uneven and low if seen by themselves. It is only if one uses as a yardstick comparison with the standards of societies at an earlier stage of development that the change becomes apparent.

Systematic comparative studies not only show that the public and personal control of strong emotive actions have increased but also that, with the advancing differentiation of societies, public and private crisis situations have become more sharply differentiated than they used to be. Public crises have become more impersonal. In these large-scale societies, many types of public crisis situations – in fact most of them apart from wars and the comparatively rare transformation of internal tensions and conflicts into open group violence – fail to stir up any spontaneous excitement although careful organization and propaganda may produce a semblance of it. In advanced industrial societies, bad local harvests have ceased to be a catastrophe that elicits despair in the face of hunger and death. Nor do abundant harvests elicit great rejoicings. Their equivalents in these societies are economic fluctuations and crises which, in the increasingly affluent societies of our time, are less liable to elicit strong, spontaneous excitement. Fluctuations of this type, by comparison with the type of fluctuations which recur in predominantly agrarian societies, are more impersonal. The fluctuations of feeling, and the sorrows and the joys connected with them, are in a different key. In these advanced industrial societies, people may not be cushioned against unemployment but they are usually cushioned against hunger and starvation. The ups and downs of this type have the character of comparatively long, slow and low waves, of changes from a relatively temperate air of well-being and prosperity to an equally temperate air of feeling low and depressed, as compared with the short, fast and high waves of rejoicing and dejection, with relatively quick and sudden transitions from one extreme to another, which one can observe in less differentiated and predominantly rural societies, for instance in connection with gluts and famines.

Even in the great private crisis situations of people's lives, sudden eruptions of strong feelings, as far as they still occur, are usually hidden away in the intimacy of one's own private circle. Social rituals and ceremonies at weddings and funerals, at the birth or coming of age of children and on similar occasions, hardly provide any longer, as those of simpler societies often do, for conspicuous excitement in public. Great fear and great joy, great hatred and great love have to be whittled away in outward appearance. Only children jump in the air and dance with excitement; only they are not immediately censored as uncontrolled or abnormal if they publicly cry and shake with tears in their sudden grief, if they panic in wild fear, or if they clench their fists and beat or bite the hated enemy with complete abandon when they get excited. To see grown-up men and women shaken by tears and abandon themselves to their bitter sorrow in public, or panic in wild fear, or beat each other savagely under the impact of their violent excitement has ceased to be regarded as normal. It is usually a matter of embarrassment for the onlooker and often a matter of shame or regret for those who have allowed themselves to be carried away by their excitement. To be rated as normal, adults brought up in societies such as ours are expected to check the rising upsurge of their excitement in good time. As a rule, they have learned not to show too much of it to others. Often enough, they are no longer able to show it at all. The control they exercise upon themselves has become, in part, automatic. The control – in part – is no longer under their control. It has become part of their built-in personality structure.

II

In advanced industrial societies, leisure activities form an enclave for the socially approved arousal of moderate excitement behaviour in public. One cannot understand the specific character and the specific functions which leisure has in these societies if one is not aware that, in general, the public and even the private level of emotional control has become high by comparison with that of less highly differentiated societies. As far as one can tell, social and personal restraints of some kind can be found in all human societies. But the relatively strong and even cover of restraints characteristic of people in more differentiated and complex societies, as has been shown elsewhere,[2] emerged in the course of a specific transformation of social and personal structures. It is symptomatic of a fairly long civilizing process which in turn stands in circular interdependence with the advancing effectiveness of the specialized controlling organization of complex societies, of the organization of the state.

As far as one can see, leisure activities as a social area for loosening non-leisure restraints are to be found in societies at all stages of development. The Dionysian festivals of the ancient Greeks – the religious excitement or 'enthusiasm', as Aristotle called it – and the carnivals of medieval Christian communities are examples. In former days, many types of religious activities had functions analogous to those which leisure activities have today – many leisure activities of our own time, particularly those of the 'mimetic' class, have functions akin to those which some types of religious activities had in former days. But while pressures and restraints as well as special leisure areas for relieving and loosening them appear to exist in all known societies, their character and the whole balance between them changes in the course of a civilizing process. In the course of such a process, restraints upon the behaviour of people become all-embracing. They become more even, fluctuate less between extremes, and become internalized as a personal armour of more or less automatically operating self-control. However, close analysis of the long-term civilizing process indicates that social developments in this direction produce counter-moves towards a balancing loosening of social and personal restraints. One can observe balancing counter-moves of this kind in some areas of contemporary life, among them in the field of leisure. New developments in music and the theatre and new forms of singing and dancing are examples. Perhaps the more active spectator participation in sports events which is observable even in countries which are traditionally rather reserved such as Britain is another. They represent a moderate break through the ordinary cover of restraints and, particularly among the young, an enlargement of the scope and the depth of open excitement.

In contemporary societies of this type, as one can observe, it is no longer a framework of religious activities and beliefs which provides scope for a balancing relaxation of restraints. But whatever their character, the compensatory excitement and emotionality which assert themselves in some of the leisure activities in these societies – in connection with specific changes in their structure and particularly in the distribution of power between different age-groups – are themselves tempered by civilizing restraints. At the same time, the greater public tolerance with regard to the display of overt excitement in recent times shows only in a more pronounced and direct manner the general function of leisure activities, particularly that of the specific class we have mentioned. As a precise sociological term for this class is lacking, we have called it the 'mimetic' class. Most, though not all, leisure activities belong to it, from sports to music and drama, from murder films to Westerns, from hunting and fishing to racing and painting, from gambling and chess to swinging and rocking, and many others. Here, as elsewhere, the quest for excitement, for the Aristotelian 'enthusiasm', in our leisure activities is complementary to the control and restraint of overt emotionality in our ordinary life. One cannot understand the one without the other.

III

The polarization which begins to emerge here differs considerably from the standard polarization which at present dominates discussions of leisure – that between leisure and work. Today, the notion that leisure activities can be explained as complementary to work often appears self-evident. It is rarely considered problematic; it is often treated as a seemingly self-evident point of departure for research into leisure but is hardly ever treated itself as a subject for research. The traditional popular stereotype expressed in phrases which come readily to the lips such as 'work and leisure' has thus been elevated without critical examination to the status of a scientific axiom. Moreover, familiarity tends to obscure the imprecision of the two concepts 'leisure' and 'work'. As things stand, the characteristics which distinguish them from each other are far from clear. Both concepts are distorted by a heritage of value judgements. Work, according to this tradition, ranks high as a moral duty and an end in itself; leisure low as a form of idleness and indulgence. The latter, moreover, is often identified with pleasure, and pleasure too gets low marks in the nominal value-scale of industrial societies. Despite the recent concern with problems of job-satisfaction, work is usually regarded as inherently antithetic to pleasure, as an heirloom of Adam's curse. Kant's reasoning that duty, if pleasurable, ceases to be moral, still finds a faint echo in the contemporary polarization of 'work' and 'leisure', the latter seemingly all pleasure, the former none at all. Yet, in the highly organized state societies of our time where the pressure of external and internal controls of a relatively permanent type is all-embracing, leisure satisfaction – or the lack of it – may turn out to be of greater importance for the well-being of people, as individuals and as societies, than the relatively low value so far attached to leisure would have us believe. As far as one can see, the survival of the tendency to regard leisure activities merely as an adjunct to work owes more to the survival of a traditional scheme of values than to any systematic examination of the two concepts and of the social structures and functions of the human activities to which they refer.

If one begins to examine them, it is easy to recognize that, even in sociological discussions, the concepts of 'work' and 'leisure' are often used rather loosely. Present usages make it difficult to decide whether a housewife's duties, or for that matter a professor's gardening, are to be rated as work, or the play of a professional footballer as leisure. If theoretical and empirical work in the sociology of leisure are not as advanced as one might wish, it is due in no small degree to this value heritage and the conceptual ambiguities which result from it.

IV

In the conventional polarization of work and leisure, the term 'work' usually refers only to a specific type of work – to the type of work which people perform in order to earn a living. In more differentiated and urbanized societies this is a strictly time-regulated and, in most cases, highly specialized type of work. At the same time, members of these societies usually have a good deal of unpaid work to do for themselves in their spare time. Only a portion of their spare time can be devoted to leisure in the sense of a freely chosen and unpaid occupation of one's time – chosen primarily because it is enjoyable for oneself. At a guess, half of people's spare time is usually devoted to work in societies such as ours. One of the first steps towards the development of a theoretical frame of reference for the study of leisure which is more closely attuned to the observable facts, is a sharper distinction and a clearer definition of the relations between spare time and leisure. Spare time, according to present linguistic usages, is the whole time free from occupational work. In societies such as ours, only part of it can be devoted to leisure activities. Broadly one can distinguish five different spheres in people's spare time which shade into each other and overlap in a variety of ways but which nevertheless represent different classes of activities and, to some extent, raise different problems.

Sparetime Activities: Preliminary Classification[3]

(1) *Private work and family management* To this class belong the many household activities including the provision of a home itself. All major and minor purchases, all the various personal financial transactions, all planning for the future belong here. So does the management of one's children, the whole family strategy including family disputes and many related tasks. All these activities require special aptitudes which have to be learned. This sphere as a whole tends to take up more time as the standard of living rises. As a field of research, apart from such problems as those of household expenditure, the field of private work and family management is still largely unexplored. Many of the activities connected with it are hard work. Much of it has to be done whether one likes it or not. After a time, it tends to become routinized in each family to a greater or lesser extent. One can hardly call it leisure.

(2) *Rest* To this class of activities belong sitting and smoking or knitting, day-dreaming, pottering about the house, doing nothing in particular and, above all, sleeping. One may call this class of activities leisure, but it is clearly distinct from a host of other leisure activities mentioned later as representative of the mimetic class such as sport and theatre.

(3) *Catering for biological needs* To leave no room for misunderstanding: all the biological needs for which we have to cater, in our spare time as elsewhere, are socially patterned – eating and drink-

ing as well as defecating, love-making as well as sleeping. These needs recur: one tries to satisfy them. They rise; they demand fulfilment. The fulfilment is pleasurable. They are stilled and abate, only to rise again later when the rhythm is repeated. Eating, drinking and love-making irradiate into other classes, directly or indirectly, particularly the class of sociability. They can all be – and they usually are – routinized up to a point but they can be and could also be in fact de-routinized from time to time in a more deliberate manner than is often the case. At the same time, they all have this in common with the mimetic class: they can provide heightened enjoyment provided one is able to cater for them in a non-routine manner, such as eating out for a change.

(4) *Sociability*   This, too, is non-work though it may involve considerable effort. It ranges from highly formal to highly informal sociability with many intermediary grades. To this class belong activities which are still work-related such as visiting colleagues or superiors, going for an outing with the firm, as well as others which are not work-related such as going to a pub, to a club, to a restaurant or a party, gossiping with neighbours, being with other people without doing much else, as an end in itself. The types of sociability as a form of spending one's spare time, as far as one can see, differ greatly in different strata of society. Like classes 1 and 2, this class of spare-time activities still remains largely unexplored.

(5) *The class of mimetic or play activities*[4]   Many enquiries into and discussions about leisure activities are focused on activities of this type. The others are often taken for granted. This enquiry, too, is mainly concerned with this class, for although a growing number of investigations are devoted to it, the distinguishing characteristics of this type of activities do not, in any of them, stand out very clearly for our understanding. Much attention has been devoted to single aspects or to single problems, relatively little to the basic structure, to the common characteristics of this class of activities. The activities themselves show great diversity. To this class belong such leisure activities as going to the theatre or a concert, to the races or the cinema, hunting, fishing, bridge, mountaineering, gambling, dancing and watching television. Activities in this class are spare time activities which have the character of leisure whether one takes part in them as actor or spectator, as long as one does not take part in them as a specialized occupation from which one earns a living; in such a case, they cease to be leisure activities and become a form of work, entailing all the obligations and restraints characteristic of work in societies of our type – even if the activities as such are felt to be highly enjoyable.

This typology, provisional as it is, can serve as a point of departure for a number of theoretical clarifications. It illustrates the insufficiences, for practical purposes as well as for purposes of study, of a conceptualization which uses the terms 'spare time' and 'leisure' more or less as synonyms. The typology shows very clearly that a considerable part of our spare time cannot be devoted to leisure. For this reason alone, the polarization of leisure and work in its traditional form is inadequate. It appears to suggest that all time not spent at work in the sense of paid occupational work, all spare time, can be devoted to leisure activities.

As the classification implies, work in the sense of paid, occupational work is only one of the spheres which require a steady and even subordination of personal feelings, however strong and passionate they may be, to impersonal social demands and tasks. The relatively even cover of restraints extends, in societies such as ours, far into the field of spare-time activities. With differences in the degree of restraint, it permeates many private social relations with people outside the inner family circle. Even within the family circle itself, the socially permitted scope for loosening restraints is relatively small. Social control, even state control, tempers the relations between husbands and wives and parents and children in societies such as ours. Passionate outbursts, a fuller relaxation of excitement control, have become rarer even within the family circle itself. In complex industrial societies with a high differentiation of social functions, the correspondingly high interdependence of all activities, public as well as private, occupational as well as non-occupational, demands and produces a cover of restraints all round. The evenness and strictness of the cover of restraints may be relaxed a little in the most intimate relationships but, compared with simpler societies, it has lost its segmentary character. It no longer has the gaps and openings for unrestrained indulgence which one encounters in less differentiated societies, among other reasons on account of the greater differences in power and status between different social strata which left a much wider scope for emotional indulgence and unrestraint, for example in the conduct of a master in relations with his slaves or servants or in that of a *pater familias* in his relations with wife and children. The cover of restraints in less inegalitarian societies such as ours now extends, with relatively small differences in degree, to all human relationships. The structure of these societies leaves little scope, even to the most powerful persons, for spontaneous and unreflected outbursts of passionate excitement. Even they can never relax the circumspection and the foresight which are the concomitants of emotional restraint without endangering their position in society.[5] The emotional restraint of occupational work extends, as an almost unshakeable habit of restraint, far into the non-occupational life of people.

The specific functions of sport, theatre, racing, parties and all the other activities and events usually associated with the term 'leisure', especially of all mimetic activities and events, have to be assessed in relation to this ubiquity and steadiness of excitement control. This is the polarity with which we are concerned here. In the form of leisure events, particularly those of the mimetic class, our society provides for the need to experience the upsurge of strong emotions in public – for a type of excitement which does not disturb and endanger the relative orderliness of social life as the serious type of excitement is liable to do.

V

It may well be that some people will detect a note of mockery in the description of our type of society as 'unexciting'. What has been said may help to give precision to the sense in which the term is used here. It refers to the type and degree of restraint which is imposed in our type of society upon the spontaneous, elementary and unreflected type of excitement, in joy as in sorrow, in love as in hatred. The extremes of powerful and passionate outbursts have been dampened by built-in restraints maintained by social controls, which, in part, are built-in so deeply that they cannot be shaken off.

However, the term 'exciting' is often used today in a less specific and more figurative sense. One would lay oneself open to misunderstanding if one did not say that, in this wider and figurative sense, our societies are far from unexciting. In this sense, one would not be wholly unjustified in regarding the societies in which we live as among the most exciting in the development of mankind. Perhaps a quotation may help to illustrate this other sense. It is taken from an article by Jean-Luc Godard:

> I am particularly glad to live . . . today, in our time, for the changes are enormous. For a 'peintre en lettres' this is immensely exciting. In Europe, and especially in France, everything today is on the move. But one must have the eye to see it. The youth, the development of cities, of the provinces, of industrialisation – we live in an extraordinary time. For me, the representation of modern life does not simply consist in an attempt at representing single inventions and industrial developments in the way some journals do; it consists in representing this total metamorphosis.[6]

This type of excitement many of us may share. It is probably true to say that, since the Renaissance, few periods have offered to those who lived in them so great a chance as ours for experimentation with new thoughts and forms, and for the gradual freeing of the imagination from traditional fetters. In spite of the threat of war, there is great promise in the air and that is exciting.

But the excitement of which we speak in this essay is of a different kind. It is less reflective, less dependent on foresight, knowledge, and on the ability to free oneself for a short while from the oppressive burden of suffering and danger which surrounds us. We are concerned with the spontaneous and elementary excitement which has probably been inimical to the orderliness of life throughout human history. In a society in which the propensities for the serious and threatening type of excitement have diminished, the compensatory function of play-excitement has increased. With the help of this type of excitement, the mimetic sphere offers again and again the chance, as it were, for a new 'refreshment of the soul' in the otherwise even tenor of ordinary social life. In certain respects, of which more will have to be said later, play-excitement differs from the other type. It is excitement which we seek voluntarily. To experience it, we have, often enough, to pay. And in contrast to the other type, it is always pleasurable excitement and in a form which, within limits, can be enjoyed with the social consent of others and with that of our own conscience.

One might be justified in pointing out that our society leaves a good deal of scope for pleasurable excitement of a thoroughly realistic kind outside the mimetic sphere. It is obvious to think of the excitement inherent in the relationship between men and women. Perhaps we can illustrate further the line of thought which has been pursued so far by taking up this challenge. In our society, the great excitement inherent in the encounter of the sexes has been hedged around in a very specific manner. In this sphere, too, brute passion and excitement contain great dangers. We are apt to forget them because, here too, a very high degree of restraint becomes second nature among those brought up in these more complex societies, and a loosening of controls tends to be classified either as anomalous or as criminal. The great, exciting experience in the knowledge of the other sex is, in accordance with the official norms and traditions of our society, regulated so as to become a unique event in a person's life. The greatest possible socially recognized excitement, symbolized by the concept of love, is fitted into the orderliness of our life by limiting it, ideally at least, to a single experience in the life of each person. Perhaps nothing illustrates so well the peculiar function of the mimetic sphere in our society than the immense part which the representation of love plays in many of its products. The apparently unending need for the representation of love stories in films, in plays and in novels is not sufficiently explained by simple references to people's libidinous propensities. What these mimetic representations provide is the renewal of the specific excitement associated with the first, and perhaps later with a new, great attachment of a man to a woman which is closed to many people in real life. It is central for the clarification of our problem to distinguish in this context between the satisfaction, including the sexual satisfaction, inherent in a long-lasting and well-ordered married life and the specific excitement inherent in the unique attachment of love which is fresh and new. What the innumerable mimetic representations of love provide is the experience or the reliving of this excitement, if only in play, the reliving of the excitement through all the tensions and conflicts to the fulfilment which is pleasurable whether the outcome of the story is happy or sad. The mimetic experience of love moves and stirs emotions which are apt to become sluggish in ordinary life, even if people do not lack sexual satisfaction in the ordinary sense.

One can see better from this example why it is not enough to treat occupational work alone as the counter-pole of leisure and to try to explain the characteristics and functions of people's leisure activities only with reference to those of occupational work. In relatively well-ordered societies such as ours, routinization captures all spheres of life, including the spheres of greatest intimacy.[7] It is not confined to factory work or to clerical, managerial and other similar activities. Unless the organism is intermittently flushed and stirred by some exciting experience with the help of strong feelings, overall routinization and restraint as conditions of orderliness and security are apt to engender a dryness of the emotions, a feeling of monotony of which the emotional monotony of work is only one example. For it is not as a property of work, but as that of the feelings engendered in those who do it that one has to assess the character of monotony. The peculiar emotional stimulation and refreshment provided by the mimetic class of leisure activities, culminating in pleasurable tension and excitement, represents a more or less highly institutionalized counterpart to the strength and evenness of emotional restraints required by all classes of purposeful activities of people in more differentiated and civilized societies. The pleasurable play-excitement which people seek in their leisure hours, thus represents at the same time the complement and the antithesis to the periodic tendency towards staleness of emotional valencies in the purposeful, 'rational' routines of life;[8] while the structure of mimetic organizations and institutions themselves represents the antithesis and the complement to that of formally impersonal and task-directed institutions which leave little room for passionate emotions or fluctuations of mood. As a complement to the world of purposeful, task-directed and highly impersonal activities, leisure institutions, whether theatres and concerts or races and cricket matches, are anything but representatives of an 'unreal' fantasy world. The mimetic sphere forms a distinct and integral part of social 'reality'.

VI

With this polarization as the point of departure, one can see more clearly the basic problem with which one is faced in studying leisure. It resolves itself, broadly speaking, into two interdependent questions:

(1) What are the characteristics of the personal leisure needs developed in the more complex and civilized societies of our time?
(2) What are the characteristics of the specific types of leisure events developed in societies of this type for the satisfaction of these needs?

It seemed useful, in order to clear the way for closer and more detached examination, to single out the need for a particular type of pleasurable excitement and to place it in the centre of the first problem. One can show that the need for it is at the core of most play needs. Excitement is, as it were, the spice of all play-enjoyment.

It is perhaps not so easy to see the aims and implications of question two. One of the reasons why it seemed necessary to use a specific term for all leisure events which can reasonably be classified as mimetic, was the recognition that all these events have a specific structure which enables them to satisfy specific leisure needs. It seemed useful to conceptualize as inherent in their structure the characteristics which make leisure events such as sports, concerts, films and television fit to serve people's needs for leisure enjoyment. It is, we hope, not presumptuous to say that, although one is used to speaking of the structure of factories or of families, one has not yet got to a point where one is used to speaking of the structure of leisure events. Yet once one reaches this point, it is not difficult to see that the heart of the problem of leisure lies in the relationship between the structure of the leisure needs characteristic of our type of society and the structure of the events designed to satisfy these needs.

We were first confronted with this problem in our studies of football. In the course of these studies we could not help noticing that a particular type of group dynamics, a specific tension-balance in the game, in short a structure which could be clearly analysed, was experienced as immensely exciting and enjoyable, while another type of figuration, equally open to clear figurational analysis, was regarded as unexciting and disappointing. It was in this context that we were first confronted with the problem which, *mutatis mutandis*, can be raised with regard to all mimetic events; the problem which we have already formulated, of the correspondence between socially generated leisure needs and the structure of the socially instituted leisure events which are designed to fulfil them. We are not suggesting that raising and clarifying the problem is by itself enough to indicate a definite solution. It is a complex problem and some of the difficulties one encounters in exploring it will have to be stated explicitly. But while we do not suggest that we can or shall present a complete solution in this essay, what we hope to be able to do is to take a few steps towards a solution.

One of the main difficulties with this type of problem, and probably one of the reasons why one has so far made little progress with it, lies in the fact that it is a problem which straddles the frontiers of several sciences. It is a moot point whether one can call it an interdisciplinary problem, for it does not arise as a problem if one pursues one's enquiries strictly within the traditional frontiers of any one of the human sciences. The problem has its physiological, its psychological, and its sociological aspects. But although these distinctions are real enough in terms of present disciplinary boundaries, they often go hand in hand with the illusion that the object of each of the different disciplines has a separate existence. In terms of the reality which we set out to explore, the problem areas with which these three specialisms are concerned, though distinguishable, are inseparable and interdependent. They are all concerned with human beings and human beings do not consist of separate and independent compartments. What has been taken to pieces for purposes of study, for purposes of study has to be put together again.

(1) Some physiological aspects of the excitement syndrome have been studied by specialists such as Walter B. Cannon and others.[9] They provide a picture of the principal somatic changes of animals and humans when confronted with a sudden critical situation. The picture is sufficiently clear to enable us, at least tentatively, to suggest possibilities of correspondence between the organic structures of an excitement reaction and the social structures of the events which elicit them. But physiological enquiries have been concentrated on the more unpleasurable types of excitement. The results have been summed up with the help of concepts such as 'emergency' or 'alarm' reactions.[10] The physiological apparatus of excitement has been studied almost entirely in connection with hunger, fear, rage, and, in general, as a specific reaction to sudden danger. We appear to know relatively little about the excitement syndrome associated with pleasure. But in spite of this limitation,

physiological investigations show, as nothing else can do, the excitement syndrome as a change of gear which concerns the whole organism on all levels; and without at least some understanding of the overall change in the multi-polar tension balance of the whole organism, one cannot understand the isomorphism between the structure of exciting leisure events, for instance an exciting football match, and the 'change of gear' in the mass of spectators which we conceptualize as excitement.

(2) Psychological aspects of the excitement syndrome have been studied explicitly, as far as one can see, only in areas nearest to the physiological level, that is in very small children. There is some evidence that a generalized excitement reaction is one of the earliest to occur in infants.[11] Studies of excitement in infancy suggest that body-rocking and other rhythmical movements are among the earliest manifestations of an excitement syndrome. They can have a soothing effect and can be connected with pleasurable sensations. It is probably not too far-fetched to assume that one type of enjoyable leisure activity, the play-excitement through rhythmically repetitive movements in some forms of dancing, is derived from the very elementary excitement which one can observe in infants.

For the rest, psychologists as such have contributed very little to the understanding of these problems. Systematic experimental studies of control as well as studies of the counter-moves towards a loosening of controls and all the questions of the fluctuating tension-equilibria connected with moves towards greater control and the corresponding counter-moves, are still an open field. In that respect we have had to rely on our own resources.

(3) One can say more or less the same with regard to the sociological study of leisure events. The structure of these social events and particularly the properties which find resonance in the satisfying play-enjoyment of actors and spectators, often rising to a climax, are mostly unexplored. We have already referred to the attempt we have made to clarify this type of structure with reference to football.

VII

It may help towards a better understanding of the difficulties which one encounters in dealing with problems which do not fit into the boundaries of one or another of the present academic specialisms if one looks at the way in which much the same problems were approached at a stage where this division of labour, this splitting-up of the quest for knowledge into different specialisms, had not yet occurred. At an earlier stage, such problems were considered within the all-embracing matrix of philosophy. One of the best examples of this pre-specialization approach to the very same problem can be found in Aristotle. If one finds it strange, and perhaps a little suspect in this advanced scientific age, that one refers in a sociological enquiry to the Aristotelian approach to the problems of leisure excitement, a short and necessarily cursory summing-up of his hypothesis may show the advantages.

In accordance with the different structure of Greek society, the Greek concept of 'leisure' did not have quite the same meaning as our own. It is an added advantage of this glance back that one can see in better perspective the limitations of our own somewhat stereotyped concepts of leisure and work by confronting them with corresponding concepts from another society.

Aristotle devoted a good deal of effort to the study of what we would call problems of leisure.[12] Translators, however, are apt to obscure the different experience and the different value-scheme represented by his manner of thinking and writing; they usually try to translate not only his words into our words but also his manner of thinking into our manner of thinking without any clear understanding of the different character of his experience in a different society. Take the very words which Aristotle used to discuss problems of leisure and work. The Greek word for 'leisure' is the direct ancestor of our word 'school'. It is *schole*. The term could also refer to the occupations of men of leisure, to that for which they employed their leisure time – to conversation, to learned disputations and discussions, to lectures, or to a group to whom lectures were given. In that way it gradually approached the meaning of our term 'school'. But it only approached it. For learning was and remained largely a privilege of 'men of leisure'.

However, members of the Greek leisure classes had a number of things to do which kept them away from *schole*, understood as leisure, such as the management of their estates, civic affairs, war and military service. These and many other occupations took up a good deal of their time and when they referred to them they used their word for work. Nothing illustrates better the difference between their value-scheme and ours than their word for the work of a gentleman. They could only express it negatively by forming a word which means 'having no leisure' – *ascholia*. Without reference to the actual Greek words, one cannot understand such statements of Aristotle as this: 'We work in order to have leisure'; which simply meant: we work in order to have time for better and more meaningful things.

Only fragments of Aristotle's theory of leisure survive,[13] but they are often illuminating enough. His theory centres on the effect on people of music and tragedy. Today one might still hesitate to explain the effects of leisure events such as these, which rank very high in our value-scale, in terms modelled on the effects of a purgative. Aristotle, for whom they ranked hardly less high, had no hesitation in doing so. In fact, one of the main differences between the contemporary scientific approach to human problems and that of Aristotle and of many other philosophers of antiquity was this: many contemporary human scientists appear to be looking over their shoulders at the haunting paradigms of the non-human sciences, above all those of physics. Perhaps the most reliable fund of empirical knowledge to which many of the great thinkers of antiquity looked as a model was medicine. It is not surprising, therefore, that Aristotle, in assessing the effects on people of music and drama, took his cue from the factual observations of physicians. His theory of the effects of music and drama has, as a centre-piece, the concept of 'catharsis'. It was derived from the medical concept used in connection with throwing out harmful substances from the body, in connection with cleansing the body through a purgative. In a figurative sense, Aristotle suggested, music and tragedy do something similar to people. They also have a curative effect which they bring about, not through a movement of the bowels but through a 'movement of the soul' (*kinesis tes psyches*). If people are overexcited or tense, exciting music will help to calm them. If they are numb with despair and despondency, they can find relief in the stirring-up of their feelings through mournful tunes. The essence of the curative effect of these mimetic events is that the excitement which they produce, in contrast to the excitement in seriously critical situations, is pleasurable. Aristotle explicitly used the term *pharmakon* in this context. He could still see what has perhaps been suppressed or mostly forgotten in the tradition of European thinking, in spite of the absorption of Aristotelian thinking into the traditions of the Christian Church: that pleasure in the comparatively temperate form provided by mimetic events can have a curative effect. Without the hedonic element of 'enthusiasm', of the excitement produced by music and by drama, no catharsis is possible.

It would be well worthwhile to consider other aspects of the Aristotelian theory of the effects of leisure events on people. What has been said here may be enough to show that, at that stage, one could still see very clearly a problem which is much more difficult to see at a stage of development where the study of human beings is sharply divided among a number of different specialisms whose relationship with each other is uncertain and lacks any redeeming scheme of integration. It is perhaps also useful – in a period in which, even in the scientific theories of psychology and sociology, problems of pleasure in general and problems of pleasurable excitement in particular, if they are treated at all, are apt to be treated rather gingerly – to see how seriously Aristotle considered the restorative effect of leisure enjoyment. Given the much larger fund of factual knowledge available today, it is not surprising that we can advance beyond him. But, as a point of departure, his approach is suggestive. It is difficult to believe that one can develop an adequate theory of leisure without paying attention to the pleasurable aspects of leisure activities.

VIII

Aristotle propounded his thesis that pleasure is a necessary ingredient of the curative, the cathartic, effect of the leisure occupations which were foremost in his mind without placing any particular stress on that fact. He put forward his thesis in a matter of fact manner. It was polemically directed against other Greek philosophers such as Plato and the Stoics who were inclined to regard the affects of people with suspicion if not with outright contempt but it did not have to contend with a heritage of social taboos. Within the context of a tradition such as ours, discussions of problems of pleasure are apt to become unbalanced: the tendency to banish pleasure as a topic from serious conversation or research is matched by the tendency to overstress its relevance, which is characteristic of the effort needed' when one approaches a zone of taboos. It may well be due to such difficulties of finding the right balance that, even today, the function of leisure activities as sources of pleasure is not often regarded as significant, if it is mentioned at all.

However, even in the European tradition, the Aristotelian thesis has, from time to time in past centuries, helped those who fought the tendency to diminish or suppress pleasure-giving activities as such to fight their battles. An example is Milton. When his Puritan friends aimed at suppressing, not only light theatrical entertainment, but even the performance of tragedies, he wrote this:

> Tragedy, as it was antiently compos'd, hath ever been held the gravest, moralest, and most profitable of all other Poems: therefore said by ARISTOTLE to be of power by raising pity and fear, to purge the mind of those and such like passions, that is to temper and reduce them to just measure with a kind of delight, stirr'd up by reading or seeing those passions well imitated. Nor is Nature wanting in her own effects to make good his assertion: for so in Physic things of melancholic hue and quality are us'd against melancholy, sowr against sowr, salt to remove humours.[14]

The cathartic effect of strong passions aroused in play and as such diffused with delight, however undelightful and terrible the same passions are in real life – the Aristotelian problem and the Aristotelian thesis – were still known to learned people in Milton's time. Their concordance with homoeopathic medicine still made them sound familiar and convincing. In the light of the much more developed research techniques of our time and the very much greater fund of knowledge available today, Aristotle's theory must appear simple and unsophisticated, but it brings to mind aspects of the problem of leisure which today are often forgotten. One of them is the fact that most leisure events arouse emotions which are related to those which people experience in other spheres: they arouse fear and compassion, or jealousy and hatred in sympathy with others but in a manner which is not seriously perturbing and dangerous as is often the case in real life. In the mimetic sphere they are, as it were, transposed into a different key. They lose their sting. They are blended with a 'kind of delight'.

The term 'mimetic' refers to this aspect of a specific type of leisure events and experiences. Its most literal meaning is 'imitative', but already in antiquity it was used in a wider, more figurative sense. It referred to all kinds of artistic forms in their relation to 'reality' whether they were representational in character or not.

However, the mimetic aspect which is the common characteristic of all leisure events classified under that name, high or low according to current evaluations, from tragedies and symphonies to poker and roulette, is not that they are representations of 'real-life' events, but rather that the emotions – the affects aroused by them – are related to those experienced in 'real-life', situations, only transposed in a different key and blended with a 'kind of delight'. Socially and personally, they have a different function and a different effect on people. Comparison between the excitement generated in 'real-life' situations and that aroused by leisure events shows similarities as well as differences clearly enough. Although physiological research along these lines has hardly got under way, there is some reason to think that the basic physiological aspects of an excitement syndrome are the same in both cases. It would be interesting and rewarding to find out what the specific differences are. Psychologically and socially, the difference is easier to recognize. In serious, non-mimetic excitement people are liable to lose control over themselves and to become a threat, both to themselves and to others. Mimetic excitement is socially and personally without danger and can have a cathartic effect. But the latter can transform itself into the former. Examples are excited football crowds or pop fans who get out of hand.[15]

The term 'mimetic' is thus used here in a specific sense. It might be taken to refer primarily to the relationship between the mimetic events themselves and certain seriously critical situations which they seem to resemble, but in point of fact the connectedness to which the term 'mimetic' refers, as it is used here, is, in the first place, the connectedness between the affects aroused by mimetic events and by specific serious life situations. Thus, the conflicts, the victories and defeats represented dramatically and tragically in a theatrical performance such as Euripides' *Trojan Women* may or may not bear any direct relationship to the life situations of a public in the twentieth century, but the affects to which they appeal can be immediate, strong, spontaneous and, if one can use this phrase, wholly contemporary. It is they, the affects aroused by the whole range of events characteristic of the sphere of that name, which bear, in a playful and pleasurable fashion, a resemblance to affects experienced in seriously critical situations, even if the mimetic events themselves in no way resemble 'real' events. The pattern and the character of play events is certainly not the same in all societies. The strength and pattern of emotional needs differ according to the stage a society has reached in a civilizing process. The mimetic events which serve these needs differ accordingly. But the fact that certain types of mimetic events such as theatrical plays or musical compositions can be enjoyed in societies of very different types is one of the observations which indicates why the allusion to imitation contained in the term 'mimetic' would be misunderstood if interpreted to mean imitation of real life situations by the mimetic events themselves. This relationship is often very slender while a very special and very direct relationship exists between the feelings to which mimetic events are attuned and feelings attuned to seriously critical situations.

IX

It is not only the matter-of-fact way in which people of former ages treated enjoyment and delight as essential ingredients in the emotional resonance of leisure events which makes the return to their reflections rewarding but also their clear understanding of the apparent paradox which the emotional resonance of leisure events presents. Aristotle mentioned the fear-arousing qualities of tragedies and the suffering in sympathy, the compassion, to which they give rise. St Augustine in his *Confessions*, reproaching himself for having frequented theatres and other places of entertainment, asked himself the very incisive question why it should be that we regard as entertainment performances which arouse in us fear, anxiety, rage, anger, and a good many other feelings which, if we could, we would avoid in real life like the plague.[16] In the light of such reflections of past ages, some of those of our own time on the very same problems make odd reading. It is not rare to find in our day such explanations of leisure events as 'recuperation from work', 'relaxation from the fatigue of daily life', and above all, 'release from tension'. Here are two examples. M. H. and E. S. Neumayer, for instance, have argued that leisure events are

> activities which recreate the body and mind resulting in recreation of one's exhausted powers through relaxation from the more serious pursuits of life. When a person is tired of physical and mental labour and still does not want to sleep, he welcomes active recreation.[17]

And G. T. W. Patrick claimed that

> all plays are pastimes, but not all pastimes are play. Some of these seem merely to satisfy a longing for excitement. Why is it since our whole modern life is so exciting compared with former ways of living, that in our leisure time we seek exciting pastimes? . . . Fortunately, the psychologists have worked out the problem for us and we now understand fairly well the psychology of play. We have learned that it is not excitement that we seek in play, but release from those forms of mental activities which are fatigued in our daily life of grind.[18]

Not only the observations of the ancients but also almost all observations in our own time point to the fact that what people seek in their mimetic leisure activities is not release from tension but, on the contrary, a specific type of tension, a form of excitement often connected, as Augustine clearly saw, with fear, sadness and other emotions which we would try to avoid in ordinary life. One could give a very wide range of examples in order to show that the arousal of tensions is an essential ingredient of all types of leisure enjoyment in the mimetic sphere, but it may be enough for present purposes to give three from different types of mimetic events. Here is a concentrated representation by a poet of a pattern of crowd behaviour during a performance by the Beatles:

> *The Beatles at Shea Stadium*
> Preliminary sounds
> lick the sixty
> thousand into one
> body
> ululating
> on the rim
> of knowledge
> . . . .

Jangled nerves await
exploratory chords
the plunge is immediate
protracted climax
. . . .
Bacchic girls drop,
thrashing frenzy,
or faint, arms flopping.
Scratched faces
grimace to believe
flat against a fence,
clawing, heave,
arched bodies lean,
arms, pleading, reach
to cross the void between.[19]

This poem describes very well one particular pattern which repeats itself in a good number of mimetic events: the gradual working up of tension-excitement reaching, as the poet says, a protracted climax, in the case of a pop audience, of near frenzy, which then slowly resolves itself. One can find a similar pattern in many plays, a gradual rising of tensions leading, through a climax, to a form of tension-resolution. Take as an example the summing up of play and audience reaction in the following theatre review:

It was not a very comfortable evening that they gave us . . . But for those who were prepared to take it, it was magnificently rewarding. The battle-field, of course, was married life, and the first requirement for a production worthy of the author was two players capable of giving compelling, larger than life performances as Edgar the husband and Alice the wife, who during the play fight out the last and climactic scenes of the war they have been engaged in during twenty-five years of marriage. One could have guessed with complete confidence that Edgar, commander of a small detachment of troops on an island where hatred and frustration have every opportunity to fester and to turn to violence, would be a part that would give Sir Laurence Olivier a chance to pull out all the stops and give a crashing performance.

One could not have anticipated quite so certainly that Miss Geraldine McEwan would be able to generate enough force to carry her plausibly to the inevitable Strindberg victory of woman's guile over man's power. She did though. Its effect was in no way lessened or spoiled by occasional outbreaks of nervous laughter in the audience. It was obvious that the laughers did so not in mockery, but because they needed some relief from tensed up feelings.[20]

The release from tension mentioned in this review is much more specific and has a much more testable character than the rather vague and ill-defined concept of release from tension often used as a hypothetical explanation for leisure activities. The tension mentioned here is that which has been worked up by the leisure event itself. The laughter mentioned has the function of a safety valve. It prevents the mimetic tension from becoming too strong. In the usual social setting of a theatre, an audience cannot let itself go to the same extent as the pop audience at Shea Stadium. Outwardly, a theatre audience is normally more restrained. The movements which form an integral part of a spontaneous excitement syndrome are kept under firmer control. The excitement is confined more rigidly to what we usually call the feeling level. There are evidently considerable differences between different age-groups and different classes in the openness with which they show their tension and excitement through bodily movements. There are differences in the whole social setting of different mimetic events. All this offers great scope for sociological enquiry. But this, above all, is evident: that it is not enough to rely, for an explanation of problems such as these, on hypotheses in terms of 'release from tension' or 'recuperation from work' which might be more appropriate if most people spent their spare time in activities characteristic of sphere (2), if they just pottered around, relaxed, or had a rest.

X

We came across this problem first in connection with the study of football. At a later stage, one will have to consider the differences among types of mimetic events which we rank as higher and lower in the hierarchic order attributed to them. But in order to arrive at a stage of enquiry where that may be possible, it is first necessary to determine with greater precision the characteristics which mimetic events of all kinds have in common. One can perhaps see the problem better if one adds an example from the field of sport to those which have already been given. People may speak of the pleasurable excitement for which they look in all these pastimes in different terms. Young people may say after a performance by the Beatles that they 'got a kick' out of it. Older and more sedate people may say after a play they liked, 'I was greatly moved'. Football fans may tell you that they were 'thrilled'. But although there are differences which have to be explored, a strong element of pleasurable excitement and, as a necessary ingredient of the pleasure, a degree of anxiety and fear, is always present whether it is the tension-excitement derived from going to the races, especially when one has a little flutter on the side, or the much quieter but more profound excitement one may derive from listening to Beethoven's Ninth Symphony when the choir, singing Schiller's 'An die Freude', works up to its tremendous climax.

There are great variations in the way in which the pleasurable excitement, the enjoyable stirring of the emotions provided by leisure activities, can express itself, and, until we have studied in greater detail the connections between the structure of the leisure activities and that of the emotional resonance they find in actors or spectators, it would be premature to put forward even tentative explanations for the varieties of enjoyment provided.

The study of football, we found, with all its limitations, lends itself rather well, and perhaps better than many others, to a clarification of at least some of the basic problems which one encounters in the mimetic field. Here one can study very closely the rather complex correspondence between the dynamics of the mimetic event itself and the psychological dynamics of the spectators.

Take the following extract from one of our case studies:

> The home team had rather unexpectedly scored the first goal. The tightly packed crowd, overwhelmingly supporters of the home team, was jubilant. They waved their banners and rattles excitedly and sang, loud and triumphantly, in support of their favourites. The much smaller group of supporters who had travelled with the guest team, noisy and excited, too, at the beginning, was stunned into silence.
>
> The guest team, regarded in the country at large as the better team, did not counter-attack immediately. They concentrated on tight marking of the home team's attack, bringing their inside-forwards and, at times, even their wingers back to play defensive roles. First a few, then more and more of the guest supporters started to chant in unison, 'Attack! Attack! . . . Attack! Attack! Attack!' But the players evidently had their plan and were biding their time. The counter-chorus of the home supporters took up the challenge. They sang: 'We are the champions', mocking the rival team and prodding their own.
>
> For a time, the game swayed indecisively to and fro. Its tonus was low. Tension among the spectators flagged accordingly. People shrugged their shoulders. They became restless. They talked about last week's game. Suddenly, attention returned. The ball was hit by the guest team right-half far down the wing; it was taken up like lightning by an unmarked colleague. He centred quickly before the home team could reach him. The centre forward had an open goal before him. Leaving the goalkeeper no chance, he hit the ball hard and accurately into the net. Few had expected it. Shouts of surprised delight went up from the guest supporters, mingled with angry outbursts on the other side. There was a short battle of words on the terraces, with cat-calls and waving of banners. Three excited little boys ran on to congratulate their heroes and

were chased off by the police. One could hear some of the supporters swearing from the corners of their mouths. Others, clapping their hands to their heads in despair, cursed audibly. One-all, and only twenty minutes left!

If one looked at the faces of the home team players when they took up their positions again, one could see that they were angry and determined. Play became fast and furious. The guest centre-forward, once again storming through, was hacked down in the penalty area just as he seemed certain to score. The referee's whistle blew. The right half stood there, the fate of the game at his feet. A hush came over the crowd. He missed: the ball hit a post and was quickly scrambled away by the home team. There were sighs of relief and loud jeers from its supporters. Then came a lengthy melee in front of the home team's goal: they broke it and got the ball away with a clever combination of passing and dribbling. Now they had the initiative. Heads and bodies in the crowd moved to and fro with the ball. Roars went up here and there, becoming louder and louder with the growing tenseness of the game. The ball changed possession, moving fast from one end of the field to the other. The tension mounted, it became almost unbearable. People forgot where they were standing. They were pushed, and pushing back, were again jostled back and forth, up and down the terraces. There was a tussle to the left of the guest team's goal, a quick centre, a header. Suddenly the ball was in the net, and the joy, the delight of the home supporters went up in a thundering roar that one could hear over half the town, a signal to everyone, 'We've won!'

It may not be easy to find a clear consensus with regard to the characteristics of plays or symphonies which provide a high and low degree of audience satisfaction, although the difficulties may not be insuperable even in the case of concerts in spite of the greater complexity of the problems. With regard to sport-games such as football, the task is simple. If one follows the game regularly one can learn to see, at least in broad outline, what kind of game figuration provides the optimum enjoyment: it is a prolonged battle on the football field between teams which are well matched in skill and strength. It is a game which a large crowd of spectators follows with mounting excitement, produced not only by the battle itself but also by the skill displayed by the players. It is a game which sways to and fro, in which the teams are so evenly matched that first one, then the other scores and the determination of each to score the decisive goal grows as time runs out. The tension of the play communicates itself visibly to the spectators. Their tension, their mounting excitement in turn communicates itself back to the players and so on until tension reaches a point where it can just be borne and contained without getting out of hand. If, in this manner, the excitement approaches a climax, and if then suddenly one's own team scores the decisive goal so that the excitement resolves itself in the happiness of triumph and jubilation, that is a great game which one will remember and about which one will talk for a long time – a really enjoyable game.

There are many shades and degrees of enjoyment and fulfilment which the *cognoscenti* can find in such a leisure activity. Not all, by any means, provide optimum fulfilment. A very exciting game may be lost by one's own side. In that case people as a rule will still carry home the after-taste of their pleasurable excitement, but this enjoyment will not be quite as unmixed as it is in the first case. Or a very good game might end in a draw. At this point, one already begins to enter an area of controversy. The consensus – very high in the cases we have mentioned – is likely to diminish until one reaches the other end of the scale where one finds again a high degree of consensus. In football, as in all other mimetic events, there are undoubted flops. For an enquiry into leisure satisfactions, it is no less relevant to study the distinguishing characteristics of flops than it is to study those which provide optimum fulfilment. Unsatisfactory games are for instance those where one side is so superior to the other that the tension is lacking; you know beforehand more or less who is going to win. There is hardly any surprise in the air and without surprise, no excitement. People do not get much pleasure out of such a game. One could give other examples, but the essentials have been mentioned.

It would not be difficult, then, to map the mimetic events of a particular type along a scale. One of its poles can be represented by leisure events which provide optimum enjoyment, the other by those which, with a high degree of consensus, are considered a flop. The majority of events, evidently, would lie between the two poles, but a good deal of information can be gained from an analysis of the two extremes. It could serve, and it has in fact served us to some extent, as a pilot study for the preparation of studies on a larger scale. Enquiry into the structure of events providing maximum and minimum satisfaction by itself contributed a great deal to the understanding of the correspondence between the social dynamics of a particular type of leisure event such as football and the personal dynamics leading to greater or lesser enjoyment on the part of individual participants. Although we are apt to classify the latter as psychological and the former as sociological, they are in fact wholly inseparable, for the greater or lesser enjoyment of those who participate in a particular type of leisure event, as actors or spectators, is the *raison d'être* for the existence of these events. It provides the criterion for the distinctive structure of leisure events, for distinguishing those which are successful and those which are a flop. Again, one can well imagine the development of leisure events which, on their part, open and educate their public to greater perceptiveness and enrichment. Academic divisions thus need not prevent the recognition of the intimate relationship between what may otherwise be separated in the form of physiological, psychological and sociological problems.

It would not be too difficult to design types of enquiries with regard to football and other sports which would make it possible to attack the same problem from the individual and the social levels at the same time, provided one is ready to use a unified theoretical framework. What has been said points in that direction. It would be quite possible, for instance, at least at the physiological level, by measuring changes in the pulse rate, heartbeat and breathing of spectators during a football game, to determine the most elementary aspects of the rising and falling waves of excitement among them. It would be equally possible, particularly if one were to use films, to determine the rising and falling waves in the tension-balance of a game. One could try to find out whether and in what ways the physiological aspects of spectator enjoyment and excitement differ in the presence of games at the optimum from those at the opposite end of the scale. Nor would it be difficult to design survey enquiries in order to enlarge our understanding of these correspondences between the social dynamics of games and the individual and crowd dynamics of spectators.

These examples indicate one of the ways in which empirical enquiries in the relatively controllable field of sport could serve as models for enquiries into other mimetic leisure activities from dog-racing to tragedy, from pushpin to poetry. By and large, we are still at a stage where ideas as to what people *should* do with their leisure time are apt to take precedence over studies of what they do in fact. Hence the former are not always based on a firm knowledge of the nature and the structure of existing leisure activities as they actually are.

XI

Nor can one say that we already have a reasonably adequate knowledge about the needs they serve. We have tried to indicate what appears to us to be the central problem with regard to these needs and have made a preliminary proposal showing the direction in which one might look for an answer. Even if the latter is found insufficient, it seems useful as a means for putting the problem itself in clearer perspective. We have assembled a number of examples from different types of mimetic events, indicating as a common characteristic not release from tension but rather the production of tensions of a particular type, the rise of an enjoyable tension-excitement, as the heart-piece of leisure enjoyment.

A recurrent need for the stirring up of strong enjoyable emotions which rises and, if it finds satisfaction, abates only to rise again after a time, makes itself felt in our society as in many others. Whatever the relation of this need may be to other, more elementary needs such as hunger, thirst, and sex – all the evidence points to the fact that it represents a much more complex, much less purely biological phenomenon – one may well find that the neglect of paying attention to this need is one of the main gaps in present approaches to problems of mental health.

The problem is to some extent obscured by the negative undertones with which the concept of tension is used both in sociological and psychological discourse. We have already pointed out that a game of football itself constitutes a form of group dynamics with a built-in tension.[21] If this tension, if the 'tonus' of the game becomes too low, its value as a leisure event declines. The game will be dull and boring. If the tension becomes too great, it can provide a lot of excitement for the spectators but it will also entail grave dangers for players and spectators alike. It passes from the mimetic to the non-mimetic sphere of serious crisis. Already in this context one has to discard the negative undertones of the conventional concept of tension and to replace it by another which allows for a normal optimum tension which can, in the course of the figurational dynamics, become too high or too low.

This more dynamic concept of tension applies not only to the game of football as such but also to the participants. Individual people, too, can live with a built-in tension which is higher than normal or lower than normal, but they are only without tension when they die. In societies such as ours which require an all-round emotional discipline and circumspection, the scope for strong pleasurable feelings openly expressed is severely hedged in. For many people it is not only in their occupational but also in their private lives that one day is the same as another. For many of them, nothing new, nothing stirring ever happens. Their tension, their tonus, their vitality, or whatever one might call it, is thus lowered. In a simple or complex form, on a low or a high level, leisure activities provide, for a short while, the upsurge of strong pleasurable feelings which is often lacking in the ordinary routines of life. Their function is not simply, as is often believed, a liberation from tensions but the restoration of that measure of tension which is an essential ingredient of mental health. The essential character of their cathartic effect is the restoration of normal mental 'tonus' through a temporary and transient upsurge of pleasurable excitement.

The effect cannot be wholly understood unless one is aware of the very great risk which people take if they allow themselves to become excited. It is the antithesis of self-control, to rational or reasonable conduct. Those responsible for law and order, as one can discover if

2

Leisure in the Spare-time Spectrum

Norbert Elias and Eric Dunning

I

That human decisions interlace is probably clear to anyone but a philosopher.[1] But the way in which they interlace is different in people's occupational work and in their spare-time activities. Furthermore, within the latter it is different in activities which are devoted to leisure and in those which are not. In some of their aspects, all decisions, all activities of an individual, have other individuals as their frame of reference; in others, the frame of reference is the actor him or herself. In the case of work activities, the balance between these two aspects is tilted in favour of the former, in the case of leisure activities in favour of the latter. That is to say, in their occupational work, as it is structured in societies such as ours, people's decisions to do this or that are always made to a very large extent with regard to others of whom they can say 'they', or even with regard to more impersonal units of which they can say 'it', though, of course, the 'I' aspect is never entirely lacking.[2] In decisions about leisure activities, although, as we shall see, references to others are more relevant than may at first appear, regard for oneself can have much more weight than it can in the case of occupational work or in those spare-time activities which do not have the character of leisure. When choosing one's leisure activities, consideration for one's own pleasure, for one's own satisfaction, can, within certain socially prescribed limits, be paramount. What kinds of satisfactions they provide and how they provide them remains to be seen.

In the present sociological literature, one can notice a tendency to regard leisure merely as an adjunct to work.[3] The pleasurable satisfaction provided by leisure activities tends to be treated as a means to an end – to the end of giving relief from the strain of work and of improving people's capacity for it. However, if one asks primarily what the function of leisure is for work, the possibility of discovering what its function is for people tends to be obscured. To point out that, in a working society, leisure is the one public sphere where individual decisions can be taken primarily with regard to one's own pleasurable satisfaction already represents a step towards removing that blockage. It is a step towards a critique of the prevailing sociological approaches to problems of leisure, both theoretical and empirical. We do not wish to burden this essay with an elaboration of such a critique. It seems more desirable to use the available space for indicating positively how far one can get if one sheds these limitations. But it may be advantageous to sum up briefly some of the critical points.

(1) The prevalence of a work-centred approach to problems of leisure ensures a certain consistency in their treatment, but this consistency is largely due to a common value and belief system which is widely taken for granted and therefore remains unquestioned. It would not be entirely unjustified to say that it is the consistency of a leisure ideology: the actual essence, the good and valuable thing in a person's life, which seems to be the gist of it, is the work which he/she does. During the hours in which people do not need to work, they do things which are of lesser value or inherently valueless, and society makes allowance for their inclination to the pleasures of idleness. But, fundamentally, this is merely done so as to ease the strain and tension of work. The main function of leisure activities, according to this leisure ideology, is relaxation from these strains.

As a scientific proposition, this kind of reasoning, the idea that leisure activities are to be regarded as auxiliaries to work is, to put it at its highest, an hypothesis which requires examination. At present, no one seems to have a clear idea of what the strains of work are from which people seek relief in their leisure unless what is meant is simply physical fatigue, in which case it would be far better to go to bed than to the theatre or a football game. And since one does not know what kind of 'strain' or 'tension' work produces in people, one also does not know how our leisure activities manage to provide relaxation. Instead of blindly accepting the conventional hypotheses embodied in everyday language, it is surely much better to make a fresh start and to say to oneself: 'Here is an open problem.' One need accept neither the traditional contention that the function of leisure activities is to allow people to work better, nor even the idea that the function of leisure is a function only for work. This looks suspiciously like a value-judgement represented as a statement of fact. There is a good deal of evidence which suggests that the structures and functions of leisure activities cannot be understood without considering them as social phenomena in their own right, interdependent with non-leisure activities but functionally not of lesser value, not subordinate to them. Both leisure and non-leisure activities evidently have functions for people. The task is to find out what these are.

(2) It is probably a symptom of the same traditional value scheme that, in spite of the growing part which leisure activities play in the actual lives of people in societies such as ours, leisure remains relatively neglected as an area of sociological research. A further manifestation of these evaluative undertones can be found in statements which stress that leisure is 'unreal', 'fantasy' or simply a 'waste of time', and which imply that only work is 'real'.[4] Most present theories of societies show the impact of these assumptions. The models of human relations embodied in their concepts – in concepts such as 'role', 'structure', 'function', 'system' and many others as commonly used – are developed primarily with an eye to the type of human relations found in what one might call the 'serious business of life', in non-leisure life. They rarely take notice of the somewhat different type of relations to be found, as we shall see, in many leisure activities. Without accounting for different types of relationships such as those to be found in leisure and in work, sociological theories can hardly be said to match the observable facts of life.

(3) The tendency to explain leisure activities in terms of their function as a means of providing 'relaxation from tension', or 'recuperation from the strains of work', is indicative of an assumption, fairly widespread in contemporary sociological writings, that tensions are to be evaluated as something negative. They are not perceived primarily as facts to be investigated but rather as something to be 'got rid of'. Thus, enquiries which approach leisure primarily as a way to get rid of tensions are apt to mislead; their authors' preemptive evaluations take the place of factual enquiry into functions. If tensions are to be evaluated purely and simply as disturbances of which people try to rid themselves, why in their leisure time do they again and again seek a specific heightening of tensions? Instead of condemning tensions as a nuisance, should one not rather explore people's need for a measure of tension as a normal ingredient in their lives? Should one not try to distinguish more clearly between tensions which are felt to be pleasant and tensions

which are felt to be unpleasant? That a common denominator of almost all leisure events is that of arousing pleasurable tension is easy enough to see. What, then, does it mean if one says that the function of leisure is to provide relaxation of tension? That is one of the questions which requires examination.

(4) Sociological enquiries into problems of leisure tend to suffer from considerable confusion in the use of terms. Sometimes, for example, no clear distinction is made between 'leisure' and 'spare time' as sociological concepts.[5] Both terms are often used interchangeably. The types of activities to which they are applied vary widely. An adequate classification of these types does not exist. Yet without it the place of leisure in people's spare time and the relationship between the various types of spare-time activities remain obscure. The 'spare-time spectrum' has been designed as an attempt to provide such a classification.

(5) The deficiencies we have mentioned have had a number of consequences for the design and direction of research into problems of leisure. It may be enough to give two examples:

(a) Sociological research efforts tend to be highly concentrated into certain limited areas of leisure activities. For example, mass media are a favourite topic of research. Theatre, sport, social dances, pub-going, concerts, bull-fighting and a wide field of other leisure activities have rarely been treated as the central topics of enquiry. Concentration of research on television, radio, newspapers and other media may be due partly to their importance as media of political socialization and social control, and partly to the assumption that, as leisure activities, they take up a greater part of people's spare time than others. However, even if the latter were the case, one cannot assume without further investigation that the time spent by people on a specific type of spare-time activity is necessarily a measure of its significance for them. It is not impossible to imagine that the mass media, in a period when spare time has perhaps increased faster than people's ability to use it for their leisure, serve to some extent as time-fillers, as another form of 'pottering around', and that this is one of the reasons for the amount of time devoted to them.

(b) A central theory of leisure capable of serving as a common framework for enquiry into all kinds of specific leisure problems is lacking. One may doubt whether it can be developed as long as empirical research is largely confined to very limited areas of leisure activities. On such a slender basis one can neither determine nor explain the characteristics and the functions which all leisure activities have in common. One cannot say what distinguishes leisure activities as such from all other human activities. This essay is designed as a step in that direction. It is a move towards a unified theory of leisure. As we shall see, by clarifying the common characteristics of leisure activities, it is possible also to bring out more fully the characteristics which distinguish different types of leisure activities from each other.

II THE SPARE-TIME SPECTRUM

Critical observations such as these already indicate that a certain reorientation of thinking is required before one can perceive the relationships and differences between all the various spare-time activities, leisure activities among them. The 'spare-time spectrum' which one finds in the following pages is an attempt to trace a brief outline of these relationships and differences. It is designed to provide what has so far been lacking, namely a fairly comprehensive and detailed typology of spare-time activities. It shows at a glance that leisure activities are only one type among others. At the same time, it indicates the relationship between leisure and other spare-time activities. As one can see, the distinction is fairly obvious: all leisure activities are spare-time activities but not all spare-time activities are leisure activities. Seen in isolation, this statement is not particularly revealing. Its relevance becomes apparent only in the context of the wider theoretical scheme embodied in this essay. Oddly enough, without such a theoretical scheme, the fact that a great number of spare-time activities are not devoted to leisure is not clearly perceived. It does not, as it were, appear to strike fully home.

Any classification of observable data which is arbitrary is useless. If the classificatory scheme of the spare-time spectrum does not agree with the results of further enquiries in this field one may bury it; but only if one is able on this new basis to give it a better-fitting successor. As it is, the spare-time spectrum indicates at least some of the structural characteristics which link the various classes of spare-time activities to each other and which distinguish them from non-spare-time activities, from occupational work. The basic theoretical scheme embodied in it will emerge by and by in the course of this essay. We began to work it out initially in 'The Quest for Excitement in Leisure' (chapter 1). In the current essay, we develop it further with reference to a more comprehensive range of leisure as well as of other spare-time activities. One should not think that the unifying theory underlying the spare-time spectrum formed an a priori point of departure for developing this classificatory scheme. It emerged only very gradually in constant cross-fertilization with a widening range of observations about spare-time activities. Like Brisaeus in relation to Earth, theoretical thinking retains its force as part of sociological enquiry only as long as it does not lose touch with the terra firma of empirical facts.

We have called the typology which follows a 'spectrum' because the various types of spare-time activities, like colours in the colour spectrum, shade into each other; they frequently overlap and fuse. They often combine characteristics of several classes. But the properties of such amalgams, of all borderline and transitional types, can only be understood from their character as such. Once one starts afresh and the problem is set, the discovery of common structural characteristics in apparently diverse leisure activities, of characteristics which distinguish them as leisure activities from non-leisure activities, is not particularly difficult. As an example, as a pointer to the drift of the theoretical thread which runs through the spectrum, one can say that all leisure activities embody a controlled decontrolling of restraints on emotions. The classes of the spare-time spectrum as a whole, as one can see, can be distinguished by the degree of routinization and de-routinization, or, in other words, by the different balance between the two embodied in them. De-routinization goes farthest in leisure activities but even there it is a question of balance. De-routinization and the de-controlling of restraints on emotions are closely related to each other. A decisive characteristic of leisure activities, not only in highly ordered industrial societies but, as far as one can see, in all other types of societies too, is that the de-controlling of restraints on emotions is itself socially and personally controlled.

The Spare-Time Spectrum[6]

(1) Spare-time routines
    (a) *Routinized catering for one's own biological needs and care of one's body* e.g. eating, drinking, resting, sleeping, lovemaking, exercising, washing, bathing, dealing with ailments and sickness.
    (b) *Household and family routines* e.g. keeping one's house in order, getting-up routines, doing one's laundry, buying food and clothes, making preparations for a party, dealing with taxes, house administration and other forms of private (i.e.

non-occupational) work for oneself and one's family; coping with family strains and stresses; feeding, training and looking after children; looking after pets.

(2) Intermediary spare-time activities mainly serving recurrent needs for orientation and/or self-fulfilment and self-expansion

    (a) *Private (i.e. non-occupational) voluntary work primarily for others* e.g. participating in local affairs, elections, church and charity activities.

    (b) *Private (i.e. non-occupational) work primarily for oneself of a relatively serious and often impersonal nature* e.g. private study with a view to occupational advancement, technical hobbies without obvious occupational value, but which require perseverance, specialized study and skill, such as building radios or amateur astronomy.

    (c) *Private (i.e. non-occupational) work primarily for oneself of a lighter, less demanding type* e.g. hobbies such as amateur photography, woodwork, and stamp-collecting.

    (d) *Religious activities*

    (e) *Orientation activities of a more voluntary, socially less controlled and often casual character* ranging from more serious, less entertaining, to less serious, more entertaining forms of absorbing knowledge, with many intermediary shades, such as reading newspapers and periodicals, listening to political talks, attending adult education lectures, watching informative programmes on television.

(3) Leisure activities

    (a) *Purely or mainly sociable activities*

        (i) participating as a guest in more formal gatherings such as weddings, funerals or banquets; being entertained to dinner in the house of a superior;

       (ii) participating in relatively informal 'leisure-gemeinschaften' with a level of friendly and open emotionality considerably above that of other spare-time and of work activities, e.g. pub and party gatherings, family gatherings, gossip communities.

    (b) *'Mimetic' or play activities*

        (i) participating in (relatively) highly organized mimetic activities as a member of the organization, e.g. in amateur theatricals, club cricket, club football. In such cases, one arrives at the core of the de-routinizing, de-controlling mimetic activities and experiences through a shell of voluntarily accepted and shared routines and controls. Most of the mimetic activities in this category involve a degree of de-routinization and loosening of restraints through movement of body and limbs, that is through motility;

(ii) participating as a spectator in highly organized mimetic activities without being part of the organization itself, with little or no participation in its routines and, accordingly, with relatively little de-routinization through motility, e.g. watching football or going to a play;

(iii) participating as an actor in less highly organized mimetic activities, e.g. dancing and mountaineering.

(c) *Miscellaneous less highly specialized leisure activities, largely of a pleasurable de-routinizing character and often multi-functional* e.g. holiday travelling, eating out for a change, de-routinizing love relations, 'lying in' on a Sunday morning, non-routine bodily care such as sun-bathing, going for a walk.

The spare-time spectrum represents a classificatory scheme which indicates the main types of spare-time activities in societies such as ours. With its help, one can see at a glance facts which are often obscured by the tendency to equate spare-time and leisure activities: some spare-time activities have the character of work, though they form a type of work which can be distinguished from occupational work; some, but by no means all, spare-time activities are voluntary; not all of them are enjoyable and some are highly routinized. The special characteristics of leisure activities can only be understood if they are seen, not merely in relation to occupational work, but also in relation to the various non-leisure spare-time activities. In this way, the spare-time spectrum helps to give greater precision to the problem of leisure.

The field of exploration opened up by the spare-time spectrum is fairly wide. Central for it, as one can see, is the degree of routinization characteristic of its various bands. We understand 'routines' to be recurrent channels of action enforced by interdependence with others, and which impose upon the individual a fairly high degree of regularity, steadiness and emotional control in conduct and which block other channels of action even if they correspond better to the mood, the feelings, the emotional needs of the moment. The degree of routinization can vary. In general, occupational work is highly routinized and so are a number of spare-time activities classified under 1, less so those classified under 2, still less those classified under 3.

Some of the other spare-time activities, as one can see, shade over into leisure activities. In the long run, we may not be able to proceed without paying attention to them. However, since one can only proceed step by step, a considerable number of problems raised by the spare-time spectrum cannot be taken up here.

The distinguishing characteristics at the core of leisure activities have already been mentioned. In a society where most activities are routinized in connection with a compelling interdependence between great numbers of people and with the corresponding types of personal and impersonal aims which demand a high subordination of immediate emotional needs to the regard for others or for an impersonal task, leisure activities provide – within certain limits – opportunities for emotional experiences which are excluded from the highly routinized parts of people's lives. Leisure activities are a class of activities where, more than in any other, the routine restraint of emotions can, up to a point, be relaxed publicly and with social approval. Here, an individual can find opportunities for an acute arousal of pleasurable emotions of medium strength without danger to himself or herself and without danger, or lasting commitment, to others, whereas in other spheres of life activities accompanied by strong, acute affects either commit an individual beyond the moment of strong arousal or incur grave dangers and risks – if they are not altogether blocked by the routinized subordination of immediate personal feelings to the regard for aims outside oneself. In leisure activities, the regard for oneself and especially for one's own emotional satisfaction, in a more or less public and at the same time socially approved form, can take priority over all other considerations.

Also, the degree of social compulsion towards participation is markedly lower and the scope for voluntariness and individual choice correspondingly higher in leisure activities than in other spare-time activities, particularly of type 1, to say nothing of occupational activities. A gradient of more or less decreasing social compulsion – with many intermediary varieties and shades between these types of compulsion and individual voluntariness – runs through the whole spectrum, with leisure activities at the lower end. As understood here, leisure occupations offer more scope than any other types of public activities for acute and relatively spontaneous personal short-term enjoyment. They represent a sphere of life which gives people greater opportunities for individual choice than any other. They all provide chances for experiencing a pleasurable stirring-up of emotions, an enjoyable excitement which can be experienced in public and shared with others and which can be enjoyed with social approval and in good conscience. In many cases, the arousal of pleasurable emotion in leisure activities is connected with specific types of enjoyable tension, with forms of pleasurable excitement which are specific to this sphere of life, though one would expect them to be genetically connected with other types of

excitement. As we shall see, leisure excitement entails a risk of transforming itself into these other types. The risk – going to the brink – is
constitutive for many leisure activities. It often forms an integral part of
the enjoyment.

How and why leisure institutions and events offer opportunities for
this type of experience is one of the problems which require exploration. But one can already say that this function is a key aspect of most,
if not all, of them. They all embody a peculiar type of risk-taking. They
are apt to provoke the sterner order of people's routinized life without
endangering their livelihood or their status. They enable people to ease
or to tease the norms of their non-leisure life and they do all this
without offending conscience or society. They involve 'playing with
norms' as one 'plays with fire'. Sometimes they go too far. The emotional refreshment provided by this playing with norms deserves closer
examination, as much for its own sake as for the sake of what we may
learn from it about ourselves.

III

That leisure institutions and events are structured so as to provide
enjoyable excitement or at least a pleasurable stirring of emotions in
combination with a relatively high degree of individual choice is easy to
see. The question is, how do they manage to provide this type of
experience and why does it offer a specific form of emotional refreshment? Why is the need for this type of refreshment so widespread and,
at least in our type of society, so urgent that people spend a great deal
of money in search of it? What is the function for people of the specific
stirring up of emotions which they appear to expect from their leisure
occupations? And what correspondence exists between the structure of
leisure institutions and events and the structure of human beings, of the
persons who seek these specific satisfactions by participating in them?

In order to answer these questions in a general way before considering them in a more detailed manner with the help of some specific types
of leisure activities, it will be useful to consider for a moment certain
wider assumptions which are fairly common in contemporary sociological theories. Without critically examining these assumptions, one cannot hope to explore this type of question. Here, one encounters one of
the areas where the bearing of the sociology of leisure on the general
problems of sociological theory and, in a wider sense, on one's image of
human beings, becomes apparent.

The examination which is needed can best be undertaken in two
steps. The first is to examine certain assumptions often implied by the
present use in sociological theories of concepts like 'norms' and

'values'. According to this convention, one is inclined to think and to speak, for instance, as if the human beings who form a society with each other were ruled in all their activities by a single set of norms.[7] It is easy to see that, in fact, people in society often follow different norms in different spheres of their lives. Norms, in other words, are to some extent 'sphere-bound': conduct which may be normal in one sphere may be deviant in another. If one considers leisure as one sphere, non-leisure as another, this is precisely what one observes: in both spheres human beings follow certain norms, but the norms are different, sometimes contradictory. Thus, when Laurel and Hardy bring a Christmas tree to a customer and it gets stuck in the door and they tear the door down and the customer hits them and they all go mad in an orgy of destruction, we scream with laughter, although they and we are acting counter to the norms of non-leisure life, they by hitting each other, we by laughing about it. In a boxing match, norms of non-leisure life such as that which prohibits physical attack on others are suspended and other norms take their place. Drinking communities, too, develop leisure-specific norms; for instance, that you can drink more but must not drink less than others and that you can get a little but not too drunk. One cannot, in short, determine the functional interrelationships of leisure and non-leisure activities without embodying in one's theoretical model the plurality of interdependent codes appropriate to each of them. This is the first step that needs to be taken towards a critique of an assumption fairly widespread in contemporary sociology, of the assumption that the norms of every society are monolithic and all of a piece.

But one has to go a little further in the critical examination of concepts such as 'norms' and 'values'. On closer scrutiny, one soon discovers how surprisingly vague and imprecise the use of these terms remains. One cannot entirely bypass this fact even if one is only concerned with the sociology of leisure. Thus, as used today, the sociological term 'norm' can refer to a good many different types of phenomena. It can refer purely and simply to moral prescriptions which are believed to be valid for all human beings. It can refer to norms followed in a particular national group but not in others. It can be applied to linguistics. People may say: 'You should form the first person singular "I am" and not "I be".' Or in other cases (for grammatical norms are by no means the only type of linguistic norms): 'This is how you should pronounce it: "Beaver" not "Belvoir".'[8] Again, the term can refer to the rules of a game. Thus, norms need not have the form of highly generalized prescriptions such as 'Soldiers should obey the orders of their commanding officers' which Parsons mentions as an example of his concept of norms;[9] they can, for instance, also take the form of a framework for the interlacing moves of players on a chess-board or on a football field. Thus, in a particular game you may not be able to make move A if your opponent is capable of making move B, but you are allowed to make it if your opponent is not in a position to make move B. Contrary to norms of the moral law type which appear not to be bound by specific figurations, norms of the game-rule type are figuration-bound.[10] This is one of the many instances which indicate that statements about what people ought or ought not to do need not follow from the highly generalized model which often seems to determine the use of the term 'norm' in sociological discourse, the model of a general moral law for identical individual cases. They can also follow models representing a lower level of generality and a different type of abstraction such as the rules of a game. There is no reason, except that of an unexamined philosophical tradition, to assume that lesser generality is identical with lesser epistemological or scientific value.

One can examine the characteristics of different types of norm, such as the moral law type and the game-rule type, irrespective of any evaluative associations. Both are social regulations of individuals acting in groups. However, the former is modelled on highly internalized regulations. Like the commands of one's conscience, social norms of this type appear neither to require nor to be capable of any further explanation. One does not ask how they originate or whether they can change and develop and, if so, what makes them do so. They are perceived as the spring and fountainhead of social action which, again like one's own conscience, seems to come from nowhere – which, while causing people to cohere in societies, seems to be neither descended from nor dependent on anything else. Norms of this type have the character of general laws for decisions which each individual has to take by himself or herself independently of all others.

The other type of norm which it is useful to consider here, the type of norm conceived in the image of game rules, has in many respects different characteristics. While both represent regulations of individuals acting in groups, norms of the moral law type are individual-centred, those of the game-rule type group-centred. Being individual-centred, moral law type norms do not explicitly refer to specific groups. Game-rule norms, on the other hand, are quite explicitly prescriptions for individuals in specific limited groups. The former usually refer to single acts of individuals at a given moment in time, the latter to the dynamics of interlacing individual acts, to individual strategies in the sequence of time, to the moves of players in a changing figuration of people.

Moreover, while the former, in accordance with the conscience model, are usually conceived as absolute, rigid and unalterable, the latter represent an elastic framework for group activities within which each player can develop rules of his or her own or even new rules as he or she goes along. Thus, a soccer player or a netball player may evolve their own technique, an individual style of playing or, in other words, norms which they themselves develop and follow in the concrete situations of their game experiences. A specific team of players may evolve their own tradition, a manner of playing embodying norms of their own, which are thus norms within norms, that is within the rules according to which all games of Association Football or netball are played. These, in turn, are rules within wider rules on many levels, for instance within the rules common to all amateur players of games as set out by the Olympic Committee, or within the legal rules of a country which on their part may embody certain unwritten moral prescriptions believed to be valid for all human beings, and so forth.

In time, no doubt, one will see how inadequate is the one-level concept of norms modelled on highly internalized individual prescriptions. Not only the analysis of a particular team sport but closer analysis of the interlacing strategies of individuals in groups generally reveals norms on several levels – norms within norms or rules within rules – which may change in accordance with new developments and experiences in society. Empirical investigations such as those of the civilizing process and the development of football show very clearly that, in fact, norms develop as part of the structure of society.[11] In sociological theories up till now, however, norms have usually been treated as absolutes, as the end of all questions: that is how the norms of conscience are perceived in the immediacy of one's own experience, even though one may know – on the level of reflection – that they have become assimilated and internalized through learning in the course of a process of socialization. There is no zero-point, no beginning of game-involvement for human beings, and therefore also no beginning of norms or rules. A human being becomes involved from the outset in an ongoing game with others, and together with others he or she may, knowingly or not, contribute to a change in the rules according to which it is played.

IV

The second of the two steps mentioned before is that of using games as a model for the relationship between leisure and non-leisure activities. By proceeding in this way, and undeterred by hidden and untested evaluations, one may find it easier to perceive the relationship between them; one may have less difficulty in understanding that both are not simply the activities of individuals but the activities of individuals in

specific groups. This is quite obvious if one studies the leisure activities
of less urbanized and less differentiated societies, which are almost
always communal. It is less obvious but no less correct with regard to
highly differentiated urban and industrial societies, even though there
the scope for individual choice with regard to leisure activities is very
much wider. For however wide, it is by no means unlimited. An
individual's choice of leisure activities in more developed societies too
depends on socially preformed opportunities and these activities themselves are usually fashioned by strong needs for social stimulation, for
direct or mimetic leisure companionship. The theory of leisure set out
here would remain incomprehensible if it were not clearly understood
that individual leisure activities are social activities in highly differentiated no less than in simpler societies. Even if they take the form of a
person's withdrawal from others, they are intrinsically directed either
from others to that person, as is the case when he or she listens to a
record or reads a book, or from that person towards others – whether
they are present in the flesh or not – as is the case when he or she writes
poetry or plays the violin alone. They are, in short, communications
received from or sent out by people in specific group figurations. That is
what the games model is meant to convey. The constitutively social
character of leisure activities is often overlooked in reflections on this
modality, on the question whether leisure activities are 'real' or 'mere
fantasies'. It is not infrequent, for example, that one finds statements
such as that by William Stephenson, according to which the distinction
between work and play 'turns on what is fantasy and in some sense
unreal, which is play, and what is real in the world which is work'.[12]
One can also point to Roger Caillois who frequently stresses the
'unreality' of games.[13]

The difficulties inherent in all these discussions are essentially due to
two factors. The first is the implicit evaluation which frequently determines what is regarded as 'real' and what is not. Thus, the assessment
of work as real and of leisure as unreal is closely connected with the
traditions and values of a society in which work is one of the highest
values while leisure is often treated as a useless frill. Representatives of
societies with a different value system, for instance Aristotle, who
valued leisure more highly than work, would hardly have agreed with
the assessment of leisure as 'unreal'. The second factor is the failure to
take account of the one context in which the term 'real' has a factual
meaning which can be checked in the light of testable evidence. That is
the use of the concept 'real' as an antonym to that of purely individual
dreams and fantasies, particularly the dreams and fantasies of insane
people which are not communicable in the ordinary sense of that word,
which do not make sense to others except perhaps to a doctor. In that

sense, 'realness' is a property of all human activities which are subject to the discipline of communication, 'unrealness' of all individual fantasies not shared by others. This clarification no longer stipulates a static and absolute division between what is real and what is unreal; it leaves room for different types and degrees of reality. It implies that all human activities which are based on communications, which have the character of moves in a game played by people with each other, are real.

The groupings of people in leisure and the groupings of people outside their leisure activities are undoubtedly different from each other. It is this difference which we are trying to express by saying that leisure and non-leisure are games played by groups of people with each other according to different rules. There is no doubt that in leisure games fantasies and emotions of all kinds are allowed a greater part than in people's non-leisure life, but they are fantasies which are socially patterned and communicated, fantasies crystallized into a theatrical play, a painting, a game of football, a symphony, into horse-racing, dancing and gambling. In contradistinction to purely private, not socialized fantasies they are as real in terms of the human beings participating in them as the spare-time care of one's children or one's wife or, for that matter, as one's work.

Perhaps one can facilitate the understanding of this essentially simple clarification by means of a slight change in the use of terms. One may hesitate to consider paintings, novels, plays and films as 'real' as long as one groups them mentally under the heading of 'leisure activities'; one may find it easier to accept them as 'real' by grouping them mentally under the heading of 'culture'. One is often debarred from grasping the obvious simply by value differences hidden away in the meaning of words.

But if the fact that both leisure and non-leisure activities are social activities, that both are games played by groups of people with each other, assures their reality, they are, nevertheless, games of a different type. The task, therefore, is to determine their functional interdependence in society as well as their distinguishing characteristics (of which a good deal has already been said). It helps towards a better understanding of societies such as ours to see that in this case as in others people play not only one but several interdependent games with each other with different rules. Leisure and non-leisure games are one example of these complementary games. There are many others. In some cases two or more games are played simultaneously, as for example in the case of 'formal' and 'informal' relationships. In others several interdependent games are played at different times, as in the case of 'war games' and 'peace games'. The relationship between leisure and non-leisure is of the latter type. The distinguishing structures of the two types of games, their relationships with each other, as well as the functions of each of them for those who play, require closer scrutiny. Certain aspects of these differences can be stated quite briefly. The spare-time spectrum and the comments which followed were designed to indicate them. The dominant activities in non-leisure games are aim-directed. They have the character of straight-line vectors. Their primary functions are functions for others, for 'them' or for impersonal organizations such as business houses or nation states, although they also have secondary functions for oneself. This may, and in fact usually does, involve satisfaction through messages and stimulation received from others, but personal satisfaction for those involved in the game remains their primary function. In that sense, one can say that leisure constitutes an enclave of socially permitted self-centredness in a non-leisure world which demands and enforces the dominance of other-centred activities. While the latter are aim-directed and vector-like, the former, figuratively speaking, have a 'wavy' character. The feelings aroused by leisure activities are tensed between opposites such as fear and elation, and they move, as it were, to and from one and the other. It is only the inadequacy of our traditional concepts and of our linguistic tools generally which makes it difficult to express and to understand that, in leisure occupations, seemingly antagonistic feelings such as fear and pleasure are not simply opposed to one another (as they 'logically' seem to be), but are inseparable parts of a process of leisure enjoyment; for leisure satisfactions can only be conceptualized as processes. In that sense, one can say that no satisfaction can be had from leisure occupations without short wisps of fear alternating with pleasurable hopes, brief flutters of anxiety alternating with anticipatory flutters of delight, and in some cases, through waves of this kind, working up to a cathartic climax in which all fears and anxieties may resolve themselves temporarily, leaving, for a short while only, the taste of pleasurable satisfaction in possession.

This is why forms of excitement play a central part in leisure activities. It is only thus that one can understand the de-routinizing function of leisure. Routines embody a high degree of security. Without exposing oneself to a degree of insecurity, to some more or less playful risk, the encrustation of routines could not be loosened or removed even temporarily and the function of leisure activities would be lost.

However, specific leisure activities can lose their de-routinizing function. They retain it only in relation to a given set of routines. Activities which have a de-routinizing function today can become routinized through repetition or through too strict a measure of control and thus lose the function of providing a measure of excitement. They lose, in that case, the function of providing a degree of insecurity, of satisfying the expectation of something unexpected and the risk, the tension, the flutter of anxiety which goes with it. These up and down, short or long waves of playfully antagonistic feelings such as hope and fear, elation and despondency, are one of the springs of the emotional refreshment of which we have spoken before. Even preparing for a holiday in a place that is new – which on the face of it may seem straightforward pleasure – implies savouring in anticipation the unexpected which one might encounter there and at the same time fearing perhaps the slight uncertainty, the possibility of disagreeable encounters with unpleasant people or uncomfortable quarters, or the hope of making some new, wholly delightful acquaintances. Thus even in this case there are wisps of anxiety blended with a flutter of anticipatory delight.

One can already see that the functional interdependence of leisure and non-leisure (for which we possess at present no adequate classificatory term), between the routine parts of our lives and the de-routinizing enclaves within them, can only be expressed in terms of balances. Leisure activities might easily become routinized themselves, they might easily become de-functionalized if there were nothing else.

And routines? Could we pursue an evenly routinized life without leisure enclaves? To ask this question goes to the heart of the problem. We do not mean to say that there are no people who do not live in such a way. It is possible that in societies such as ours great numbers of people live a wholly routinized, wholly unexciting life without relief, not only old people, among whom forms of leisure starvation seem to be fairly frequent – partly because while they are still alive their lives become by degrees less 'real' as they cease to participate in work games but cannot find or cannot open themselves to appropriate participation in leisure games – but also among people of middle age, though perhaps less among the young. There is some evidence which suggests that a lack of balance between non-leisure and leisure activities entails some human impoverishment, some drying up of emotions which affects the whole personality. Perhaps one can see here more clearly the dangers inherent in any classification of leisure activities as 'unreal'.

One can go one step futher in working out at least a provisional model of the balancing function of non-leisure and leisure activities in societies such as ours. The prevailing conceptualization of this functional interdependence between leisure and non-leisure in terms of relaxation from strain or tension is misleading, among other reasons because it implies that occupational work as well as highly routinized spare-time activities produce tensions while the nature of these tensions remains obscure. In a vague manner, the term 'tension' often apperar in this context to be identified with fatigue. On that basis, the character of leisure activities, the fact that they themselves create tensions, that they answer to needs for stimulation, to a quest for excitement, as we have said before, remains incomprehensible. What kind of tension is it that is counter-balanced by and finds a resolution through the other kind of tension, which is aroused and, perhaps, pleasurably resolved by leisure activities?

V

One cannot answer questions such as these without taking into consideration aspects of leisure which, according to the present conventions of research, lie outside the field of sociology. The problem which one encounters here has made itself felt throughout this enquiry. It is time to bring it into the open. Is it at all possible, that is the question, to work out a reasonably adequate theory of leisure within the framework of any single human science such as sociology, psychology, or for that matter, human biology, if their relationship remains as obscure as it is today? The problems of leisure, in fact, belong to that large class of problems which, at the present stage in the development of scientific specialization, fall not merely between two but between several stools. They do not fit wholly into the frame of reference of any one of these sciences as they are at present constituted, but rather belong to the unexplored no-man's land between them. If sociology is considered as a science which abstracts from the psychological or the biological aspects of human beings, if psychology or human biology are regarded as sciences which can proceed on their own without taking account of the sociological aspects of people, the problems of leisure will be left out on a limb. In fact, they indicate in the clearest possible manner the limitations inherent in the compartmentalization of human beings as a subject of scientific study. As a classificatory model, the spare-time spectrum has already indicated that it can never be enough to distinguish different aspects of people as separate without an overall frame of reference indicating their relationship. The present conception of the various social sciences suffers from this very defect: each of these sciences deals with aspects of people as if they *in fact* existed independently of each other. The separation is complete. There is no overall frame of reference indicating how these various aspects fit into each other. By placing leisure activities within the wider framework of the spare-time spectrum, we have already indicated that the problems confronting the investigator here, though they require a distinction, do not allow a separation to be made between the aspects of people usually allotted to one or another of the different human sciences.

If people go to the theatre, if they go to a dance, to a party, or to the races, it is, as we have said before, because in leisure, they can choose to occupy themselves in a manner which promises to give them pleasure. Thus, people's pleasure, the prospect of a specific type of enjoyable stimulation, is constitutive for the social structure of these institutions, of the theatre, of dancing, of parties, of racing and of all the many others which have been mentioned in the course of this enquiry. Problems of pleasure, one might say, belong in the realm of psychology or physiology; problems of leisure, however, fall into the sociologist's sphere of competence. Throughout the history of their science, sociologists have aimed at distinguishing their own types of problems from those studied by psychologists and biologists. It was indispensable, for a time, to establish the fact that social phenomena represent a level of enquiry with distinct characteristics of its own. In that sense, the fight of sociologists for the relative autonomy of their subject-matter has proved fruitful. But one may think that this autonomy is by now firmly enough established for sociologists to consider not only the distinctiveness of their problems but also their relationships to those of neighbouring fields. It has shown itself to be fruitful for sociologists in their enquiries to abstract from the psychological and biological problems which they encounter and, for a time, to travel along a separate road towards a better understanding of human beings. But this separation, inevitably, has led to the neglect of large groups of problems, one of which is the problem of leisure. The present enquiry is an example of the kind of blockage which one encounters if one tries to deal with sociological problems without looking beyond the frontiers of the field. In the case of leisure events and institutions, whose *raison d'être* is a specific psychological experience, any attempt to abstract from it must defeat its own end. Here, the study of social structure and that of emotions cannot be pursued in separate compartments.

However, this does not mean that one can dissolve the one into the other. Biologists and psychologists are sometimes inclined to believe that, ultimately, they will be able to answer all sociological problems in their own – in biological or psychological – terms. In that respect, the sociologists' struggle for the autonomy of their own problems has been well justified. Perhaps one may think that not even all contemporary sociologists are able to see clearly the relative autonomy, the irreducibility of sociological problems in relation to biological and psychological ones.[14] There is evidently a good deal of confusion as to how one should steer a path between the idea that the study of society is totally autonomous and therefore completely unrelated to that of psychology and biology, and the idea that the problems of society as a field of study will all be solved sooner or later through the psychological and biological study of individuals alone.

The study of leisure, as we have said, is one of the many instances in which it is not possible to disregard the problem of the actual relationship between phenomena on the sociological level and those on the psychological and physiological levels. Here, one cannot escape from the task of a multi-level analysis, from the task of considering, at least in broad outlines, how in the study of leisure the three levels – the sociological, the psychological and the biological – connect.

VI

Theories about the psychological and physiological aspects of emotions are numerous and one cannot say that they all agree with each other. But, for our purposes, it may be enough to point to certain comparatively elementary aspects which are fairly well established. In their most elementary form, in very small children, emotional reactions appear to have the character of an undifferentiated excitement response probably connected, according to circumstances, with pleasant and unpleasant feelings without any specific emotional differentiation. Fear, love and rage reactions, once regarded as the original trio of emotions, probably emerge gradually from the generalized excitement pattern as part of a process of differentiation.

But however that may be, a glance at the emotional reactions of young children brings to mind very clearly one fact which is often overlooked if, in speaking of emotions, one has in mind only the emotions of adults. Adults in societies such as ours often do not show their emotions. Small children of all societies do. With them, the feeling state to which we refer as emotion is one aspect of a stirred-up state of the whole organism in response to a stimulating situation. Feeling and acting, namely moving one's skeletal muscles, one's arms and legs and perhaps one's whole body, are not yet divorced. This, one can say, is the primary character of the feeling state to which we refer as emotion. It appears in people's experience as a feeling state only gradually when they learn to do what small children are never able to do, namely not to move their muscles – not to act – in accordance with the emotional impulse to act. In popular discourse, we speak of people 'controlling their feelings'. In actual fact, one does not control one's feelings but rather the movement, the acting part of a stirred-up state of the whole organism. The feeling part of this state may actually assume the character of an emotion partly because it cannot discharge itself in movements. But we do not stop feeling. We only prevent or delay our acting in accordance with it.

Grown-up people as a rule, at least in societies such as ours, become so accustomed to not acting in accordance with their feelings that this restraint often appears to them as the normal, the natural state of human beings, especially as with themselves the restraint becomes to a large extent automatic. They cannot relax the ingrown control even if they want to. They have largely forgotten how hard it once was for them not to do what they felt like doing, how the grown-ups strove, with a raising of their eyebrows, with hard and sweet words, and perhaps with worse than words, to control their actions until the control, according to the pattern customary in their society, no longer required an effort. It became second nature and appeared as a self-understood part of their persons, as something with which they were born. The degree and the pattern of this training for self-control varies from society to society in accordance with the stage in the specific pattern of their development. In general, one can say that the type of socialization characteristic of highly industrialized societies results in a stronger and firmer internalization of individual self-control, that it results in an armour of self-control which operates relatively evenly and comparatively moderately – but without many loopholes – in all situations, in all spheres of life.

It would be a great help for sociological enquiry into problems of leisure, which is one of the few enclaves where, even in industrial societies, people are able to look – still with moderation but with full public approval – for emotional excitement and where they can even show it up to a point in a socially regulated form, if one could find psychological and physiological enquiries into the various problems of self-control which have been raised here. However, not only sociologists but also psychologists and physiologists, though for different reasons, avoid enquiry into problems intermediary between these various fields. And in its present form, even social psychology is of little help with regard to problems such as these. There is a vast psychological and physiological literature on problems of learning but comparatively little on the structuring of the personality through learning. And the establishment of controlling impulses which interpose themselves – as a learned development of unlearned human potentialities – between the recurrent upsurge of drives and emotional impulses from lower biological levels and the skeletal motor apparatus towards which they are directed is almost unexplored.

Strong evidence of a pre-scientific type pointing in that direction is not entirely lacking. There is enough of it to enable us at least to indicate, though not, of course, to solve, the problem which shows the links between the phenomenon of socially induced control of emotions and the special provision for emotional refreshment in leisure activities. The civilizing self-controls which play a comparatively large part in the life of highly developed societies are not the outcome of any deliberate and critical planning. They have grown into the shape they have now, as has been shown elsewhere,[15] more or less blindly over a long period of time. It is often taken for granted, though it has never been shown, that these controls have a necessary part to play in the functioning of industrial societies. The mounting revolt against some of them, particularly among the younger generation, will, one may hope, contribute to a more systematic enquiry into the question of whether internalized controls as well as external social constraints, and which aspects of them, have positive functions for the operation of society and which have not. Some of the problems of leisure which we have explored here are closely connected with this type of question. What happens in a society where the pressure both of social constraints and of built-in self-controls upon individuals becomes so strong that its negative consequences outweigh its positive functions?

This enquiry must be left to a later date. But this short excursus into some of the elementary aspects of self-control makes it possible to advance a little further what has been said before about the relationship between non-leisure and leisure activities. One may remember that the neatest, though of course not the only and certainly not an exhaustive formulation of the differences between the two types of activities referred to the two types of function which all activities have for actors: namely a function (or functions) for the actors themselves and a function (or functions) for other people, sometimes though not always in the form of functions for an impersonal social unit such as a nation. The difference between the two types of activities to which we are referring, to put it briefly, is that in non-leisure activities the function for oneself is subordinated to the function for others; in leisure activities, the function for others is subordinated to the function for oneself. In more psychological terms, this means that non-leisure activities require throughout – not only if they have the character of occupational work but also if they have the character of non-leisure spare-time activities as classified in the spare-time spectrum – a relatively very high degree of emotional control because consideration for others is demanded by the often very complex interdependence of these activities with the activities of others. This is why we spoke of them as 'routinized'. By comparison with less highly developed societies, most intertwining activities in societies such as ours are extremely well and firmly regulated. It is only if one has experience – either direct through participation or indirect through study – of what it means to live in a less well-regulated society that one can assess the relative orderliness of highly developed societies and the part played in them by the comparatively high internalization of individual controls. On the other hand, this internalization, whether it takes the form of conscience, of a more or less obsessional orderliness, or of any of the other consequences of the implicit socialization for this absorption of social controls as part of individual personality, undoubtedly results in specific frustrations, a good deal of distress and suffering, and probably a number of illnesses. This means that in the more developed state societies, a double ring of constraints keeps the behaviour of individuals within the conduct boundaries of their group: external constraints, represented for instance by the ubiquitous threat of the law and its agents, and internal controls, represented by such personal controlling agencies as conscience and reason. These terms – which like so many others appear almost as if they were some kind of substances, 'ghosts in the machine', instead of as controls learned from others and absorbed as a result of socialization – refer precisely to those types of impulses which we mentioned before and which interpose themselves between the more elementary, more directly biogenetic impulses to which we refer as drives, affects or emotions, and to the motor apparatus. They give us control over ourselves; that is to say, they enable us not to move our muscles, not to act immediately we feel driven to act, or to act in a different way from that to which our spontaneous drives and emotions direct us. They thus not only enable us to direct and to time our movements in accordance with the highly complex structure of our interdependencies; they also give us greater freedom from the upsurge of momentary impulses and also greater scope for decisions. On the other hand, by preventing drives, affects, emotions from seeking and finding direct and immediate satisfaction, they create tensions of a specific kind.

If, however, one looks at the present psychological and psychiatric literature on the affective aspects of human behaviour and experience, one may notice after a time that, with very few exceptions, the translation of facts into theories is hampered by a traditional concept of human beings which, as the framework of all theoretical propositions, is more or less taken for granted and never systematically examined with regard to its appropriateness. We have referred to it before. It is the image of people as a kind of non-social machine. It is sometimes represented by the metaphor of a 'black box': we can observe how the black box behaves but we do not know what goes on inside it. In many cases, the implicit assumption is that people react to specific stimuli with specific responses. On the basis of this assumption, one may be led to assume that human beings would not react in this manner unless the stimulus or the releaser elicited a particular reaction pattern. However, there is a great deal of evidence which indicates that human beings do not merely wait passively for specific stimuli. In fact, from a growing mass of available evidence it is fairly clear that the human organism requires stimulation in order to function satisfactorily, particularly stimulation through the company of other human beings. The significance for the concept of human beings of the many experiences we have gained about the effects of extreme isolation has, perhaps, not always been fully expressed.[16] They indicate that the need of one human being for arousal through other human beings is not confined to that specialized sphere which we call sexuality. It is a broader, far less specialized need for social stimulation. It may or may not be libidinal in origin. Its genesis needs exploration; but, whatever it is, the 'black box' is not quiescent when it is not stimulated. Each human being, in his or her whole constitution, is directed towards other human beings – towards the emotional stimulation which only other human beings can provide, although there can be substitutes such as pets or stamp collections. Perhaps the most salient point for perceiving the interdependence between the aspects of human beings explored by psychologists and psychiatrists on the one hand, and by sociologists on the other, is the understanding that the 'black box' is not closed, that it is open and that it sends out feelers ready to fasten onto others and to reciprocate in the same manner to the feelers which others send out.[17] In fact, one cannot quite understand the nature of drives and emotions unless one is aware that they represent one line in a two-way traffic. Each human being, in his or her whole constitution, is directed towards others – towards emotional stimulation through living human beings – and pleasurable stimulation of this kind, the stimulation one receives from being together with others either in actual fact or in one's imagination, is one of the most common elements of leisure enjoyment. If one were to try to sum up metaphorically the difference between the image of human beings appropriate to observations such as these and the image of human beings of which the 'black box' metaphor is representative, one would have to say that a better simile – if people are to be compared with any mechanical device at all – is that of someone equipped with a radio transmitter and receiver who constantly sends out messages which elicit responses which he or she in turn can receive and to which he or she in turn can respond. Put a child alone for days in a room and see what happens. It 'wilts', however good the food it gets. The reason is that this elementary need for such 'two-way' traffic of all that which we call, still very imperfectly, 'drives' or 'emotions', the need for a stimulating emotional response to one's own emotional messages, is cut off. The suffering, the pain inflicted on small children by this cutting off or merely by the non-fulfilment of this almost insatiable need to fasten the vectors of their affections onto others, eliciting an affectionate response which will fasten onto them and which will, on their part, elicit a reinforced response of the affections and so on and so forth, is very great indeed. In short, the vectors sent out towards others in search of an anchorage, whether we call them 'drives', 'libido', 'affections' or 'emotions', are part of an interpersonal, a social process. So far as children are concerned, if these processes are interrupted or merely disturbed, the whole personality development of the child will be more or less severely damaged. In the course of the process of growing up, of the 'civilizing process' which individuals undergo in societies such as ours, they are taught to control most severely and in part automatically the always unstilled need of human beings for the kind of stimulation gained from the sending and receiving of emotionally significant messages which, for the human young, is as vital as their food. Grown-ups in our type of society have, in their non-leisure life, to curb most severely the sending out of emotional messages. They are, in that sphere of their lives, debarred from sending out and from receiving messages on certain wavelengths. Leisure activities, on the other hand, give a certain scope for sending and above all for receiving messages on those wavelengths to which we crudely refer as emotional. But since the lessening of controls in human societies of all kinds, but particularly in societies so well ordered and complex as ours, always entails risks, the de-controlling function of leisure activities which opens up the way for the refreshment of emotions is on its part too surrounded with precautionary rules so that it can be socially tolerable.

From all this, one of the central aspects of the relationship between non-leisure and leisure activities emerges more clearly. Perhaps one can sum it up conceptually by reference to a specific polarity which runs through the whole of life in the form of a fluctuating tension-balance. We are referring to the tension-balance between emotional control and emotional stimulation. The form in which this tension-balance manifests itself varies from society to society. In our type of society where control of the whole feeling-continuum, from animalic drives to the most sublime emotions, is, in part, strongly internalized, the external control of emotions is relatively moderate and the emotional stimulation provided with public approval in leisure activities is, by and large, equally moderate in character. Both, in short, require a considerable degree of emotional maturity.

But the short reference above to the fact that sociability is, one might say, a permanent feature of children's life can serve as a reminder of one of the principal functions of leisure activities in societies such as ours; namely that they help to temper the very great severity of conscious or unconscious self-control required of all participants by the type of occupational activities and non-leisure activities generally to which we have to accommodate ourselves, by allowing us to engage, in an adult form, in activities which prevail in the lives of children. Psychoanalysts might speak in such a case of a 'socially permitted regression' to childhood behaviour, but statements such as this merely reveal the inadequacy of any psychological theory which embodies the idea that adult behaviour is all of a piece, that it follows the same pattern in all activities. In fact, through the institution of leisure, social development itself has left scope for a moderate loosening of adult controls, a temperate 'de-controlling' of individuals by means of an equally moderate excitation of affects – a temperate emotional arousal which can help to counteract the stifling effect controls can easily have without such social institutions.

VII

One can best visualize the relationship between non-leisure and leisure activities as a fluctuating tension-balance. In the highly routinized and well-regulated spheres of life where the function for 'you' or for 'them' dominates the function for oneself, we cater for the long-term requirements of our highly complex societies and thereby also of ourselves. But we do so at the expense of a number of immediate and spontaneous needs and their satisfaction. We do not tell this man or woman – our boss, our customer, our colleague or even our subordinate – how we dislike them, how we despise and loathe them. We do not tell this man or woman – our secretary, our colleague from another department, our customer, our bank or insurance official – how much we like them, how attractive they are and that we would like to go out with them. There are a hundred and one ways in which we starve our emotions – for a very good reason. If everyone loosened or lost restraint, the whole fabric of our society would break down and all the long-term satisfactions which we derive from it in terms of comfort, health, variety of consumption and leisure satisfactions and many other privileges compared with less developed countries – privileges which we often no longer experience as such – would be lost.

We have got used to thinking, without any more precise model of the relationship, that the counterbalance to the impersonal type of relationship that prevails in the more highly routinized sectors of our social life is provided in the family. Up to a point, this is probably correct. The family can provide a number of emotional balances which counteract the relative emotional restraint required particularly in the occupational life of people. In fact, if one considers the relative loss of functions which the family as an institution has suffered in connection with such processes as urbanization and industrialization, one can add that it has gained functions as one of the social agencies for the satisfaction of people's instinctual and emotional needs in a type of society in which elsewhere they are perhaps more strongly controlled than is the case in many other types of societies. But there are many indications that the family by itself is not enough to cater for all those needs which are otherwise severely restrained. One of the reasons is that family life itself in societies such as ours is highly routinized and, although it is a social locus for a specific, socially approved relaxation of the restraints which keep our drives in check, it is also necessary to recognize that it has, in connection particularly with the greater equality of power between the sexes and the generations, produced new types of restraints and new types of tensions. Another reason is the fact that, within the framework of the family, the counterbalancing function – the satisfaction of drives and emotions which it provides – is associated with a very strong and almost inescapable commitment. This commitment has a three-layered character. Of the three, a ring of two is typical of the many commitments in more developed societies. Husband and wife in their relations with each other, parents in relation to their children, are committed to each other by all kinds of social pressures, not least those of neighbours or friends and those of the law. Husband and wife are committed to each other and to their children, as we say, by a 'sense of responsibility' or, in other words, by their own conscience. They are also, in some cases, committed to each other emotionally by the mutual affection and perhaps by the love which they feel for each other. Very little is known about the way in which these three layers of family commitment affect each other. It is often surmised that the first and also the second of these commitments are necessary so that the third can form itself or last. If we were honest with ourselves, we would say that we know exceedingly little about the nature of the lasting emotional attachment of a couple to each other. Although sexual satisfaction plays a part in it – and this is characteristic of the whole make-up of human beings – such a long-lasting attachment has quite a different character from the short-lasting sexual act. Theoretically, we have hardly begun to scratch the surface in our exploration of the nature and conditions of the long-lasting emotional commitment of human beings to each other. If it is mutual, it is probably among the most satisfying of human experiences but this statement has to be qualified since, so far as the problem of love is concerned, it is still extremely difficult to penetrate through the ideal to the fact itself. Nor has one even begun to explore the relationship between the effects on emotional commitment of institutional pressures and commitment through one's own conscience. Even to arrive at this stage of conceptual clarification has proved difficult. If one could go on from here, if one knew more about the functional interdependence of these three layers of family commitment, one might be able to face up to and to deal with the changing conditions of family life more realistically than one can at present. But however this may be, one can understand better the peculiar character of leisure as an enclave where emotional refreshment of a kind can be found without any of these commitments if one sees it in relation to the family, where emotional refreshment of a different kind can be found but only in connection with emotional and other commitments.

Without reference to the fact that leisure activities demand no compulsory commitment, one cannot quite understand the specific functions which they perform in the life of industrial societies. The instinctual and emotional satisfactions provided within the framework of the family are bound up with strong institutional and normative restraints. Because these satisfactions are long lasting, they themselves are apt to become routinized to some extent. Personal satisfactions are in part subordinated to consideration for others who, on their part, are the providers of these satisfactions. Leisure satisfactions are confined to the moment to a far higher extent. They are highly transient. At the same time, they offer the chance of counteracting the emotional restraint, the comparative lack of openly expressible emotional stimulation characteristic of the major sectors of people's activities in more differentiated societies by another type of activity whose primary function is that of providing enjoyment for oneself. They are able to counteract the normal emotional constraints without any commitment except that which an individual is willing to take on voluntarily at any given time. But this very lack of commitment, combined with a high degree of emotional stimulation which, together, give many leisure activities the characteristics to which we refer as 'play' or 'playfulness', raises specific problems.

We have already referred to the fact that in all more or less well-ordered societies situations which stimulate strong emotions are treated with suspicion, particularly by those responsible for preserving good order. What has been said before about the nature of emotions as driving forces of action explains this tendency. Under the impact of strong feelings, people are apt to act in a manner which they themselves can no longer control and which, therefore, the guardians of good order in society may also find it difficult to control. All areas in a society, and particularly in a highly complex society where the dovetailing of activities through long chains of interdependencies has to be maintained, are, for that reason, usually hedged in by regulations and sanctions designed to prevent the arousal of emotions from getting out of hand. The way in which most societies couple the legitimization of sexual and other emotional satisfactions within the framework of the family, with a socializing training, with beliefs, with direct restraints and prohibitions counteracting the dangers to others of any liberation of instinctual and emotional forces in a person, has already been mentioned. It is perhaps not always fully realized that the same problems arise with regard to leisure activities. We have already mentioned that many types of leisure activities embody as one of their integral features an element of risk-taking, a 'playing with fire'. At first glance, this may seem to be risk only for those engaged in any particular activity themselves – the risk of gambling to the gambler, of motor racing to the racing driver. But this is not the whole story. Leisure activities, as we have tried to show, constitute an enclave where, up to a point, emotional controls can be relaxed, excitement stimulated and openly shown. In societies so well regulated as ours, the legitimization of any loosening of self-control entails risks, not only for the persons involved themselves, but also for others, for the 'good order' of society. In investigating the development of football, for example, we came across the fact that in the Middle Ages the kings and the authorities of towns tried for centuries to put a stop to the playing of football, among other reasons because it almost invariably ended in bloodshed or, if played in the streets of a town, at least in lots of broken windows.[18] The inability of the authorities to put a stop to all this was largely due to the fact that the people concerned took very great pleasure in the excitement of the game, the loosening of restraints. The control organization of the state was simply not effective enough to counteract the attraction which the emotional excitement of the game had for the players.

Today, the effectiveness of the restraining power of the state has become very much greater, but the very fact that it is so great must be remembered if one is to understand some of the structural characteristics and recurrent problems of leisure activities in our time. The tension-balance between the desire for emotional refreshment on the part of those engaged in leisure activities and the state authorities who keep a watchful eye on them so that no harm may come from this relaxation of control, either to the leisure-seekers themselves or to others, is as fundamental a characteristic of the organization and conduct of leisure activities today as it was in the medieval societies which we have mentioned. But the fact that state control is so much more effective has had certain consequences for these activities. For the time being, it may be enough to point to the fact that the need for a high degree of regulation appears to have induced a stronger tendency towards the sophistication and sublimation of the emotional·responses to which leisure institutions are intended to appeal. The whole mimetic aspect of leisure occupations in our time cannot be quite understood without reference to the fact that the appeal of many, though not all, of them is no longer to emotional or instinctual needs in their most elementary form, though it may appear to be just that, but rather to complex sets of affective demands where blends of composite feelings come into play. But the fact that state control is so much more effective also means that its operation is more even and more predictable. It often operates only as a 'guardian in the wings', relying to a consider- able extent on the self-control of the 'guarded'. A sociological analysis of leisure activities would be very fragmentary if it did not take account of the fact that two of the three layers of commitment mentioned before with reference to the family also play the part of a controlling framework in leisure activities.

VIII

In the light of the theoretical framework we have begun to set out above, the structural unity behind the variety of leisure occupations becomes more visible. In its centre stands the fairly rigid separation imposed by the character of highly differentiated societies upon their members between a sphere of social life where activities and experi- ences directed towards impersonal aims predominate – where the functions of everything one does for others have strict priority over functions for oneself and where emotional satisfactions are strictly subordinated to cool reflection – and a sphere where the opposite order of priorities prevails: relatively unemotional and impersonal thought processes are weakened, emotional processes are strengthened and functions for oneself are given greater weight than those for others. Leisure activities fulfil these functions by a variety of means. For want of a better word, we shall call them the 'elements of leisure'. Basically, there are three of them: sociability, motility and imagination. If one looks at the types of leisure activities indicated in the spare-time spectrum, one can see at a glance that there are none where all of these three elementary forms of emotional activation are absent. One can also see that two or three of these elements often combine although, in any given activity, one of them may be dominant. Each of these elements, in its own way, can serve as a means of loosening the controls which, in the non-leisure sphere, keep the affective propensities of people sev- erely in check. Consideration of them points back to the general model of human beings as in an unstable tension-equilibrium between a sphere where impersonal intellectual activity and the control of emo- tions which goes hand in hand with it prevail over the activation of emotional activities, and another sphere where the pleasurable exci- tation of such emotional processes prevails and the inhibitory controls are weakened. It may be enough here to illustrate the functions of these elements of leisure by discussion of two of the primary spheres of leisure activities in societies such as ours: those we have called the 'sociability' and the 'mimetic' spheres.

(1) Sociability as a basic element of leisure plays a part in most if not in all leisure activities. That is to say, an element of the enjoyment is pleasurable arousal through being in the company of others without commitment, without any obligations to them apart from those one takes on voluntarily. This type of stimulation plays a part if one goes to the races, if one trains for an athletic contest, if one goes to a gambling club, to a hunt, to a dance, and even if one goes to a restaurant with one's husband or wife: even there, as we have said before, the fact that one eats out among others, although one may not know any of them, plays a part in one's enjoyment, even though it may be secondary to other primary elements in the leisure situation. Sociability itself plays the primary part in gatherings such as parties, pub-going, visits to friends, and so on. One can find many incidental observations on problems of sociability in the sociological literature; however, socio-logical enquiries based on a consistent theory of leisure which have problems of sociability as their central theme are lacking. The rele-vance of this type of enquiry for a theory of society is easy to see. Many sociable gatherings have the characteristics of what, for want of a better word, may be called 'leisure-gemeinschaften': they provide opportuni-ties for closer integration on a level of overt and – in intent – friendly emotionality which differs markedly from that regarded as normal in occupational and other non-leisure contacts between people. These differences in the emotional level of sociable gatherings such as pub-gemeinschaften, parties or drinking sociability in an officers' mess, and that of non-leisure groupings such as workshop assemblies or com-mittee meetings, are easy to observe but less easy to conceptualize. It is perhaps not inappropriate to apply to them by way of abbreviation the concept of *Gemeinschaft*, giving it a slightly different turn of meaning by comparison with its traditional use. With the examples we have given in mind, it is easy to discard the romantic connotations tradition-ally associated with the term *Gemeinschaft*. People who, in their leisure time, find it satisfying to join a 'pub-gemeinschaft' or who enjoy going to parties which encourage integration on a higher level of overt and more or less friendly emotionality are not necessarily of the same frame of mind as those who romantically long for a return to the village *Gemeinschaft* of former days. There is a structural relationship of sorts – which need not be discussed here – between the tendencies towards leisure-gemeinschaften in urban-industrial societies and the romantic longing for village-gemeinschaften, but the differences are fairly clear. It is doubtful whether adults today who like to form recurrent but transient leisure-gemeinschaften with each other would wish to give

them permanence to the exclusion of the emotionally more restrained types of relations that prevail in their non-leisure life. It is not unlikely that many people who enjoy the sociable gatherings of their leisure time might not enjoy them so much or might not enjoy them at all if they became a permanent form of living. The characteristic alternation between participation in a non-leisure *Gesellschaft* and in transient leisure-gemeinschaften in the life of many adults points to the complementary character of the two types of relationships in societies such as ours.

Conceived in that way, the term leisure-gemeinschaften opens up a fairly wide field for investigation. In industrial societies, these transient enclaves of greater overt affectivity and of relatively spontaneous though impermanent integration are among the ordinary, socially standardized institutions into which many people's leisure requirements are canalized with fair regularity. Here, in contradistinction to mimetic leisure institutions, people join each other without necessarily possessing any specialized skills, without 'performing' for others or for themselves (though that can occasionally happen), quite simply to enjoy each other's company, to enjoy, that is, a higher level of emotional warmth, of social integration and of stimulation through the presence of others – a playful stimulation without serious commitments and the risks inherent in them – than is possible in any other sphere of life.

At the same time, leisure sociability, like mimetic activities, is indicative of specific structural characteristics of industrial societies. Leisure-gemeinschaften counteract in particular the routinization inherent in the relatively impersonal contacts which are prevalent in the non-leisure spheres of these societies. There, emotional barriers between people, like the emotional restraints required of people generally, are usually high. The existence of leisure-gemeinschaften of a variety of types points to a recurrent need for lowering these barriers, for human contacts in a climate of higher overt emotionality with a marked preponderance, in intent if not always in actual fact, of the positive aspects of otherwise ambivalent relationships. But again, in leisure-gemeinschaften as in other leisure events, the lowering of the barriers, the raising of the level of emotionality as a counter-agent to the encrustation of routines, entails a certain risk. As most people know, the socially permitted degree of de-routinization can be overstepped.

There is no need for purposes of this essay to speak of the wider research possibilities opened up by this approach to the problem of leisure sociability. One area of research problems, however, deserves discussion at some length. In many cases, the pleasure which people take in sociable gatherings appears to be enhanced by the communal consumption of alcoholic drinks. What is the function that alcohol has as a normal ingredient of many of these gatherings? If the satisfaction derived from the sociable gatherings is connected with a lowering of the barriers between people, with a pleasurable raising of the level of emotionality, why do people need drink to produce or at least to heighten the pleasures of sociability? Can one say that communal drinking serves an integrating function? What satisfactions do people themselves expect from their participation in such drinking-gemein-schaften? What are the common characteristics of these gatherings? What is their normal, what their optimal course? What courses are found to be disappointing? And under what conditions does communal drinking serve a disintegrating rather than an integrating function?

If our provisional assumptions are correct, one will probably find that, in this case too, people expect from their leisure pursuits not simply, as it is often put, 'relaxation' but rather stimulation and exhila-ration. Again, medical approaches to problems such as these appear to us incomplete without complementary sociological investigations. There is a good deal of evidence to suggest that in this type of leisure activity too people look for pleasurable emotional arousal and excite-ment, in short for the production of specific types of heightened tension in the company of others.

These apparently fairly ubiquitous needs of human beings for forms of stimulation which can only be provided by other human beings can easily be neglected if one looks primarily, as is often done in the traditional medical approach to people, at the individual organism as a self-contained system. It is for that reason that medical attempts at explaining drinking as a normal ingredient of leisure gatherings are apt to be somewhat inadequate. It is not quite enough to point to the fact that the 'depression of the inhibitory centres of the brain' due to the consumption of alcohol 'produces a transient feeling of well-being' if one tries to explain the social functions of drinking. If it were merely a feeling of well-being which people were seeking from the use of alco-hol, they could just as well stay at home and drink their alcohol there. It is much more likely that people drink alcohol in company because, by depressing the inhibitory centres of the brain, it facilitates the friendly reciprocal stimulation on a relatively high level of emotionality which is the essence of leisure sociability. A glass or two enables people to loosen relatively quickly the often rather deeply ingrown armour of restraints and thus to open themselves to the mutuality of playful arousal which serves as a counter-agent to the relative loneliness of the fully armoured individual and to his or her commitments and routines in non-leisure spheres including that of family life. Thus, leisure-gemeinschaften reinforced by drinking provide, like many other leisure events, opportunities for raising the level of overt emotionality in public, in the presence of others. The excitement thus generated is usually expected not to go beyond certain limits. As in other leisure events, it can get out of hand. The risk is always there. It may well be that 'playing with fire' in this case too is part of the pleasure. As in a number of other forms of leisure activities, this playing with fire, this risk, appears to contribute to the pleasurable excitement and in that way to the enjoyment of leisure-gemeinschaften. Approaching the border of what is socially permissible and sometimes transgressing it, in short a limited breaking of social taboos in the company of others, probably adds spice to these gatherings.

The ubiquity of enclaves where human beings can reciprocally 'loosen their armour' together with others suggests that the needs of people for emotional human stimulation, even if it is unspecific, undemanding, and relatively mild, are far stronger and far more general than is usually recognized. The consumption of alcohol evidently acts as a help to people who, without it, might not be able so quickly, or perhaps not at all, to move from the type of groupings dominated by relatively impersonal contacts, by highly routinized tasks and by aims outside themselves, to the relatively less well-ordered and more personal companionship of the leisure-gemeinschaft with no other aim but itself.

(2) The distinguishing characteristics of sociability as a sphere of leisure are fairly clear. Those at the core of the class of leisure activities which we have called mimetic are perhaps a little less clear and need some comments. The term 'mimetic' underlines the fact that a number of leisure institutions and activities which are usually classified as diverse on a lower level of generality have specific structural characteristics in common. As we use it here, the term refers to the fact that the events and activities grouped together under that name share the following structural characteristics: they arouse emotions of a specific type which are closely related to, yet in a specific way different from, those which people experience in the ordinary course of their non-leisure life. In the context of mimetic events, people can experience, and in some cases act out, fear and laughter, anxiety and love, sympathy and antipathy, friendliness and hatred, and many other emotions and sentiments which they may also experience in their non-leisure life. But in the mimetic context, all the sentiments, and, if it comes to that, the emotional acts connected with them, are transposed. They lose their sting. Even fear, horror, hatred and other ordinarily far from pleasant feelings and the corresponding actions are associated in the mimetic setting, to a greater or lesser extent, with feelings of enjoyment. The experiences and behaviour of people in a mimetic context thus represent a specific transposition of experiences and behaviour characteristic of the so-called 'serious' business of life, whether this

term refers to occupational work or to other spare-time activities. The term 'mimetic' is an expression of this special relationship between the non-mimetic business of life and this type of leisure activities. It does not mean that the latter is an imitation of the former or that it mirrors the former. It refers to the fact that, in the mimetic context, the emotional behaviour and experiences of ordinary life take on a different colour. In this context, one can experience and in some cases act out strong feelings without running any of the risks normally connected with all activities under the impact of strong emotional excitement, particularly in highly civilized societies, but to some extent in all others too. In fact, the arousal of a specific type of excitement is the core of all mimetic leisure activities. Outside the mimetic context, the public arousal of strong excitement and a show of excited behaviour are usually severely controlled; they are hedged in by social controls as well as by people's own conscience. In the mimetic context, pleasurable excitement can be shown with the approval of one's fellows and of one's own conscience as long as it does not overstep certain limits. One can experience hatred and the desire to kill, defeating opponents and humiliating enemies. One can share making love to the most desirable men and women, experience the anxieties of threatened defeat and the open triumph of victory. In short, one can tolerate, up to a point, the arousal of strong feelings of a great variety of types in societies which otherwise impose on people a life of relatively even and unemotional routines and which require a high degree and great constancy of emotional controls in all human relationships.

Thus, mimetic activities share with the other two types of leisure activities the function of an antidote to the routines of life. But in their case one encounters, at least in highly industrialized societies, a great variety of institutions and organizations particularly specialized for their leisure task, for the arousal of mimetic excitement as a crystallizing point for a wide range of other experiences. This highly specialized task binds together mimetic institutions and activities which are usually grouped into separate compartments such as entertainment and culture, sports and art. It will certainly be necessary to look more closely into their differences, but that can hardly be done without at the same time investigating their common characteristics not only as leisure events, but as mimetic leisure events.

3

The Genesis of Sport as a Sociological Problem

Norbert Elias

I

Many types of sports which today are played in a more or less identical manner all over the world originated in England.[1] They spread from there to other countries mainly in the second half of the nineteenth and first half of the twentieth centuries. Football, in the form which became known in England as 'Association Football' or, by a popular abbreviation, as 'soccer', was one of them. Horse-racing, wrestling, boxing, tennis, fox-hunting, rowing, croquet and athletics were others. But none of the others was quite as widely and, in many cases, quite as rapidly adopted and absorbed by other countries as their own as the soccer type of football. Nor did they enjoy quite as much popularity.[2]

The English term 'sport', too, was widely adopted by other countries as a generic term for this specific type of pastimes. That 'sports', the specific type of English pastimes which spread to many other countries mainly between 1850 and 1950, had certain distinguishing characteristics in common which justified their designation as such, namely as 'sports', has probably been noted more in other countries than in England itself. A German commentator wrote in 1936:

> As is well known, England was the cradle and the loving 'mother' of sport . . . It appears that English technical terms referring to this field might become the common possession of all nations in the same way as Italian technical terms in the field of music. It is probably rare that a piece of culture has migrated with so few changes from one country to another.[3]

That 'sport' – the social datum as well as the word – was initially a stranger in other countries can be shown from many examples. The timing of a process of diffusion and adoption is always a significant datum in the context of a sociological diagnosis. Thus in Germany in 1810, an aristocratic writer who knew England was still able to say, '"Sport" is as untranslatable as "gentleman".'[4] In 1844 another German author wrote with regard to the term 'sports', 'we have no word for this and are almost forced to introduce it into our language.'[5] The diffusion of the English term 'sport' as an expression which German people could understand as a matter of course continued to be slow up to the 1850s. It gradually gained momentum in conjunction with the increase of sports activities themselves. Finally, in the twentieth century, 'Sport' became fully established as a German word.

In France, the *Larousse du XIXiéme Siécle* characterized the term 'sport' thus: 'Sport – sportt – English word formed from the old French "desport", pleasure, diversion . . . ' It complained about the importation of such terms 'which obviously corrupt our language but we have no customs barriers in order to prohibit their importation at the frontier.'[6] Other imports from England to France, factual as well as verbal, were 'turf', 'jockey', 'steeplechase', 'match', 'sweepstake' and 'le boxe'. Already under Louis XVIII horse-racing and betting became more regularized in France in accordance with English models. The fashion disappeared during the revolution but was revived with the re-establishment of a more or less aristocratic upper class. A jockey club was founded in Paris in 1833. In fact, the aristocratic or 'Society' type of pastimes, which dominated the meaning of the term 'sport' in England itself in the first half of the nineteenth century, spread to other countries and was adopted there by corresponding social elites before the more popular types such as football developed the characteristics of a 'sport', were perceived as such in England itself and spread in that form to other countries, as a pastime of middle- and working-class groups. In Germany as in France, some English terms which belonged to the language of the upper-class type of sport were taken up as early as the eighteenth century. From about 1744 on, an older term 'baxen' appeared in the more literate form of 'boxen'. It is as significant for our understanding of the development of European societies as it is for that of sport itself that the first types of English sports which were taken up by other countries were horse-racing, boxing, fox-hunting, and similar pastimes, and that the diffusion of ball games such as football and tennis and of 'sport' generally in the more contemporary sense began only in the second part of the nineteenth century.

The transformation of a polymorphous English folk game into Association Football or 'soccer' had the character of a fairly long development in the direction of greater regulation and uniformity. It culminated in the codification of the game more or less on a national level in 1863. The first German football club playing according to English rules was founded, characteristically enough in Hanover, in 1878. In the Netherlands, the first football club was founded in 1879/80, in Italy about 1890. Football federations were founded in Switzerland in 1895, in Germany in 1900, and in Portugal in 1906, indicating the increase in the number of clubs in each country. In the Netherlands alone, 25 different football clubs with more than ten members each existed as early as 1900/01. By 1910/11, the number of clubs had risen to 134. From 1908 onwards, football became – with interruptions – a regular part of the Olympic Games.

As the game spread to other countries, the term 'football' itself, often suitably transformed and, in most, though not all cases, associated with the 'soccer' type of English football, entered other languages. In France it retained its original form. In Germany it was transformed without great difficulty into 'Fussball'. In Spain it became 'futbol' with characteristic derivatives such as 'futbolero' and 'futbolista'. In Portugal it became 'futebol', in Holland 'voetbal'. In the United States, too, the term 'football' was for a time connected with the soccer type of game, but there the term changed its meaning in accordance with the changing fortunes of the game itself. The dominant American style of playing football gradually changed from the soccer type. Some of the leading American universities, so it seems, diverged from its rules, at first influenced by a Canadian variant of the English rival of soccer, 'rugby' football or 'rugger', which they then developed further in their own way. But the term 'football' remained attached to the different style of playing the game which evolved gradually and finally became standardized in the States while the Association type of the game became known there purely and simply as 'soccer' in contrast to the continued use of 'futbol' and 'futebol' for this form of the game in the Latin-American states.

One could give many other examples of this diffusion from England and the absorption by other countries of sport and the terms associated with it. As a first approach, these few may be enough to indicate the problem.

II

What accounts for the fact that, mainly in the nineteenth and twentieth centuries, an English type of pastimes called 'sport' set the pattern for a world-wide leisure movement? Pastimes of this type evidently corresponded to specific leisure needs which made themselves felt in many countries during that period. Why did they emerge in England first?

What characteristics in the development and structure of English society account for the development there of leisure activities with the specific characteristics which we designate as 'sport'? What are these characteristics? And what distinguished pastimes which came to possess them from earlier pastimes?

At first glance, one may well feel that this array of questions is based on wrong assumptions. Surely, contemporary societies are not the first and not the only ones whose members have enjoyed sport? Did not people play football in England and in other European countries in the Middle Ages? Did not the courtiers of Louis XIV have their tennis courts and enjoy their 'jeu de paume'? And above all the ancient Greeks, the great pioneers of 'athletics' and other 'sports', did they not, like ourselves, organize local and inter-state game-contests on a magnificent scale? Is not the revival of the Olympic Games in our own times a sufficient reminder of the fact that 'sport' is nothing new?

It is difficult to clarify the question whether the type of game-contests which developed in England under the name 'sport' during the eighteenth and nineteenth centuries and which spread from there to other countries was something relatively new or whether it was a revival of something old which had unaccountably lapsed, without looking briefly into the question of whether in fact the game-contests of ancient Greece had the characteristics of what we now regard as 'sport'. The term 'sport' is at present often used rather loosely to cover game-contests of many kinds. Like the term 'industry', it is used both in a wider and a narrower sense. In the wider sense, it refers, like the term 'industry', to specific activities of pre-state tribal societies and pre-industrial state-societies as well as to corresponding activities of industrial nation-states. If one uses the term 'industry' in this wider sense, one is at present nevertheless well aware of its narrower and more precise meaning, of the fact that the 'industrialization process' of the nineteenth and twentieth centuries is something rather new and that the specific types of production and work which have developed in recent times under the name 'industry' have certain unique structures that can be determined sociologically with considerable precision and clearly distinguished from other types of production. If one speaks of 'sport', however, one still uses the term indiscriminately both in a wider sense in which it refers to the game-contests and physical exercises of all societies and in a narrower sense in which it refers to the specific type of game-contests which, like the term itself, originated in England and spread from there to other societies. This process – one might call it the 'sportization' of game-contests if that did not sound rather unattractive – points to a problem which is fairly clear: can one discover in the recent development of the structure and organization of those leisure activities which we call 'sport' trends which are as unique as those in the structure and organization of work which we refer to when we speak of a process of industrialization?

This is an open question. One can easily misread it. Given the prevailing evaluation of work as something of much higher value than leisure activities of all kinds, it can easily suggest that any transformation, whether of leisure activities in general or of game-contests in particular, which has taken place in the last 200 years or so must have been the 'effect' of which industrialization was the 'cause'. The implicit expectation of causal connections of this type closes the issue before it has been properly opened. One may, for instance, consider the possibility that both industrialization and the transformation of specific leisure occupations into sports are interdependent part-trends within an over-all transformation of state societies in recent times. But only if one ceases to treat changes in social spheres which rate higher in the value scale of one's society as 'causes', and changes in lower ranking spheres as 'effects', can one hope to clarify the problem which one encounters here. And the clarification of the problem itself – that of the genesis of sport – is the main task of this essay. In this as in other cases, it is easier to find solutions if one is quite clear what the problem is.

III

The following excerpt from the article on athletics in a recent edition of the *Encyclopaedia Britannica* can probably be regarded as a reasonable summary of the conventional views on this problem:

> The earliest historical records of athletics are of the Grecian Olympic Games (*c*.800 BC) . . . terminated by order of the emperor Theodosius in AD 394. The history of athletics between the fall of Rome in the 5th century and the 19th century is quite sketchy. Religious festivals in the Middle Ages were often accompanied by crude ball games between rival towns or guilds. These were the forerunners of the great spectator sports of the 20th century: soccer, baseball, tennis, football, etc. The coming of the Industrial Revolution in the mid-18th century and the later introduction of sports as a regular extra-curricular activity in public schools by Thomas Arnold (*c*.1830) provided a spur which led to the great development of sport during the Victorian age of England. Capping the athletic revival of the 19th century was the restoration of the Olympic Games at Athens in 1896. As the 20th century dawned, interest in all competitive sports reached a peak and despite two world wars and numerous minor hostilities, this interest continues to grow.

This summary, as one can see, states a number of reasonably well-documented facts. It occasionally hints at an explanation such as the spur supposedly given to sport through the initiative of Dr Arnold. But it is hardly designed to open the eyes of a reader to the many unsolved problems buried under the smooth surface of the narrative. How, for instance, is it to be explained that the religious festivals of the Middle Ages were accompanied by games which were 'crude' while the religious festivals in antiquity at Olympia and elsewhere were apparently less crude and thus more akin to those of the nineteenth and twentieth centuries? And how is it to be determined that these are less crude? How can one determine, with a reasonable degree of precision, variations in 'crudeness', in civilizing standards in the performance of games? And how can one explain them? How can one explain the 'great development of sport', the 'athletic revival of the nineteenth century'? If one remembers the tournaments of the Middle Ages or the innumerable folk-games of that age – unsuppressed and, in fact, unsuppressable even if the authorities disapproved of them, as the recurrent edicts against playing football in England and other European countries indicate – one can hardly say that there was not a very lively interest in game-contests as such. Was the difference between the game-contests that people enjoyed prior to the eighteenth century and those which they enjoyed in the age of the 'industrial revolution' simply a question of a higher or lower degree of 'crudeness'? Was it due to the fact that the latter were less savage, that they were more 'civilized'? And is that one of the distinguishing characteristics of 'sport'? But in that case, is it justified to speak of a 'revival'? Is the sports movement of the nineteenth and twentieth centuries another 'Renaissance', an unexplained 'rebirth' of something which existed in antiquity, perished in the Middle Ages and, for unknown reasons, was simply reborn in our time? Were the game-contests of antiquity less 'crude' and less savage? Were they, like ours, relatively restrained and representative of a comparatively high sensitivity against playfully inflicting serious injuries on others for the delight of spectators? Or is the tendency to present the modern sports movement as the revival of a similar movement in antiquity one of those benevolent ideological legends innocently used as a means for strengthening the unity of a movement that is full of tensions and conflicting tendencies and for heightening its glamour and prestige? In that case, would it not perhaps be preferable to examine realistically the specific conditions which account for the genesis and rise of the sports movement of our time, to face up to the fact that game-contests of the type which we call 'sport', like the industrial nation-states where they take place, have certain unique characteristics which distinguish them from other types, and to start the difficult task of enquiring into and explaining the nature of these distinguishing characteristics?

IV

On closer inspection, it is not difficult to see that the game-contests of classical antiquity, which are often represented as the great paradigm of sport, had a number of features and grew up under conditions which were very different from those of our own game-contests. The ethos of the contenders, the standards by which they were judged, the rules of the contests, and the performances themselves differed markedly in many respects from those characteristic of modern sport. Many of the relevant writings of today show a strong tendency to minimize the differences and maximize the similarities. The result is a distorted picture of our own as well as of Greek society and a distorted picture of the relationship between them. The issues are confused not only by the tendency to treat the game-contests of antiquity as the ideal embodiment of contemporary sport but also by the corresponding expectation to find confirmation for this hypothesis in the writings of antiquity and the tendency to neglect contradictory evidence or to treat it automatically as a reference to exceptional cases.

It may be enough here to point to one of the basic features characteristic of the differences in the whole structure of game-contests of classical antiquity and those of the nineteenth and twentieth centuries. In antiquity the customary rules of 'heavy' athletic events, such as boxing and wrestling, admitted a far higher degree of physical violence than that admitted by the rules of the corresponding types of sport-contests. The rules of the latter, moreover, are very much more detailed and differentiated; they are not primarily customary rules but written rules, explicitly subject to reasoned criticism and revision. The higher level of physical violence in the games of antiquity itself was anything but an isolated datum. It was symptomatic of specific features in the organization of Greek society, especially in the stage of development reached by what we now call the 'state' organization and by the degree of monopolization of physical violence embodied in it. A relatively firm, stable and impersonal monopolization and control of the means of violence is one of the central structural traits of contemporary nation-states. Compared with it, the institutional monopolization and control of physical violence in the city-states of Greece was still rudimentary.

The clarification of problems such as these is not difficult if their investigation is guided by a clear theoretical model such as that provided by the theory of civilizing processes.[7] According to it, one expects that state formation and conscience formation, the level of socially permitted physical violence and the threshold of repugnance against using it or witnessing it, differ in specific ways at different stages in the development of societies. It is striking to find how fully the evidence in the case of classical Greece confirms these theoretical expectations. In this way, theory and empirical data together remove one of the main obstacles to the understanding of developmental differences such as those which exist between ancient and contemporary game-contests, namely the feeling that one casts a slur on another society and lowers its human value by admitting that the level of physical violence tolerated there even in game-contests was higher, and the threshold of revulsion against people wounding or even killing each other in such a contest to the delight of spectators correspondingly lower than our own. In the case of Greece, one is thus torn between the high human value traditionally attached to its achievements in philosophy, the sciences, the arts and poetry, and the low human value which one seems to attribute to the ancient Greeks if one speaks of their lower level of revulsion against physical violence, if one seems to suggest that they were, compared with ourselves, 'uncivilized' and 'barbarous'. It is precisely the misunderstanding of the factual nature of civilizing processes, the prevailing tendency to use terms like 'civilized' and 'uncivilized' as expressions of ethnocentric value judgements, as absolute and final moral judgements – we are 'good', they are 'bad', or vice versa – that leads our reasoning into seemingly inescapable contradictions such as these.

We ourselves are brought up, in accordance with the specific social organization and control of the means of violence within the industrial nation-states of our time, with specific standards of self-control with regard to impulses of violence. We measure transgressions automatically by these standards – whether they occur in our own or in other societies at a different stage of development. Internalized, these standards afford protection and strengthen our defences against lapses in a variety of ways. A heightened sensibility with regard to acts of violence, feelings of repugnance against seeing violence committed beyond the permitted level in real life, guilt-feelings about our own lapses, a 'bad conscience', all these are symptomatic of these defences. However, in a period of incessant violence in inter-state affairs, these internalized defences against impulses to violence inevitably remain unstable and brittle. They are continuously exposed to conflicting social pressures – those encouraging a high level of self-control of violent impulses in human relations within one and the same state-society, and those encouraging a loosening of the self-control of violent impulses and even a training for violence in the relations between different state-societies. The former account for the relatively high degree of physical security, though not, of course, of psychological and other forms of security, enjoyed by citizens of more developed nation-states within their own societies. They constantly conflict with the demands made on the citizens of these states as a result of the absence of any effective monopolization and control of physical violence in inter-state relations. A double morality, a split and contradictory conscience formation, is the result.

No doubt discrepancies of this type can be found at many stages in the development of societies. The level of violence control within social groups at the tribal stage is almost always higher than that of violence control between social groups of this type. It was certainly no different in the case of the Greek city-states. But in their case the disparity between the two levels was relatively small compared with that characteristic of our own time. There is a good deal of evidence to suggest that this gradient, the disparity between the level of physical security and of both social and self-control of violent impulses, with the corresponding conscience formation reached today in intra-state relations, and the level of physical security and social regulation of overtly violent feelings and – intermittently – of overt acts of violence in inter-state relations is greater today than ever before. The level of physical security within the more advanced industrial nation-states, though it may appear low enough to those who live in them, is, in all likelihood, normally higher than in less developed state societies, while the insecurity in inter-state relations has hardly decreased. Violent inter-state conflicts at the present stage of social development are still as unmanageable for those involved in them as they always were. Standards of civilized behaviour, accordingly, are relatively low and the internalization of social taboos against physical violence, the conscience formation, is in that respect transient and comparatively unsteady. That conflicts and tensions within industrial nation-states have become – normally – less violent and somewhat more manageable is the result of a long unplanned development; it is certainly not the merit of the present generations. But present generations are apt to regard it as such; they are inclined to sit in judgement **over** past generations whose conscience formation, whose level of revulsion against physical violence, for instance in the relations between ruling elites and ruled, was lower, as if their own, higher level of revulsion was simply their own personal achievement.

The level of violence to be observed in the game-contests of past ages is often judged in this manner. We often fail to distinguish between individual acts of transgression against the standards of violence control within our own society and individual acts of a similar kind committed in other societies in accordance with *their* socially permitted level of violence, in accordance with the norms of *those* societies. Thus our immediate, our almost automatic emotional response often induces us to judge societies with different standards of violence control and of revulsion against violence as if the members of these societies had been free to choose between *their* standards and *their* norms and ours, and, having had this choice, had taken the wrong decision. We enjoy, in relation to them, the same feeling of 'being better', of moral superiority often experienced in relation to individual offenders in our own society if we call their conduct 'uncivilized' or 'barbarous', in this manner expressing our feeling of moral superiority. We treat their adherence to social norms which permit forms of violence that are condemned as repulsive in our own societies as a blot on their moral character, as a sign of their inferiority as human beings. Another society is thus judged and evaluated by us as a whole as if it were an individual member of our own. As a rule, we do not ask and, as a result, we do not know how changes in the level of violence control, in the social norms regulating violence, or in the feelings associated with violence occur. Nor, as a rule, do we ask and therefore we do not know why they occur. We do not know, in other words, how they can be explained or, for that matter, how our own, higher level of sensitivity with regard to physical violence, at least in intra-state relations, can be explained. At the most, we explain them vaguely by the choice of our expressions rather than explicitly and critically, for example as a 'flow' in the nature of the groups concerned, or as an unexplainable characteristic of their 'racial' or ethnic make-up.

V

The customary levels of violence used and permitted in the game-contests of societies at different stages of development thus illuminate a much wider and a very fundamental problem. A few examples may help to give it precision.

Take the case of wrestling as performed in our own days and in antiquity. Today, the sport is highly organized and highly regulated. It is governed by an International Wrestling Federation with head-quarters in Switzerland. According to the Olympic rules of January 1967, among the foul holds of free-style wrestling are the stranglehold, the half-strangle, and the double nelson with pressure applied straight down or with the use of legs. Punching, kicking, butting with the head are all forbidden. A bout, lasting not more than nine minutes, and divided into three periods of three minutes each with two intervals of one minute, is controlled by a referee, three judges and a timekeeper. In spite of these very tight regulations, free-style wrestling appears to many people today as one of the less refined, 'cruder' types of sport. Performed as a spectator sport by professionals, a slightly rougher though often pre-arranged version is still highly popular. But the

professionals rarely inflict serious injuries on each other. In all likelihood, the public would not enjoy seeing bones broken and the blood
flow. But the performers make a good show of hurting one another,
and the public seems to like the make-believe.[8]

Among the game-contests of the ancient Olympic Games was the
pancration, a kind of ground wrestling which formed one of the most
popular events. But the level of permitted violence represented by the
customary duel of the pancration was very different from that permitted in contemporary free-style wrestling. Thus Leontiskos of Messana,
who twice in the first half of the fifth century won the Olympic crown
for wrestling, obtained his victories not by throwing his opponents but
by breaking their fingers. Arrhachion of Phigalia, twice Olympic victor
in the pancration, was strangled in 564 during his third attempt to win
the Olympic crown, but before being killed he succeeded in breaking
the toes of his opponent and the pain forced the latter to give up the
struggle. The judges, therefore, crowned Arrhachion's corpse and
proclaimed the dead man victor. His compatriots subsequently erected
a statue of Arrachion in the market-place of their town.[9] This, apparently, was the customary practice. If a man was killed in a game-contest
of one of the great festivals, the dead man was crowned victor. But
apart from loss of the crown – a very severe loss – the survivor was not
punished. Nor, as far as one can see, was any social stigma attached to
his action. To be killed or to be very severely wounded and perhaps
incapacitated for life was a risk a fighter in the pancration had to take.
One can assess the difference between wrestling as a sport and wrestling as an 'agon' from the following summary:

> In the pancration, the competitors fought with every part of their body,
> with their hands, feet, elbows, their knees, their necks and their heads; in
> Sparta they even used their feet. The pancratiasts were allowed to gouge
> one another's eyes out . . . they were also allowed to trip their oppo-
> nents, lay hold of their feet, noses and ears, dislocate their fingers and
> arms and apply strangle-holds. If one man succeeded in throwing the
> other, he was entitled to sit on him and beat him about the head, face and
> ears; he could also kick him and trample on him. It goes without saying
> that the contestants in this brutal contest sometimes received the most
> fearful wounds and that not infrequently men were killed! The pan-
> cration of the Spartan epheboi was probably the most brutal of all.
> Pausanias tells us that the contestants quite literally fought tooth and nail
> and bit and tore one another's eyes out.[10]

There was a judge but no timekeeper and no time limits. The
struggle lasted until one of the opponents gave up. The rules were
traditional, unwritten, undifferentiated and, in their application, probably elastic. It seems that, traditionally, biting and gouging were forbid-

den. But before the judge could drive an offender, caught up in the fury of the battle, away from his opponent, the damage was probably done.

The old Olympic Games lasted more than a thousand years. Standards of violence in fighting may have fluctuated throughout this period. But whatever these fluctuations were, throughout antiquity the threshold of sensitivity with regard to the infliction of physical injuries and even to killing in a game-contest and, accordingly, the whole contest ethos, was very different from that represented by the type of contest which we nowadays characterize as 'sport'.

Boxing is another example. Like the pancration type of wrestling, it was very much less hedged in by rules and was therefore to a much higher extent dependent on physical strength, on spontaneous fighting passion and endurance, than sport boxing. One did not distinguish between different classes of boxers. One did not try, therefore, to match people according to their weight either in this or in any of the other contests. The only distinction made was that between boys and men. Boxers did not only fight with their fists. As in almost all forms of boxing, the legs played a part in the struggle. Kicking the shins of an opponent was a normal part of the boxing tradition in antiquity.[11] Only the hand and the upper parts of four fingers were bound with leather thongs fastened to the forearm. Fists could be clenched or fingers stretched and, with hard nails, rammed into the opponent's body and face. As time went on, soft leather thongs gave way to harder thongs specially made from tanned ox-hide.[12] These were then fitted with several strips of hard thick leather with sharp projecting edges. The statue of a seated boxer by Apollonius of Athens (first century BC), now in the Museo Nazionale delle Terme in Rome, shows the arrangement fairly clearly. But perhaps boxing is a misleading term. Not only the manner but also the aim and the ethos of this kind of fighting was different from those in sport boxing. Significantly enough, the fighting ethos of these pugilistic matches, like that of the Greek *agones* generally, was far more directly derived from the fighting ethos of a warrior aristocracy than is the case with the fighting ethos of sport contests. The latter stemmed from the tradition of a country which, more than most other European countries, developed a distinct organization of sea-warfare[13] very different from that of land-warfare, and whose land-owning upper classes – aristocracy and gentry – developed a code of behaviour less directly concerned than that of most other European upper classes with the military code of honour of the officer corps of land-armies.

Greek 'boxing', in common with the other forms of agonistic training and practice in the Greek city-states, but unlike English boxing in the eighteenth and nineteenth centuries, was regarded as a training for warfare as well as for game-contests. Philostratos mentions that the fighting technique of the pancration stood the Greek citizen-armies in good stead in the battle of Marathon when it developed into a general mêlée, and also at Thermopylae where the Spartans fought with their bare hands when their swords and spears had been broken.[14] In the time of Imperial Rome in which he wrote, wars were no longer fought by citizen armies. They were fought by professional soldiers, by the Roman legions. The distance between military technique and the conduct of war on the one hand, and the traditional agonistic technique of the game-contests on the other hand, had become greater. The Greek Philostratos looked back to the classical age with understandable nostalgia. Perhaps even there, in the period of the hoplite armies, the fighting techniques of war and those of the game-contests were no longer quite as connected with each other as he suggests, but their connection was very much closer than that between the fighting techniques of sport-contests and the fighting techniques of warfare in the age of industrial nation-states. Philostratos was probably very near the mark when he wrote that, in former days, people had regarded the game-contests as an exercise for war and war as an exercise for these contests.[15] The ethos of the game-contests at the great Greek festivals still reflected that of the heroic ancestors as represented in the Homeric epics and perpetuated to some extent from generation to generation by their use in the education of the young. It had many characteristics of the display ethos which rules the status and power rivalries of noble elites in a great number of societies. Fighting, in games as in war, was centred on the ostentatious display of the warrior virtues which gained for a man the highest praise and honour among other members of his own group and for his group – for his kin-group or his city – among other groups. It was glorious to vanquish enemies or opponents but it was hardly less glorious to be vanquished, as Hector was by Achilles, provided one fought with all one's might until one was maimed, wounded or killed and could fight no longer. Victory or defeat was in the hands of the gods. What was inglorious and shameful was to surrender victory without a sufficient show of bravery and endurance.

It was in line with this warrior ethos that a boy or a man killed in one of the Olympic boxing or wrestling matches was often crowned as victor to the glory of his clan and his city and that the survivor – the killer – was neither punished nor stigmatized. The Greek games were not ruled by a great concern for 'fairness'. The English ethos of fairness had non-military roots. It evolved in England in connection with a very specific change in the nature of the enjoyment and excitement provided by game-contests as a result of which the all-too brief pleasure in the outcome of a sports battle, in the moment of consummation or victory, was extended and prolonged by the equal pleasure and excitement, derived from what initially was foreplay, from participating in or from witnessing the tension of the game-contest itself. Greater emphasis on the enjoyment of the game-contest, and the tension-excitement it provided as such, was to some extent connected with the enjoyment of betting which, in England, played a considerable part both in the transformation of 'cruder' forms of game-contests into sports and in the development of the ethos of fairness. Gentlemen watching a game-contest played by their sons, their retainers or by well-known professionals, liked to put money on one side or the other as a condiment of the excitement provided by the contest itself which was already tempered by civilizing restraints. But the prospect of winning one's bet could add to the excitement of watching the struggle only if the initial odds of winning were more or less evenly divided between the two sides and offered a minimum of calculability. All this required, and in turn was made possible by, a higher organizational level than that reached in the city-states of ancient Greece:

> The boxers of Olympia were not classified according to weight any more than the wrestlers were. There was no boxing ring, the bouts being fought on an open piece of ground inside the stadium. The target area was the head and the face . . . The fight went on until one of the two contestants was no longer able to defend himself or acknowledged defeat. This he did either by raising his index finger or extending two fingers towards his opponent.[16]

Representations on Greek vases usually show boxers in a traditional stance so close to each other that each stands with one foot forward next to or even behind that of the other. There was little scope for the footwork which enables modern boxers to move quickly, now to the right or left, now backwards, now forwards. To move backwards, according to the code of warriors, was a sign of cowardice. To avoid the enemy's blows by moving out of his way was shameful. Boxers, like warriors at close quarters, were expected to stand fast and not to give way. The defences of skilful boxers might be impenetrable; they might tire their opponents and win without receiving injuries. But if the fight took too long, a judge could order the two opponents to take and to give blow for blow without defending themselves until one of them was no longer able to continue the fight. This agonistic type of boxing, as one can see, accentuated the climax, the moment of decision, of victory or defeat, as the most important and significant part of the contest, more important than the game-contest itself. It was as much a test of physical endurance and of sheer muscular strength as of skill. Serious injuries to the eyes, ears and even to the skull were frequent; so were swollen ears, broken teeth and squashed noses. We hear of two boxers who agreed to exchange blow for blow. The first struck a blow to the head which his opponent survived. When he lowered his guard, the other man struck him under the ribs with his outstretched fingers, burst through his side with his hard nails, seized his bowels and killed him.[17]

VI

'Of all the Olympic contests the one which is most alien to us today is boxing; no matter how hard we try we are still unable to conceive how a highly cultivated people with such discriminating aesthetic tastes could derive pleasure from this barbaric spectacle in which two men beat one another about the head with their heavily mailed fists . . . until one of them acknowledged defeat or was reduced to such straits that he was unable to continue to fight. For not only under the Romans, but under the Greeks as well this form of contest was no longer a sport; it was a deadly serious business . . . More than one Olympic competitor lost his life in the stadium.'

This critique, made in 1882 by Adolf Boetticher, one of the early Olympic scholars, is valid today. Like their colleagues in the wrestling and the pancration, the boxers were determined to win at all costs.[18]

The facts are not in doubt but the evaluation is. The quotation represents an almost paradigmatic example of the misunderstanding that results from the unquestioned use of one's own threshold of repugnance in the face of specific types of physical violence as a general yardstick for all human societies regardless of their structure and of the stage of social development they have reached, especially the stage they have reached in the social organization and control of physical violence: this is as significant an aspect of the development of societies as the organization and control of 'economic' means of production. One encounters here a very striking example of the barrier to the understanding of societies produced by the dominance of heterono-mous[19] evaluations over the perception of functional interdependen-cies. Classical Greek sculpture ranks highly in the value scale of our time. The types of physical violence embodied in Greek game-contests such as the pancration, according to our value scale, receive high negative marks. The fact that we associate with the one a high positive value, with the other a high negative value, makes it appear to those who allow their understanding to be guided by preconceived value judgements that these data cannot possibly be connected with each other. It confronts those who judge the past in terms of this type of evaluation with an insoluble problem.

However, if one is concerned with the sociological analysis of the connections between different aspects of the same society, one has no reason to assume that only those manifestations of that society to which, as an outside observer, one attributes the same value, be it positive or negative, are interdependent. One can discover in all societies factual interdependencies between aspects to which an observer on the one hand and the people themselves who form these societies on the other attach opposite values. The beauty of Greek art and the relative brutality of Greek game-contests are an example. Far from being incompatible, they were closely connected manifestations of the same level of development, of the same social structure.

The emergence of Greek sculpture from its archaic mould and the idealistic realism of the sculptures of the classical period remain incomprehensible without an understanding of the part which the physical appearance of a person played as a determinant of the social esteem in which he was held among the ruling elites of the Greek city-states. In that society it was hardly possible for a man with a weak or misformed body to reach or to maintain a position of high social or political power. Physical strength, physical beauty, poise and endurance played a very much higher part as determinants of the social standing of a male person in Greek society than they do in ours. One is not always aware that the possibility for a man who is physically handicapped to rise to, or to maintain, a position of leadership or high social power and rank is a relatively recent phenomenon in the development of societies. Because 'body image' or physical appearance ranks relatively low, much lower, for example, than 'intelligence' or 'moral character', in the value-scale which, in societies such as ours, determines the ranking of men and the whole image we form of them, we often lack the key to the understanding of other societies in which physical appearance played a much greater part as a determinant of the public image of a man. In ancient Greece this was undoubtedly the case. One can perhaps convey the difference by pointing to the fact that in our society physical appearance as a determinant of the social image of an individual still plays a very high and perhaps a growing part as far as women are concerned but with regard to men, although television may have some impact on the problem, physical appearance and particularly bodily strength and beauty do not play a very great part in the public esteem of a person. The fact that one of the most powerful nations of our time elected a paralysed man to its highest office is in this respect symptomatic.

It was different in the society of the Greek city-states. From childhood on, human beings who were weak or misformed were weeded out. Weak babies were left to die. A man who was unable to fight counted for little. It was very rare for a man who was crippled, ailing or very old to gain or to maintain a position of public leadership. The term used in classical Greek society as one of the expressions of their ideal, the term *arete*, is often translated as 'virtue'. But in fact it did not refer, as the term 'virtue' does, to any moral characteristics. It referred to the attainments of a warrior and a gentleman among which his body image, his qualification as a strong and skilled warrior, played a dominant part. It was this ideal which found expression in their sculptures as well as in their game-contests. Most Olympic victors had their statues erected in Olympia and sometimes also in their home town.[20]

It is merely another facet of the same distinguishing characteristic of Greek society during the classical age that the social position of athletes was very different from that which they hold in our own society. The equivalent of sport, the 'culture' of the body, was not to the same extent a specialism as it is today. In contemporary societies a boxer is a specialist; and if we apply the term to those who gained fame as 'boxers' in antiquity, the mere use of the word is apt to conjure up in our minds a similar picture. In fact, the men who proved their physical strength, their agility, their courage and their endurance through their victories in the great festivals, of which those at Olympia were the most famous, stood a very good chance of gaining a high social and political position in their home society if they did not already hold it. For the most part the participants in the game-contests of Olympia probably came from 'good families', from the relatively wealthy elites of their home towns, from groups of landowners and perhaps from wealthier peasant families. Participation in these game-contests demanded a long and arduous training which only relatively wealthy people could afford. A promising young athlete who lacked the money for such a training might find a wealthy patron; or a professional trainer might advance him the money. But if he gained a victory at Olympia, he brought fame to his family and his home town and had a strong chance of being counted from then on as a member of its ruling elite. Probably the most famous wrestler of classical antiquity was Milon of Croton. He gained a considerable number of victories at Olympia and other panhellenic festivals. He was a man of prodigious strength which in time became proverbial. He is also mentioned as one of the best pupils of Pythagoras and as commander of the army of his home town in its victorious battle against the Sybarites which ended in the furious mass-killing of the latter after their defeat. We find the same picture in reverse if we notice that men who today are remembered above all for their intellectual achievements, were often remembered in their own time also in connection with their attainments as warriors or athletes. Aeschylus, Socrates and Demosthenes went through the hard school of hoplite fighting. Plato had victories in some of the athletic festivals to his credit. Thus, the idealization of the warrior in Greek sculpture, the representation even of the gods in accordance with the ideal physical appearance of the aristocratic warrior, and the warrior ethos of the game contests were, indeed, not only compatible; they were closely connected manifestations of the same social group. Both are characteristic of the social position, the manner of life and the ideals of these groups. But the understanding of this factual interdependence does not impair the enjoyment of Greek art. If anything, it enhances it.[21]

VII

A comparison of the level of violence represented by the game-contests of classical Greece, or for that matter by the tournaments and folk-games of the Middle Ages, with those represented by contemporary sport-contests shows a specific strand in a civilizing process, but the study of this strand, of the civilizing of game-contests, remains inadequate and incomplete if one does not link it to that of other aspects of the societies whose manifestations game-contests are. In short, the fluctuating level of civilization in game-contests must remain incomprehensible if one does not connect it at least with the general level of socially permitted violence, of the organization of violence-control, and with the corresponding conscience formation in given societies.

A few examples may help to bring this wider context into focus. In the twentieth century, the mass slaughter of conquered groups by the German Nazis has aroused almost world-wide revulsion. The memory of it for some time tarnished the good name of Germany among the nations of the world. The shock was all the greater because many people had lived under the illusion that, in the twentieth century, such barbarities could no longer happen. They had tacitly assumed that people had become more 'civilized', that they had become 'morally better' as part of their nature. They had taken pride in being less savage than their forefathers or than other peoples that they knew without ever facing up to the problem which their own relatively more civilized behaviour posed – to the problem of why they themselves, why their behaviour and their feelings had become a little more civilized. The Nazi episode served as a kind of warning; it was a reminder that the restraints against violence are not symptoms of the superiority of the *nature* of 'civilized nations', not eternal characteristics of their racial or ethnic make-up, but aspects of a specific type of social development which had resulted in more differentiated and stable social control of the means of violence and in a corresponding conscience-formation. Evidently, this type of social development could be reversed.

This does not necessarily imply that there are no grounds for evaluating the results of this development in human behaviour and feelings as 'better' than the corresponding manifestations of earlier developmental stages. Wider understanding of the nexus of facts provides a much better, indeed provides the only secure basis for value judgements of this type. Without it, we cannot know, for example, whether our manner of building up individual self-controls against physical violence is not associated with psychological malformations which, themselves, might appear highly barbaric to a more civilized age. Moreover, if one evaluates a more civilized form of conduct and feeling as 'better' than less civilized forms, if one considers that mankind has made progress by arriving at one's own standards of revulsion and repugnance against forms of violence which were common in former days, one is confronted by the problem of why an unplanned development has resulted in something which one evaluates as progress.

All judgements about standards of civilized behaviour are comparative judgements. One cannot say in any absolute sense: we are 'civilized', they are 'uncivilized'. But one can say with great confidence: 'the standards of conduct and feeling of society A are more, those of society B, less civilized', provided one has worked out a clear and precise developmental gauge. The comparison between the Greek agon-contests and contemporary sport-contests provides one example. Standards of public revulsion in the face of mass murder provide another. As it showed itself in recent times, the almost universal feeling of repugnance against genocide indicates that human societies have undergone a civilizing process, however limited in scope and however unstable its results. Comparison with past attitudes show this very clearly. In Greek and Roman antiquity, the massacre of the whole male population of a defeated and conquered city and the sale into slavery of its women and children, though they might have aroused pity, did not rouse widespread condemnation. Our sources are incomplete but even they show that cases of mass slaughter recurred with fair regularity throughout the whole period.[22] Sometimes the battle fury of a long-threatened or frustrated army played its part in the wholesale massacre of enemies. The destruction of all the Sybarites they could lay their hands on by the citizens of Croton under the leadership of Milon, the famous wrestler, is a case in point. Sometimes 'genocide' was a calculated act aimed at destroying the military power of a rival state, as in the case of Argos, whose military power as a potential rival of Sparta was more or less annihilated by the wholesale destruction of all men who could bear arms on the orders of the Spartan general, Cleomenes. The massacre of the male population of Melos at the order of the Athenian Assembly of Citizens in 416 BC, vividly described by Thucydides, resulted from a figuration very similar to that which led to the Russian occupation of Czechoslovakia in 1968. The Athenians regarded Melos as part of their empire. It had a specific strategic significance for them in their struggle with Sparta. But the inhabitants of Melos did not wish to become part of the Athenian empire. Therefore the Athenians killed the men, sold the women and children into slavery, and settled the island with Athenian colonists. Some Greeks regarded war as the normal relationship between city-states. It could be interrupted by treaties of limited period. Gods, through the mouths of their priests, and writers might disapprove of massacres of this kind. But the level of 'moral' repugnance against what we now call 'genocide' and, more generally, the level of internalized inhibitions against physical violence, were decidedly lower, the feelings of guilt or shame associated with such inhibitions decidedly weaker, than they are in the relatively developed nation-states of the twentieth century. Perhaps they were entirely lacking.

There was no lack of compassion with the victims. The great Athenian dramatists, above all Euripides in his *Trojan Women*, expressed this feeling with a vividness which was all the stronger because it was not yet overlaid by moral repugnance and indignation. Yet one can hardly doubt that the sale into slavery of the women of the defeated, the separation of mother and child, the killing of male children, and many other themes of violence and warfare in their tragedies possessed very much greater actuality for an Athenian public in the context of their lives than they possess for a contemporary public in the context of ours.

Altogether, the level of physical insecurity in the societies of antiquity was very much higher than it is in contemporary nation-states. That their poets showed more compassion than moral indignation is not uncharacteristic of this difference. Homer, already, disapproved of the fact that Achilles, in his grief and fury at the death of Patroclus, had not only sheep, cattle and horses but also 12 young Trojan nobles killed and burned on the funeral pyre of his friend as a sacrifice to his ghost. But, again, the poet did not sit in judgement and condemn his hero from the high throne of his own moral righteousness and superiority because he had committed the barbarous atrocity of human sacrifice. The poet's criticism of Achilles did not have the emotional colour of moral indignation. It did not cast doubt on what we call the 'character' of his hero, on his value as a human being. People do 'bad things' (*kaka erga*) in their grief and fury. The bard shakes his head but he does not appeal to the conscience of his listeners; he does not ask them to regard Achilles as a moral reprobate, a 'bad character'. He appeals to their compassion, to their understanding of the passion which seizes even the best, even the heroes, in times of stress and makes them do 'bad things'. But his human value as a nobleman and a warrior is not in doubt. Human sacrifice did not have for the ancient Greeks quite the same odour as something horrible that it has for the more 'civilized' nations of the twentieth century.[23] Every schoolboy of the Greek educated classes knew of the wrath of Achilles, of the sacrifices and the game-contests at the funeral of Patroclus. The Olympic game-contests stood in a direct line of succession from these ancestral funeral con- tests. It was a very different line of descent from that of contemporary sport-contests.

VIII

Nor, as far as one can see, was the normal level of passion and violence of the Homeric heroes and gods or, expressed differently, their normal developmental level of built-in self-control, of 'conscience', more than a few steps behind that reached in Athens during the classical period. The surviving stones, the temples and the sculptures of Greek gods and heroes have all contributed to the image of the ancient Greeks as a peculiarly even-tempered, balanced and harmonious people. The term 'classical' itself, in phrases such as 'classical antiquity', conjures up the picture of Greek society as a model of balanced beauty and equipoise which later generations can never again hope to emulate. This is a misconception.

One cannot set out here with the precision it deserves the place of classical Greece in the development of 'conscience', of internalized controls with regard either to violence or to other spheres of life. It must be enough to say that even classical Greece still represents the 'dawn of conscience', a stage where the transformation of a self- controlling conscience represented by communal images of external superhuman persons, of commanding or threatening demon-gods who told human beings more or less arbitrarily what to do and what not to do, into a relatively impersonal and individualized inner voice speaking in accordance with general social principles of justice and injustice, right and wrong, was still rather the exception than the norm. Socrates' *daimonion* was perhaps the closest approximation to our type of conscience-formation in classical Greek society but even this highly individualized 'inner voice' still had in some measure the character of a tutelary genius. Moreover, the degree of internalization and individual- ization of norms and social controls which we encounter in Plato's representation of Socrates was, in his time, without doubt a very exceptional phenomenon. It is highly significant that the classical Greek language lacked a differentiated and specialized word for 'con- science'. There are a number of words such as *synesis*, *euthymion*, *eusebia* and others which are occasionally translated as 'conscience', but, on closer inspection, one soon becomes aware that each of them is less specific and covers a much broader spectrum, such as 'having scruples', 'piety', and 'reverence towards god'. But a single concept as highly specialized as the modern concept of 'conscience', denoting a highly authoritative, inescapable and often tyrannical inner agency which, as part of his or her self, guides an individual's conduct, which demands obedience and punishes disobedience with 'pangs' or 'bites' of guilt-feelings, and which, unlike 'fear of the gods' or 'shame', acts on its own, seemingly coming from nowhere, seemingly without deriving power and authority from any external agency, human or superhuman – this concept of conscience is absent from the intellectual equipment of ancient Greece. The fact that this concept of 'conscience' had not yet developed in Greek society can be regarded as a very reliable index of the fact that conscience-formation in that society had not yet reached a stage of internalization, individualization and relative autonomy in any degree comparable to our own.

If one wants to understand the higher level of violence embodied in Greek game-contests and the lower level of revulsion against violence in Greek society generally, this is one of the clues that one needs. It is symptomatic of the fact that, within the social framework of a Greek city-state, individuals were still to a much higher extent dependent on others, on external agencies and sanctions as means of curbing their passions, that they could rely less on internalized barriers, on themselves alone, for controlling violent impulses, than people in contemporary industrial societies. One must add that they, or at least their elites, were already capable to a much higher extent of restraining themselves individually than their forefathers in the pre-classical age had been. The changing images of Greek gods, the critique of their arbitrariness and ferocity, bear witness to this change. If one bears in mind the specific stage in a civilizing process represented by Greek society in the days of self-ruling city-states, it is easier to understand that – compared with ours – the very high passionateness of the ancient Greeks in action was perfectly compatible with the bodily balance and equipoise, the aristocratic grace and pride in movement reflected in Greek sculpture.

As a last step, it may be useful to point briefly to one other link in the chain of interdependencies which connect the level of violence embodied in the Greek type of game-contests and of warfare with other structural characteristics of Greek society. It is quite significant for the stage which state organization had reached in the period of the Greek city-states that the protection of the life of a citizen against attacks by another was not yet treated in the same way as it is treated today, as a monopoly concern of the state. Even in Athens it was not yet treated in this manner. If a person was killed or maimed by a fellow citizen, it was, even in classical times, still a matter for his or her kinsmen to avenge and settle the account. By comparison with our own time, the kin-group still played a much larger part in protecting an individual against violence. This meant, at the same time, that every able-bodied male person had to be prepared for the defence of his kinsmen or, if it came to that, for an attack in order to help or to avenge his kinsmen. Even within a city-state, the general level of physical violence and insecurity was comparatively high. This, too, helps to account for the fact that the level of revulsion against inflicting pain and injuries on others, or of seeing it done, was lower and that feelings of guilt about acts of violence were less deeply bred into the individual. In a society so organized they would have been a severe handicap.

A few sayings of a great Greek philosopher, Democritus, may perhaps help to give a little more depth to the understanding of these differences. They are symptomatic of the common social experience of people in that situation. They show that – and they indicate why – 'right' and 'wrong' cannot mean quite the same thing in a society such as ours as in a society where every individual may have to stand up for himself and for his kinsman in defence of their lives. It is right, said Democritus, according to the rules of custom to kill any living thing which has done an injury; not to kill it is wrong. The philosopher expressed these views wholly in human and social terms. There is no appeal to the gods; nor to righteousness and holiness as can be found later in Socrates' dialogue with Protagoras – if one can trust Plato. Nor, as one can see, is there any appeal for protection to law courts, to state institutions, to governments. People were, then, far more on their own with regard to sheer physical survival than we are. This is what Democritus said:

68 (B257)

As to animals in given cases
of killing and not killing the rule is as follows:
if an animal does wrong
or desires to do wrong
and if a man kill it
he shall be counted exempt from penalties.
To perform this promotes well-being
rather than the reverse.

3 (B258)

If a thing does injury contrary to right
it is needful to kill it.
This covers all cases.
If a man do so
he shall increase the portion in which he partakes of right
and security
in any [social] order.

5 (B256)

Right is to perform what is needful
and wrong is to fail to perform what is needful
and to decline to do so.

6 (B261)

If men have wrong done to them
there is need to avenge them so far as is feasible.
This should not be passed over.
This kind of thing is right and also good
and the other kind of thing is wrong and also bad.[24]

4

An Essay on Sport and Violence

Norbert Elias

A few centuries ago, the term 'sport' was used in England, together with the older version 'disport', for a variety of pastimes and entertainments. In *A Survey of London* written at the end of the sixteenth century,[1] we read about the 'show made by the citizens for the disport of the young Prince Richard', or of the 'sportess and passtimes yearly used, first in the Feaste of Christmass . . . There was in the Kinges house . . . a Lord of Misrule, òr Maister of merry disports . . . '[2] In course of time, the term 'sport' became standardized as a technical term for specific forms of recreation in which physical exertion played a major part – specific forms of recreation of a type which first developed in England and which, from there, spread all over the world. Was the spread of these English spare-time occupations connected with the fact that the societies where people adopted them underwent structural changes similar to those which England had undergone before? Was it due to the fact that England was in advance of other countries with regard to 'industrialization'? The parallel pattern of these two processes, of the diffusion from England of industrial models of production, organization and work, and the diffusion of spare-time occupations of the type known as 'sport' and of the types of organization connected with it is certainly striking. As a first hypothesis, it does not seem unreasonable to assume that a transformation of the manner in which people used their spare-time went hand in hand with a transformation of the manner in which they worked. But what were the connections?

Much thought has been given to processes of industrialization and their conditions. To speak of processes of 'sportization' may jar upon the ear. The concept sounds alien. Yet it fits the observable facts quite well. In the course of the nineteenth century – and in some cases as early as the second half of the eighteenth century – with England as the model-setting country, some leisure activities demanding bodily exertion assumed the structural characteristics of 'sports' in other countries too. The framework of rules, including those providing for 'fairness', for equal chances to win for all contestants, became stricter. The rules became more precise, more explicit and more differentiated. Supervision of the observance of the rules became more efficient; hence, penalties for offences against the rules became less escapable. In the form of 'sports', in other words, game-contests involving muscular exertion attained a level of orderliness and of self-discipline on the part of participants not attained before. In the form of 'sports', moreover, game-contests came to embody a rule-set that ensures a balance between the possible attainment of a high combat-tension and a reasonable protection against physical injury. 'Sportization', in short, had the character of a civilizing spurt comparable in its overall direction to the 'courtization' of the warriors where the tightening rules of etiquette played a significant part and with which I have dealt elsewhere.[3]

The widespread tendency to explain almost everything that occurred in the nineteenth century as a result of the Industrial Revolution makes one a little wary of explanations in these terms. No doubt industrialization and urbanization played a part in the development and diffusion of spare-time occupations with the characteristics of 'sports', but it is also possible that both industrialization and sportization were symptomatic of a deeper-lying transformation of European societies which demanded of their individual members greater regularity and differentiation of conduct. The growing length and differentiation of chains of interdependence may have had something to do with it. This process found its expression in the submission of both people's feeling and their acting to a minutely differentiated regulatory time-schedule and to an equally inescapable accountability in terms of money. It is possible to think that European societies, broadly speaking from the fifteenth century onwards, underwent a transformation which enforced among their members a slowly increasing regularity of conduct and sentiment. Maybe the ready acceptance of the sport type of pastimes in continental countries was a sign of the growing need for more orderly, more highly regulated and less physically violent recreational activities in society at large? Future research may help to give an answer to these questions. For the moment, it must be enough to clarify and to straighten some of the questions surrounding the early development of sports themselves. In the past the term 'sport' has often been used indiscriminately with regard to specific types of modern leisure activities and to the leisure activities of societies at an earlier stage of development as well, just as one often referred to modern 'industry' and, at the same time, to the 'industry' of Stone Age peoples. What I have said may be enough to bring out more clearly that sport is something relatively recent and new.

II

If one begins to work one's way further back from this brief vision of the spread of the sports movement beyond England to the preceding development of sport in England itself, one has to think about the best way to proceed. How does one find reliable evidence about processes of growth – about the development of games and other leisure activities into the form to which we now apply the term 'sport'? So much of these developments, one may think, has gone unrecorded. Are there enough records left for the reconstruction of the processes in which pastimes acquired the characteristics of sports and in which each sport in turn acquired its own distinguishing characteristics?

It is not evidence so much which is lacking. But, in looking for it, one is often prevented from taking note of such evidence as there is by preconceptions about history-writing in general and about writing the history of sports in particular. Thus, in studying the development of a sport, one is often guided by the wish to establish for it a long and respectable ancestry. And, in that case, one is apt to select as relevant for its history all data about games played in the past which bear some resemblance to the present form of the particular sport whose history one is writing. If one finds in a twelfth century chronicle that, already at that time, the young people of London went on certain days into the fields in order to play with a ball, one is apt to conclude that these young people were already then playing the same game which, under the name of 'football', has now become one of the major games of England and which has, in that form, spread all over the world.[4] But, by thus treating the leisure activities of the fairly distant past as more or less identical with those of one's own time – the 'football' of the twelfth century with the football of the late nineteenth and twentieth centuries – one is prevented from placing at the centre of one's enquiry the questions of how and why playing with a large, leather ball grew into this particular form? One is prevented from asking how and why the particular rules and conventions developed which now determine the conduct of players when they play the game and without which the game would not be 'football' in our sense of the word. Or how and why the particular forms of organization developed which provided the most immediate framework for the growth of such rules and without which they could not be maintained and controlled.

In all these regards, the training, the study and the outlook to which we now apply the term 'sociological', directs attention to problems, and consequently to evidence, which are not always regarded as centrally relevant within the dominant tradition of history-writing. The sociologist's history is not the historian's history. Attention to the rules and norms which govern human behaviour at a given time, and to the organizations within which such rules are maintained and their observance controlled, has become a fairly normal task of sociological enquiries.

What is at present still rather unusual is attention to rules or norms in development. The problem as to how and why rules or norms have become what they are at a given time is not often systematically explored. Yet without exploration of such processes, a whole dimension of social reality remains beyond one's reach. The sociological study of sport-games, apart from its intrinsic interest, also has the function of a pilot scheme. One encounters here in a field which is relatively limited and accessible, problems of a type which are often encountered in other larger, more complex and less accessible areas. Studies in the development of sports provide experiences in many ways and sometimes lead to theoretical models which can be of help in the exploration of these other areas. The problem as to how and why rules develop is an example. The static study of rules or norms as something given has often led in the past, and still leads today, to an equivocal and somewhat unrealistic picture of society.

If one tests current theories of society, one discovers strong tendencies to regard norms and rules – in the succession of Durkheim – almost as if they had an existence independently of persons. One often speaks of norms or rules as if they were data which account by themselves for the integration of individual persons in the form of societies and for the particular type of integration, for the pattern or structure, of societies. In short, one is often given the impression that norms or rules, like Plato's ideas, have an existence of their own, that they exist, as it were, somehow by themselves and constitute, therefore, the point of departure for reflections on the way in which living persons form themselves into societies.

If one enquires into the way in which rules or norms develop, one is better able to see that the Durkheimian approach, which explains the cohesion, the interdependence and the integration of human beings and groups in terms of the rules or norms which they follow, still has a strong nominalistic ring about it. It lends itself to a misconception about the nature of society which is now fairly widespread. According to it, the sharp evaluating distinction between forms of human conduct and human grouping which agree with the set norms and others which run counter to them, is uncritically taken over into the conceptual apparatus of those whose task it is to study, and as far as possible to explain, problems of society. Sociological studies aimed at explaining the connection of events in society would fail in their task if they were to classify events in this way. For, in terms of explanation, activities and groupings which agree with the set norms, and others which deviate from them – 'integration' and 'disintegration', 'social order' and 'social disorder' – are interdependent and constitute exactly the same kind of events.[5]

If one enquires into the processes in which norms and rules develop, this factual interdependence of 'order' and 'disorder', of 'function' and 'dysfunction', becomes strikingly clear. For in the course of such processes, one can see again and again how specific rules or norms are set by human beings in order to remedy specific forms of malfunctioning, and how malfunctionings in turn lead to other changes in norms, in the codes of rules governing the conduct of people in groups.

One can see more clearly, too, the illusionary character of any conception of society which makes it appear that norms or rules have a power of their own, as if they were something outside and apart from the groups of people, and could serve as such as an explanation for the way in which people group themselves as societies. The study of the development of 'sport-games'[6] and, as one aspect of it, the development of their rules, enabled me to explore in a comparatively manageable field the technique of sociological research for which I use, as an appropriate name, the term 'figurational' analysis and synthesis, and to show how I think it should be used. More particularly, such a study shows very clearly one of the basic facts about the structure of societies generally, namely that – given unchanging non-human conditions – the specific forms in which people group themselves can only be explained in terms of other specific forms in which people group themselves. At the present stage, it still sounds rather odd if one says that what one studies as 'social patterns', 'social structures' or 'figurations' are patterns, structures or figurations formed by human beings. Linguistic usages and habits of thinking make us inclined to speak and to think of such patterns, structures, figurations almost as if they were something outside and apart from the people who form them with each other.

Many sociological standard terms, of course, have reached a high degree of appropriateness to observable structures. Among them is the term 'structure' itself. And yet I have some reservations with regard to standard expressions such as that which we use when we say a society or group *has* a structure. One can easily interpret this manner of speaking as if the group were something apart from the people who form it. What we call 'structure' is, in fact, nothing but the pattern or figuration of interdependent individual people who form the group or, in a wider sense, the society. What we term 'structures' when we look at people as societies, are 'figurations' when we look at them as individuals.

Figurations form the core of what one investigates if one studies sports. Every sport – whatever else it may be – is an organized group activity centred on a contest between at least two parties. It requires physical exertion of some kind. It is fought out according to known rules, including, if physical force can be used at all, rules which define the permitted limits of violence. The rules determine the starting figuration of the players and its changing pattern as the contest proceeds. But all kinds of sports have specific functions for the participants, for spectators or for their countries at large. When the given form of a sport fails to perform these functions adequately, the rules may be changed.

Sports differ in accordance with their different rules and, therefore, the different pattern of the contest or, in other words, of the different figurations of individuals concerned as determined by their respective regulations and the organizations controlling adherence to them. The problem is evidently what distinguished the English type of 'playing the game' – the type of games contest, of rules and organization, to which we now refer as 'sports' – from other types of games contest. How did they come into being? How did the distinguishing character of the rules, the organizations, the relationships, the groups of players in action peculiar to 'sports' develop in the course of time? Evidently this was one of those processes in the course of which specific structures of group relations and activities developed over many generations through the concourse of the actions and aims of many individuals even though none of the participating people, as individuals or as groups, intended or planned the long-term outcome of their actions. Thus it is not merely a manner of speaking if one envisages the emergence of sports as a developmental and not merely as an historical problem. In history books, the history of sports is often presented as a series of almost accidental activities and decisions of a few people. What appears to lead up to the 'final', the 'mature' form of the game is put into the limelight. What is different from or opposed to the 'ultimate' pattern is often left as irrelevant in the shade. As one shall see, the growth of the 'mature' form of a sport cannot be adequately presented if it is envisaged largely as a haphazard medley of activities and decisions of a few known individuals or groups. Nor can it be adequately presented in the manner suggested by current sociological theories as a series of 'social changes'. The changes which one can observe in the development of sports such as cricket and football as well as fox-hunting and horse-racing, have both a pattern and a direction of their own. That is the aspect of the history of sports to which one refers if one speaks of it as a 'development'. But in using this term, one has to dissociate oneself from its philosophical or metaphysical use. What is meant by social development can only be found out with the help of detailed empirical studies. It can only be found out in this specific context if one enquires into the way in which fox-hunting, boxing, cricket, football and other sports in fact 'developed'. I have used, provisionally and in quotes, the expression 'mature' or 'ultimate' form of the game. It was one of the discoveries made in the course of enquiries of this kind that a game may reach in the course of its development a peculiar equilibrium stage. And when this stage has been reached, the whole structure of its further development changes. For to have reached its 'mature' form, or however one cares to call it, does not mean that all development stops; it merely means that it enters upon a new stage. However, neither the existence of this stage, nor its characteristics, nor, for that matter, its significance for the whole concept of social development, can be determined in any other way except through the empirical study of the evidence itself. On the other hand, the preliminary knowledge that what one is looking for if one studies the history of a sport is not merely the isolated activities of individuals or groups, and not only a number of unpatterned changes, but a patterned sequence of changes in the organization, the rules and the actual figuration of the game itself, leading over a certain period to wards a specific stage of tension-equilibrium which has been provisionally called here the 'mature stage' and whose nature has yet to be determined. This knowledge itself, used flexibly and with the possibility of its inadequacy always in one's mind, can guide one's eye in the selection of data and help in perceiving connections.

III

As has been said, whatever else it may be, a sport is an organized group activity centred on a contest between at least two parties. It requires physical exertion of some kind and is fought out according to known rules, including, where appropriate, rules which define the permitted limits of physical force. The grouping of contestants is arranged in such a manner that a specific pattern of group dynamics recurs at each meeting – a pattern which is elastic, sometimes more, sometimes less, and hence variable and, preferably, not wholly calculable in its course and its outcome. The figuration of people in such a contest is so arranged that it engenders as well as contains tensions. In a mature form it embodies a complex of interdependent polarities in a state of unstable tension-equilibrium and allows – in the best of cases – moderate fluctuations that offer all the contenders chances to gain the upper hand until one of them succeeds in breaking the tension by winning the game. It is one of the characteristics of a sport-game in its mature state that the period of tension is neither too short nor too long. Most sports, like good wines, needed a good deal of time to grow into that shape, to grow to maturity and to find an optimal form. It is rare – though it has been done – to invent a satisfactory sport-game.[7] As a rule, they have gone through a period of trial and error before reaching a form which secured sufficient tension for sufficient time without fostering tendencies towards stalemate. Both precipitate victories and recurrent stalemates can occur for a variety of reasons, some of which, but not all, may lie in the construction of the game-pattern, of the figuration and its dynamics themselves. The necessary tautness of the figuration will be lacking if one of the opponents is too superior to the other in strength and skill, for in such cases the game will quickly end in the defeat of the weaker side. If the opponents are too evenly matched in strength and skill, the contest may drag on. In that case, it is likely to end in a stalemate and the tension-excitement will not be able in good time to find its release in the climax of victory. In these cases, it is the temporary figuration of players, not the more permanent figuration set up by the instituted game-pattern itself, which is responsible for imperfections in the complex tension-equilibrium that is characteristic of sport-games. In other cases, tendencies towards precipitate victory or stalemate are due to the instituted figuration of the players in the game itself. In the development of a sport-game, one can often find a period during which the figurational arrangements favour the attackers at the expense of the defenders or vice versa. In the first case, the attackers are apt to win all the games and to win them too quickly. The middle stump of the wicket, it is reported, was introduced into cricket when bowlers developed a technique which got the ball too often and, it seemed, too easily through the wicket.[8] In the second case, games frequently end in a stalemate.[9] Thus, the adequacy of the tension-equilibrium and of the dynamics of the figuration in a sport-game depends, among others, on arrangements which ensure that the contestants, as well as attacking and defending, have equal chances to win and to lose. But they are not the only polarities on which the tension-equilibrium of the game depends. If players do not control themselves sufficiently, they are likely to break the rules and victory may go to their opponents. If they restrain themselves too much, they will lack the verve and the drive necessary for victory. If they follow the rules slavishly, they risk losing through lack of inventiveness; if they dodge or stretch them to the utmost, they risk losing by breaking the rules. They have to find the right middle way between carefully following rules and conventions, and dodging them or stretching them to the utmost and playing near the breaking-point. If, for the sake of a fair game and good sport, they do not exploit every chance of winning, they may lose the chance of victory; if they go all out for victory, the game itself may deteriorate.

In the earlier stages of the development of sport-games, when relatively small local groups of players or their patrons made their own rules, it was relatively easy to change the rules to suit the needs of the players and their public. But when national organizations became the law-givers, the polarity between the players' tendency to follow the rules and to dodge or stretch them had its counterpart on a new level in a polarity between two different groups, between, on the one hand, the makers of the rules at the centre of a national organization and, on the other, the players themselves. The former legislated with an eye on the overall situation of the game and its relation to the general public; the latter, often remote from the centre of power and in the interest of their own chances of winning games, used the elasticity of all verbal rules by looking for loopholes and by dodging the intentions of the law-givers.

The disequilibria in one or another of these polarities are factors in the development of sport-games towards greater tension-equilibrium. At least three levels play a part in the dynamics of this process: games played at a given time by individuals that one can name; the set game-patterns according to which a game is played at a given stage in its development, together with the organization (or organizations) which controls it; and the process of the developing game-pattern throughout the existence of the game. The dynamics of the individual game, the built-in dynamics of the game-pattern at a given time, and the dynamics of the formative long-term process of the game up to maturity and after maturity has been reached, form a complex pattern. Conceptually these levels can be distinguished, though factually they are inseparable. But for purposes of observation and study, it is useful to enquire whether changes in the game-pattern are due to what are felt to be deficiencies in the game-pattern itself at a time when the conditions for playing the game in society at large remain largely unchanged, or whether changes in the game-pattern are due to felt deficiencies which arise largely from changing conditions of the game in society at large. A sport-game, in other words, particularly when it has reached maturity, can have a degree of autonomy in relation to the structure of the society where it is played; hence, the reasons for changes can lie in the game-pattern itself. But the autonomy is limited. The development of sport in general, as well as that of particular sports, can be seen as a strand within the larger development of the societies where they are played and increasingly, as they are played internationally, in the development of world society.

Enough has been said in these preliminary remarks to indicate the complexity of the basic figurational characteristics of sport-games. They all – tennis, football, boxing, hockey, and many other forms of sport, including the English form of hunting – show similar character-istics in certain respects. Figurational analysis helps to sharpen the perception of such characteristics and to conceptualize their dis-tinguishing properties with greater precision. One can see from these preliminary considerations at least some of the distinguishing charac-teristics of sport in better perspective. The centrepiece of the figuration of a group engaged in sport is always a mock contest with the controlled tensions engendered by it and the catharsis, the release from tension, at the end. According to the dominant tradition of thinking and feeling, tensions as social phenomena are apt to be regarded as something which runs counter to the norms – as abnormal, as harmful and undesirable. The figurational analysis of sport shows that group ten-sions of a well-tempered kind are a normal ingredient. In fact, they are a central element of all leisure activities. A sport is an organized form of group-tension, even though the group pursuing it at a given time may be only a group of two. 'Tension-equilibrium' is a term introduced in order to express the idea that the basic figuration of a sport is designed to produce as well as to contain tensions. The techniques for maintain-ing within a set figuration of people an equilibrium of forces in tension for a while, with a high chance of catharsis, or release from tension, in the end, remain to be studied. Whatever these techniques are, the figuration in action is poised between the Scylla of a precipitate victory and the Charybdis of a stalemate.

Evidently, these and other basic characteristics of sport have not been planned. It was not once the expressed and clearly conceptualized aim of specific groups to design as leisure activities dynamic figurations of people with these characteristics. Yet, unplanned and largely unin-tended, many pastimes in England, largely during the eighteenth and nineteenth centuries, developed in that direction. The sociologist's task is evidently first to get in a general way a clearer picture of the specific group dynamics, the game-pattern, the figurations of people character-istic of sport, and then, as far as possible, to see in greater detail how specific pastimes gradually developed the distinguishing characteristics of sport from a state where they lacked them, and finally to determine the specific characteristics in the development of a country, of society at large, which account for the development of pastimes in this particular direction.

That, at least, is the long-term task. What follows are some steps along that road.

IV

One of the earliest examples of a pastime with the distinguishing characteristics of a sport was the English form of fox-hunting. In our own time hunting of any kind is regarded by many people as, at most, a marginal form of sport. In the eighteenth and early nineteenth centuries in England fox-hunting was decidedly one of the principal pastimes to which the term 'sport' was applied. One can understand better what was meant by 'sport' if one studies the peculiar character of this type of hunting. It was far removed from the simpler, less highly regulated and more spontaneous forms of hunting of other countries and earlier ages where people themselves were the principal actors, where the hounds were mere adjuncts and where foxes were not the only animals hunted.

In England fox-hunting became a highly specialized pastime with an organization and conventions of its own. While hunting the fox, gentlemen strictly refrained from pursuing and killing any other animals which came their way[10] – to the amazement of foreign spectators who were unable to understand the reasons for this restraint. Even the hunting gentlemen of England themselves, secure in the knowledge and enjoyment of their customs, were mostly unable or unwilling to explain their hunting rituals. To go after a fox and to disregard any other animal that came one's way, even though it might have served as a most desirable delicacy at one's table, was simply part of their social code. A gentleman did not go hunting in order to bring home delicacies for the table. He did it for sport. They told each other with considerable amusement stories which showed the lack of comprehension of English fox-hunting amongst foreigners, particularly amongst Frenchmen. There was the story of the French *chasseur* who witnessed a fox-hunt in England and expressed both surprise and derision when he observed some young hounds being whipped off the scent of a hare which they were just about to catch; or the story of another French gentleman who heard an Englishman during a hunt exclaim: 'How admirable! the sport which the fox has shown in this charming run of two hours and a quarter.' He replied: '*Ma foi*, he must be worth catching when you take so much trouble. *Est-il bon pour un fricandeau?*'[11]

This, as one can see, was 'sport' – the fine run, the tension, the excitement, not the *fricandeau*.

In earlier days the pleasurable excitement of the hunt had been a kind of forepleasure experienced in anticipation of the real pleasures, the pleasures of killing and eating. The pleasure of killing animals was enhanced by its utility. Many of the hunted animals threatened the fruits of people's labour. For the greater part of the eighteenth century, wild animals, and among them foxes, were still abundant in most countries. Hunting was necessary in order to keep them down. Foxes in particular were a constant menace to the chicken-run, to the geese and ducks of peasantry and gentry. They competed with the poachers for the hares in the field. In earlier days hounds were allowed to hunt deer, hares, marten-cats and foxes indiscriminately. The fields and forests were full of them and they were all regarded as vermin. They also provided food. In times of drought and famine, poor people might be less inclined to waste the meat of a fox because it had a fairly strong taste. "'The meat of the fox", according to a French source, is less disagreeable than that of the wolf; "dogs as well as men eat it in autumn, especially if the fox has fed and grown fat on grapes."'[12]

Earlier forms of hunting thus imposed on their followers few restraints. People enjoyed the pleasures of hunting and killing animals in whatever way they could and ate as many of them as they liked. Sometimes masses of animals were driven near the hunters so that they could enjoy the pleasures of killing without too much exertion. For the higher ranking social cadres, the excitement of hunting and killing animals had always been to some extent the peacetime equivalent of the excitement connected with killing humans in times of war. As a matter of course people used for both purposes the most suitable weapons at their disposal. One shot foxes just like other animals ever since firearms had been invented.

A glance back at the earlier forms of hunting shows the peculiarities of English fox-hunting in better perspective. It was a form of hunting in which the hunters imposed on themselves and their hounds a number of highly specific restraints. The whole organization of fox-hunting, the behaviour of the participants, the training of the hounds, was governed by an extremely elaborate code. But the reasons for this code, for the taboos and restraints which it imposed upon the hunters, were far from obvious. Why were the hounds trained not to follow any scent other than that of the fox and, as far as possible, not of any fox other than the first that they discovered? The ritual of fox-hunting demanded that the hunters should not use any weapons. Why was it regarded as a major social crime to shoot foxes and as improper for gentlemen hunting foxes to use any weapons at all? Fox-hunting gentlemen killed, as it were, by proxy – by delegating the task of killing to their hounds. Why did the fox-hunting code prohibit the killing of the hunted animal by the people themselves? In the earlier forms of hunting, when people had themselves played the main role in the hunt, hounds had played a subordinate role. Why was the main role in English fox-hunting left to the hounds, while the human beings confined themselves to the secondary role of followers and watchers or perhaps of controllers of the hounds?

As a result of this delegation of the primary hunting roles and the consequent need of the hunters to identify themselves, to some extent, with the hounds – as if they had externalized part of themselves and sent it out for the blood and the killing instead of doing it themselves – many huntsmen were linked to their hounds by an affection that was often mutual. They knew their hounds individually by name. They assessed and discussed their individual qualities and compared them with each other. They admired their prowess, their fierceness and intrepidity, and encouraged their rivalries.

'They should', wrote Beckford, 'both love and fear the huntsman. They should fear him much, yet they should love him more. Without doubt hounds would do more for the huntsman if they loved him more.'[13] An intimate and personal relationship between hunters and hounds, including a degree of projection of the hunters' feelings, formed an integral aspect of the basic figuration of fox-hunting.

> Mind Galloper, how he leads them! It is difficult to distinguish which is first, they run in such a style; yet he is the foremost hound; the goodness of his nose is not less excellent than his speed. How he carries the scent! . . . There – now – now he's at head again.[14]

And the end:

> Now Reynard, look to yourself – How quick they all give their tongues! – Little Dreadnought, how he works him! The terriers, too, they are now squeaking at him – How close Vengeance pursues! How terribly she presses! It is just up with him! Gods what a crush they make; the whole wood resounds! That turn was very short! There – now! – aye, now they have him! Whoo-hoop![15]

With the delegation by the humans to the hounds of the major part of the pursuit and also of the killing function, and with the submission of the hunting gentlemen to an elaborate, self-imposed code of restraints, part of the enjoyment of hunting had become a visual enjoyment; the pleasure derived from doing had been transformed into the pleasure of seeing it done.

The direction of the changes in the manner of hunting which one can find by comparing the English fox-hunting ritual with earlier forms of hunting shows very clearly the general direction of a civilizing spurt.[16] Increasing restraints upon the use of physical force and particularly upon killing, and, as an expression of these restraints, a displacement of the pleasure experienced in doing violence to the pleasure experienced in seeing violence done, can be observed as symptoms of a civilizing spurt in many other spheres of human activity. As has been shown, they are all connected with moves in the direction of the greater pacification of a country in connection with the growth, or with the growing effectiveness of, the monopolization of physical force by the representatives of a country's central institutions. They are connected, furthermore, with one of the most crucial aspects of a country's internal pacification and civilization – with the exclusion of the use of violence from the recurrent struggles for control of these central institutions, and with the corresponding conscience-formation. One can see this growing internalization of the social prohibition against violence and the advance in the threshold of revulsion against violence, especially against killing and even against seeing it done, if one considers that, in its heyday, the ritual of English fox-hunting, which prohibited any direct human participation in the killing, represented a civilizing spurt. It was an advance in people's revulsion against doing violence, while today, in accordance with the continued advance of the threshold of sensitivity, not a few people find even this representative of an earlier civilizing spurt distasteful and would like to see it abolished.

The nature of a civilizing process is sometimes misunderstood as a process in which the restraints or, as it is sometimes put, the 'repressions' bred into people increase and in which people's capacity for pleasurable excitement and enjoying life correspondingly decrease. But perhaps this impression is, to some extent, due to the fact that people's pleasurable satisfactions have attracted less attention as a worthy and interesting object of scientific research than the restricting rules – than social constraints and their instruments such as laws, norms and values. An enquiry into the development of sports can help to redress the balance. Every now and then one can find in the literature short statements which are very much to the point. Thus hunting has been recognized quite often as a substitute activity for warfare. It has also sometimes been recognized quite clearly that the form it assumed in England represented a moderation of less civilized aspects of hunting. It corresponded better to the sensitivity of civilized gentlemen to let the hounds do the killing and confine their own activity to assisting them, to the anticipatory excitement and to watching the killing. Beckford wrote:

Such as are acquainted with the hounds and can at times assist them, find

the sport more interesting and have the satisfaction to think that they
themselves contribute to the success of the day. This is a pleasure you
often enjoy; *a pleasure without any regret attending it*. I know not what
effect it may have on you; but I know that my spirits are always good
after a good sport in hunting; nor is the rest ever disagreeable to me.
What are other sports compared to this which is full of enthusiasm!
Fishing is in my opinion a dull diversion. Shooting, though it admit of a
companion, will not allow many. Both, therefore, may be considered as
selfish and solitary amusements, compared with hunting to which as
many as please are welcome . . .

For hunting is a kind of warfare; its uncertainties, its fatigues, its
difficulties and its dangers rendering it interesting above all other diversions.[17]

This illuminating passage points in several ways to the core of the
problem. Since Beckford's days the civilizing process has moved, in
some sections of the population, in the same direction and beyond the
point represented by Beckford and the section of society in which he
moved. That section has ceased to be the dominant, the model-setting
section. If, in his own society, conscience and the corresponding sensitivities had grown into a form which made it distasteful for them to kill
the fox with their own hands, today sections of the population have
grown more powerful and vocal whose sensitivities and identification
with the hunted animal are so strong that the hunting and killing of
foxes for the sake of human pleasure alone is, to them, altogether
distasteful.

In Beckford's time internal pacification – the stability and effectiveness of the protection which the central agencies of a society and their
organs could give to individuals, particularly against physical threats of
all kinds – together with the corresponding restraints upon individuals,
external and internal, had not gone quite so far as they have today. But
compared with earlier forms of hunting and of pastimes generally, the
direction of the change in conduct and sensitivity was the same. Killing
and the use of physical violence generally, even physical violence in
relation to animals, had become hedged in more elaborately by taboos
and restraints. Nothing is more characteristic of one of the central
problems of a civilizing trend than the statement that the indirect form
of violence, the killing by proxy, the fact that one could at times assist
the hounds in doing what one no longer wanted to do oneself, made it
possible to enjoy 'a pleasure without any regret attending it'.

What Beckford observed here was, indeed, one of the central aspects
of sport and particularly of sport-games. They are all dynamic figurations of people, and sometimes of animals as well, which make it
possible for people to fight a contest directly or indirectly involving

their whole persons (as one used to say, 'body and soul') in such a manner that they can enjoy the excitement of the struggle without any regret – without bad conscience.

Sport is, in fact, one of the great social inventions which human beings have made without planning to make them. It offers people the liberating excitement of a struggle involving physical exertion and skill while limiting to a minimum the chance that anyone will get seriously hurt in its course.

In the eighteenth century the threshold of revulsion against directly or indirectly injuring others in connection with the pleasurable excitement that one derived from the mimetic battle of a sports contest had not gone so far and was in many cases at a lower level than that attained in many advanced state-societies today. But the direction of the change in conduct and sentiment which one can observe there was the same as that which one can observe in more recent times.

One of the crucial problems confronting societies in the course of a civilizing process was – and remains – that of finding a new balance between pleasure and restraint. The progressive tightening of regulating controls over people's behaviour and the corresponding conscience-formation, the internalization of rules that regulate more elaborately all spheres of life, secured for people in their relations with each other greater security and stability, but it also entailed a loss of the pleasurable satisfactions associated with simpler and more spontaneous forms of conduct. Sport was one of the solutions to this problem. The innumerable people who anonymously contributed to the development of sports may not have been aware of the problem with which they wrestled in the general form in which it presents itself now in retrospect to the reflecting sociologist, but some of them were well aware of it as a specific problem which they encountered in the immediacy of their own limited pastimes. The figuration of fox-hunting – of hunting transformed into a sport – shows some of the ways in which people still managed to derive pleasure from a pursuit that involved physical violence and killing at a stage in which, in society at large, even wealthy and powerful people had become increasingly restricted in their ability to use force without the licence of the law and in which their own conscience had become more sensitive with regard to the use of brute force and the spilling of blood.

How was it done? How could one manage to have one's pleasure without bad conscience in spite of the fact that the socially built-in conscience had become stronger, almost all-embracing and, though still less sensitive with regard to violence than tends to be the case in advanced industrial societies today, far more sensitive than it had been in earlier days? The problem was less difficult to solve when the violence was done to animals rather than to humans. That the threshold of sensitivity in the wake of a civilizing trend had advanced so as to include animals was surprising enough. The tightening of external social controls as expressed in formal laws and regulations concerned only humans. That the sensitivity with regard to violence came to affect animals was characteristic of the irradiation of feeling beyond the initial target which is a general feature of conscience-formation. The advance, at this stage, had been sufficient for people to enjoy the killing of the hunted animal indirectly as participant observer rather than directly as the executing agent.

But if one studies the figuration of fox-hunting more closely and compares it with earlier forms of hunting, one soon notices a highly characteristic shift in emphasis with regard to the pleasure-giving activities. In earlier forms of hunting, the main sources of pleasure had tended to lie in the killing and subsequent eating of the hunted animal. It was characteristic of the English form of fox-hunting that the pleasure of eating as a motive for hunting had disappeared and that the pleasure of killing, though by no means negligible, had become attenuated. It was a pleasure by proxy. The killing was done by the hounds, and the pleasure of the pursuit itself had become, as it were, the principal source of entertainment and the central part of the exercise. The ultimate killing of the fox – the triumph of victory – still remained the climax of the hunt. But it was no longer by itself the main source of pleasure. That function had shifted to the hunting of the animal, to the pursuit. What, in the simpler and more spontaneous forms of hunting, had been a fore-pleasure enjoyed in anticipation of killing and eating, had gained much greater significance than before. In relation to all the other ends of hunting, the tension of the mock battle itself and the pleasure it gave to the human participants had reached a high degree of autonomy. Killing foxes was easy. All the rules of the hunt were designed to make it less easy, to prolong the contest, to postpone victory for a while – not because it was felt to be immoral or unfair to kill foxes outright, but because the excitement of the hunt itself had increasingly become the main source of enjoyment for the human participants. To shoot foxes was strictly forbidden; in the circles where this form of hunting originated, in the aristocracy and gentry, it was regarded as an unforgivable solecism, and the tenant farmers had, willy-nilly, to follow the rules of their betters even though foxes were stealing their chickens or their geese. Shooting foxes was a sin because it deprived gentlemen of the tension-excitement of the hunt; it spoiled their sport.

What had once been a fore-pleasure, preparatory to the main pleasure of killing and eating the hunted animal, had now become the central part of the pleasure, culminating and ending in the killing of the animal, while the animal itself no longer played any part at all in the subsequent dining and drinking, except as a subject of conversation. The meaning which the term 'sport' assumed during the eighteenth century was profoundly affected by this peculiar shift in people's enjoyment of their pastimes; it represented a profound sublimatory transformation of feeling. In the Middle Ages the term 'sport' had had a far less specific meaning. It could be applied to many different diversions and entertainments. During the eighteenth century it became a more highly specialized term: it transformed itself into a *terminus technicus* for a specific type of pastimes which developed at that time among landed gentlemen and aristocrats and of which the highly idiosyncratic form of fox-hunting which developed in those circles was one of the most prominent. Perhaps its most characteristic feature was the tension-excitement of a mock battle which involved physical exertion and the enjoyment which the mock battle gave to human beings as participants or spectators.

The fox-hunting groups, as far as one can see, were not wholly unaware of the peculiar autonomy of their 'sport' – of the relative detachment of the joys of the mimetic battle from any other social purpose or function. Expressions such as 'the fox gave us good sport', or 'our sport depends entirely on that exquisite sense of' smelling so peculiar to hounds', show quite clearly how closely at that time the term 'sport' was associated with the tension of the mock battle as such and the pleasure derived from it.[18]

Nor were the followers of fox-hunting entirely unaware of the fact that the pleasurable tension-excitement which was the essence of 'good sport' could only be expected of a fox-hunt because its basic figuration ensured a moderately unstable tension-equilibrium, a transient balance of power between the contestants. According to a sports manual,

> The noble science, as foxhunting is called by its votaries, is by common consent allowed to be the perfection of hunting. The animal hunted is just fast enough for the purpose, and is also full of all kinds of devices for misleading its pursuers. He leaves a good scent, is very stout, and is found in sufficient abundance to afford a reasonable chance of sport.[19]

English fox-hunting is used here as an empirical model in order to demonstrate some of the original distinguishing characteristics of the type of pastimes which are called 'sport'. That may help one to perceive better certain structural characteristics of sport as a source of pleasurable tension-excitement which later often came to be explained in utilitarian terms alone. The fox-hunting groups had already developed a specific 'ethos' which is one of the characteristics of all sports. But at this stage the 'sports ethos' was not the kind of ethos of working middle classes to which one applies terms like 'moral' or 'morality'. It was the ethos of wealthy, sophisticated and comparatively restrained leisure classes who had come to value the tension and the excitement of well-regulated mock battles as a major part of their pleasure. The rules of fox-hunting, devised and observed by gentlemen, and rigorously enforced against offenders, ensured that the hunt would give them the essentials of good 'sport', a sufficiency of enjoyable tension and battle excitement. They ensured that the conditions for the pleasurable tension-excitement which one wanted and needed could be produced with great regularity by the dynamics of a figuration in which horse-riding hunters, hounds and fox were bound together.

Today one is apt to explain the relative evenness of the chances of both sides that is characteristic of all sports largely in terms of a 'moral' postulate by reference to the 'fairness' of such an arrangement. But, in this as in other cases, the 'moral' aspects are apt to conceal the sociological aspects, the structure or function of such an arrangement. Without a figuration that was able to maintain for a time a moderately unstable equilibrium of chances for opponents, one could not expect to have 'good sport'; without such a 'fair' arrangement, the pleasure and excitement provided by the tension of the battle, which was the main function of the sport, would be too short and could not be expected with a high degree of regularity. Thus fox-hunting already showed in essentials that people had learned a specific technique for organizing themselves which is used in sport of all kinds – a technique for maintaining for a while within a set figuration of participants an equilibrium of forces in tension with a high chance of catharsis, of a release from tension, in the end.

Another of the recurrent problems of sport generally, which sportsmen encountered fairly early in connection with fox-hunting, was that of finding the appropriate balance between the chances for the more extended tension-excitement of the battle itself and the chances for the relatively short culminating pleasure of the catharsis, of the climax and release from tension. The problem of the emphasis on one or the other of these two poles, like that on the corresponding polarities of other sports, gave rise to controversies between people who laid greater stress on the hunting itself and others who laid greater stress on killing the fox – between the advocates of 'good sport' and the advocates of 'winning victories'. The persistence with which homologous discussions occur in different sports at different times is an index of the persistence of the basic structure of sport. As has already been said, the figurational dynamics of a sport must be equilibrated so as to avoid, on the one hand, the frequent recurrence of precipitate victories and, on the other, the frequent recurrence of stalemates. The former cut short the pleasurable tension-excitement; they do not give it time enough to rise to an enjoyable optimum. The other draws out the tension beyond its optimum and lets it get stale without any climax and the 'cathartic' release from tension which follows. As long as the basic figuration of a sport ensured a fair equilibrium between these two marginal possibilities, sportsmen could take their choice by putting more weight on one side or the other.

With regard to fox-hunting, Beckford discussed this problem as early as the end of the eighteenth century. He himself stressed the importance of the climax, of the killing of the fox. But that did not mean that he contemplated the pleasure and excitement of the killing independently of the pleasure and excitement of the preceding hunt. Explaining why he recommended that one should go out with one's pack early in the morning, particularly if one's hounds were 'out of blood', he wrote:

> The morning is part of the day which generally affords the best scent; and the animal himself, which, in such a case, you are more than ever desirous of killing (the hounds being out of blood) is then least able to run away from you. The want of rest, and perhaps a full belly, give hounds a great advantage . . . I expect, my friend, that you will reply to this, 'that a foxhunter, then, is not a *fair sportsman*' – he certainly is not; and what is more, would be very sorry to be mistaken for one. He is otherwise from principle. In his opinion, a fair sportsman, and a foolish sportsman, are synonymous; he, therefore, takes every advantage of the fox that he can. You will think, perhaps, that he may sometimes spoil his own sport by this? It is true, he sometimes does, but . . . the whole art of foxhunting being to keep the hounds well in blood, sport is but a secondary consideration with the 'foxhunter'; the first is, *the killing of the fox*; hence arises the eagerness of the pursuit, chief pleasure of the chase; – I confess, I esteem blood so necessary to a pack of foxhounds that with regard to myself, I always return home better pleased with but an indifferent chase, with death at the end of it, than with the best chase possible, if it ends with the loss of the fox. Good chases, generally speaking, are long chases; and if not attended with success, never fail to do more harm to hounds than good. Our pleasures, I believe, for the most, are greater during the expectation than the enjoyment: in this case, reality itself warrants the idea, and your present success is almost a sure fore-runner for a future sport.[20]

One of the devices upon which people stumbled when confronted in the course of a civilizing process by the need for a new balance between pleasure and restraint, was a greater capacity for enjoying the extended excitement of the struggle and tension that lead up to the climax in comparison with the short enjoyment of the climax and the attendant release from tension itself. The statement, 'our pleasures . . . for the most, are greater during the expectation than the enjoyment', though not necessarily correct as a diagnosis, points clearly enough to the shift in the weight between tension-enjoyment and consummation-enjoyment that is indicated in the development of such pastimes as hunting and that is, more generally, characteristic of a civilizing trend. The term 'sport', as one saw, became the technical term attached to what had formerly been the preparatory part of a hunt or game, together with the anticipatory pleasure one expected from it. To say that the fox 'gave us good sport' was an expression which referred simultaneously to the figurational dynamics themselves and to the degree of enjoyable excitement they provided; the expression referred to the contest between fox and hounds and the attendant huntsmen, as well as to the satisfaction it gave to the latter. Beckford could still say unashamedly what most people would probably have said as a matter of course in earlier centuries and what fewer and fewer people were likely to say in the following – that the first thing that the fox-hunter desired was killing the fox and that sport was a secondary consideration.

Moreover, as the weight of the longer tension and tension-enjoyment increased in comparison with the short final act – with the killing and its pleasures – the pleasure itself became more varied. It became, in fact, a composite pleasure. The basic figuration of the fox-hunt, like that of many other kinds of sport, was so arranged that the excitement and enjoyment derived from it rested not only on one, but on several contests taking place simultaneously. As usual, the primary contest was that between hunter and hunted. But in the case of fox-hunting, the figuration was formed not only by two but by three types of participants, by the group of horse-riding humans, by the pack of hounds and by the fox. The struggle between the hounds and the fox was the primary contest, and the tension, the excitement, engendered by it dominated all the others. But closely linked to this primary contest was a secondary contest, the contest among the hounds. The hunters followed and watched the hounds eagerly. The bravest and fastest, with the best noses and which kept close to the fox, swelled the pride of master and owner. They were admired and fondled. High prices were paid for their offspring. And, finally, another secondary contest inherent in the figuration was that among the human hunters themselves. The question was: who could stick closest to the pack? Who would take short cuts, even if they were dangerous? Who flinched before fences, rivers or other obstacles? Who was present at the kill?

The excitement evoked by the contest between fox and hounds was greatly heightened by that between the huntsmen. In the eighteenth and early nineteenth centuries a fox-hunt was often considerably more exacting and wilder than it is today. It was a test of courage, robustness and skill for gentlemen, and sometimes for ladies. In the heat of the hunt the huntsmen often dared each other to the utmost. They took risks, even though they knew that they might have to pay for the pleasure of the excitement with a fall, with injuries, or even with their lives. English fox-hunting was fashioned by noblemen and gentlemen in a period when the integral status rivalry of their social cadre was, increasingly, less fought out in the form of duels and other forms of direct physical combat – though these were still quite frequent among the younger set – and more by means of such weapons as conspicuous consumption and conspicuous prowess. Fox-hunting gave opportunities for both. For many of its adherents, its conventions assumed the character of a ritual, almost a cult.

The eighteenth century was a period in England – and not in England alone – in which the pacification and domestication of the landed classes and, with it, the refinement of their manners, advanced noticeably. The threat of civil war had receded. Memories of the internal strife of the previous century lingered on for a while.[21] As so often in the aftermath of civil strife, many people feared its recurrence. They were tired of violence among humans. More often than not in a period following internal dissensions, one particular group emerges as the strongest. But in England that was not the case. The progressive monopolization of physical force on which the internal pacification of a country everywhere depended, particularly the pacification of its ruling groups, took a different course in England from that in most other countries of Europe. The administration and utilization of the institutionalized monopoly of physical force and the twin monopoly of taxation on which, among other things, the effectiveness of legal procedures in the country depended, had not become the permanent monopoly of one of several competing establishments. It had certainly not become, as it had in France and other autocratic states, the monopoly of king and court. What had resulted in England from the more violent period of social conflicts was a moderately unstable tension-equilibrium between several competing ruling groups, none of which was any longer willing, or appeared strong enough, to challenge the combined forces of the others by a direct test of physical strength. Instead, a tacit agreement gradually developed between the rival establishments in society at large. They agreed on a set of rules according to which they could take turns in forming governments and in administering or utilizing the centrepieces of all governmental functions – the monopoly of physical force and the levying of taxes. Certainly, the working out of these rules did not occur overnight. Sporadic fights and clashes between the followers of different establishments occurred till at least the middle of the eighteenth century but, gradually, the fear that one of the contending groups and its followers would physically injure or annihilate the others receded. The agreement not to fight for governmental office and its power resources by means of violence, but only, according to agreed rules, by means of words, votes and money, began to hold. It is worth noting that this agreement, too, embodied a moderately unstable tension-equilibrium between several groups. An important part in the transition to such a complicated arrangement was played by the fact that none of the contending parties, not even the king, had at its disposal the unrestricted control of a standing army.

It took time to solve the central problem which has always been, and which still is, the main stumbling block in the transition from a period of violence between several interest groups to a regime embodying non-violent institutional means for settling conflicts. The problem is always the same; it is how to overcome the reciprocal fear and suspicion that one's opponents, once they have gained control of the governmental offices and the power resources vested in them, will cease to play the game according to the agreed rules, will try to stay in power regardless of these rules, and will use the power resources of government to weaken or annihilate their opponents. How and why the competing social groups which had used or threatened each other with physical violence in their struggles for dominance ceased, by and large in the first half of the eighteenth century, to do so, how and why a parliamentary regime embodying changes in government by non-violent means and in accordance with agreed rules then began to function with considerable regularity and almost without regressions, is a problem which, in this context, need not be explored. But one cannot wholly omit to point to the fact itself. It is relevant to point to the peculiar form which access to governmental offices and the control of their principal power resources – the monopolies of physical force and of taxation – assumed in England in this period. One is used to referring to this form of government as 'pluralism' or 'parliamentary government'. But such routinized words can easily conceal the central problem that has to be solved in order to allow such a regime to function. That is the problem of the non-violent transition from one government to another in accordance with set rules. How is one to induce the members of a government to abandon the very considerable power resources which governmental office put at their disposal if that becomes necessary according to the agreed rules? How can one be sure that they will obey the rules in spite of the proportionally very great military and financial power resources which they can command as controllers of the central monopolies of the state?

The development and relatively smooth functioning of a multi-polar parliamentary regime in England during the eighteenth century, after a period of bitter civil strife and dissension, solved that problem. The gradual establishment of a parliamentary regime represented a very pronounced pacifying spurt. It required the higher level of self-restraint which is necessary if all the groupings concerned steadfastly renounce the use of violence even if the agreed rules demand that one's opponents can take office and enjoy its fruits and power resources. It is hardly an accident that the relatively more violent and less well-regulated pastimes of the landed classes transformed themselves into the relatively less violent and more minutely regulated pastimes which came to give the expression 'sport' its modern meaning in the same period in which the same social classes came to renounce violence and learned the heightened form of self-restraint demanded by the parliamentary form of controlling and especially of changing governments. In fact, the parliamentary contests themselves did not entirely lack the characteristics of a sport; nor did these largely verbal and non-violent parliamentary battles lack opportunities for enjoyable tension-excitement. There were, in other words, obvious affinities between the development and structure of England's political regime in the eighteenth century and the sportization of English upper-class pastimes in the same period.

Like the transformation of parliament from the end of the seventeenth and beginning of the eighteenth century onwards, that of upper-class pastimes in the eighteenth century reflected a specific problem that was characteristic of the overall changes that were occurring in the structure of the country at large. It was a problem which made itself increasingly felt as pacification progressed, as the pressure for self-restraint, particularly on the politically most powerful landed classes of England, increased and as the social apparatus for the prevention of unlicensed violence, an apparatus largely controlled by members of these classes themselves, became a little less ineffective. Without the increased security provided in this way, without advances in internal pacification, economic growth and increasing commercialization could hardly have got very far. Pacification and commercialization, between them, contributed to and demanded greater regularity in the personal conduct of people and not just in their occupational affairs. This trend towards greater regularity in the conduct of life was not only sustained by external controls but also by socially induced self-controls.[22] In the seventeenth century, perhaps with the exception of Cromwell's commonwealth, the culture, the ideals and standards of conduct of courtiers and citizens, in spite of some cross-links, were still recognizably set apart. With a slight exaggeration, one might say that manners without morals stood on one side, morals without manners on the other. Early in the eighteenth century the two traditions began to move closer to each other. The attempt made by Addison and Steele to reconcile morals and manners was only one manifestation of a wider trend. Not only citizens but the landed classes, the aristocracy and the gentry were affected by the pressures which the restraints on the use of physical force and the pressure for greater regularity in the conduct of life imposed on individuals in a politically more stable and rapidly commercializing country.

However, with the trend towards greater regularity, life tended to become duller. Conditions of strong individual excitement, particularly of socially shared excitement which might lead to loss of self-control, now became rarer and socially less tolerable. The problem was how to enable people to experience to the full the pleasurable excitement which appears to be one of the most elementary needs of human beings without the attending social and personal dangers for others or oneself, and in spite of a conscience-formation that was apt to clamp down on many forms of excitement which, in former ages, had been sources of high pleasurable gratification as well as of upheavals, injuries and human suffering. How could one ensure for human beings in an increasingly regularized society a sufficiency of pleasurable excitement as a shared experience, without the risk of socially intolerable disorders and mutual injuries? One of the solutions to this problem in England, as one saw, was the emergence of pastimes in the form that became known as 'sport'. The English form of fox-hunting was only one example among others of this transformation but it shows very vividly an early stage in the solution of that problem. The change from the emphasis on winning the contest to the greater emphasis on the long pleasurable excitement of the contest itself was, in this respect, highly significant. At a later stage, it found its expression in the well-known sports ethos according to which it was not the victory but the game itself which mattered. The fox-hunters were still able actually to injure and kill, if only by proxy and only animals. Other forms of sport, such as cricket and football, show how the problem was solved in cases where all the participants were human beings.

5

Folk Football in Medieval and Early Modern Britain

Norbert Elias and Eric Dunning

Reasonably reliable references to a ball-game called 'football' can be found in English sources from about the fourteenth century onwards, but identity of the name does not in the least vouchsafe identity of the game itself.[1] All that we know of the way in which it was played points to a very different type of game. The majority of references to football in medieval English sources come either from official prohibitions of the game in the edicts of kings and civic authorities or from reports of court cases against people who had broken the law by playing the game despite these official prohibitions. Nothing can be more revealing about the kind of game played at that time under the name of football than the constant and, by and large, apparently quite unsuccessful attempts of state and local authorities to suppress it. It must have been a wild game, suiting the temper of the people of that age. The comparative helplessness of those among the authorities who made themselves responsible for maintaining the peace of the land is extremely instructive for outlining the difference in the position of state and local authorities *vis-à-vis* ordinary citizens and above all in the effectiveness of the social machinery for the enforcement of laws in a medieval as opposed to a modern state.

One of the earliest prohibitions of the game occurred in London in a proclamation of 1314 issued in the name of King Edward II by the Lord Mayor. It reads as follows:

Proclamation issued for the Preservation of the Peace . . . Whereas our Lord the King is going towards the parts of Scotland, in his war against his enemies, and has especially commanded us strictly to keep his peace . . . And whereas there is great uproar in the City, through certain tumult arising from great footballs in the fields of the public, from which many evils perchance may arise – which may God forbid – we do command and do forbid, on the King's behalf, upon pain of imprisonment, that such game shall be practised henceforth within the city.[2]

An order from King Edward III in 1365 to the Sheriffs of the City of London also illustrates how strongly the authorities disapproved of these unruly pastimes. They were evidently in their eyes a waste of time as well as a threat to peace and they wished to canalize the energies of the people into what they regarded as more useful channels. They wanted the people to train in the use of military weapons instead of indulging in these unruly games. But the people, already at that time, apparently preferred their games to military exercises:

> To the Sherriffes of London. Order to cause proclamation to be made that every able bodied man of the said city on feast days when he has leisure shall in his sports use bows and arrows or pellets and bolts . . . forbidding them under pain of imprisonment to meddle in the hurling of stones, loggats and quoits, handball, football . . . or other vain games of no value; as the people of the realme, noble and simple, used heretofore to practise the said art in their sports when by God's help came forth honour to the kingdom and advantage to the King in his actions of war; and now the said art is almost wholly disused and the people engage in the games aforesaid and in other dishonest, unthrifty or idle games, whereby the realme is likely to be without archers.[3]

However wild and riotous their traditional ball-games were, the people liked them. Their tug-of-war with the authorities in the matter of these pastimes continued intermittently for centuries. The reasons given by the authorities for their opposition to these sports vary. The danger to public order and the competition with military training in archery are among the most prominent.

The following selected list may give an idea of the frequency of these edicts. Their recurrence indicates the relative powerlessness of the authorities at that stage in the development of English society to enforce permanently the legal prohibition of what today we might perhaps call a form of 'deviant behaviour'. By applying this term to breaches of the law in a different age, one can see more clearly that, sociologically speaking, the concept of 'deviant behaviour' is quite inadequate. The recurrence of special types of law-breaking implies not so much an accidental or arbitrary failure of individuals, as an inability of a society which is organized as a state to allow individual needs to be canalized in a way which is at the same time socially tolerable and individually satisfactory.

1314	Edward II	London
1331	Edward III	London
1365	Edward III	London
1388	Richard II	London
1409	Henry IV	London
1410	Henry IV	London
1414	Henry V	London
1424	James I of Scotland	
		Perth
1450		Halifax
1454		Halifax
1457	James II of Scotland	
		Perth
1467		Leicester

1471	James II of Scotland	
		Perth
1474	Edward IV	London
1477	Edward IV	London
1478		London
1481	James III of Scotland	
		Perth
1488		Leicester
1572		London
1581		London
1608		Manchester
1609		Manchester
1615		London

Although it appeared as asocial behaviour to the authorities, it remained for centuries a favourite pastime of the people in many parts of the country to amuse themselves with a football, broken bones and bloody noses or not. As one can see, the state apparatus for the enforcement of such edicts was as rudimentary as their ability to find other, equally satisfying leisure outlets for the citizens. Some people were fined or sent to prison for taking part in one of these riotous games. Perhaps here or there the custom lapsed for a time. If so, it continued in other places. The exciting game itself did not die out.

We still have records of many court cases against offenders. Two selections from these records, for the years 1576 and 1581, may be enough to show what often happened when the people of these times played with a football although, unfortunately, they do not show in detail the kind of game they played:

That on the said day at Ruyslippe, Co., Midd., Arthur Reynolds, husbandman, (with five others) all of Ruyslippe afsd., Thomas Darcye of Woxbridge, yeoman, (with seven others, four of whom were husbandmen, one a taylor, one a harnis maker, one a yeoman) all seven of Woxbridge afsd., with unknown malefactors to the number of one hundred assembled themselves unlawfully and played a certain unlawful game called football, by means of which unlawful game there was amongst them a great affray, likely to result in homicides and serious accident.

Coroner's inquisition – post mortem taken at Southemyms, Co., Midd., in view of the body of Roger Ludford, yeoman, there lying dead, with the verdict of the jurors that Nicholas Martyn and Richard Turvey both late of Southemyms, yeomen, were on the third instant between three and four p.m. playing with other persons at footeball in the field called Evanses Feld at Southemyms, when the said Roger Ludford and a

certain Simon Maltus, of the said parish, yeoman, came to the ground,
and that Roger Ludford cried out, cast him over the hedge, indicating
that he meant' Nicholas Martyn, who replied come thou and do yt'. That
thereupon Roger Ludford ran towards the ball with the intention to kick
it, whereupon Nicholas Martyn with the forepart of his right arm and
Richard Turvey with the forepart of his left arm struck Roger Ludford a
blow on the fore-part of the body under the breast, giving him a mortal
blow and concussion of which he died within a quarter of an hour and
that Nicholas and Richard in this manner feloniously slewe the said
Roger.[4]

A number of reports show the recurrent tug-of-war between the
people who clung to their violent customs and the authorities who tried
to suppress or to change them. Thus, a document dated 10 January
1540, issued by the mayor and corporation of Chester, mentions that it
was customary in that town on a Shrove Tuesday for the shoemakers to
challenge the drapers to a match with a 'ball of letter [leather], caulyd a
foutbale'. The mayor and corporation pronounced in the strongest
terms against these 'evill disposed persons' who caused such 'grete
inconvenience' in the city. They tried instead to introduce a footrace,
supervised by the mayor, with what success we do not know.[5]

An order prohibiting football promulgated in Manchester in 1608
and repeated almost literally a year later shows very much the same
picture. One reads there of the great harm done by a 'company of lewd
and disordered persons usinge that unlawfulle exercise of playing with
the ffotebale in ye streets'. The order mentions the large numbers of
windows which they broke, how they wronged other inhabitants and
committed many 'great inormyties'.[6]

It is probably useful to add at least one example not connected with
football in order to show, in general, the relatively greater ease with
which restraints were loosened in medieval England and, accordingly,
with which people, within their own country or town, behaved violently
in relation to each other:

The King having a resolve to go abroad in 1339 granted a commission to
the mayor, aldermen and commonalty of London for the conservation of
the peace in the city during his absence and invested them with power to
cause due and speedy punishment to be done upon any malefactors and
disturbers of the peace in the said city.[7] Soon after the King's departure,
a contest arose between the Companies of the Skinners and Fishmongers
which terminated in a bloody skirmish in the streets. The mayor with his
officers hastened to the place of riot and apprehended several of the
disturbers of the peace as required by his office and duty; but Thomas
Hounsard and John le Brewerer, with some of their accomplices, resisted
the power of the magistrates, and not only rescued the malefactors, but

Thomas, with a drawn sword, violently assaulted Andrew Aubrey, the mayor, and endeavoured to overthrow him; and in the meanwhile, the said John grievously wounded one of the city officers. They were, after a struggle, secured and conveyed without delay to the Guildhall where they were indicted and tried before the mayor and aldermen, having severally pleaded guilty, they were condemned to die and being forthwith conveyed to West Cheape or Cheapside were there beheaded. This sovereignty of the mayor was so well timed for the preservation of peace within the city and for preventing the riots and outrages so frequent in those days . . . that it gave great satisfaction to the King, who, by his writ dated 4th June '15 Edward III at the tower, not only pardoned the mayor for beheading the above parties, but also approved and confirmed the same.[8]

The chronicles of medieval England, like those of other medieval societies, describe many scenes such as this. Without reference to the frequency of outbreaks of uninstitutionalized violence in the Middle Ages one cannot understand the more institutionalized forms of which football was one.[9] Semi-institutionalized fights between local groups arranged on certain days of the year, particularly on Saints' Days and Holy Days, were a normal part of the traditional pattern of life in medieval societies. Playing with a football was one of the ways of arranging such a fight. It was, in fact, one of the normal annual rituals of these traditional societies. To remember this institution helps us to see their manner of life in better perspective. Football and other similar encounters in those times were not simply accidental brawls. They constituted an equilibrating type of leisure activity deeply woven into the warp and woof of society. It may seem incongruous to us that, year after year, people engaged in a kind of fight on Saints' Days and Holy Days. Our forefathers, at a different stage in the civilizing process, evidently experienced it as a perfectly obvious and obviously enjoyable arrangement.

People today, preoccupied with the disagreeable sides of life in big towns and with the disadvantages of living in a mass society, occasionally look back nostalgically to the times when most people lived in small communities which resembled in character and social structure what we would call large villages or small market towns. There were, of course, exceptions of which London is perhaps the most outstanding example. But, even in the sociological literature, a notion persists about the way of life in these 'traditional' or 'folk' societies according to which they were permeated by feelings of great 'solidarity'. This can easily be interpreted and is, in fact, quite often taken to mean, that tensions and conflicts were less strong and harmony greater within them than is the case with our own societies.[10] The difficulty about the use of such categories is not that they are wrong but that all such general terms as 'solidarity' applied to a different kind of society are apt to mislead the reader. Types of institutions and of conduct which appear to be incompatible in contemporary industrial societies are by no means always equally incompatible in the eyes of people accustomed to the life in societies of a different type. Our language, therefore, when applied to other societies reflects our own distinctions which may not be applicable to societies at a different stage of development. Thus, the term 'solidarity' evokes in us the impression of permanent unity, of friendliness and the absence of strife. 'As they intimately communicate with each other, every member [of a folk society] claims the sympathy of all the others,' as a writer on the subject put it.[11] One can, indeed, often observe expressions of strong and spontaneous 'fellow feeling' in traditional societies. But such expressions of what we might conceptualize as 'strong solidarity' were perfectly compatible with equally strong and spontaneous enmities and hatreds. What was really characteristic, at least of the traditional peasant societies of our own Middle Ages, was the much greater fluctuation of feeling of which people were then capable and, in connection with this, the relatively greater instability of human relationships in general. In connection with the lesser stability of internalized restraints, the strength of passions, the warmth and the spontaneity of emotional actions were greater in both directions: in the direction of kindness and readiness to help as well as in that of unkindness, callousness, and readiness to hurt. That is why terms such as 'solidarity', 'intimacy', 'fellow-feeling', and others like them used to describe attributes of pre-industrial folk societies are rather inapt. They only show one side of the picture.

Even many institutional traditions were 'double-faced' in our sense of that term. They allowed for the expression of intimate unity and solidarity and for the expression of equally intimate and intense hostility, without giving the slightest impression that the participants themselves saw anything contradictory or incompatible in these fluctuations.

Shrove Tuesday football, a ritualized and, according to our notions, fairly savage brawl between neighbouring groups, is a striking example of this compatibility between emotionally charged activities which seem to be incompatible according to present standards. As we have seen, the secular authorities tried, fairly early and for a long time without much success, to suppress these riotous fighting games of the people. But one cannot wholly understand the strong survival power of such customs if one sees in them merely games in our sense of the word. Medieval football formed part of a traditional ritual. It belonged to the Shrove Tuesday ceremonial which was to some extent a Church ceremonial and was closely linked to the whole cycle of Saints' Days and

Holy Days. In this respect, too, a differentiation which appears almost self-evident to us, the differentiation between religious and secular activities in medieval society, had not reached the same stage as in contemporary societies. One can occasionally read that everything medieval people did was 'steeped in religion'. The same writer has even gone so far as to say that one can express 'the essence of a folk-society by applying to it the term "sacred society"'.[12] This sort of statement can easily give the impression that everything done in these societies had the character of earnest and highly disciplined solemnity which prevails in Church services today. The truth is that even Church services in the Middle Ages were often noisier, less disciplined and far less removed from people's daily lives than is the case today. On the other hand, people's daily lives were permeated to a higher extent, for better or for worse, by beliefs in the nearness of God, the Devil, and their various helpers – saints, demons, spirits of all kinds, good or bad – which they hoped to influence by various forms of prayer as well as by white or black magic. With regard to this field, too, the application of abstract terms such as 'religious' or 'secular' which appear to us as exclusive alternatives, blocks the understanding of a kind of life which does not conform to our standard of institutional and conceptual differentiation into religious and secular activities. If one must express the lesser degree of differentiation in our terms, one can only say that, in the folk societies of the Middle Ages, secular activities were more religious and religious activities more secular than in contemporary societies.

   The same applies to the medieval folk game of football. It reflected potential for greater solidarity as well as for conflict and strife. Frictions between neighbouring communities, local guilds, groups of men and women, young married and younger unmarried men were often en-demic. If tempers ran high, they could, of course, lead at any time to outbreaks of open fighting. But in medieval society, in contrast to ours, there were traditional occasions when some of these tensions between groups within a community or between neighbouring village communi-ties could find expression in a form of fighting which was sanctioned by tradition and probably also for a considerable time by the Church and local magistrates. Again and again the old reports show that fighting between representatives of local groups, with or without a football, formed part of an annual ritual. One gets the feeling that the young members of such groups were often spoiling for a fight and, unless the tension exploded beforehand, waited with pleasurable anticipation for the coming of Shrove Tuesday or for any other day in the year which was earmarked for such a public encounter. Throughout this period, the game of football provided one of these outlets for standing tensions between local groups. The fact that such a game formed part of a traditional ritual did not prevent one side or the other from bending the traditions in its own favour if their feelings against the other side ran high enough. In the year 1579, for example, a group of Cambridge students went, as was customary, to the village of Chesterton to play 'at foteball'. They went there, so we are told, peacefully and without any weapons but the townsmen of Chesterton had secretly hidden a number of sticks in the porch of their church. After the match had started, they picked quarrels with the students, brought out their sticks, broke them over the heads of the students and gave them such a severe beating that they had to run through the river in order to escape. Some of them asked the Constable of Chesterton to keep the 'Queene's peace' but he was among those playing against them and, in fact, accused the students of being first to break the peace.[13]

This is a good example of the way in which football was used as an opportunity for paying off old scores. If we speak of traditions, of rules and rituals, these words can easily conjure up the picture of regulative institutions which work in a fairly strict and impersonal manner, for that is the connotation of these words in our own time. But if one uses the same words with reference to medieval societies one must not lose sight of the fact that the regulative institutions to which they refer – including what we call 'traditions' – although people clung to them more firmly than we do to ours, were at the same time far more dependent in their actual working on the changeable personal feelings of people and on passions of the moment. This explains on the one hand the extraordinary tenacity with which the people of medieval England played their Shrove Tuesday games year after year in the traditional manner despite all the proclamations of kings and fulminations of local magistrates against them, while they were quite capable at the same time of breaking the traditional conventions when their feelings ran high and of playing a trick or two on their opponents as they did in Chesterton.

A report from Corfe Castle, Dorsetshire, dated 1553, shows in greater detail some aspects of the type of folk ritual which was embodied in a game of football. The Company of Freeman Marblers or Quarriers played annually with a football as part of a whole series of Shrovetide ceremonies. First, the company officers were elected, then the apprentices were initiated. Each member of the company who had married in the previous year paid a 'marriage shilling' which gave his wife the right to have apprentices work for her in the case of his death. However, the man who had married last was excused from payment of the shilling. Instead, he had to provide a football. Then, on the next day, Ash Wednesday, the football was carried to the Lord of the Manor and a pound of pepper was given to him as a customary payment for an ancient right of way which the Company claimed. When the gift of pepper had been delivered, a game of football was played over the ground for which the company claimed this right.[14] An example such as this, and there are many others, shows very clearly that the people of this age saw nothing incongruous in the fact that a wild and riotous customary game should form part of a solemn ritual. Official solemnities and uproarious celebrations often shaded into each other as a matter of course.

Closely connected with the less impersonal character of all activities and with the higher levels of open emotionality was a peculiar variability of traditional customs, including games. People were deeply attached to their traditional ways of life. One reason for this was because a great many of the tension and conflict situations which today are formally regulated by a unified code of laws discussed and executed in relatively impersonal law courts, were then still the subjects of often highly personal decisions in the context of the local group. But the unwritten customary traditions, although they had to some extent, similar regulative functions to the written laws of our time, were by no means as completely immutable as they appear from a distance today. They could change, either imperceptibly if the group relations with which they were concerned changed, or perhaps more radically under the impact of wars, civil strife, epidemics and other events which often deeply disturbed the life of medieval communities. People would then develop new customs. They soon came to regard them as their traditions, whether or not they were identical with those which they had possessed before the disturbances. The greater part of these medieval folk traditions were handed on from one generation to another by word of mouth. They were oral traditions. The majority of the people concerned with them were non-literate. It was not customary to put any of the rules of games such as football formally in writing. The sons played as the fathers played or, in the case of disturbances, as they thought their fathers had played.

As there were neither written rules nor any central organizations to unify the manner of playing, references to football in medieval documents do not imply, as similar references would in the documents of our own time, that the game played with a football in different communities was everywhere the same. How people actually played was dependent on local customs not on common national rules. The organization of the game was much looser than it is today. The emotional spontaneity of the struggle was much greater; traditions of physical fighting and the few restraints – imposed by custom rather than by highly elaborate formal regulations which require a high degree of training and self-control – determined the manner of playing and made

for a certain family likeness among all these games. The differences
between games which were differently named were not necessarily as
sharply drawn as they are between different sport-games today. It is not
unlikely that the reason why medieval documents referred to some of
these local games as 'football' while others were known by different
names was primarily the fact that they were played with different
implements. Indeed, references to 'football' usually appear quite literally to be references to a particular type of ball and references to a type
of game only in so far as a different kind of ball or of playing implements in general might dictate a different manner of playing. Some
medieval documents do in fact refer to playing 'with a football' and not
to 'playing football'.[15] And, as far as one can see, the ball which was
called a 'football' had this in common with that used in football games
today: it was an inflated bladder sometimes, but not always, encased in
leather. Peasant communities the world over have used such balls as a
device for their amusement. Records of their use certainly exist for
most parts of medieval Europe. If it has the right size and resilience,
and is neither too small nor too large, such an inflated animal bladder,
whether encased in leather or not, probably lends itself better than a
small solid ball to kicking with the feet. But there is no reason to
assume that the medieval 'football' was only propelled by foot or,
conversely, that the medieval 'handball' was only propelled by hand.
Again, the primary reason for such differences in the names of these
games may simply refer to the fact that they were played with balls
which were different in size and shape or that they were played with
sticks or with other implements of a similar kind. But the elementary
characteristics, the character of the game as a struggle between different groups, the open and spontaneous battle-enjoyment, the riotous-
ness and the relatively high level of socially tolerated physical violence,
as far as one can see, were always the same. And so was the tendency to
break whatever customary rules there were, if passions moved the
players. Thus, since the family likeness of all these games in some of
their aspects was very great, one can gain a vivid impression of the
manner in which people played with a football, of which we have no
really detailed report, from the few more extensive reports that have
come down to us from this period even though they were not actually
played with a football but with other implements.

One of these more extensive reports, which is well worth reading, is
that of a Cornish game which had the still familiar name of 'hurling'. It
shows very vividly how much less strict, how much more personal and
informal the handling of traditional customs and rules was in medieval
societies than the handling of rules and even of customs and traditions
is in our own time.

The report speaks for itself. No paraphrase can emulate the impression of the game and of its atmosphere which it conveys:

Hurling

Hurling taketh his denomination from throwing of the ball, and is of two sorts, in the East parts of *Cornwall*, to goales, and in the West, to the countrey.

Hurling to goales.

For hurling to goales, there are 15, 20 or 30 players more or lesse, chosen out on each side, who strip themselves into their slightest apparell, and then joyne hands in ranks one against another. Out of these ranks they match themselves by payres, one embracing another, and so passe away: every of which couple, are specially to watch one another during the play.

After this, they pitch two bushes in the ground, some eight or ten foote asunder; and directly against them, ten or twelve score off, other twayne in like distance, which they terme their Goales. One of these is appoynted by lots, to the one side, and the other to his adverse party. There is assigned for their gard, a couple of their best stopping Hurlers; the residue draw into the midst betweene both goales, where some indifferent person throweth up a ball, the which whosoever can catch, and cary through his adversaries goale, hath wonne the game. But therein consisteth one of *Hercules* his labours: for he that is once possessed of the ball hath his contrary mate waiting at inches, and assaying to lay hold upon him. The other thrusteth him in the breast, with his closed fist, to keepe him off; which they call Butting, and place in weldoing the same, no small poynt of manhood.

If hee escape the first, another taketh him in hand, and so a third, neyther is hee left, untill having met (as the Frenchman sayes) *Chaussera son pied*, hee eyther touch the ground with some part of his bodie, in wrastling, or cry, Hold; which is the word of yielding. Then must he cast the ball (named Dealing) to some one of his fellowes, who catching the same in his hand, maketh away withall as before; and if his hap or agility bee so good, as to shake off or outrunne his counter-wayters, at the goale, hee findeth one or two fresh men, readie to receive and keepe him off. It is therefore a very disadvantageable match, or extraordinary accident, that looseth many goales; howbeit, that side carryeth away best reputation, which giveth most falles in the hurling, keepeth the ball longest, and presseth his contrary nearest to their owne goale. Sometimes one chosen person on eche party dealeth the ball.

The Hurlers are bound to the observation of many lawes, as, that they must hurle man to man, and not two set upon one man at once: that the Hurler against the ball, must not *but*, nor hand-fast under the girdle: that hee who hath the ball, must *but* onely in the others brest: that he must deale no Fore-ball, *viz.* he may not throw it to any of his mates, standing neerer the goale, than himselfe. Lastly, in dealing the ball, if any of the other part can catch it flying, between, or e're the other have it fast, he thereby winneth the same to his side, which straightway of defendant becommeth assailant, as the other, of assailant falls to be defendant. The least breach of these lawes, the Hurlers take for a just cause of going together by the eares, but with their fists onely; neither doth any among them seek revenge for such wrongs or hurts, but at the like play againe. These hurling matches are mostly used at weddings, where commonly the ghests undertake to encounter all commers.

Hurlinge to the countrie.

The hurlinge to the Countrey, is more diffuse and confuse, as bound to few of these orders: Some two or more Gentlemen doe commonly make this match, appointing that on such a holyday, they will bring to such an indifferent place, two, three, or more parishes of the East or South quarter, to hurle against so many other, of the West or North. Their goales are either those Gentlemens houses, or some townes or villages, three of four miles asunder, of which either side maketh choice after the neernesse to their dwellings. When they meet, there is neyther comparing of numbers, nor matching of men: but a silver ball is cast up, and that company, which can catch, and cary it by force, or sleight, to their place assigned, gaineth the ball and victory. Whosoever getteth seizure of this ball, findeth himself generally pursued by the adverse party; neither will they leave, till (without all respects) he be layd flat on Gods deare earth: which fall once received, disableth him from any longer detayning the ball: hee therefore throweth the same (with like hazard of intercepting, as in the other hurling) to some one of his fellowes, fardest before him, who maketh away withall in like maner. Such as see where the ball is played, give notice thereof to their mates, crying Ware East, Ware West, etc. as the same is carried.

The Hurlers take their next way over hilles, dales, hedges, ditches; yea, and thorow bushes, briers, mires, plashes and rivers whatsoever; so as you shall sometimes see 20, or 30 lie tugging together in the water, scrambling and scratching for the ball. A play (verily) both rude and rough, and yet such, as is not destitute of policies, in some sort resembling the feats of warre: for you shall have companies layd out before, on the one side, to encounter them that come with the ball, and of the other party to succor them, in the maner of a foreward. Againe, other troups lye hovering on the sides, like wings, to helpe or stop their escape: and where the ball it selfe goeth, it resembleth the joyning of the two mayne battels: the slowest footed who come lagge, supply the showe of a rereward: yea, there are horsemen placed also on either party (as it were in ambush) and ready to ride away with the ball, if they can catch it at advantage. But they must not so steale the palme: for gallop any one of them never so fast, yet he shall be surely met at some hedge corner, crosse-lane, bridge, or deep water, which (by casting the Countrie) they know he must needs touch at: and if his good fortune gard him not the better, hee is like to pay the price of his theft, with his owne and his

horses overthrowe to the ground. Sometimes, the whole company run-
neth with the ball, seven or eight miles out of the direct way, which they
should keepe. Sometimes a foote-man getting it by stealth, the better to
scape unespied, will carry the same quite backwards, and so, at last, get
to the goale by a windlace: which once knowne to be wonne, all that side
flocke thither with great jolity: and if the same bee a Gentlemans house,
they give him the ball for a *Trophee*, and the drinking out of his Beere to
boote.

The ball in this play may bee compared to an infernall spirit: for
whosoever catcheth it, fareth straightwayes like a madde man, struggling
and fighting with those that goe about to holde him: and no sooner is the
ball gone from him, but he resigneth this fury to the next receyver, and
himselfe becommeth peaceable as before. I cannot well resolve, whether
I should more commend this game, for the manhood and exercise, or
condemne it for the boysterousnes and harmes which it begetteth: for as
on the one side it makes their bodies strong, hard, and nimble, and puts a
courage into their hearts, to meete an enemie in the face: so on the other
part, it is accompanied with many dangers, some of which do ever fall to
the players share. For proofe whereof, when the hurling is ended, you
shall see them retyring home, as from a pitched battaile, with bloody
pates, bones broken, and out of joynt, and such bruses as serve to
shorten their daies; yet al is good play, and never Attourney nor
Crowner troubled for the matter.[16]

Such a description is of very great help if one wants to form a
reasonably clear idea of the distinguishing characteristics – of the
different 'structure' – of games in an earlier, in the late medieval and
early modern stages in the development of English society. It also helps
to illuminate differences in the wider structure of English society at that
stage in its development. In some respects, a folk-game tradition as it
has been described here must have been affected by one very influential characteristic of British society, though it is not possible to know
exactly in what ways. Only comparative studies of other societies and
the structure of their games could reassure us in this respect. The folk
game as we see it here reflects a very specific relationship between
landowners and peasantry. As one can see, the landowners themselves
made it their business to organize, to act as patrons of folk games of this
kind. The game as we see it here, brutal and disorderly as it may appear
to us, is not simply a game played between villagers and townsmen
without any reference at all to people of higher authority who could
check what, according to the standards of that time, might have
appeared as excessive violence. It is, as one knows, characteristic of the
pattern of social development on these islands, that on the one hand, a
rural population which consisted of peasants living in varying degrees
of serfdom transformed themselves into a rural population of more or

less free peasants; and that on the other hand, side by side with a class of landowning noblemen, there emerged a class of landowners who were untitled, a class who were only 'gentlemen'. This, as far as one can make out, is the setting of the game as we see it here: a local amusement for a population of more or less free peasants promoted by local landowners who often, though perhaps not always, were non-nobles. If some bones were broken in the course of the game, if perhaps occasionally someone died as a result of injuries received in the game, if in short the whole affair infringed the king's laws and was frowned on by the king's representatives, the local people, peasantry and gentry together, enjoyed it and were, as one can see, quite prepared to snap their fingers at them. One can still hear the sly undertones in the voice of Carew when he spoke of pitched battles, bloody pates and bones broken – yet, 'never Attourney nor Crowner troubled for the matter'. This was a local tradition. Both peasantry and gentry meant to keep it up and to enjoy it.

Its violence was by no means unmitigated and completely lawless, however. There were in fact already, as we learn from this account, customary 'laws' or, more strictly speaking, rules. A rudimentary sense of what became known as 'fairness' was already there and it is most likely that this peculiar social setting, relatively free peasants and middle-class landowners, had something to do with it. If there was a fight between the player with the ball and his opponents, the 'laws' stipulated that only one should attack him at a time, not two. Another rule decreed that players should not hit each other below the belt: the chest was the only legitimate target. However, there was no formal organization outside and apart from the players themselves to ensure that the rules were obeyed. There was no referee, no outside arbiter in the case of disputes. In some respects, this manner of playing a game shows us an aspect of the social life of early communities which is otherwise difficult to grasp. As we have seen already, it is often said of them that they were more closely integrated or had a special kind of solidarity feeling compared with ours. However, these peasant communities had their conflicts, either within their own ranks or with neighbouring communities. The manner of settling them was considerably more violent as a rule than became the case at a later stage. And football and other folk games, as we have seen, were one way of releasing the tension. But the fact that there were no written rules or central authorities and no referees to supervise the players or to arbitrate did not mean that they played without any rules at all. Traditional rules, customary regulations, as one can see, which had developed over the centuries as a kind of communal self-restraint, took the place of our more elaborate and often more carefully thought-out institutional rules and it may well be that people in these earlier societies clung to their traditions and among them to the few customary restraints of tensions and conflicts as tenaciously as we know they did, precisely because to lose them would often have meant to lose a very essential part of such restraints against their own passions as were available to them. But if these customary restraints were broken they had no one but themselves to keep the offenders in check. What one encounters here is a very early type of democracy – a kind of village democracy. The manner of punishing offenders against the 'laws' of the game, as Carew describes it, is a small-scale paradigm of this self-regulating peasant democracy, with relatively little supervision by outside officials. One has the impression that, by our standards, this way of preventing people from breaking the customary rules was perhaps not very efficient. A breach of the rules, as Carew describes it, was often enough just another occasion for a fairly violent fight – probably with few holds barred.

One can also see fairly clearly from Carew's description that the traditions of what are today two different and, apparently, quite unrelated types of sports still formed an undifferentiated game-pattern in some of these ancestral folk games. Hurling, in fact, contained elements of a ball-game on the one hand, and of unarmed mock- or display-combat on the other. In such a folk game it was quite evidently accepted by all participants and spectators as a normal element of the game and as part of the fun that people engaged in some kind of physical fighting with each other. However, even hand-to-hand fighting in societies of the 'medieval' type followed some sort of regulating tradition which provided both a mutual attunement of the movements of the combatants and some limitation on the injuries they inflicted on each other. In Cornwall at the time of this hurling game, one type of mock and display fighting, called wrestling, still formed one of the standing amusements of village life. The ordinary Cornish wrestlers proclaimed each other locally the best and most famous in the country. It is not surprising to see, therefore, that wrestling techniques played a part in the ball-game of hurling. One of the factors taken into account in determining the winner of a game, as Carew describes it, was the number of 'falles' inflicted on the other side; and 'to give a falle', to put an opponent on his back and make him touch the ground with a shoulder on one side and with a heel on the other was in fact one of the main aims in hurling. Skill and success in this respect enhanced the reputation of a village team. One can imagine how the teams and the communities which they represented must have afterwards discussed who got the better of the other in this respect, and that they sometimes had an extra row about it.

Even in 'hurling to goales', however, the more regulated of the two types of hurling described by Carew, the criteria for winning were not as clearly defined and as calculable as the winning of sport-games is in our own time, for the latter is usually connected with some unequivocal measurement such as the 'goal', the 'point' or the 'run'. The determination of the winner in a folk game such as hurling, as one can see from Carew's description, was far less precise and sharply regulated and, in a way, this is symptomatic of the distinguishing character of these traditional folk games from modern sport-games generally. Even at the turn of the sixteenth century, European societies were not yet 'measuring' societies. What is most important to note, however, is that, while compared with our sport-games, the hurling game, including its wrestling component, was far less highly regulated, it was certainly not completely anarchic. Our conceptual vocabulary is not yet developed enough, our perception not yet trained enough to enable us to distinguish clearly and precisely between different degrees and types of regulation. It is clear that a series of detailed comparative studies both with other folk games in our own society and with the folk games of different societies at a comparable stage of social development would perform a useful service in this respect.

6

Dynamics of Sport Groups with Special Reference to Football

Norbert Elias and Eric Dunning

It happens quite often in the development of a science, or of one of its branches, that a type of theory which has dominated the direction of research for some time reaches a point where its limitations become apparent.[1] One begins to see that a number of significant problems cannot be clearly formulated and cannot be solved with its help. The scientists who work in this field then begin to look round for a wider theoretical framework, or perhaps for another type of theory altogether, which will allow them to come to grips with problems beyond the reach of the fashionable type of theory.

What is called 'small group theory' in contemporary sociology appears to be in that stage. It is fairly evident that a good many problems of small groups are beyond the reach of small group theory in its present form, to say nothing of its limitations as a model-setting theory for the exploration of larger social units. It did not, at any rate, prove of great help to us when we tried to investigate problems of small groups engaged in sport-games such as football. Confronted with the study of sport groups *in vivo*, small group theory failed us.[2]

We therefore set out – in connection with a wider investigation of the long-term development of football – to explore some of the theoretical aspects of the dynamics of groups engaged in games of this type. It appeared to us that sport-games in general, and football in particular, could serve as a useful point of departure for the construction of models of small group dynamics which are somewhat different from those offered within the framework of present-day small group theories. Some aspects of such a model are presented in this paper. Although it is built primarily with reference to football, the concepts derived from our analysis may perhaps be of wider use. They almost certainly apply not only to football, but also to other group games.

In studying football and other sport-games, one encounters from the start certain semantic difficulties. People often speak of a game of football as if it were something outside of, and apart from, the group of players. It is not entirely incorrect to say that a game such as football can be played by many different groups. As such, it is partly independent of any one of them. At the same time, the pattern of each individual game is itself a group pattern. In order to play a game, people group themselves in specific ways. As the game runs its course, they continually regroup themselves in a manner similar to the ways in which groups of dancers regroup themselves in the course of a dance. The initial figuration from which the players start changes into other figurations of players in a continuous movement. It is to this continuous movement of the figuration of players to which we refer when we use the term 'game-pattern'. The term can be misleading if it makes one forget what one actually observes when watching a game: one observes small groups of living human beings changing their relations in constant interdependence with each other.

The dynamics of this grouping and regrouping of players in the course of a game are fixed in certain respects and elastic and variable in others. They are fixed, because without agreement among the players on their adherence to a unified set of rules, the game would not be a game but a 'free-for-all'. They are elastic and variable, otherwise one game would be exactly like another. In that case, too, its specific character as a game would be lost. Thus, in order that group relations can have the character of a game, a very specific balance must be established between fixity and elasticity of rules. On this balance depend the dynamics of the game. If the relations between those who play the game are too rigidly or too loosely bound by rules, the game will suffer.

Take the initial figuration of players in Association Football. It is regulated by certain rules. Thus, the wording of one of the 1897 rules about the 'kick-off' figuration, which with some qualifications is still valid, is this:

> The game shall be commenced by a place-kick from the *centre of the field of play* in the direction of the opponents' goal-line; *the opponents* shall not approach within ten yards of the ball until it is kicked off, nor shall any player on either side pass the centre of the ground in the direction of his opponents' goal until the ball is kicked off.[3]

It is easy to see how much room for manoeuvring this kind of rule leaves to the two sides – how elastic it is. Within the framework of the kick-off rules, players can group themselves in a 'W-formation' (2–3–5) or in the form of a 'horizontal H' (4–2–4). If they want to, the defending side may even mass themselves solidly in front of their own goal, although in practice this is rarely done. How the players actually position themselves at the kick-off is determined by formal rules as well as by convention, by their experience of previous games, and often by their own strategic plans coupled with their expectations of the intended strategy of their opponents. How far this peculiar character-istic, this blend of firmness and elasticity applies to the regulation of human relations in other spheres is a question which may deserve more attention than it has received so far.

From the starting position evolves a fluid figuration formed by both teams. Within it, all individuals are, and remain throughout, more or less interdependent; they move and regroup themselves in response to each other. This may help to explain why we refer to this type of game as a specific form of group dynamics. For this moving and regrouping of interdependent players in response to each other *is* the game.

It may not be immediately clear that by using the term 'group dynamics' in this context we do not refer to the changing figurations of each of the two groups of players as if they could be considered in separation, as if each had dynamics of its own. That is not the case. In a game of football, the figuration of players on the one side and that of players on the other side, are interdependent and inseparable. They form in fact one single figuration. If one speaks of a sport-game as a specific form of group dynamics, one refers to the overall change in the figuration of the players of both sides together. Few aspects of the group dynamics of football show as clearly as this the relevance of sport-games as models for the dynamics of groups in many other fields.

A fundamental characteristic, not only of football, but of practically all sport-games, is that they constitute a type of group dynamics which is produced by controlled tensions between at least two sub-groups. For this reason alone, traditional sociological small group theory is not of very great help in the exploration of the sort of problems which confronted us here. These require specific concepts different from those used so far in the sociological study of small groups, and perhaps a little more complex than those commonly used in discussions about sport-games. According to present conceptual usage, one might be content with saying that a game of football is played by two different groups. This is one of those linguistic conventions which induce people to think and to speak as if the game were something apart from the human beings concerned. By stressing that the game is nothing but the changing figuration around a moving ball of the players themselves, one brings into focus at the same time that it is not the changing figuration of each of the two teams seen separately, but of the players of *both* teams together in their struggle with one another. Many people who watch a game of football may know that this is what they try to follow – not merely one team or the other, but the fluid pattern formed by both. This *is* the pattern of the game – the dynamics of a group in tension.

As such, this model of group dynamics has theoretical implications beyond the study of small groups. It may be of help for the study of such varied problems as, for example, that of marital tensions, or of union-management tensions. There, as in the case of sport groups, tensions are not extraneous, but intrinsic to the figuration itself; there too, they are to some extent controlled. How and to what degree they are, and how they came to be controlled, is a problem to be studied. Inter-state relations are another example of a figuration with built-in tensions. But in that case effective and permanent tension control has not yet been achieved and, at the present level of social development and of sociological understanding of groups-in-tension, perhaps cannot be achieved. Among the factors which prevent the achievement of better control is certainly the widespread inability to perceive and to investigate two states in tension or a multi-polar state system as a single figuration. One usually approaches such a system as the involved participant of one side and is therefore not quite able to visualize and to determine the paramount dynamics of the figuration which different sides form with each other and which determines the moves of each side. The study of sport-games like football can thus serve as a relatively simple introduction to a figurational approach to the study of tensions and conflicts – to an approach in which attention is focused, not on the dynamics of one side or the other, but of both together as a single figuration in tension.

Today, sociological thinking with regard to problems of this kind often seems to revolve around two alternatives: problems of group tension stand on one side, problems of group co-operation and harmony on the other. Group tensions appear to be one phenomenon; group co-operation and harmony another. Because one has different words, it appears almost as if the phenomena themselves were different and independent of each other. An analysis of sport-games illuminates the inadequacy of this approach. The group dynamics of a game presuppose tension and co-operation on a variety of levels at the same time. Neither would be what it is without the other.

Traditional small group theory is apt to lead attention away from problems of this type. Its representatives often select for study small group problems in which tensions play no part at all, or if they select for study problems of tension, they confine themselves to specific types of individual tension such as individual competition. In reading their arguments, one often has the feeling that their discussions on the subject of group tensions and conflicts are discussions about questions of political philosophy and political ideals rather than about conclusions derived from strictly scientific enquiries. In this case as in others, contemporary sociology appears at times to be threatened by a polarization between those who are blind to the role of tensions in social groups – or at least who greatly underplay this role – and those who overplay the role of tensions and conflicts to the neglect of other, equally relevant aspects of group dynamics. Homans, for example, has developed a small group theory in which conflict and tension play at most a marginal part. It is probably not unfair to suggest that this harmonistic tendency is connected with a pre-established scheme of values, a kind of sociopolitical *Weltanschauung* which sets the course for theoretical arguments and empirical observations alike. It almost appears as if Homans has developed an emotional allergy to the discussion of tensions and conflicts. Thus, he wrote:

> if we confine ourselves to behaviour . . . (concerned with the exchange of rewarding activities), we are sure to call down upon our heads the wrath of the social scientists who make a profession of being tough-minded. 'Never play down conflict,' they would say. 'Not only is conflict a fact of social life, but conflict has positive virtues and brings out some of the best in men.' It turns out that these very scientists are no more willing than is the rest of mankind to encourage conflict within any body of men they themselves are responsible for. Conflict is good for other people's subordinates, not their own. But we must refrain. It is all too easy to ask men to practise what they preach. A trap that none can escape is no fun setting.[4]

This, as one can see, is an emotionally charged argument. It shows how greatly Homans himself misunderstands the character of sociological analysis. Without doubt, some writers who focus attention on problems of conflict, do so because they wish to encourage conflict – that is, for reasons extraneous to the sociological study of such problems. But to suggest, as Homans seems to do, that the encouragement of conflict is the only reason why sociologists try to determine the nature of tensions and conflicts in the social life of people implies a fundamental misunderstanding of the task of sociological analysis. Although Homans writes, 'no one can deny . . . that conflict is a fact of social life', he obviously finds it difficult to deal with this fact simply as such, as one fact of life among others.

In this respect, the study of sport-games can be of considerable help. A specific type of tension plays a significant part in such games. In studying them, one cannot overlook tensions whether one likes them or not. It seemed useful to determine the character of sport-games like football as figurations with tensions of a specific type and we thought that 'groups-in-controlled-tension' would be an appropriate term to express it.

At the present stage of theoretical development one is confronted by a dilemma in these matters which, in a somewhat different context, has been most clearly formulated by Dahrendorf. We have already referred to the tendency to treat conflict and co-operation as independent phenomena and to form different and separate theories, one for each of them. Dahrendorf encountered a similar problem with regard to integration and coercion, and posed in this connection a significant question:

> Is there, or can there be, a general point of view that synthesises the unsolved dialectics of integration and coercion? So far as I can see there is no such general model; as to its possibility, I have to reserve judgement. It seems at least conceivable that unification of theory is not feasible at a point which has puzzled thinkers ever since the beginning of Western philosophy.[5]

The same might be said with regard to tensions and co-operation. Some sociological theories are woven around problems of conflict and tension without much regard for those of co-operation and integration; others pay regard above all to problems of co-operation and integration, treating conflict and tension more or less as marginal phenomena. From closer range, it is easy to see the reason. Both procedures are based on a reification of values: because one attaches different values to conflict and co-operation, one is apt to treat these phenomena as if they had a separate and independent existence.

A study of sport-games is thus a useful point of departure for an approach to these problems which may allow the passions to calm down. It is easier in this field to move outside the battle of extraneous evaluations and to keep in close touch with testable, factual evidence in framing theoretical propositions. It is less difficult, therefore, to move towards a unified theoretical framework within which both tension and co-operation can find their place as interdependent phenomena. In football, co-operation presupposes tension, and tension co-operation.

However, one can clearly perceive their complementary character only if one studies how the game has developed to its present form where tensions and co-operation are related to each other through firm types of control. The study of the long-term development of football enabled us, in fact, to see in a limited field one aspect of the interplay between tension and tension-control without which the relevance of sport-games as a theoretical model cannot be fully understood. It showed how tensions which were at one time uncontrolled and probably uncontrollable were gradually brought under control.

In its present form, one of the central characteristics of Association Football and many other sport-games is certainly the manner in which the often fairly high group tensions engendered in the game are kept under control. But this is a fairly recent attainment. In former days, tensions between players, which were and are at all times characteristic of games, were often far less well controlled. This transformation, the development of a highly regulated, relatively non-violent form of group tension, from an earlier stage where the corresponding tensions were much more apt to discharge themselves in one or another form of violence, is at the core of the long-term dynamics of the game of football. It is representative – one might almost say symbolic – of certain aspects of the long-term development of European societies. For within many of these societies the general level of overt violence has diminished over the ages. There, too, one encounters, as one does in the development of football, both a higher level of organization and higher levels of self-restraint and of security compared with the past. How and why this long-term development towards more 'civilized' standards of human relations occurred in society at large need not concern us here.[6] But we were able to find out some of the reasons why a game like football developed, in connection with similar trends in society at large, from a more to a less violent and uncontrolled form and correspondingly to a different form of game-pattern, of group dynamics. This understanding of the long-term dynamics of football greatly assists that of the short-term dynamics of the game as played today.

As played in earlier ages, not only in England but also in many other countries, football, like most ball games, was a very wild game indeed.[7]

Centuries later, between 1845 and 1862, when the playing of football, at least in some of the leading public schools, had become much more highly regulated, the level of permitted violence was still very much higher than it is today and the dynamics of group tensions were therefore rather different.[8]

As late as 1863, the incipient Football Association split because the majority proposed to eliminate 'hacking' altogether from the game, while a minority of the founder members held to the view that the abolition of hacking would make the game 'unmanly' and opposed it. This was not the only, but certainly one of the major points which led to the development of two types of football in England. Association Football, or 'soccer', on the one hand, and Rugby Football, or 'rugger', on the other. It is interesting to note that even in the rugby game, although the general level of violence remained somewhat higher than in Association Football, hacking was also 'outlawed' not very long after the break occurred.

The problem we encountered here – a problem not entirely without theoretical significance – was that of the reasons why one of the two types of football, namely 'soccer', gained very much wider recognition and success than the other, not only in England but almost the world over. Was it because the level of violence in soccer was lower than in rugby? In order to answer questions such as this one needs a very clear idea of at least one of the central problems that resulted from the lowering of violence for the whole pattern of the game, for its group dynamics. The danger of this decrease of permitted violence was quite obviously that the game in its changed form would become uninteresting and dull. The survival of the game evidently depended on a peculiar kind of balance between, on the one hand, a high control of the level of violence, because without it the game was no longer acceptable to most players and most spectators in accordance with the now prevailing standards of 'civilized' behaviour, and, on the other hand, the preservation of a sufficiently high level of non-violent fighting without which the interest of players and public alike would have flagged. The whole development of most sport-games, and certainly that of football, centred to a very large extent on the solution of this problem: how was it possible to maintain within the set game-pattern a high level of group tension and the group dynamics resulting from it, while at the same time keeping recurrent physical injury to the players at the lowest possible level. The question was and still is, in other words, how to 'steer the ship', as it were, between the Scylla of disorderliness and the Charybdis of boredom. People who have acted as coaches or managers in the game may appreciate that this is a problem of great practical significance. A good number of people in that position are used to thinking in terms of figurations as a matter of course if they plan ahead; for that is the most realistic way of envisaging a game and most appropriate for the working out of strategies. Thus, in preparing his team for a game, a manager may say that the opponents are likely to use a '4–2–4 system', that their own task is to prevent the opponents from dominating the mid-field play; in order to achieve this, he may assign to two of his players the task of 'blotting out' the opponents' 'link' men, so that the rest can concentrate on the task of attack. However, although trained by his immediate experience to envisage the game as a fluctuating figuration of players it is neither his aim nor his task to stand back and to reflect on the characteristics and regularities of these figurations as such. The Committee of the Football Association, who decided in 1925 to change the offside rule, were probably aware that under the old rules the 'tone' of the game had become too low, as people on other occasions noticed that the game had begun to stray from the middle course between disorderliness and dullness. But up to now the concepts available for dealing with such problems are not very articulate. In order to see their wider significance – their significance for a small group theory or for a sociological game theory in general – it is necessary to work out comparatively new concepts as a framework for observation and to change the meaning of some of those which already exist.

Let us start with the concept of 'figuration'. It has already been said that a game is the changing figuration of the players on the field. This means that the figuration is not only an aspect of the players. It is not as one sometimes seems to believe if one uses related expressions such as 'social pattern', 'social group', or 'society', something abstracted from individual people. Figurations are formed by individuals, as it were 'body and soul'. If one watches the players standing and moving on the field in constant interdependence, one can actually see them forming a continuously changing figuration. If groups or societies are large, one usually cannot see the figurations their individual members form with one another. Nevertheless, in these cases too people form figurations with each other – a city, a church, a political party, a state – which are no less real than the one formed by players on a football field, even though one cannot take them in at a glance.

To envisage groupings of people as figurations in this sense, with their dynamics, their problems of tension and of tension control and many others, even though one cannot see them here and now, requires a specific training. This is one of the tasks of figurational sociology, of which the present essay is an example. At present, a good deal of uncertainty still exists with regard to the nature of that phenomenon to which one refers as 'society'. Sociological theories often appear to start from the assumption that 'groups' or 'societies', and 'social pheno-mena' in general, are something abstracted from individual people, or at least that they are not quite as 'real' as individuals, whatever that may mean. The game of football – as a small-scale model – can help to correct this view. It shows that figurations of individuals are neither more nor less real than the individuals who form them. Figurational sociology is based on observations such as this. In contrast to sociologi-cal theories which treat societies as if they were mere names, a *flatum vocis*, an 'ideal type', a sociologist's construction, and which are in that sense representative of sociological nominalism, it represents a sociolo-gical realism.[9] Individuals always come in figurations and figurations are always formed by individuals.

If one watches a game of football one can understand that it is the fluctuating figuration of the players itself on which, at a given moment, the decisions and moves of individual players depend. In that respect concepts such as 'interaction' and its relatives are apt to mislead. They appear to suggest that individuals without figurations form figurations with each other *a posteriori*. They make it difficult to come to grips with the type of tensions one encounters in the study of football. These tensions are different in character from those which may arise when two formerly independent individuals, 'ego' and 'alter', begin to inter-act. As has already been said, it is the figuration of players itself which embodies a tension of a specific type – a controlled tension. One can neither understand nor explain its character from the 'interaction' of individual players.

In societies such as ours, it is one of the characteristics of a game that the tension inherent in the figuration of players is neither too high nor too low: the game must last for a while, but must finally be resolved in the victory of one side or the other. There can be 'drawn' games, but if they occur too often, one would suspect that something in the construction of the game was faulty.

Thus, in present-day industrial societies, a game is a group figuration of a very specific type. At its heart is the controlled tension between two sub-groups holding each other in balance. This is a phenomenon one can observe in many other fields. It appears to deserve a special name. We have called it a 'tension-balance'. Just as the mobility of a human limb is dependent on the contained tension between two anta-gonistic muscle groups in balance, so the game process depends on a tension between two at the same time antagonistic and interdependent sets of players keeping each other in a fluctuating equilibrium.[10]

The mechanics of figurations with a tension-balance at their centre are far from simple. Two examples may be enough to illustrate them: the flexible tension-balance in a game process cannot be produced and maintained at just the right level if one side is very much stronger than the other. If that is the case, the stronger side will probably score more frequently, the game tension – the 'tone' of the game – will be relatively low, and the game itself will be slow and lifeless. But it would be a mistake to think that in studying the group dynamics of a game one is mainly concerned with questions arising from the qualities of individual teams or of individual players. What we have primarily studied are the development and the structure of the game-pattern as such. This pattern has, at a given time, a specific form maintained by controls at various levels. It is controlled by football organizations, by state and local authorities, by the spectators, by the teams mutually, by the players individually. One need not enumerate them all or analyse their interplay in this context. In theoretical discourse, one is apt to consider the controls preserving a particular figuration, and above all the tension-balance of a figuration, in terms of rules or norms only. But, as in other cases, rules and especially formal rules are only one of the 'instruments' of control responsible for the relative stability of groups-in-controlled-tension. And, whatever they are, group rules or group norms, here as elsewhere, are no absolutes.

Rules or norms as devices for the control of tensions do not float outside and above social processes as is sometimes suggested in present discussions. The group dynamics which rules help to maintain may, on their part, determine whether rules persist or change. The development of football regulations shows very strikingly how changes of rules can depend on the overall development of that which they rule. The dynamics of such figurations have what one might call a 'logic' of their own. Thus, in football the tension level may flag, not simply because of the distinguishing characteristics of individual playing groups or of their individual members, but because of set characteristics of the figuration which they form with one another. This is a phenomenon which one encounters again and again if one surveys the development of a game. In 1925, for example, the offside rule in soccer was changed. Until then, the rule was this: a player could only legitimately receive a ball passed forward to him by another member of his side if at least three members of the opposing team stood between him and their goal. If less than three were so positioned, he was ruled offside and a free kick was awarded to the opponents. In 1925, the number was reduced to two. The elasticity of the older rule, skilfully exploited, had led to a stage where stalemates had become increasingly frequent. What had happened was that the balance had moved too far in favour of the defence. Games tended to drag on without decision, or scores were low. The reason was not any particular quality of individual players: the figuration of players as stabilized by a variety of controls, among which the formal rules held a key position, had itself proved deficient. Hence, the attempt was made, by means of a change of rules, to establish a more fluid figuration of the players which could restore the balance between attack and defence.

This is one example of a number of polarities which in football, and probably also in all other sport-games, are built into the established figuration of the game process. Such polarities operate in close connection with each other. In fact, a complex of interdependent polarities built into the game pattern provides the main motive force for the group dynamics of a football game. In one way or another they all contribute towards maintaining the 'tone', the tension-balance of the game. Here is a list of some of them:

(1) the overall polarity between the two opposing teams;
(2) the polarity between attack and defence;
(3) the polarity between co-operation and tension of the two teams;
(4) the polarity between co-operation and competition within each
       team.

Polarity (4) can express itself in a variety of ways. One of them is that
between individual team members and the team as a whole, shown in
the following examples:
   (a) In the 1860s and 1870s individual dribbling was the centrepiece
of soccer. The fluctuating tension-balance between team interests and
individual interests was geared in favour of the latter. This corresponded to the social characteristics of the game during that period. It
was then a game primarily played by public school old-boys and by
other middle- and upper-class people for their own enjoyment. In the
last two decades of the nineteenth century this technique gave way to a
different manner of playing. Team co-operation became accentuated at
the expense of opportunities for the individual to shine competitively
within the team. Thus, the balance between individual and team interests changed. Individual dribbling receded and passing the ball from
one member of a team to another came to the fore. It is possible to
analyse the reasons for this change with considerable stringency. An
increase in the number of teams, the establishment of formal competi-
tions, increased competitive rivalry among teams, and the beginning of
playing for a paying public were among them.
   (b) Even after the balance between the team members' consideration for the team's interests and that for their individual interests had
moved strongly in favour of the former, the polarity continued to play
its part. Every game pattern leaves to some players considerable scope
for decisions. In fact, without the capacity to take decisions quickly, an
individual cannot be a good player. But again and again, in taking his
decisions, the individual player must decide between the need for co-
operating with other members for the team's sake and that for contributing to his personal reputation and advancement. The present conceptualization in cases such as this is dominated by absolute alternatives such as 'egoism' and 'altruism'. As instruments of realistic
sociological analysis they have little to recommend them. As one can
see, thinking in terms of balances and polarities makes it easier to come
to grips with what one actually observes.
   Other polarities are of a slightly different type. These are a few
examples:

(5) the polarity between the external controls of players on a variety of
       levels (by managers, captains, team-mates, referees, linesmen,

spectators, etc.), and the flexible control which the individual player exercises upon him- or herself;

(6) the polarity between affectionate identification and hostile rivalry with the opponents;

(7) the polarity between the enjoyment of aggression by the individual players and the curb imposed upon such enjoyment by the game pattern;

(8) the polarity between elasticity and fixity of rules.

These are some aspects of the theoretical model, and some examples of the type of concepts which emerge from the study of game figurations. They may help to bring into focus a few of the distinguishing characteristics of this type of group. Such groups differ from the types of groups usually employed as empirical evidence for small group studies not only because they are groups-in-controlled-tensions, but also because they are more highly structured and organized. Theories derived from studies of relatively loosely structured, *ad hoc* groups specially formed for the purpose of studying groups are frequently marred by a confusion between properties of groups which are mainly due to those of their individual members and properties inherent in the figuration of people itself. In the case of more highly structured and organized groups, it is easier to determine the dynamics inherent in the figuration as such – and to distinguish it from variations due to differences on the individual level. It is easier, for instance, in the case of football to distinguish the dynamics inherent in the game figuration as such from variations due to the characteristics of different nations, of different teams, or of different players.

Ad hoc groups have little autonomy in relation to the society where they are formed and this lack of autonomy can impair the validity of the results derived from studies of such groups. Thus, small groups formed in the United States with the aim of studying problems of leadership, generally, may in fact provide information only about aspects of leadership in the United States. It is an open question how far similar experiments undertaken, say in Russia or in Ghana, would produce similar results.

Games such as football are played everywhere in the same manner and the basic figurational dynamics are everywhere the same. One can study them as such and one can study at the same time the variations which arise from the playing of different nationalities, of different teams, of different individuals.

Like *ad hoc* groups, sport groups have definite limitations as evidence for the study of small group problems or of problems of group dynamics in general. Among them are the limitations due to the fact that games are largely ends in themselves. Their purpose, if they have a purpose, is to give people pleasure. In that respect, they differ greatly from those groupings of people which are usually regarded as the centrepieces of social life and which hold a correspondingly central position in sociology, from groupings such as factories with the purpose of producing goods, bureaucracies with that of administering states or other enterprises, and from other, equally useful figurations of people which are not normally regarded as ends in themselves or supposed to give people pleasure. It agrees with this scheme of values that sociologists often try to define organizations and social units in general, in the first place by means of their goals.

But if it is a limitation of the study of sport-games – compared with that of social units concerned with the serious business of life – that they have no purpose except perhaps that of providing enjoyment, and are often pursued as ends in themselves, it is also an advantage. It may serve as a corrective to the teleological fallacy still fairly widespread in sociological thinking. In a simplified manner, this can be described as a confusion between the individual level and the group level. With regard to games of football this distinction is fairly clear. Individual players and teams have aims, scoring goals is one of them. The enjoyment of playing, the excitement of spectators, the hope of rewards may be others. But the concatenation of purposeful actions results in a figurational dynamics – in a game – which is purposeless. One can determine it as such and to some extent that has been done here. But this could not have been done if one had attributed the aims of individual players to the changing figuration which the players form with each other.

How far this is true of other figurations of people need not be discussed here. But one can say that even state organizations, churches, factories, and other figurations of the more serious kind, whatever the aims of the people who form them, are at the same time ends in themselves with dynamics of their own. What, after all, are the purposes of nations? It is not entirely frivolous to say that even they resemble a game played by people with one another for its own sake. To neglect this aspect by focusing attention in the first place on their purposes, means overlooking the fact that, as in football, it is the changing figuration of people itself on which at any given time the decisions, the purposes, and the moves of individuals depend. This is particularly so in the case of tensions and conflicts. They are often explained only in terms of the intentions and aims of one side or the other. Sociologists would perhaps be better able to contribute to an understanding of those tensions and conflicts which have so far proved uncontrollable if they would investigate them as aspects of the purposeless dynamics of groups.

7

The Dynamics of Modern Sport: Notes on Achievement-Striving and the Social Significance of Sport

Eric Dunning

I INTRODUCTION

The subject of this essay is what I take to be, world-wide, the dominant trend in modern sport, namely a trend, at all levels of participation but most conspicuously in top-level sport, towards growing competitiveness, seriousness of involvement and achievement-orientation.[1] Expressed differently, the trend I am referring to involves the gradual but seemingly inexorable erosion of 'amateur' attitudes, values and structures, and their correlative replacement by attitudes, values and structures that are 'professional' in one sense or another of that term. Viewed from yet another angle, it is a trend in which, in countries all over the world, sport is being transformed from a marginal, lowly valued institution into one that is central and much more highly valued, an institution which, for many people, seems to have religious or quasi-religious significance in the sense that it has become one of the central, if not *the* central, sources of identification, meaning and gratification in their lives.

Resistance to this trend has been offered on several occasions, in Britain perhaps most notably in the attempt since the end of the nineteenth century to maintain Rugby Union as a player-centred amateur sport based on voluntary organization and an informal framework of 'friendly' matches, that is as a sport in which the rules are designed to secure enjoyment for players rather than spectators, organization at the club, regional and national levels is undertaken as an unpaid avocation, and there is no structure of formal competition, of 'cups' and 'leagues'.

However, the attempt to maintain such a structure has been conspic-uously unsuccessful. Despite strenuous efforts by the game's ruling groups, top-level matches are now played in front of large crowds and several spectator-oriented rules have been introduced. Clubs also com-pete annually for the John Player Cup and a number of local ones besides, and there is a system of 'merit tables' which are leagues in all but name. Moreover, the national controlling body, the Rugby Football Union, and many top clubs are financially dependent on revenue from match attendances and commercial sponsorship. The RFU also employs a number of permanent officials, and there have been repeated rumours of players who are paid. In short, in this as in other cases, the resistance has been overcome, a fact which suggests that the trend towards growing seriousness and competitiveness or, alternatively, towards the 'de-amateurization' of sport, is a compelling social process.[2]

To say this is not to claim that resistance has died out altogether. Conflict over the issue of play-oriented, amateur versus achievement-oriented, professional forms and conceptions of sport continues in Rugby and elsewhere, hence attesting to the fact that this process is not simply a thing of the past. Moreover, besides being compelling and ongoing, this process was, and is, conflictual, a fact which shows that it is an example of what Elias would call a 'blind' or 'unplanned' long-term social process.[3] That is, it is not the result of the intended acts of any single individual or group but, rather, the unintended outcome of the interweaving of the purposive actions of the members of several interdependent groups over several generations.

What I want to do in this paper is to sketch in the outlines of a sociogenetic explanation of this long-term process, i.e. an explanation of the manner in which it was and continues to be socially or structur-ally generated. This means, positively, that I shall seek an explanation in terms of the immanent structure and dynamics of social relation-ships *per se*, and, negatively, that I shall eschew three kinds of sociolo-gical explanations that are common, namely: (1) explanations in terms of psychological or 'action' principles that ignore the patterns of inter-dependence within which human beings live; (2) explanations in terms of ideas and beliefs that are conceptually treated as 'free-floating', that is to say in abstraction from the social settings in which ideas are always developed and expressed; and (3) explanations in terms of abstract and impersonal social forces – for example 'economic' forces – that are reified and considered as existing independently of the interdependent human beings who generate them. In order to accomplish this task, I shall employ the 'figurational' method developed by Elias[4] and, to illustrate what this means, I shall begin by reviewing the article on the 'Dynamics of Sport Groups' that Elias and I published in 1966.

II THE 'DYNAMICS OF SPORT GROUPS' – A BRIEF REVIEW

The central contention of that article is that sport groups are a type of social figurations and that their dynamics are best conceptualized as a tension-balance struck between the opposites in a whole complex of interdependent polarities. What this means is that, viewed sociologically, a sport or game is a 'structure' or 'pattern' that a group of interdependent human beings form with one another. This structure, pattern or, more properly, figuration comprises: (1) the two individuals or teams who co-operate with one another in more or less friendly rivalry; (2) controlling agents such as referees and linesmen; and (3) sometimes, but not always, a greater or lesser number of spectators. However, the immediate figuration formed by those who participate directly in and are present at a game forms part of a wider figuration that consists, on one level, of the club organizations that pick the teams and are responsible for such matters as the provision and maintenance of playing facilities and, on another, of the legislative and administrative bodies that formulate the rules, certify and appoint the controlling officials, and organize the overall competitive framework. In its turn this figuration forms part of the wider figuration constituted by members of the society as a whole and, in its turn, too, the societal figuration exists in an international framework. In short, sports and games as social figurations are organized and controlled as well as watched and played. Moreover, they are not socially detached and free-floating, unconnected with the wider structure of social interdependencies but closely, often intricately, interwoven with the fabric of society at large and with the manner in which that fabric is woven into the structure of international interdependencies.

The concept of the dynamics of sport-groups refers to games as processes, that is to the fluid, changing pattern formed, as it were 'body and soul', by the interdependent participants as a game runs its course. It is a pattern which they form with their whole selves, that is intellectually and emotionally and not just physically. The concept of a tension-balance is based on an organic analogy. Thus, just as the mobility of an animal limb depends on the contained tension between two balancing yet antagonistic muscle groups, so, we suggested, the game-process depends upon a tension between two simultaneously antagonistic and interdependent players or sets of players who keep each other in a fluctuating equilibrium. And this tension-equilibrium is best conceptualized as a balance struck between the opposites in a whole complex of interdependent polarities. Among these interdependent polarities – although this was not intended to constitute an exhaustive list – we specified the following:

(1) the overall polarity between the two opposing teams;
(2) the polarity between attack and defence;
(3) the polarity between co-operation and tension between the two teams;
(4) the polarity between co-operation and competition within each team;
(5) the polarity between the external control of players on a variety of levels (for example by managers, captains, team-mates, referees, linesmen, spectators, and so on) and the flexible control which the individual player exercises on himself or herself;
(6) the polarity between affectionate identification with and hostile rivalry towards the opponents;
(7) the polarity between the enjoyment of aggression by the individual players and the curb imposed upon such enjoyment by the game-pattern;
(8) the polarity between elasticity and fixity of rules.

It is, we hypothesized, the tension-balance between interdependent polarities such as these which determines the 'tone' of a game, that is whether it is experienced as exciting or dull, or whether it remains a 'mock-fight' or breaks out into fighting in earnest. It is also implicit in our conceptualization that such a tension-balance is partly a consequence of the relatively autonomous dynamics of specific game-figurations, and partly a consequence of the manner in which such figurations are articulated into the wider structure of social interdependencies.

This discussion must be enough for present purposes to illustrate this conceptualization. It remains, I think, a fruitful one, yet, in retrospect, it strikes me that it depended partly on assumptions that derive from an amateur conception of sport, from what Elias would regard as a specific 'heteronomous evaluation'.[5] These assumptions, whilst not leading us astray, did, I think, limit our vision and prevent us from developing the analysis further in at least one important respect. In order to show how this was so, it is necessary first to recall our objects in writing on the dynamics of sport groups. In writing such an essay, we did not hope to contribute simply to the sociology of sport but wanted, rather, to suggest to sociologists more generally that sport groups can serve as a means of illustrating the dangers, firstly of treating conflict and consensus as crudely dichotomous opposites, and secondly of committing the teleological fallacy in conceptualizing group dynamics – of attributing 'purposes' to reified social constructs. It was in the context of a discussion of these issues that our dependency on amateur values became arguably apparent. Thus, in a passage where we contrasted sport groups with industrial, administrative and other associations concerned with what are generally regarded as the 'serious' sides of life, we wrote that the 'purpose' of sport groups, 'if they have a purpose, is to give people pleasure'[6] and we went on to mention, as other goals or purposes of the people involved in sport-groups, striving for rewards of a financial or status kind, and providing excitement for spectators. But we did not discuss the fact that these purposes involve different forms of valency, that is of bonding, or, more simply, of relationships, between the immediate play-group and others. Thus, enjoyment-seeking is, on balance, self-directed or egocentric, whilst reward-striving and providing excitement for spectators are, on balance and in different senses, other-directed. This suggests three things: (1) that these purposes emerge as the principal goal of sport within different patterns of interdependence; (2) that they can, under specific circumstances, be incompatible with one another, and hence, the source of strain and conflict; and (3) that the list of interdependent polarities involved in the dynamics of sport groups can be extended by at least the following two, namely: (a) the polarity between the interests of players and the interests of spectators; (b) the polarity between 'seriousness' and 'play'.

As I hope to show, these two polarities are closely interrelated. They are also crucial in the sense that they have ramifying effects on the other interdependent polarities involved in the dynamics of a game. Thus, if players participate seriously in a game, the tension-level will be raised and, beyond a certain point, the incidence of hostile rivalry both within and between teams is likely to be increased; that is the game is likely to be transformed from a mock-fight in the direction of a 'real' one and players are liable to transgress the rules, to commit acts of 'foul' play. Or, to the degree that spectators become seriously identified with the teams they support, they are less liable to contemplate defeat with equanimity and may act in ways that are intended to affect the outcome of the contest. Again, once a certain point is reached, they may even invade the pitch in an attempt to suspend the contest altogether.

III SOME THEORIES OF MODERN SPORT: A BRIEF CRITIQUE

The polarity between the interests of players and spectators, and that between 'seriousness' and 'play', have already formed the subjects of theory-building exercises in the sociology of sport, most notably, from a historical-philosophical standpoint by Huizinga;[7] from a symbolic interactionist perspective by Stone;[8] and from a Marxist standpoint by Rigauer.[9] In his own way, each of these authors argues that the balance between these polarities has been upset in modern sport, and a critical review of what they wrote will, I hope, provide a basis for demonstrating the superiority of Elias's figurational approach as a means for obtaining an 'object-adequate' analysis of what constitutes a central trend in modern sport, that is an analysis that accounts for and explains this trend simply as such, without ideological embroidering or distortion.

Huizinga's central contention is that, prior to the nineteenth century, Western societies maintained a balance between the polarities of seriousness and play. However, with industrialization, the growth of science and the emergence of egalitarian social movements, he argues that seriousness began to gain the ascendancy. At first glance, the fact that the nineteenth century witnessed the large-scale growth of sports would seem to contradict his thesis but Huizinga contends that it tends to confirm it since, in modern sports as he puts it, 'the old play factor has undergone almost complete atrophy.' As part of the decline of the play-element in modern civilization generally, sports have experienced what he calls a 'fatal shift towards overseriousness'. The distinction between amateurs and professionals is, he contends, the clearest indication of this trend. That is because professionals lack 'spontaneity and carelessness' and no longer truly play whilst, at the same time, their performance is superior, leading amateurs to feel inferior and engage in imitative action. Between them, according to Huizinga, these two groups

> push sport further and further away from the play-sphere proper until it becomes a thing *sui generis*, neither play nor earnest. In modern social life sport occupies a place alongside and apart from the cultural process . . . [it] has become profane, 'unholy' in every way and has no organic connection with the structure of society, least of all when prescribed by the government . . . However important it may be for the players or spectators, it remains sterile.[10]

But apart from descriptively relating it to a general trend and pointing to what he regarded as the destructive effects of the interaction between amateurs and professionals, Huizinga failed to address himself to the dynamics, the sociogenesis of the presumed trend towards 'sterility', 'overseriousness' and 'profaneness' in modern sport. This issue is tackled more satisfactorily by Stone, who modifies Huizinga's arguments, suggesting that modern sports are subject to a twofold dynamic that results, partly from the manner in which they are caught up in the 'contests, tensions, ambivalences and anomalies' of the wider society, and partly because of certain features inherent in their structure. Only the latter aspect of his analysis need concern us here.

'All sport', Stone contends, 'is affected by the antinomial principles of play and display', that is oriented towards producing satisfaction either for players or spectators. But 'display' for spectators is 'dis-play', according to Stone, destructive of the play-character of sport. Whenever large numbers of spectators attend a sports event, it is transformed into a spectacle, played for the spectators and not the direct participants. The interests of the former take precedence over the interests of the latter. Enjoyment from playing becomes subordinate to the production of crowd-pleasing moves. The sport begins to lose its uncertainty, spontaneity and character of playful innovation, becoming a type of ritual, predictable, even predetermined in its outcome.

Rigauer's analysis depends heavily on Marxist assumptions about the exploitative character of work in capitalist societies, a category that he extends to societies such as the Soviet Union presumably because he believes them to be 'state-capitalist' or 'state-socialist' in character and not essentially different from capitalist societies of a 'purer' type. Modern sport, he argues, is a 'bourgeois' product, a type of recreation initially pursued by members of the ruling class for their own enjoyment. For them, it functioned as a counter to work but, with increasing industrialization and the spread of sport down the social hierarchy, it has come to take on characteristics which resemble those of work. Thus, like forms of work in industrial societies, Rigauer maintains, sport is coming to be characterized by achievement-striving. This is seen in the drive to break records, in the hours of gruelling training that are employed towards that end, and in the application of scientific methods to the goal of improving performance. Moreover, training techniques such as 'interval' and 'circuit' training replicate the 'alienating' and 'dehumanizing' character of assembly-line production. Even in the 'individual' sports, the role of sportsman is being reduced to one in a whole constellation of trainers, coaches, managers and doctors, a tendency which is doubly apparent in the team sports where the modern sportsman is compelled to fit into a fixed division of labour and comply with the demands of a prescribed tactical plan. He plays little part himself in working out this plan.

His scope for the exercise of initiative is correspondingly reduced. That is even more true of the administration of sports for, increasingly, it is full-time officials and not sportsmen themselves who decide matters of policy. The result, says Rigauer, is a steady constriction of the scope for private decision-making and dominance over the majority by a bureaucratic elite.

It follows from this diagnosis that sport must increasingly be unable to function as a means of providing relief from the strains of work. It has become, Rigauer contends, demanding, achievement-oriented and alienating. The belief that it functions as a counter to work survives but it is a 'masking ideology' that hides from the participants its 'real' function, namely that of reinforcing in the leisure-sphere an ethic of hard work, achievement and group loyalty which is necessary for the operation of an advanced industrial society. In this way, according to Rigauer, sport helps to maintain the status quo and to bolster the dominance of the ruling class.

These three diagnoses – that sport is growing more 'serious'; that 'display' is coming to predominate over and destroy 'play'; and that sport is becoming indistinguishable from work – seem, at first glance, apposite as descriptions of a central trend in modern sport. However, elements of value-bias enter each of these analyses, casting doubts on their adequacy. It is, for example, difficult to believe that sports could have managed to sustain their popularity, indeed, to increase it as, in fact, they have done in countries all over the world, if the play-factor in them had atrophied to the extent that Huizinga asserts, or if, as Rigauer contends, they had become as alienating and repressive as work, or again if, as Stone would have it, the balance between play and display had been so seriously upset. It is possible, of course, that forms of compulsion and/or of rewards other than direct personal enjoyment may have played a part in their spread, hence offsetting to some extent the deleterious effects of growing seriousness of involvement. That such balancing counter-trends have, in fact, occurred is implicit in the arguments put forward later in this essay. But for the moment, it is sufficient just to note that Huizinga, Rigauer and Stone pay no attention to such a possibility.

Moreover, Huizinga is a romantic who yearns for an 'organic' society. It is also implicit in his analysis that the 'democratization' of sports is the main reason for their 'decay'. In short, he implies that creativity and high moral standards are restricted to elites. His critique of modern sports strikes home, especially, although he exaggerates it, his contention that a 'shift towards overseriousness' has occurred. Yet, apart from relating it to what he regards as a general cultural trend, he makes no attempt to analyze the sociogenesis of this putative transformation of sport, to relate it firmly to its social structural sources.

Similar considerations apply to Rigauer's critique. He makes no attempt to analyse empirically the manner in which the alleged structural correspondence between sport and work has been brought about. Nor does he distinguish between forms of work, forms of sport and different countries in this respect, or make any attempt to determine whether different groups are proponents, on the one hand, of achievement-oriented values or, on the other, of values which stress the pleasure-giving, leisure character of sport. Nor does he attempt to document empirically the changes which, he maintains, have occurred over time in the balance between these values. Instead, he simply paints a blanket picture which asserts that all sports in all industrial countries have developed work-like characteristics and hence serve ruling interests to the same extent.

Although, like Huizinga, he lays stress on the deleterious effects of the democratization of sports, Stone's analysis is sociologically more satisfactory. Yet there is reason to believe that his analysis of the balance between 'play' and 'display' may not reach to the heart of the matter. Viewed figurationally, this is not simply a question of the presence or absence of spectators or, where the latter are present, of the interaction between them and the players, but, more crucially, of the *patterns of interdependence* among the participating groups. Thus, the presence of spectators at a sports-event may *induce* players to engage in display but it cannot *constrain* them to do so. The play-element in a sport is more likely to be seriously threatened when players become *dependent* on spectators – or on external agencies such as commercial interest groups and the state – for financial and other rewards. Under such conditions, whether the sport is openly profess-ional or nominally amateur, the pressures to allow the interests of spectators to assume an important role, for the 'game' to become a 'spectacle', are likely to be compelling.

In fact, in examining the development of modern sport, neither Huizinga, Rigauer nor Stone has dealt satisfactorily with the dynamics of that process. Their analyses are, in a sense, curiously impersonal. Each of them postulates a trend connected with industrialization, but they pay little or no attention to clashes of group interest and ideology. It almost appears in their analyses – this is especially true of Huizinga and Rigauer – as if the old values and forms of sport were fading away without conflict. That such a conceptualization is oversimplified, what-ever its merits as a first approximation to a sociological theory of the dominant trend in modern sport, will, I hope, emerge from a figura-tional analysis of this trend.

In what follows, I want to suggest that the growing seriousness of modern sport can be in large part attributed to three interrelated processes, namely, state-formation, functional democratization and the spread of sport through the widening network of international interde-pendencies. The first two are, of course, the deep-structural processes, both interwoven with the lengthening of interdependency chains, by means of which Elias principally explains the sociogenesis of the civiliz-ing process.[11]

This suggests that there may be a connection between the civilizing process and the trend towards growing seriousness of involvement in sport; for example the latter may consist partly in the fact that, by virtue of his or her socialization into the more restraining standards of the more complex and constraining modern system of social interdependencies, the more restrained and civilized modern individual is less able to participate spontaneously and uninhibitedly in sport than his or her less civilized and more emotionally unrestrained forebear who lived in a less complex and less constraining system of social interdependencies. It seems plausible to maintain that this is so. Yet it remains necessary to spell out precisely what the connections were between, on the one hand, the growing seriousness of sports participation and, on the other, state-formation, functional democratization and the civilizing process. It also remains to show how this trend was connected with the international spread of sport, and how these deep-structural processes can provide a more satisfactory account of it than was achieved by Huizinga, Rigauer and Stone.[12] It is to the first of these tasks that I shall now address myself.

IV A FIGURATIONAL ANALYSIS OF THE TREND TOWARDS GROWING SERIOUSNESS IN SPORT

In order to accomplish such a demonstration, I shall first discuss the amateur ethos and attempt to explain sociogenetically both it and its dissolution, that is the trend towards growing seriousness in sport. I shall then, briefly and in general terms, discuss sport in pre-industrial Britain in order to show why, in such a social figuration, it was possible for groups at all levels of the social hierarchy, to have what were, on balance, 'self-directed' or 'egocentric' forms of sports participation, that is why it was possible for them to participate in sport for fun. Next, I shall attempt to show why, with the emergence of urban-industrial-national-states, more 'other-directed' sport-forms connected more with achievement-orientation, identity-striving and the struggle for pecuniary rewards came to develop. Finally, I shall discuss what I take to be the growing social significance of sport and the part played by its spread internationally in this overall social process.

The amateur ethos is the dominant sports ideology in modern Britain and, I think I am right in saying, of ruling groups in sport across the world, for example of the International Olympic Committee and its various national affiliates. The central component of this ethos is the ideal of playing sports 'for fun'. Other aspects, such as the stress on 'fair play', voluntary adherence to rules and non-pecuniary involvement, are essentially subordinate, designed to facilitate the achievement of that end – to make sporting contests 'play-fights' in which pleasurable excitement can be generated. The earliest example I have found of the explicit use of this ethos to criticize the trend towards growing serious-ness in sport appears in a book by Trollope, published in 1868:

> [Sports] are being made too much of, and men who follow them have allowed themselves to be taught that ordinary success in them is not worth having . . . All this comes from excess of enthusiasm on the matter; – from a desire to follow too well a pursuit which, to be pleasurable, should be a pleasure and not a business . . . [This] is the rock against which our sports may possibly be made shipwreck. Should it ever become unreasonable in its expenditure, arrogant in its demands, immoral and selfish in its tendencies, or, worse of all, unclean and dishonest in its traffic, there will arise against it a public opinion against which it will be unable to hold its own.[13]

It is, of course, likely that earlier examples could be found, but this mobilization of amateur values, with their stress on pleasure as the essential ingredient of sport, came at an early stage in the development of the modern forms of sport, above all at a time when professional sport as we know it today hardly existed. It was then possible for some men to earn a precarious living as prize-fighters, jockeys and cricketers, but the fact that they were only a handful suggests that Trollope's critique was directed mainly at a trend towards growing seriousness within *amateur* sport. And it is possible that one of his principal targets was what historians have called the 'public school games cult',[15] a movement in the public schools that involved five main components: (1) a tendency to appoint and promote staff in terms of sporting rather than academic criteria; (2) the selection of prefects, that is the leading boys in a school, principally on the basis of ability at sport; (3) the elevation of sport to a prominent and, in some cases, pre-eminent position in the curriculum; (4) the educational rationalization of sport, especially team-games, as an instrument of 'character-training'; and (5) participation by members of staff in the organization and playing of their pupils' games. It is, of course, likely that such a movement could only have arisen in elite schools, the majority of whose pupils were not dependent on an academic education for their future careers. But that is less relevant for present purposes than the fact that the public school games cult shows clearly that the trend towards growing seriousness in sport in Britain was, in its earliest stages, a phenomenon connected with amateur and not professional sport and that it did not derive its initial momentum from the conflict between amateurs and profession-als adduced by Huizinga. In fact, I should like to hypothesize that the amateur ethos was articulated as an ideology in opposition to the trend towards growing seriousness and that it received its most explicit and detailed formulation when, as part of that trend, the modern forms of professional sport began to emerge.

In Britain prior to the 1880s, the amateur ethos existed in a relatively inchoate form. That is, it was an amorphous, loosely articulated set of values regarding the functions of sport and the standards believed necessary for their realization. However, with the threat posed by the incipient professionalization of new sports such as soccer and rugby, a process that began in the North and Midlands and drew low-status, regionally based, middle- and working-class groups as organizers, players and spectators into the ambit of sports that had hitherto been the exclusive preserve of the 'public school elite',[15] the national ruling class, the amateur ethos began to crystallize as an elaborate and articulate ideology. That is, it was a collective representation developed by the members of one collectivity in opposition to the members of another which they perceived as a threat both to their organizational and playing pre-eminence and the forms of sport as they wished to see it played. In short, I am suggesting that, even though the public school elite tended to couch their pronouncements in sport-specific terms, claiming to be solely interested in preserving what they regarded as the essential, 'fun-oriented' character of sport, class and regional hostility and resentment over the loss of their erstwhile dominance played an important part in their articulation of the amateur ethos as an explicit ideology. However, if I am right, the social situation in which they found themselves was increasingly inconducive to the full-scale, unbridled realization of self-directed, pleasure-oriented forms of sport and that, in articulating and mobilizing the amateur ethos in response to the growing threat from below, they were trying to maintain forms of sports participation which they regarded as their right as members of a ruling class and which had, in fact, been possible for ruling and even subordinate groups in the pre-industrial era but which were increasingly impossible for them.

Support for this view comes from the fact that many of the 'abuses' that the public school elite claimed to detect in professional sport were at least equally evident in the games cult in the schools they had attended. Further support – although there were symptomatic exceptions such as 'the Corinthians' soccer team[16] – comes from the fact that, in an increasing number of sports, the public school elite withdrew into their own exclusive circles, revealing by their fear of being beaten by professionals that they played in order to obtain the kudos of being recognized as successful sportsmen as much as they did for fun. Of course, this separatist trend was probably, in part, occasioned by the fact that contests between professional and amateur teams would frequently have been unbalanced and lacking in tone owing to the skill discrepancy that usually exists between full-time players who are following their occupation and part-time players who are merely participating in a leisure activity. But that this is not the whole story is suggested by the fact that a further separatist trend by members of the public school elite occurred within the ranks of *amateur* sport. That is, they were unwilling to submit themselves regularly to the possibility of defeat at the hands of working-class amateur teams and, by hiving off into their own exclusive circles, they showed, not only class prejudice, but that they took part in sport seriously and in order to win – the success goal had come to take precedence in their hierarchy of sporting values over the goal of participating primarily for fun. Further support for such a view comes from a figurational analysis of sport in eighteenth-century Britain.

The overall social figuration of Britain in the eighteenth century, indeed, the overall pattern of social interdependencies in pre-industrial Britain generally, was one in which there was relatively little structural pressure on groups, whether high or low in the status order, towards success-striving and achievement-orientation, that is towards 'other-directed' forms of participation, in the sporting or in other fields. The relatively low degree of state-centralization and national unification, for example, meant that 'folk games', the games of the ordinary people, were played in regional isolation, competition traditionally occurring between contiguous villages and towns or between the sections of towns. But there was no national competitive framework. The aristocracy and gentry formed a partial exception in this regard. They were, and perceived themselves as, national classes and did compete nationally among themselves. As a result, a certain degree of other-directed competitive pressure in sporting activities was generated within their ranks. But they were subject, in a general and sporting sense, to effective pressure neither from above nor from below. The level of state-formation at that stage in the development of British society was relatively low and, in a very real sense, the aristocracy and gentry 'were the state', that is able effectively to use the state apparatus in their own interests. They had established the precedence of parliament over the monarchy and ruled over a society in which the balance of power between classes involved gross inequalities. As a result, there was no effective challenge to their position as the dominant class. The secure character of their dominance was conducive to a high degree of status security on their part and this meant, in turn, that individual aristocrats and gentlemen were, as a rule, in no way seriously threatened by contact with social subordinates. Whatever the context, they knew who was master and so did everybody else – the gross power imbalance between classes led to patterns of deference from subordinates.

Such status-security was extended to the leisure-sphere, including sport. The aristocracy and gentry took part in folk games both in an organizational and playing capacity, and used their patronage to develop forms of professional cricket, prize-fighting and horse-racing. The type of sports career that grew up under such conditions was based on unequivocal subordination of the professional to his patron and total dependency as far as life-chances were concerned of the former on the latter. No threat was posed by professionalism of that type to the interests and values of the ruling class. Professional sport was neither morally nor socially suspect and there was no need to fight against or hide the fact that pecuniary advantage could be obtained from games, whether as an occupational wage or from gambling on the outcome of contests. Above all, whether playing among themselves or with their hirelings, the aristocracy and gentry could participate in sport for fun; that is, their social situation – the power and relative autonomy they enjoyed – meant that they could develop self-directed or egocentric forms of sports participation and that, although they were not constrained to develop the amateur ethos as an explicit ideology, they came close to being amateurs in the 'ideal typical' sense of that term.

If this diagnosis is correct, it follows that the overall social figuration of pre-industrial Britain and, I think one can safely say, of other preindustrial societies, too, was not conducive to the generation of intense competitive pressure in sporting relations, whether within or between ruling and subordinate groups. It also follows that the sociogenesis of the pressure towards other-directed, achievement-oriented forms of sports-participation has to be sought in the social figuration brought into being in conjunction with industrialization. I shall now endeavour to point out what the connections between these two social processes were, that is between industrialization and the long-term trend towards increasing seriousness of involvement and achievement-striving in sport. Briefly, and in anticipation of the analysis that follows, it can be said that the key to this relationship lies in the process that Elias calls 'functional democratization' – in the equalizing change in the balance of power within and between groups that occurs contingently upon the interrelated processes of state-formation and lengthening of interdependency chains. But before I explain what this means, it is necessary to contrast Elias's approach to the division of labour with that of Durkheim.

V INDUSTRIALIZATION AND THE DEVELOPMENT OF
ACHIEVEMENT-ORIENTED FORMS OF SPORT

According to Durkheim, the structure of industrial societies is characterized by high 'material' and high 'moral' or 'dynamic' density, that is by a highly concentrated population and a high rate of social interaction between individuals and groups.[17] He believed that the competitive pressures generated in such a society would be reduced and perhaps eliminated by the division of labour. The division of labour, he suggested, would have that effect in two main ways: by creating 'bonds of interdependence' and by siphoning competitively generated tensions into specialized occupational spheres. However, his analysis contains a fundamental flaw that derives from his failure to recognize that functional interdependence or division of labour does not lead necessarily to harmonious and co-operative integration but is conducive, even in its 'normal' forms, to conflict and antagonism. In short, his concept of the society based on 'organic solidarity' is utopian. A more realistic concept of interdependence is that proposed by Elias.

According to Elias, the long-term social transformation usually referred to by terms denoting specific aspects such as 'industrialization', 'economic growth', the 'demographic transition', 'urbanization' and 'political modernization', is in fact, a long-term transformation of the total social structure.[18] And, he contends, one of the sociologically most significant aspects of this total social transformation consists in the emergence of longer and more differentiated 'chains of interdependence'. That is, it involves the emergence of greater functional specialization and the integration of functionally differentiated groups into wider networks. Moreover, concomitantly with this, there occurs, according to Elias, a change in the direction of decreasing power-differentials within and among groups, more specifically, a change in the balance of power between rulers and ruled, the social classes, men and women, the generations, parents and children. Such a process occurs because the performers of specialized roles are dependent on others and can, therefore, exert reciprocal control. The power-chances of specialized groups are further enhanced if they manage to organize since, then, they are able to disrupt the wider system of interdependencies by collective action. It is in ways such as these, according to Elias, that increasing division of labour and the emergence of longer chains of interdependence leads to greater reciprocal dependency, and, hence, to patterns of 'multipolar control' within and among groups, that is to an overall social figuration in which specific individuals and groups are subject to increasingly effective pressure from others. Such pressure is effective because of the reciprocal dependencies involved.

The relevance of this deceptively simple theory for the present analysis is manifold. Inherent in the modern structure of social interdependencies is the demand for inter-regional and representative sport. No such demand arose in pre-industrial societies because the lack of effective national unification and poor means of transport and communication meant that there were no common rules and no means by which sportsmen from different areas could be brought regularly together. At the same time, the 'localism' inherent in such societies meant that play-groups perceived as potential rivals only groups with which they were contiguous in a geographical sense. However, modern industrial societies are different on all these counts. They are relatively unified nationally, have superior means of transport and communication, sports with common rules, and a degree of 'cosmopolitanism' which means that local groups perceive as potential rivals, and are anxious to compare themselves with others which are not geographically adjacent. Hence, such societies are characterized by high rates of inter-area sporting interaction, a process that leads to stratification internally in specific sports – to a hierarchical grading of sportsmen, sportswomen and sports teams with those that represent the largest units standing at the top.

In its turn, this means that the reciprocal pressures and controls that operate in urban-industrial societies generally are replicated in the sphere of sport. As a result, top-level sportsmen and women cannot be independent and play for fun but are forced to be other-directed and serious in their sports participation. That is, they are unable to play for themselves but constrained to represent wider social units such as cities, counties and countries. As such, they are provided with material and/or prestige rewards and facilities and time for training. In return, they are expected to produce a 'sports-performance', that is the sort of satisfactions which the controllers and 'consumers' of the sport demand, namely the spectacle of an exciting contest that people are willing to pay to watch or the validation through victory of the 'image' and 'reputation' of the social unit with which the controllers and/or consumers identify. The sheer numbers of people involved and the local, regional, national and international competitive framework of modern sport work in the same direction. They mean that high and sustained achievement-motivation, long-term planning, strict self-control and renunciation of immediate gratification, in other words constant practice and training, are necessary in order to get to, and stay at, the top. They also necessitate a degree of bureaucratic control and hence lead to the subordination of sportsmen in yet another respect.

In each of these ways, the social figuration, the pattern of inter-group dependencies, characteristic of an urban-industrial-nation-state generates constraints which militate against the practical realization of the amateur ethos with its stress on enjoyment as the central aim of sport. Or more properly, it generates constraints which militate against the realization of immediate, short-term enjoyment, against each sporting contest as an 'end in itself', and leads to its replacement, both for players and spectators, by longer-term goals such as victory in a league or cup, by satisfactions more centrally concerned with identity and prestige. Moreover, such constraints are not confined to top-level sport but reverberate down to the lowest levels of sporting achievement. That is partly because top-level sportsmen and women form a media-promoted reference group who set standards which others try to follow. It is also partly a consequence of the pressures generated by competition for the material and prestige rewards which can be obtained by getting to the top. However, it is by no means only due to pressures that are generated solely within sport but also, and perhaps, more centrally, a consequence of the deep-rooted and pervasive anxieties and insecurities generated more generally in a society characterized by multipolar pressures and controls, and in which props of identity and status connected with traditional forms of class, authority, sex and age relations have all been eroded by functional democratization, that is by the equalizing process which, according to Elias, is inherent in the division of labour.

VI SUGGESTIONS REGARDING THE GROWING SOCIAL SIGNIFICANCE OF SPORT

So far, I have provided the outlines of a figurational explanation of the trend towards increasingly serious involvement in sport. The related development in the course of which its social significance has grown remains to be discussed. This is a complex issue and can only be touched on briefly in the present context. Apart from the changing balance, ideological as well as factual, between work and leisure, a process which has increased the social significance of leisure activities generally, a constellation of at least three interrelated aspects of the emergent modern social figuration can be singled out as having contributed to the growing social significance of sport, namely: (1) the fact that sport has developed as one of the principal media for the generation of pleasurable excitement; (2) the fact that sport has come to function as one of the principal media of collective identification; and (3) the fact that sport has come to form a key source of meaning in the lives of many people.

Elias and I have suggested elsewhere that sport is a 'mimetic' leisure event in which pleasurable excitement can be generated and that, in this respect, it performs a 'de-routinizing' function.[19] There is, however, no society without controls and routines or, as Elias has put it, no 'zero-point' of civilization. In that sense, the need for de-routinization is probably socially universal. But urban-industrial societies are highly routinized and civilized, characterized by multipolar pressures and controls. Accordingly, their members are constrained continuously to exercise a high degree of emotional restraint in their ordinary, everyday lives, with the consequence that the need for de-routinizing leisure activities such as sports in such societies is particularly intense. However, this de-routinizing process, this socially permitted arousal of emotion in public, is itself subject to civilizing controls. That is, sport is a social enclave, both for players and spectators, where pleasurable excitement can be generated in a form that is socially limited and controlled.

Nevertheless, the excitement generated can be intense, especially at top-level sports events which attract large crowds and, *pace* Huizinga who argued that sport has become 'profane', it is probably this that forms the experiential basis for the widespread perception of sport as a 'sacred' phenomenon. Durkheim argued that the collective excitement or 'effervescence' generated in the religious ceremonies of the Australian aborigines formed the principal experiential source of their idea of a 'sacred' realm,[20] and it seems not unreasonable to suppose that the generation of 'collective effervescence' in sports events lies at the root of the fact that it is common, at least in Britain, to refer to football and cricket pitches, especially those used for representative matches, as the 'sacred' or 'hallowed' turf. Indeed, it would probably not be going too far to suggest that, at least for some groups in present-day society, sport has become a quasi-religious activity and that, viewed from a societal perspective, it has come, to some extent, to fill the gap in social life left by the decline of religion. An extreme but none the less indicative example of this quasi-religious character of modern sport is provided by the fact that it has apparently become a tradition in Liverpool for deceased supporters of Liverpool FC to have their ashes strewn on the Anfield pitch; they seem to wish to remain identified even after death with the 'shrine' or 'temple' at which they 'worshipped' during life. But even short of this extreme, it is clear that playing and/or watching one sport or another has come to form one of the principal media of collective identification in modern society and one of the principal sources of meaning in life for many people. In short, it is by no means unrealistic to suggest that sport is coming increasingly to form the secular religion of our increasingly secular age.

It is probably the inherently oppositional character of sport, that is the fact that it is a struggle for victory between two or more teams or two or more individuals, that accounts for its prominence as a focus for collective identification. This means that it lends itself to group identification, more precisely to 'in-group' and 'out-group', or 'we-group' and 'they-group' formation on a variety of levels, such as the levels of city, county or country. The oppositional element is crucial since opposition serves to reinforce in-group identification, that is, a group's sense of 'we-ness' or unity is strengthened by the presence of a group who are perceived as 'them', the opposing team, whether local or national, and its supporters. Indeed, within the context of domestically pacified nation-states that is in societies where the state has established an effective monopoly on the right to use physical force, sport provides the only occasion on which large, complex and impersonal social units such as cities can unite. Similarly, at the international level, sporting events such as the Olympic Games and the World Cup provide the only peace-time occasions where whole nation-states are able regularly and visibly to unite. The international expansion of sport has been predicated on the growth of international interdependence and the existence, with several notable exceptions, of a fragile and unstable world peace. Contests such as the Olympics allow the representatives of different nations to compete without killing one another, though the degree to which such contests are transformed from mock-fights into 'real' ones is a function, inter alia, of the pre-existing level of tension between the particular nation-states involved. And, of course, it is in order to participate effectively at this highest level of sporting competition that the highest levels of sustained achievement-motivation, self-control and self-denial on the part of sportsmen are required.

This brings me to my final point: namely that the social pressure on sportsmen and women in countries all over the world to strive for success in international competition is a further source of the destruction of the play-element in sport. Moreover, it is that, and the increment to national prestige that success in international sport can yield, which has contributed principally to the tendency towards the involvement of the state in sport which Huizinga deplored. It has been argued that sport is a viable substitute for war but such an idea involves viewing it as an abstraction, as something independent and apart from the figurations of interdependent human beings who take part in it. That is the crucial issue: namely, whether the figurations formed by interdependent human beings, in sport and elsewhere, are conducive to co-operation or friendly rivalry, or whether they persistently generate serious fighting. That is a subject on which sociological research has hardly yet begun. There is, however, at least one notable exception: the work of Norbert Elias on which I have tried to model this paper.

8

Social Bonding and Violence in Sport

Eric Dunning

I INTRODUCTION

It is widely believed that we are living today in one of the most violent periods in history.[1] Indeed, it is probably fair to say that, in Western societies at least, the fear that we are currently undergoing a process of 'decivilization' – with regard to physical violence if not in other respects – is deeply imprinted in the contemporary *Zeitgeist*, one of the dominant beliefs of our time. Eysenck and Nias, for example, refer to 'a number of acknowledged facts' which, they claim, 'have helped to persuade many people that the civilization in which we live may be in danger of being submerged under a deluge of crime and violence.'[2] The psychologist Peter Marsh similarly contends that recent attempts to eradicate violence have led to a decline in opportunities for socially constructive ritual violence – what he calls 'aggro' – with the consequence that uncontrolled and destructive violence has increased. There has been, he writes, 'a drift from "good" violence into "bad" violence. Men are about as aggressive as they always were but aggression, as its expression becomes less orderly, has more blood as its consequence.'[3]

A not insignificant part of the belief that we are living in an excessively violent age is the widespread feeling that violence is currently increasing in, and in conjunction with, sports. Yiannakis, McIntyre, Melnick, and Hart, for example, write that. 'There can be little doubt that both crowd and player violence in sport are increasing at an alarming rate.[4] The German sociologist, Kurt Weis, appears to agree with this diagnosis.[5] He argues that the putative trend towards growing violence on the sports field and among sports spectators represents at least a partial disconfirmation of Elias's theory of the 'civilizing process'.[6] It is with this issue – the implications of this putative trend for Elias's theory – that I shall concern myself in this chapter. For reasons that will emerge, I disagree with the view that contemporary sports and contemporary society are, unambiguously and in some simple sense, growing more violent. I also disagree with the idea that this supposed trend represents a partial disconfirmation of the theory of Elias. At the same time, however, I want to argue that the issue of violence in contemporary sports and contemporary society raises a number of complex problems and that it will only be possible to tackle these problems more adequately than has been done in the past by developing the relevant aspects of the theory of the civilizing process beyond the level reached by Elias himself. That is the goal I have set myself in this chapter. In order to move towards it, it will be necessary to raise a number of wider sociological issues. More specifically, what I shall do is:

(1) Attempt to advance beyond Elias by distinguishing between types of human violence.
(2) To argue, along with Elias, that a long-term civilizing transformation with respect to violence has taken place in the industrially most advanced societies of Western Europe. I shall try to move beyond Elias by conceptualizing this transformation as a change in the balance between some of the forms of violence distinguished in the typology.
(3) Suggest that the change in the balance between forms of violence that can be empirically observed is attributable in large measure to an observable transformation in the forms of social bonding. I shall use the concept of social bonding in the *sociological* sense introduced by Durkheim and elaborated by Elias, and not in the 'sociobiological' sense introduced, for example, by Tiger and Fox.[7] That is, I shall use it to refer to different forms of relationships that are *observably socially produced* and not to their production by some *hypothetical* but as yet *undiscovered* gene pattern that *may* have been laid down during humanity's prehistoric past. My first task, however, is to lay the foundation for a typology of violence.

II TOWARDS A TYPOLOGY OF HUMAN VIOLENCE

The types of violence engaged in by human beings, in sports and elsewhere, are diverse and complex. It seems reasonable, however, to suppose that a degree of purchase on the problem can be obtained by drawing distinctions among its separable forms and dimensions. I shall distinguish between types of violence in terms of: (a) the means employed; (b) the actors' motives, especially with reference to the forms and levels of intentionality involved; and (c) some of the social parameters which help to distinguish forms of violence from one another. As an aid in the execution of this task, I shall draw upon a modification of some aspects of Weber's typology of action. It seems that at least eight distinctions can be provisionally made among the forms of human violence, namely:

(1) Whether the violence is actual or symbolic, that is whether it takes the form of a direct physical assault or simply involves verbal and/ or nonverbal gestures.

(2) Whether the violence takes a 'play' or 'mock' form, or whether it is 'serious' or 'real'. This dimension might also be captured by means of the distinction between 'ritual' and 'nonritual' violence, though it has to be noted that, *pace* Marsh and his colleagues,[8] ritual and play can both have violent content.

(3) Whether or not a weapon or weapons are used.

(4) Where weapons are used, whether or not the assailants come directly into contact.

(5) Whether the violence is intentional or the accidental consequence of an action sequence that was not intentionally violent at the outset.

(6) Whether one is dealing with violence that is initiated without provocation or with a retaliatory response to an intentionally or unintentionally violent act.

(7) Whether the violence is legitimate in the sense of being in accordance with a set of socially prescribed rules, norms, and values, or whether it is non-normative or illegitimate in the sense of involving the contravention of accepted social standards.

(8) Whether the violence takes a 'rational' or 'affective' form, that is whether it is rationally chosen as a means for securing the achievement of a given goal, or engaged in as an emotionally satisfying and pleasurable 'end in itself'. Another way of conceptualizing this difference would be to distinguish between violence in its 'instrumental' and 'expressive' forms.

Some sociologists would call these distinctions 'ideal types' but it is better to conceptualize them in terms of interconnected polarities and balances. But let me become more empirical and apply this mode of conceptualization systematically to some of the problems of violence in sports. I shall start by considering some general issues and then make some observations about the development of modern sports.

III   SPORTS AND VIOLENCE IN DEVELOPMENTAL PERSPECTIVE

All sports are inherently competitive and hence conducive to the arousal of aggression and violence. In some, however, for example, rugby, soccer, and boxing, violence in the form of a 'play fight' or 'mock battle' between two individuals or groups is a central ingredient. Such sports are enclaves for the socially acceptable, ritualized expression of physical violence and I shall concern myself in this context solely with sports of this kind. It is important in this connection to note that, just as the real battles that take place in war can involve a ritual component – for example, the battles of tribal groups such as the Dani of New Guinea[9] – so the mock battles that take place on a sports field can involve elements of, or be transformed into, non-ritual violence. This may occur when, perhaps as a result of social pressures or the financial and prestige rewards involved, people participate too seriously in a sport. As a result, the tension level may be raised to a point where the balance between friendly and hostile rivalry is upset in favour of the latter. In such circumstances, the rules and conventions designed to limit the violence and direct it into socially acceptable channels may be suspended and the people involved may start to fight in earnest. Thus, in soccer and rugby, they may play with the aim of inflicting physical damage and pain. Or in boxing where the infliction of damage and pain is a legitimate part of the contest, they may fight after a round has finished or after the contest as a whole has been brought to an end. However, the standards governing the expression and control of violence are not the same in all societies. And in our own society, they differ between different groups and different sports and have not been the same in all historical periods. In fact, I want to argue that a central aspect of the development of modern sport has been what Elias would call a 'civilizing process' regarding the expression and control of physical violence. Centrally involved in this process – whatever short-term fluctuations there may have been – has been a long-term shift in the balance between 'affective' and 'rational' violence.

To start with, it is worth recalling some relevant aspects of Elias's theory. In a nutshell, he holds that there has occurred in Western Europe a long-term decline in people's propensity for obtaining pleasure from directly engaging in and witnessing violent acts. He refers in this connection to a dampening of *Angriffslust*, literally to a decline in the lust for attacking, that is in people's desire and capacity for obtaining pleasure from attacking others. This has entailed, firstly, a lowering of the threshold of repugnance (*Peinlichkeitsschwelle*) regarding bloodshed and other direct manifestations of physical violence; and, secondly, the internalization of a stricter taboo on violence as part of the 'superego'. A consequence of this is that guilt feelings are liable to be aroused whenever this taboo is violated. At the same time, there has occurred a tendency to push violence increasingly behind the scenes and, as part of it, to describe people who openly derive pleasure from violence in terms of the language of psychopathology, punishing them either by means of hospitalization or imprisonment. However, this same social process has increased people's tendency to plan, to use foresight, and to use longer-term, more rational strategies for achieving their goals. It has also entailed an increase in socially generated competitive pressure. Consequently, I want to suggest that it has contributed to an increase in people's propensity in specific situations to use violence in a calculated manner. Let me illustrate this complex process by reference to the development of rugby football.

Modern rugby is descended from a type of medieval folk game in which particular matches were played by variable, formally unrestricted numbers of people, sometimes considerably in excess of 1,000. The boundaries of the playing area were only loosely defined and limited by custom, and games were played both over open countryside and through the streets of towns. The rules were oral and locally specific rather than written and instituted and enforced by a central controlling body. Despite such local variation, the folk antecedents of modern rugby shared at least one common feature: they were all play-struggles that involved the customary social toleration of a level of physical violence considerably higher than is normatively permitted in rugby and comparable games today. It must be enough in the present context to substantiate this point by reference to a single example, the Welsh game of 'knappan' as described by Owen in 1603.[10]

According to Owen, the number who took part in knappan matches sometimes exceeded 2,000 and, just as in other folk games, such as Cornish 'hurling', some of the participants played on horseback. The horsemen, said Owen, 'have monstrouse cudgells, of iii foote and halfe longe, as bigge as the partie is well able to wild [wield]'. As one can see from the following extract, knappan was a wild affair:

> at this playe privatt grudges are revendged, soe that for everye small occasion they fall by the eares, wch beinge but once kindled betweene two, all persons on both sides become parties, soe that sometymes you shall see fyve or vi hundred naked men, beatinge in a clusture together . . . and there parte most be taken everyeman with his companie, so that you shall see two brothers the one beatinge the other, the man the

maister, and frinde against frinde, they . . . take upp stones and there
with in theire fistes beate theire fellowes, the horsemen will intrude and
ryde into the footemens troupes, the horseman choseth the greatest
cudgell he can gett, and the same of oke, ashe, blackthorne or crab-tree
and soe huge as it were able to strike downe an oxe or horse, he will alsoe
assault anye for privatt grudge, that hath not the Knappan, or cudgell
him after he hath delt the same from him, and when on blowe is geven,
all falleth by the eares, eche assaulting other with their unreasonable
cudgells sparinge neyther heade, face, nor anye part of the bodie, the
footemen fall soe close to it, beinge once kindled with furie as they
wholey forgett the playe, and fall to beatinge, till they be out of breathe,
and then some number hold theire hands upp over theire heades and
crye, . . . peace, peace and often times this parteth them, and to theire
playe they goe a newe. Neyther maye there be anye looker on at this
game, but all must be actours, for soe is the custome and curtesye of the
playe, for if one that cometh with a purpose onlye to see the game, . . .
beinge in the middest of the troupe is made a player, by giveinge him a
Bastonado or two, if he be on a horse, and by lending him halffe a dozen
cuffs if he be on foote, this much maye a stranger have of curtesye,
although he expecte noethinge at their handes.[11]

There is ample evidence to show that games of this type were played
in various parts of Britain from at least the fourteenth to the nineteenth
century. Moreover, the wildness so vividly depicted by Owen is amply
confirmed by other accounts.[12] That is what one would expect in a type
of game characterized by the following constellation of features: large,
unrestricted numbers of players; loosely defined and locally specific
oral rules; some participants playing on horseback while others played
on foot; the use of sticks to hit other players as well as the ball; control
of matches by the players themselves rather than by a referee; and the
absence of an outside, controlling organization to establish the rules
and act as a court of appeal in cases of dispute.

Not all of these features were present in all cases but most of them
were. As a result, such games were closer to 'real' fighting than modern
sports. As Riesman and Denney pointed out, modern sports are more
'abstract', more removed from 'serious' combat.[13] The folk antecedents
of modern rugby may have been mock battles in the sense that the lives
and life chances of the contending groups were not directly at risk and
that the infliction of serious injury and death was not their central aim.
Nevertheless, their relatively high level of open violence and the opportunity they afforded for inflicting pain may have constituted one of their
sources of enjoyment. After all, the people of pre-industrial Britain
enjoyed all sorts of pastimes – cock-fighting, bull- and bear-baiting,
burning cats alive in baskets, prize-fighting, watching public executions
– which appear 'uncivilized' in terms of present-day values. Such

pastimes reflected what Huizinga called 'the violent tenor of life' in Europe during the 'autumn' of the Middle Ages[14] and which continued until well into what historians regard as 'modern' times. They also reflected the comparatively high 'threshold of repugnance' with regard to witnessing and engaging in violent acts which, as Elias has shown, is characteristic of people in a society that stands at an earlier stage in a 'civilizing process' than our own.

By contrast with its folk antecedents, modern rugby exemplifies a game form that is civilized in at least four senses that were lacking in the ancestral forms. It is typical in this respect of modern combat sports more generally. Modern rugby is civilized by:

(1) A complex set of formally instituted written rules which demand strict control over the use of physical force and which prohibit it in certain forms, for example, 'stiff-arm' tackling and 'hacking', that is kicking an opposing player off his feet.
(2) Clearly defined intra-game sanctions, that is 'penalties', which can be brought to bear on offenders and, as the ultimate sanction for serious and persistent rule violation, the possibility of exclusion from the game.
(3) The institutionalization of a specific role which stands, as it were, 'outside' and 'above' the game and whose task is to control it, that is that of 'referee'.
(4) A nationally centralized rule-making and rule-enforcing body, the Rugby Football Union.

This civilization of rugby football occurred as part of a continuous social process. Two significant moments in it were: (a) the institution, at Rugby School in 1845, of the first written rules. These attempted, among other things, to place restrictions on the use of hacking and other forms of physical force, and to prohibit altogether the use of 'navvies' (the iron-tipped boots which had formed a socially valued part of the game at Rugby and some of the other mid-nineteenth century public schools); and (b) the formation in 1871 of the Rugby Football Union. The Rugby Union was formed partly as a result of a public controversy over what was perceived as the excessive violence of the game. One of its first acts was to place, for the first time, an absolute taboo on hacking. What happened at each of these moments was that the standards for controlling violence in the game advanced in two senses: firstly, it was demanded that players should exercise a stricter and more comprehensive measure of self-control over the use of physical force; and secondly, an attempt was made to secure compliance with this demand by means of externally imposed sanctions.

To speak of rugby as having undergone a 'civilizing process' is not to deny the fact that, relative to most other sports, it remains a rough game. Features such as the 'ruck' provide the opportunity for kicking and 'raking' players who are lying on the ground. The scrum offers opportunities for illegitimate violence such as punching, eye-gouging, and biting. Given the close packing of players that the scrum involves, it is difficult for the referee to control the interaction. Nor is the contention that rugby has undergone a limited civilizing development inconsistent with the fact that it has probably grown more violent in specific respects in recent years. It has certainly grown more competitive as is shown by the introduction at all levels of cups and leagues. Growing competitiveness means that the importance of victory has increased, and this elevation of the success goal has involved an erosion of the old amateur ethos. It has, for example, diminished considerably the significance of the idea that taking part is more important than winning. It has probably simultaneously increased the tendency of players to play roughly within the rules and to use illegitimate violence in pursuit of success. In short, it seems a priori likely that the use of *instrumental* violence in the game has recently increased.

To say this is not to claim that, in the past, the violence of the game was entirely non-rational and affective but rather that the balance between rational and affective violence has changed in favour of the former. That is because the structure of modern rugby, together with the relatively civilized personality pattern of the people who play it, mean that pleasure in playing is now derived far more from the expression of skill with the ball, in combining with team-mates and from more or less strictly controlled and muted forms of physical force, and far less from the physical intimidation and infliction of pain on opponents than used to be the case in its folk antecedents and in the mid-nineteenth-century public schools when hacking and the use of navvies remained central and legitimate tactics. But the social and personality structures that have given rise to the modern game have simultaneously increased the incidence of instrumental violence in it – for example, players who are able to gain satisfaction from the comparatively mild forms of physical force that are permitted in the modern game and who do not find pleasure in inflicting pain on others, are constrained to use violence, both legitimately and illegitimately, in an instrumental fashion. They do not gain pleasurable satisfaction from such violence *per se*. It is not engaged in as an end in itself but as a means for achieving a long-term goal, that of winning a league or cup.

The growing competitive pressure that leads to the increasing *covert* use of rational violence, is simultaneously conducive to *overt* violence, namely that which occurs when sportsmen and women momentarily lose their self-control and strike an opponent in retaliation. The fact that the tactical use of instrumental violence often forms a trigger leading to such a loss of self-control shows yet again how one kind of violence can be rapidly transformed into another.

How is this apparently paradoxical development – that a game has grown less violent in certain respects and simultaneously more violent in others – to be explained? I should like to hypothesize that it is principally a consequence of a long-term shift in the pattern of social bonding, of the manner in which the members of our society are related to one another. Let me start to illustrate what this means by returning to Elias's theory of the civilizing process.

IV   VIOLENCE AND THE TRANSFORMATION OF SOCIAL BONDS

Although Elias does not express it in these terms, it is, I think, fair to say that a central aspect of the civilizing process – the lengthening of interdependency chains – involved a change in the pattern of social bonding comparable to the one described by Durkheim as the transition from 'mechanical' to 'organic' solidarity. In order to distance the analysis from the evaluative connotations implicit in Durkheim's terminology and to convey the idea that both concepts refer to forms of interdependence, I propose to describe this aspect of the process as one in the course of which 'segmental' bonding gradually came to be replaced increasingly by 'functional' bonding. Centrally involved in this transformation was a process in which the significance of the ascriptive ties of family and residence grew gradually less while that of achieved ties determined by the division of labour grew gradually more important.

The differences between these two types of social bonding can be expressed, provisionally and formally, by means of the polar models set forth in table 8.1. They attempt to depict, not only the two contrasting types of social bonding but also the distinctive types of overall social figuration within which, respectively, segmental and functional bonding are (or were) generated and which, reciprocally, they help (or helped) to maintain.

These two models are a rather crude attempt to express some of the central structural differences between the societies of medieval Europe and those of modern times. The models are, however, very general and thus obscure differences such as those between social classes. They also ignore the existence of empirical overlaps between the two types and, to the extent that it is based on extrapolation from observable trends, the model of functional bonding exaggerates, for example, the degree of sexual equality that has so far been achieved in societies which approximate to that type.

Nor do I wish to imply by this analysis that the trend towards the increasing predominance of functional bonding has been a simple, unilinear process or that it will necessarily continue into the future. A number of interrelated preconditions facilitated such a development in the past, central among them being continuing economic growth, the ability of the state to retain an effective monopoly over the means of violence, and, despite the fact that they have often offered stiff resistance, a willingness over the long term on the part of ruling groups to compromise and grant concessions as the power of subordinate groups has grown. But such complexities are less germane for present purposes than the manner in which such types of social bonding and their wider structural correlates produce, on the one hand, a tendency towards violence with a high emotional or affective content and, on the other, a high degree of individual and social control over violence together with a tendency towards the use of violence of a more rational kind. It is to that issue that I shall now, very briefly and schematically, address myself.

V SEGMENTAL BONDING AND THE SOCIOGENESIS OF AFFECTIVE VIOLENCE

The structure of a society in which segmental bonding is the dominant type is conducive to physical violence in human relations in a number of mutually reinforcing ways. Expressed in terms of a cybernetics analogy, one could say that the various elements of such a social structure form a positive feedback cycle which escalates the tendency to resort to violence at all levels and in all spheres of social relations. The weakness of the state, for example, means that such a society is prey to outside attacks. That places a premium on military roles and that, in turn, leads to the consolidation of a predominantly warrior ruling class, a class trained for fighting and whose members, because of their socialization, derive positive satisfaction from it.

Internal relations in such a society work in the same direction. Fighting, with or without weapons, is endemic, largely because 'we-groups' are narrowly defined with the consequence that even ostensibly similar groups from the same locality are defined as 'outsiders'. So intense are the feelings of pride and group attachment generated within particular kin and local segments that conflict and rivalry are virtually inevitable when the members of two or more of them meet. And their norms of aggression, coupled with the lack of social pressure to exercise self-control, mean that conflict between them leads easily to fighting.

TABLE 8.1   Segmental and functional bonding and their structural correlates

Segmental bonding	Functional bonding
1 Locally self-sufficient communities, only loosely tied into a wider, proto-national frame-work; relative poverty.	Nationally integrated communities, tied together by extensive chains of interdependence; relative affluence.
2 Intermittent pressure 'from above' from a weak central state; relatively autonomous ruling class divided into warrior and priestly sections; balance of power skewed strongly in favour of rulers/authority figures both within and between groups; little pressure generated structurally 'from below'; power of rulers simultaneously weakened, for example, by rudimentary state apparatus and poor means of transport and communication.	Continuous pressure 'from above' from a strong central state; relatively dependent ruling class in which the secular and civilian sections are dominant; tendency towards equalization of power through the generation of multi-polar controls within and between groups; intense pressure generated structurally 'from below'; power of rulers simultaneously strengthened, for example, by relatively efficient state apparatus and relatively efficient means of transport and communication.
3 Close identification with narrowly circumscribed groups united principally by means of ascribed kinship and local bonds.	Identification with groups that are united principally by means of achieved bonds of functional interdependence.
4 Narrow range of occupations; homogeneity of work experience both within and between occupational groups.	Wide range of occupations; heterogeneity of work experience both within and between occupational groups.
5 Low social and geographical mobility; narrow experiential horizons.	High social and geographical mobility; wide experiential horizons.
6 Little social pressure to exercise self-control over physical violence or to defer gratification generally; little exercise of foresight or long-term planning.	Great social pressure to exercise self-control over physical violence and to defer gratification generally; great exercise of foresight and long-term planning.
7 Low emotional control; quest for immediate excitement; tendency towards violent mood swings; high threshold of repugnance regarding violence and pain; pleasure from directly inflicting pain on others and from seeing others suffer; violence openly displayed in everyday life; low guilt feelings after committing violent acts.	High emotional control; quest for excitement in more muted forms; relatively stable temperament; low threshold of repugnance regarding violence and pain; vicarious pleasure from watching 'mimetic' violence but not 'real' violence; violence pushed 'behind the scenes'; high guilt feelings after committing violent acts; rational recourse to violence in situations where it is perceived as undetectable.

TABLE 8.1 – *continued*

Segmental bonding	Functional bonding
8 High degree of conjugal role segregation; 'mother-centered' families; authoritarian father with low involvement in the family; high separation of male and female lives; large numbers of children.	Low degree of conjugal role segregation; 'joint', 'symmetrical' or 'egalitarian' families; father with high involvement in the family; low separation of male and female lives; small numbers of children.
9 High physical violence in relations between the sexes; male dominance.	Low physical violence in relations between the sexes; sexual equality.
10 Loose and intermittent parental control over children; violence central in early socialization; spontaneous, affective violence of parents towards children.	Close and continuous parental control over children; socialization principally by non-violent means but limited, planned recourse to rational/ instrumental violence.
11 Structurally generated tendency for 'gangs' to form around the lines of social segmentation and for them to fight other local gangs; emphasis on 'aggressive masculinity'; ability to fight the key to power and status in the gang and the local community.	Structurally generated tendency for relationships to be formed through choice and not simply on a local basis; 'civilized' masculine style, expressed, for example, in formal sport; chances for more than local power and status; status determined by occupational, educational, artistic, and sports ability.
12 'Folk' forms of sport, basically a ritualized extension of fighting between local gangs; relatively high level of open violence.	'Modern' forms of sport, that is, of ritualized play-fights based on controlled forms of violence but strong social pressure to use violence in its rational/ instrumental forms.

Indeed, fighting, both within and between such groups, is necessary for the establishment and maintenance of reputations in terms of their standards of aggressive masculinity. The best fighters tend to emerge as leaders and all the members of such groups have to fight in order to feel and prove to others that they are 'men'.

The fighting norms of such segmentally bonded groups are analogous to the vendetta systems still found in many Mediterranean countries in the sense that an individual who is challenged or feels himself slighted by one or more members of an outsider group feels that his group honour, and not simply his own, is at stake. Correspondingly, he is liable to seek revenge, not simply by retaliation against that or those particular members but against *any* member of the offending group. On both sides, furthermore, there is a tendency for others to come to the aid of the initiators of the conflict. In that way, fights between individuals tend to escalate into feuds between groups, often long-lasting ones, thus providing a clear indication of the very great degree of identification under such social circumstances of individuals with the groups to which they belong.

The endemic violence characteristic of societies of this type, together with the fact that their structure consolidates the power of a warrior ruling class and generates an emphasis on male aggressiveness and strength, is conducive to the general dominance of men over women. In its turn, male dominance leads to a high degree of separateness in the lives of the sexes and, with it, to families of the mother-centered type. The relative absence of the father from the family, coupled with the large family size which is typical in societies of this type, means that children are not subjected to close, continuous, or effective adult supervision. That, in its turn, has two principal consequences. First, because physical strength tends to be stressed in relations among children who are not subjected to effective adult control, it further increases the violence characteristic of such communities. The tendency of children in segmentally bonded communities to resort to physical violence is also reinforced by its use by their parents as a means of socialization and by the adult role models available to them in the society at large. Second, the relative lack of close adult supervision of children is conducive to the formation of gangs which persist into early adult life and which, because of the narrowly defined group allegiances characteristic of segmental bonding, come persistently into conflict with other local gangs. The sports of such communities – for example, the folk antecedents of modern rugby – are ritualized expressions of the 'gang warfare' typically generated under such conditions, an institutionalized test of the relative strengths of particular communities which grows out of, and exists side by side with, the perpetual and more serious struggles between local groups.

The positive feedback cycle by means of which high levels of violence are generated in a society characterized by segmental bonding is illustrated schematically in figure 8.1.

VI FUNCTIONAL BONDING, CIVILIZING PRESSURES AND THE SOCIOGENESIS OF RATIONAL VIOLENCE

Empirical societies which approximate closely to the model of functional bonding are, in most respects, diametrically opposite to those where segmental bonding is the dominant type. Like the latter, such

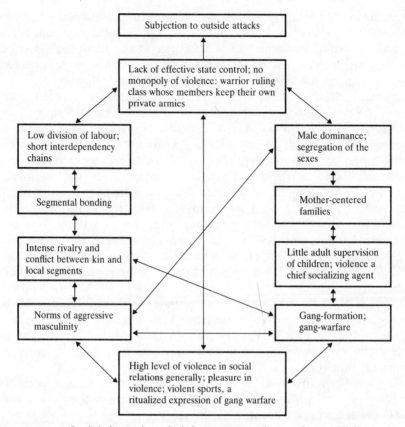

FIGURE 8.1 Social dynamics of violence generation under conditions of segmental bonding. Arrows indicate main directions of influence in positive feedback cycle.

societies are subject to a positive feedback cycle but, in this case, the cycle performs, on balance, a civilizing function, serving mainly to limit and restrain the level of violence in social relations. This does not mean necessarily that it reduces the *rate* of violence but rather that it leads to the predominance of violence in more muted forms. However, the structure of such societies simultaneously generates intense competitive pressure and a tendency for rational means to be used in goal achievement. In its turn, this combination generates a tendency for illegitimate violence and other forms of rule violation to be used rationally or instrumentally in specific social contexts, for example in highly competitive combat sports. Let me elaborate on this.

A key structural feature of a society where functional bonding is the dominant type is the fact that the state has established a monopoly on the right to use physical force. To the degree that its monopoly is stable and effective, the division of labour is permitted to grow – that is the chains of interdependence in it lengthen – and that, reciprocally, augments the power of the state, for example because central control becomes increasingly necessary as the social structure grows more complex. Both the state monopoly on physical violence and the lengthening of interdependency chains exert, on balance, a civilizing effect. The former exerts such an effect directly because the state is able to prevent citizens from openly carrying arms and to punish them for using violence illegitimately, that is in situations where it claims a monopoly for its own agents. The latter exerts such an effect indirectly because the division of labour generates what Elias calls 'reciprocal' or 'multipolar' controls. That is, bonds of interdependence allow the parties to a division of labour to exert a degree of control over one another mutually. In this sense, the division of labour exerts an equalizing or 'democratizing' effect. Such an effect is civilizing for at least two reasons: (a) because the reciprocal controls generated by interdependence are conducive to greater restraint in social relations; and (b) because a complex system of interdependencies would be subject to severe strain if all or even some personnel failed to exercise continuously a high degree of self-control. In that way, self-control is an essential precondition for the maintenance and growth of the differentiation of functions.

A society of this type is highly competitive because a complex division of labour also generates an achievement ideology and a tendency for roles to be allocated on the basis of achievement rather than ascription. This intensification of competition leads to a general increase in rivalry and aggressiveness in social relations but, to the extent that the state effectively claims a monopoly on the right to use physical force, it cannot be expressed in the form of openly and directly violent behaviour. The dominant standards generated in such a society work in the same direction by decreeing that violence is wrong and, to the extent that such standards are internalized in the course of socialization, men and women come to have a low threshold of repugnance with regard to engaging in and directly witnessing violent acts.

But, while the dominant tendency in such a society is towards a comparatively high and effective level of control over violence, competitive pressure, coupled with the fact that long chains of interdependence and the correlative pattern of socialization constrain people to use foresight, to defer immediate gratification and to use rational means of goal achievement, means that there is a parallel tendency towards the planned or instrumental use of violence by ordinary citizens in specific social contexts, most notably in crime, in sports, and, to a lesser extent, in the socialization and education of children. Only the use of instrumental violence in sports need concern us here.

The first thing to note in this connection is the fact that, in a society where a high degree of functional bonding exists, combat sports such as rugby, soccer, and boxing form a social enclave in which specific forms of violence are socially defined as legitimate. Such sports are ritualized and civilized play-fights in which the use of physical force is hemmed in by rules and conventions, and controlled, immediately, by specific officials such as referees and, at a higher level, by committees and tribunals set up by national and international ruling bodies. But, to the extent that the competitive pressure in such sports increases, either because their practitioners are competing for extrinsic rewards such as financial remuneration or the honour of winning a trophy, or because they are subject to pressure to win from the local or national groups whom they represent, there will be a tendency for the significance of victory to be raised and, correspondingly, for players to break the rules as a deliberate tactic. As part of this, there will be a tendency for them to use violence illegitimately in situations where they perceive the likelihood of detection to be low or where they take a calculated risk that the penalties incurred upon detection will not detract significantly from the achievement of their own or their team's long-term goals.

The positive feedback cycle by means of which low levels of general violence are generated in a society characterized by functional bonding, together with the generation in such a society of a tendency for people to resort to rational or instrumental violence in specific situations, is illustrated schematically in figure 8.2.

Of course, the tendency towards the rational use of violence in modern sport is counteracted, on the one hand, by general values and sport-specific norms but, on the other, because it is liable to provoke retaliation, it serves simultaneously to increase the general level of sporting violence. The complexity of the picture is further increased when one takes into account the fact that this discussion is based on a model that exaggerates the degree to which functional bonding has in fact developed in modern Britain. In particular, the model of segmental bonding still seems to be approximated fairly closely in certain sections of the British working class. It is reasonable to suppose that bonds of that type play a part in generating the norms of violent or aggressive masculinity that can be observed, for example, in the fighting of football (soccer) hooligans.

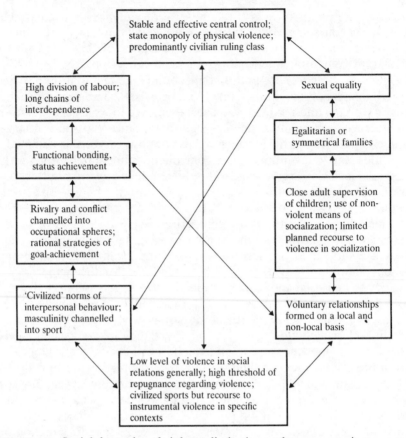

FIGURE 8.2 Social dynamics of violence limitation and recourse to instrumental violence under conditions of functional bonding. Arrows indicate main directions of influence in positive feedback cycle.

VII SEGMENTAL BONDING IN THE WORKING CLASS AND THE SOCIOGENESIS OF FOOTBALL HOOLIGAN VIOLENCE

It is commonly believed that football hooliganism first became a 'social problem' in Britain in the 1960s. Research, however, shows that no decade in the history of the game has gone by without the occurrence of disorderliness on a substantial scale. In fact, its incidence has tended to follow a U-shaped curve, being relatively high before the First World War, falling between the wars and remaining relatively low until the late 1950s. Then, in the 1960s, it increased, escalating fairly rapidly from the mid-1960s onwards, coming to form an almost 'normal' accompaniment of the professional game. Despite such variations in its incidence over time, a recurrent feature of football hooliganism is physical violence. This can take the form of assaults on players and referees, or of clashes between rival fan groups. It is clashes with rival fan groups, often with the police involved as well, that are the dominant form of football hooligan violence in its present phase. Sometimes, such violence involves the use of weapons, either in direct, hand-to-hand combat or in the form of aerial bombardment with missiles from a distance. Marsh, Rosser, and Harré suggest that football hooliganism is a form of 'ritualized aggression' and that it is not usually seriously violent except to the extent that official intervention distorts it and prevents it from taking its 'normal' form.[15] They evidently think of ritualized and 'serious' violence as mutually exclusive, for it is difficult to conceive of throwing coins, darts, beer cans, and, as has happened at matches, petrol bombs, as 'ritualized aggression'. To say this is not to deny the possible effect that official intervention may have on the forms that football hooliganism takes. The penning and segregation of rival fans, for example, have probably increased the incidence of aerial bombardment. But what Marsh and his colleagues seemingly wish to deny is the fact that such groups evidently wish to inflict serious injuries on one another of the kind, for example, that are liable to be caused by coins, darts, and petrol bombs. Alternatively, the Oxford research group may mean to imply that, independently of their violent intentions, football hooligans are restrained by instinctive mechanisms as is the case, for example, with wolves, according to the findings of ethologists such as Lorenz. But, despite Marsh's attempts to distance himself from the cruder sorts of sociobiological speculations,[16] it is reasonable to conclude that the Oxford analysis involves too close an identification of their human subjects with animals lower on the evolutionary scale. Hence it underestimates the degree to which human behaviour is normatively, that is socially, and not instinctively controlled.

I should like to hypothesize that the violent behaviour of football hooligans – whatever elements of ritual it may contain – is centrally connected with norms of masculinity that: (1) place an extreme stress on toughness and ability to fight; (2) are, in that respect, different in degree – though not in kind – from the masculinity norms that are currently dominant in society at large; and (3) that tend, as a result, recurrently to incur condemnation from socially dominant groups. In fact, such norms are reminiscent in many ways of the masculinity norms which were general in British society at an earlier stage of its development, more specifically of the norms of manliness which, if the analysis presented earlier is correct, were generated by the medieval and early modern forms of segmental bonding and their correlates in the wider social structure.

There are at least four aspects of present day football hooliganism which suggest that its core features may be generated by segmental bonds, namely:

(1) The fact that the groups involved appear to be as, and sometimes more, interested in fighting one another as they are in watching football. Indeed, their own accounts suggest that they derive positive enjoyment from fighting and that, for them, ability to fight forms the principal source of both individual and group prestige.

(2) The fact that the rival groups appear to be recruited principally from the same level of social stratification, that is from the so-called 'rough' sections of the working class. This means that, in order to account for it, one has to explain the fact that their fighting involves *intra-* as opposed to *inter-*class conflict. Segmental bonding can explain that fact, though it is necessary to state clearly that, to say this is not to deny either the fact that such groups engage in forms of inter-class conflict – for example that they fight regularly with the police who are the representatives of the dominant classes – or the fact that they are exploited victims of socially more powerful groups.

(3) The fact that the fighting of such groups takes a vendetta form in the sense that, independently of any overt action they may take, particular individuals and groups are set upon simply because they display the membership insignia of a rival group. The long-standing feuds which develop between rival groups of hooligan fans, and which persist despite the turnover of personnel that occurs within such groups, point in the same direction, that is they are an indication of the very great degree of identification of particular hooligans with the groups to which they belong.

(4) The remarkable degree of conformity and uniformity in action that is displayed in the songs and chants of football hooligans. A recurrent theme of these songs and chants is enhancement of the masculine image of the in-group, coupled with denigration and emasculation of the out-group. It is difficult to conceive of the members of more individualized groups either wishing to or being capable of engaging in such complex uniform actions and it is, accordingly, reasonable to suppose that the homogenizing effects of segmental bonding may lie at their base.

Sociological research[17] suggests that 'rough' working-class communities are characterized by all or most of the following constellation of social attributes: (a) more or less extreme poverty; (b) employment of members in unskilled and/or casual jobs, coupled with a high susceptibility to unemployment; (c) low levels of formal education; (d) low geographical mobility except for some males who travel occupationally, for example in the army or in connection with unskilled work in the building and construction trades; (e) mother-centered families and extended kin networks; (f) a high degree of conjugal role segregation and separation of the lives of the sexes generally; (g) male dominance, coupled with a tendency for men to be physically violent towards women; (h) little adult supervision of children, coupled with frequent resort to violence in socialization; (i) comparatively low ability of members to exercise emotional control and defer gratification; (j) a comparatively low threshold of repugnance towards physical violence; (k) the formation of street-corner 'gangs' which are led by the best fighters and within and between which fighting is frequent; and (l) intense feelings of attachment to narrowly defined 'we-groups' and correspondingly intense feelings of hostility towards narrowly defined 'they-groups'.

The different aspects of such figurations tend to be mutually reinforcing. That is, like their pre-industrial counterparts, working-class communities constitute a positive feedback cycle, one of the principal consequences of which is aggressive masculinity. However, these modern forms of segmental bonding are not identical with the pre-industrial forms because they are located in a society with a relatively stable and effective state, and in which there exists a complex network of interdependencies. As a result, the segmentally bonded local groups of today are subjected to 'civilizing' pressures and controls from two main sources: (1) from the policing, educational, and social work agencies of the state; and (2) from functionally bonded groups in the wider society. Pressure in the latter case occurs partly by means of the direct actions that are taken by such groups, and partly by means of the influence they are able to bring to bear on the mass media and official agencies.

In short, segmental groups in modern society are subjected to restraint *from the outside* but not, to anything like the same extent, *from within*. Internally, their members remain locked in social figurations that are reminiscent in many ways of the pre-industrial forms of segmental bonding and that correspondingly generate acute forms of aggressive masculinity. The intense feelings of in-group attachment and hostility towards out-groups of such segmentally bonded groups mean that rivalry is virtually inevitable when their members meet. And their norms of aggressive masculinity and comparative inability to exercise self-control mean that conflict between them leads easily to fighting. Indeed, much as was the case with their pre-industrial counterparts, fighting within and between such groups is necessary for the establishment and maintenance of reputations in terms of their standards of aggressive masculinity. As a result, particular individuals take positive pleasure in performing what is, for them, a socially necessary role.

Football has become a setting for the expression of such standards partly because norms of manliness are intrinsic to it. That is, it too is basically a play-fight in which masculine reputations are enhanced or lost. Its inherently oppositional character means that it lends itself readily to group identification and the enhancement of in-group solidarity in opposition to a series of easily identifiable out-groups, the opposing team and its supporters. To the extent that some fans are drawn from communities characterized by variants of segmental solidarity, football hooliganism in the form of fighting between gangs of rival supporters is a highly likely result. Indeed, it is probably correct to say that football hooliganism is a present-day counterpart to the folk antecedents of modern football, though superimposed on and intermingled in a complex manner with the more differentiated and 'civilized' Association game.

9

Spectator Violence at Football Matches: Towards a Sociological Explanation

*Eric Dunning, Patrick Murphy
and John Williams*

I INTRODUCTION

The subject of this paper is 'football hooliganism'.[1] We shall focus
centrally in this connection on the pattern of fighting between rival
groups that has come to be regularly associated with soccer, not only in
this country but in a number of others besides. In fact, although this
rarely surfaces in the press, there is scarcely a country where Association Football is played where eruptions of crowd violence have not
occurred, though English fans are currently the most feared in Europe
and the only ones who regularly cause trouble when they are travelling
abroad in support of their clubs or the national side.[2]

The research on which the paper is based was funded by the Social
Science Research Council (now the ESRC) and the Football Trust.
Before we set forth some of our results, we shall sketch in some of the
main parameters of football hooliganism as a social phenomenon.

II FOOTBALL HOOLIGANISM AS A SOCIAL PHENOMENON

As a form of behaviour, the disorderliness of football fans that has
come to attract the label 'football hooliganism' is complex and many
sided. In popular usage, for example, the label embraces swearing and
behaviour which, in other contexts, would be excused as simple 'high
spirits' or 'horseplay'. In fact, many of the fans who are arrested in a
football context have only engaged in such relatively minor misde-
meanours. In the more serious manifestations, however, the label
refers to pitch invasions that appear to be deliberately engineered in

order to halt a match and, perhaps most seriously of all, to large-scale fracas between opposing fan groups that are often violent and destructive. It is with this latter form of the phenomenon that we are principally concerned. More specifically, the evidence suggests that, although many fans are *drawn* into hooligan incidents – fans who did not set out for the match with disruptive intent – the hard core, those who engage most persistently in hooligan behaviour in a football context, view fighting and aggressive behaviour as an integral part of 'going to the match'. Such fans are frequently skilled at evading detection and arrest, and hence do not always appear in the police statistics. 'Frank', a 26-year-old lorry driver and self-confessed 'football hooligan' who was interviewed by Paul Harrison after the 1974 Cardiff City v. Manchester United game, can serve as an example. He is reported by Harrison as having said:

> I go to a match for one reason only: the aggro. It's an obsession, I can't give it up. I get so much pleasure when I'm having aggro that I nearly wet my pants . . . I go all over the country looking for it . . . every night during the week we go around town looking for trouble. Before a match we go round looking respectable . . . then if we see someone who looks like the enemy we ask him the time; if he answers in a foreign accent, we do him over; and if he's got any money on him we'll roll him as well.[3]

Frank may well have exaggerated the extent of his involvement in and enjoyment of 'aggro'. Indeed, if all his claims were true, he would probably be dubbed by other fans, even most football hooligans, as a 'nutter' or a 'loony'.[4] Nevertheless, the interest in fighting he displays, the concern with the generation of pleasurable excitement in a fight situation, has features that appear to be common to the lifestyles of 'hard-core' football hooligans. Sociologically, the point is to explain why. More specifically, why is it that adolescent and young adult males from particular groups within the socio-economically lowest sections of the working class have come to develop a strong interest in and enjoyment of fighting? Why does openly aggressive behaviour form such an important part of their lifestyle? And why has football come to form such an attractive and persistent venue for its expression? Before we turn to these complex questions, let us first sketch in some of the principal forms that football hooligan confrontations take.

III   THE FORMS OF FOOTBALL HOOLIGAN CONFRONTATIONS

Football hooligan confrontations take a number of different forms and they can take place in a variety of contexts besides the football ground itself. They can, for example, take the form of hand-to-hand fighting between just two rival supporters or between two small groups of them. Alternatively, they can involve up to several hundred fans on either side. In the most serious incidents, weapons – lightweight and easily concealed Stanley knives are favoured at the moment – are sometimes used. Football hooligan confrontations can also take the form of aerial bombardments using as ammunition missiles that range from innocuous items such as peanuts, bits of orange peel, apple cores and paper cups, to more dangerous, even potentially lethal ones, such as darts, metal discs, coins (sometimes with their edges sharpened), broken seats, bricks, slabs of concrete, ball bearings, fireworks, smoke bombs and, as has happened on one or two occasions, crude petrol bombs.

Missile throwing can take place inside or outside the ground, and, at Leicester City recently, a pitch invasion by some 200 Arsenal fans was sparked off because they were the objects of an attack with bricks and other missiles by Leicester City fans who were *outside* the ground. As a consequence of the official policy of segregating rival fans – a policy introduced in the 1960s as a means of preventing football hooliganism but which appears to have had greater success in enhancing the solidarity of 'football ends' and driving the phenomenon outside grounds – large-scale fights on the terraces became relatively rare during the 1970s and early 1980s. Small groups of fans, however, still managed frequently to infiltrate the territories of their rivals in order to start a fight or create a wider disturbance. Participating in a successful 'invasion' – 'taking' somebody else's 'end' – is a source of great kudos in football hooligan circles. More usually nowadays, however, the fighting takes place either in the unsegregated seated sections of grounds or before the match, for instance in and around town centre pubs. It also takes place after the match when the police are trying to keep the rival fans apart and to get the main body of away supporters to the railway or bus station without serious incident. It is then that the largest-scale confrontations tend to occur. These often start with a 'run', that is with a rush of as many as 200 or 300 young male fans who charge along the street looking for opposing fans or for a breach in the police defences that will enable them to make contact with their rivals. The 'hard-core' hooligans, however, those who are most committed in their desire to engage groups of the opposing team's supporters, often operate apart from the main body and use elaborate tactics in their attempts to outflank the police. If they are successful, what usually takes place is a series of skirmishes scattered over a relatively large area involving young males from either side, punching, kicking and chasing each other, dodging in and out of moving traffic and, occasionally, attacking vehicles carrying rival supporters. Confrontations can also take place when groups of rival fans *en route* to different matches meet, for instance on trains, the underground and at motorway service stations. In addition, fights also sometimes occur *within* particular fan groups, the participants in such cases being drawn, for example, from different housing estates in the same general locality.

In our research, we have been particularly interested in what the football hooligans themselves and other young fans call 'fighting crews', especially those of the 'super-hooligan' groups which have evolved in recent years at some of the larger clubs. Members of such groups – such as the self-styled 'Inter City Firm' at West Ham, the 'Service Crew' at Leeds, and the comparable groups at clubs like Newcastle United and Chelsea – often support extreme right-wing, racist organizations such as the British Movement and the National Front. They have also developed quite sophisticated forms of organization and become nationally known. One of their main distinguishing marks is the fact that they do not travel to matches on 'football specials' and official coaches but tend, instead, to use regular rail and coach services or cars and hired vans. They also eschew the forms of dress – the scarves and favours (and also the club banners) – that still tend to be widely associated with football hooliganism in popular opinion. One of their main objectives in attending matches is to confront and fight opposing fans and to 'take their end'. Fans of this kind travel without identifying colours in order to avoid advertising themselves too soon to rival fans and the police. This emerged in the case of 'Frank', the fan interviewed by Harrison, but it is also clear in the description provided by 'Howie', a 20-year-old Leicester 'hard case'. 'Howie' told us:

> If you can baffle the coppers you'll win. You've just gotta think how they're gonna think. And you know, half the time you know what they're gonna do, 'cos they're gonna take the same route every week, week in, week out. If you can figure out a way to beat 'em, you're fuckin' laughin', you'll have a good fuckin' raut [Leicester slang for a fight]. That's why I never wear a scarf, in case I go in [the opposition's] side. I used to wear a scarf but [the police] used to fuckin' come and stop me. Used to grab the scarf and go, 'bang, bang'. I thought, I ain't havin' that. Take it off, they can't grab hold of you.

'Hard cases' such as 'Frank' and 'Howie' gave up wearing scarves and identifying favours long ago, but it is worth stressing that very few fans nowadays who go to football partly or mainly for 'the action' sport such marks of identification. Nor do many of them follow the skinhead style that was so popular in the late 1960s and 1970s. Instead, and although there are regional and 'end-specific' variations, they tend to dress according to the dictates of current youth fashion, partly because the older 'hooligan uniforms' are regarded as anachronistic and lacking in 'style', and partly, as we have said, to avoid advertising themselves too soon to opposing fans and the police.

This general description of some of the main parameters of football hooliganism and some of the changes that aspects of it have recently undergone is consistent with the central point we made earlier, namely that the youths and young men involved in the most serious incidents tend to view fighting and confrontations with opposing supporters as an integral part of attending a football match. The songs and chants which form a conspicuous feature of inter-fan group rivalry, especially inside the stadium, point in the same direction. Although some of the 'hardest' lads regard singing and chanting as 'soft', and tend not to get involved in it, during a match the rival groups direct their attention as much and sometimes more to one another as they do to the match itself, singing, chanting and gesticulating *en masse* and in what one might call spontaneously orchestrated uniformity as expressions of their opposition. Their songs and chants are in part related to the match but they also have as a recurrent theme challenges to fight, threats of violence towards the opposing fans and boasts about past victories. Each fan group has its own repertoire of songs and chants but many of these are local variations on a stock of common themes. Central in this connection is the fact that their lyrics are punctuated with words like 'hate', 'die', 'fight', 'kick', 'surrender', all of which convey images of battle and conquest.[5] Apart from violence, symbolic demasculinization of the rival fans is another recurrent terrace theme, for example the reference to them and/or the team they support as 'poofs' or 'wankers', the latter accompanied by a mass gestural representation of the male masturbatory act. Yet another recurring theme is denigration of the community of the opposing fans. Let us turn now to the subject of explanation.

IV OFFICIAL EXPLANATIONS OF FOOTBALL HOOLIGANISM

Two main official explanations of football hooliganism have been proposed and both seem to be widely accepted, namely that it is caused by drinking and/or by violence on the field of play. Both have severe limitations and, to the extent that they contain partly valid elements, they need to be set within a wider explanatory framework. Drinking, for example, cannot be said to be a significant or 'deep' cause of football hooliganism for the simple reason that not every fan who drinks, even heavily, takes part in hooligan acts. Nor does every hooligan drink, though a stress, not only on fighting but also on heavy drinking, is integrally involved in the masculinity norms that are expressed in their behaviour. In fact, such fans tend to be relatively aggressive even without drink. Similarly, violence in a match is not invariably followed by hooligan incidents. Nor are all hooligan incidents preceded by violence on the field – this is obviously the case, for example, with pre-match confrontations. But to say this is not to deny the fact that drinking and on-the-pitch violence are sometimes causally implicated in the sequences of events that are typically involved in football hooligan fighting. In order to see how that is the case, one has to think in terms of a *hierarchy* of causes and, in this sense, violence on the field and drinking can be said to be causally implicated in the generation of football hooliganism in a surface sense. This is a complex issue and we do not have the space to go into details here. It must be enough to say that alcohol consumption is one of a series of conditions that can facilitate football hooligan violence, and that it does so because alcohol is an agent which lowers inhibitions. In the case of hooligan fans, it helps to generate a sense of heightened camaraderie in the group and also aids them in combating, on the one hand, their fear of being hurt in a fight and, on the other, their fear of being apprehended by the police. The latter prospect is a real one since, although football hooliganism does not constitute an offence as such, their behaviour often contravenes specific laws and takes place in public places where there is usually a large police presence designed explicitly to prevent it. In fact, the brush with the authorities – those at various levels of the football world and not just the police – can be a significant source of the excitement generated in football hooligan encounters. Football hooliganism also provides the fans involved with an opportunity to act out hostilities with the police established in a non-football context and gives them a public stage for expressing their disregard for 'respectable' values.[6]

Similarly, violence on the pitch can serve as a trigger for football hooliganism, but so can a whole series of other contingencies such as heavy and injudicious policing, a desire to avenge a defeat inflicted in fighting at an earlier match, and the desire of one fan group to knock another off the pedestal onto which the media have placed them. We are referring here to the sort of notoriety given by the media to 'Doc's Red Army', that is to Manchester United fans, in the 1970s, and to Chelsea and Leeds United fans today. In fact, the media have played a part in creating a national status hierarchy of football hooligans and a struggle for status between the different 'football ends'. In other words, there are currently two league tables as far as hooligan fans are concerned: one is official, the other unofficial and in part media-created. The first is about matches won or lost and league points gained. The second is about who ran, where and from whom, and who are currently branded by officialdom and the media as the most 'evil' and 'destructive' hooligans in the country. In short, what we are suggesting is that, whilst these popularly accepted official explanations in terms of alcohol consumption and violence on the field of play refer to factors that cannot be ruled out as elements in the determination of football hooligan behaviour, they fail to penetrate deeply into the hierarchy of causes, that is to the phenomenon's causal roots. More particularly, they say nothing about the way in which the enjoyment of fighting and a stress on the ability to 'look after oneself' are generated among hooligan fans, about the norms and standards which govern their behaviour, or about the reasons why football has come to form one of the most persistent venues for expressing them. The same is arguably true about the majority of academic explanations that have so far been proposed. It is to some among the more prominent of these academic explanations that our attention will now be turned.

V   ACADEMIC EXPLANATIONS OF FOOTBALL HOOLIGANISM

In his early work on the subject, Ian Taylor attributed football hooliganism to the effects on hard-core fans of what he called the 'bourgeoisification' and 'internationalization' of the game.[7] Working-class football fans, he suggested, believe that the league clubs used, in some sense, to be 'participatory democracies' and, he argued, the hooligans are a form of working-class 'resistance movement' which is trying to reassert control in the face of changes imposed by middle-class groups in order to secure middle-class interests.

John Clarke's analysis is similar in some respects to the early work of Taylor.[8] He attributes football hooliganism to the conjuncture in the 1960s between what he calls the 'professionalization' and 'spectaculari-zation' of the game, and changes in the social situation of working-class youth, more particularly changes, as he puts it, that 'have had the combined effect of fracturing some of the ties of family and neighbour-hood which bound the young and the old together in a particular relationship in pre-war working-class life'.[9] In other words, football hooliganism, according to Clarke, is a reaction on the part of alienated youths from disintegrated working-class communities against commer-cialized football and the increasing packaging of the game as spectacle and entertainment. As a result of the disintegration of their communi-ties, he argues, such youths now attend matches free from the control of older relatives and neighbours that used to keep them in check. Finally, Stuart Hall has examined the role of the press in creating a 'moral panic' over football hooliganism, suggesting that it has increased as a 'cause for concern' correlatively with the deterioration of the

British economy.[10] This has led, he suggests, to a clampdown on football hooliganism as part of what he and his former colleagues at the University of Birmingham describe as the current ruling-class strategy of 'policing the crisis'.[11]

We are aware, of course, that the work of Taylor, Clarke and Hall can be read as addressing the *general* phenomenon of football hooliganism and not as centring on the exploits of 'fighting crews'. This is one of the reasons why we do not wish totally to deny the validity of their explanations. However, they seem to us – and in Hall's case this emphasis is quite explicit – to be more adequate as explanations of the way in which public anxiety over football hooliganism has been generated and orchestrated than they are of the phenomenon itself. We say this partly because Hall, Taylor and Clarke all seem wrongly to believe that football hooliganism as a social phenomenon dates solely from the early 1960s, and partly because of their failure to come to grips adequately with what is, from the standpoint of the Marxian theoretical perspective that they share, one of the most puzzling aspects of football hooliganism as a social phenomenon, namely the fact that it involves a specific form of conflict *between working-class groups* and that the core participants come into conflict with the authorities and members of the more established classes largely as part of an attempt *to fight among themselves*. Hall, Taylor and Clarke, of course, could explain this aspect of the phenomenon by attributing it to 'the displacement of aggression' but, to our knowledge, with the sole exception of Taylor in his recent work, none of them has attempted to do so.[12] It is, therefore, reasonable to conclude that their explanations of football hooliganism are, at best, incomplete and, at worst, succeed only in scratching the surface of the problem.

It could be argued that an exception in this regard is provided by the work of Marsh, Rosser and Harré. In their book *The Rules of Disorder*, they do focus explicitly on football hooligan fighting, arguing that its violence is exaggerated by the media and that it is really nothing more than an 'aggressive ritual' in which people rarely get seriously hurt.[13] Lack of space prevents us from presenting a full critique of their case here.[14] It must be enough to say that their work is heavily influenced by ethology, especially the work of Desmond Morris, and based on the implicit assumption that ritual and violence are mutually exclusive as categories of behaviour. Accordingly, they seem unable to see that rituals can be *seriously violent*. In putting this criticism forward, of course, we are not denying the existence of a ritual component to hooligan behaviour. It is manifest, for example, in the aggressive posturing between rival fans and in the sequence of chanting and counter-chanting on the terraces, for, in these instances, the violence is, as Marsh *et al.* put it, 'metonymic' and 'symbolic'. What we are suggesting, rather, is that Marsh and his colleagues underestimate the seriousness of the violence which is sometimes involved in the fights between rival fans. They also neglect fighting outside and away from grounds, and the aerial bombardments which occur at football matches and which regularly include, as we said earlier, the throwing of dangerous missiles. It is difficult to believe that such missiles are thrown simply as part of an aggressive display that does not involve the intention to inflict injury, or at least the realization that serious injury could result.

As the title of their book suggests, Marsh and his associates saw it as central to their task to show that football hooliganism, an activity which is popularly perceived and portrayed by the media as 'mindless' and 'anarchic', is, in fact, governed by a set of rules. Sociologically, of course, that is hardly surprising. More to the point for present purposes, however, is the fact that their account of these rules rests at the surface level. That is, they failed to probe their social roots, the way in which they are socially generated. Consistently with this, Marsh *et al.* made no systematic attempt to examine the social origins and circumstances of the football hooligans who formed their subjects, hence contributing to the impression that, in their view, such rules are the voluntary creations of socially free-floating individuals. It is with an attempt to explain the social generation of the norms and values that are expressed in football hooligan fighting that we shall now concern ourselves. We shall draw in this connection on the work of Gerald Suttles[15] in an attempt to delineate the contours of a specific, lower working-class social figuration within which 'gangs' of adolescent and young adult males between which fighting is frequent are persistently generated and where norms of masculinity have grown up that stress toughness and ability to fight as central masculine attributes. After that, we shall offer an outline explanation of why Association Football has come to form a favoured setting for the expression of this distinctively lower working-class 'aggressive masculine style'.

VI FOOTBALL HOOLIGANISM AND THE LOWER WORKING CLASS: 'ORDERED SEGMENTATION' AND THE FORMATION OF FAN-GROUP ALLIANCES

Information on the social origins of the fans who fight at football matches is currently rather scarce, but data on those convicted for football-related offences are consistent with our own from participant observation and suggest that the phenomenon is predominantly the preserve of the lower working class. The Harrington Report, for

example, concluded in 1968 that 'the present evidence suggests that
. . . [football hooligans] are mainly from a working-class background
with the special problems inherent in large industrial cities and ports
where violent and delinquent subcultures are known to exist.'[16] Over a
decade later, Trivizas reached a similar conclusion, namely that 80 per
cent of the persons charged with football-related offences were manual
workers or unemployed.[17] Harrison's account of Cardiff City's
'committed rowdies' in 1974 had them coming from 'Canton and
Grangetown, rows of terraced houses with few open spaces, and from
Llanrumney, a massive council estate with an appalling record of
vandalism'.[18] And although, as we suggested earlier, Marsh and his
colleagues did not directly address the issue of class background in the
course of the Oxford study, some of their informants did provide
relevant comments. For example, one of them said:

> 'If you live up on the Leys [a local council estate], then you have to fight
> or else people piss you about and think you're a bit soft or something.'[19]

In fact, over half of the large contingent of Oxford fans arrested
during serious disturbances at the Coventry City v. Oxford United FA
Cup match in January 1981 came from the estate in question.[20] Evidence from Leicester supports this general picture, with one local lower
working-class council estate accounting for around one-fifth of the local
fans arrested at the Filbert Street stadium between January 1976 and
April 1980. This raises the question of what it is about the structure of
such communities and the position they occupy in society at large that
generates and sustains the pattern of aggressive masculinity that some
of their members display in a football context and elsewhere?

As we suggested earlier, a useful lead in this connection is provided
by the work of Gerald Suttles. His research was carried out in Chicago
and focused on communities whose overall pattern, as he put it, was
one 'where age, sex, ethnic and territorial units are fitted together like
building blocks to create a larger structure'.[21] He coined the term
'ordered segmentation' in order to capture two related features of the
pattern of life in such communities: firstly the fact that, while the
segments that make up larger neighbourhoods are relatively independent of each other, the members of these segments nevertheless have a
tendency regularly to combine in the event of opposition and conflict,
and that they do so without central co-ordination; and, secondly, the
fact that these group alignments tend to build up according to a fixed
sequence.[22] This pattern is similar in certain respects to what happens
in the 'segmental lineage systems' discussed by anthropologists such as
Evans-Pritchard.[23] Robins and Cohen claim to have observed a pattern
of this kind on a North London working-class estate[24] and, more

significantly for present purposes, Harrison refers to what he calls 'the Bedouin syndrome' in the contemporary football context,[25] namely a pattern in which there is a tendency for ad hoc alliances to be built up according to the following principles: the friend of a friend is a friend; the enemy of an enemy is a friend; the friend of an enemy is an enemy; the enemy of a friend is an enemy.[26]

Our own observations provide some evidence to support the existence of such a pattern both on working-class estates and in the football context. In Leicester, intra-estate conflicts involving groups of young male adolescents regularly give way to the requirements of defending the 'good name' of the estate as a whole against rival 'gangs' that represent neighbouring estates. However, lads from these estates and others from Leicester and the surrounding area stand side by side on the Filbert Street terraces and outside the ground in the cause of expressing 'home end' solidarity in opposition to visiting fans. If the challenge is perceived in regional terms, then, again, enemies may join forces. For example, Northern fans visiting London often complain about confrontations with combined 'fighting crews' from a number of metropolitan clubs. Euston Station used to be a favourite venue for encounters of this kind. David Robins even refers to alliances between fans of smaller, neighbouring clubs in London such as QPR and Chelsea, and Orient and West Ham, for purposes of confronting the fans of their larger metropolitan rivals.[27] Southerners and Midlanders visiting the North, especially the larger northern towns, also voice complaints about attacks by inter-end alliances. Finally, at an international level, club and regional rivalries tend to be subordinated to the interests of national reputation. At each of these levels, moreover, particularly if opposing groups are not present in sufficient numbers or if the challenge they offer is not, or is not perceived to be, sufficient to unite otherwise rival fans in common opposition, lower-level rivalries sometimes re-emerge. Having established how it operates in a football context, let us probe the structure of 'ordered segmentation' in greater detail.

VII 'ORDERED SEGMENTATION' AND THE FORMATION OF 'STREETCORNER GANGS'

According to Suttles, the dominant feature of a community characterized by 'ordered segmentation' is the single-sex peer group or 'streetcorner gang'. Such groups, he argues, seem 'to develop quite logically out of a heavy emphasis on age-grading, avoidance between the sexes, territorial unity, and ethnic solidarity'.[28] However, Suttles documents the regular occurrence of conflict between 'gangs' of the same ethnic group and recognizes elsewhere that ethnic differentiation and solidarity are contingent rather than necessary factors in the formation of such 'gangs'.[29] That is, age-grading, segregation of the sexes and territorial identification appear to be the crucial *internal* social structural determinants. More particularly, a strong degree of age-group segregation means that children in such communities tend to be sent into the streets to play, unsupervised by adults, at an early age. This pattern tends to be exacerbated by a variety of domestic pressures. Segregation between the sexes means that, by adolescence, there is a tendency for girls to be drawn into the home, although some form fairly aggressive 'gangs' of their own or simply 'hang around' the lads where their status tends to be subordinate. As a result of this social figuration, and apart from the attention they regularly attract from the police and other agencies, adolescent males in communities of this sort are left largely to their own devices and tend to band into groups that are determined, on the one hand, by ties of kinship and close or common residence, and on the other, by the real or perceived threat posed by the development of parallel 'gangs' in adjacent communities. According to Suttles, such communities tend to be internally fragmented but, he argues, they achieve a degree of cohesion in the face of real or perceived threats from outside. An actual or rumoured 'gang fight' engenders the highest degree of cohesion, he maintains, for such fights can mobilize the allegiance of males throughout a community.[30] But let us go beyond Suttles and explore some of the ways in which the structure of communities of this type leads to the production and reproduction within them of 'aggressive masculinity' as one of their dominant characteristics.

VIII   THE SOCIOGENESIS OF 'AGGRESSIVE MASCULINITY'

To the extent that their structures correspond to 'ordered segmentation', lower working-class communities tend to generate standards which, relative to those of groups higher in the social hierarchy, are conducive to and/or tolerate a high level of open aggressiveness in social relations. Several aspects of the structure of such communities tend to work in this direction. For example, the comparative freedom from adult control experienced by lower working-class children and adolescents, the fact that so much of their early socialization takes place in the street in the company mainly of their age peers, means that they tend to interact aggressively among themselves and to develop dominance hierarchies that are based largely on age, strength and physical prowess.[31] This pattern is reinforced by the fact that, relative to the tendency of adults higher up the social scale, lower working-class parents exert less pressure on their growing children to exercise strict and continuous self-control over aggressive behaviour. To the extent that parents in the lower working class do attempt to restrain their children in this regard, there is a greater tendency for them to resort to physical punishment. Moreover, such children become more accustomed from an early age to seeing their parents and other adults, especially males, behave in an aggressive and not infrequently violent way. As a result, they tend to grow up with a more positive attitude towards aggressive behaviour than their counterparts higher up the social scale and to be less inhibited about witnessing and publicly taking part in violent acts.[32]

Also crucial to the formation of this pattern is the tendency towards segregation of the sexes, and male dominance in communities of this sort. This means, on the one hand, that such communities tend to be characterized by a comparatively high rate of male violence towards women, and, on the other, that their male members are not consistently subjected to 'softening' female pressure. Indeed, to the extent that the women in such communities grow up to be relatively aggressive themselves and to value many of the *macho* characteristics of their men, the aggressive propensities of the latter are liable to be compounded. Further reinforcement comes from the comparative frequency of feuds and vendettas between families, neighbourhoods and, above all, 'street-corner gangs'. In short, lower working-class communities of the type we are describing, especially those sections of them to which the adjective 'rough' most literally applies, appear to be characterized by 'feedback' processes which encourage the resort to aggressive behaviour in many areas of social relations, especially on the part of males.

One of the effects of these processes is the conferring of prestige on males with a proven ability to fight. Correlatively, there is a tendency for such males to enjoy fighting. For them and their peers who strive to emulate them, it is an important source of meaning, status and pleasurable emotional arousal. The central difference in this regard between these 'rough' sections of lower working-class communities and their 'respectable' counterparts in the upper, middle and working classes appears to be that, in the latter, violence in face-to-face relations tends to be normatively condemned, whilst, in the former, there are a greater number of contexts and situations in which the open expression of aggression and violence is tolerated or positively sanctioned. A further difference is that there is a tendency in the 'respectable' classes for violence to be 'pushed behind the scenes' and, when it does occur, for it to take, on balance, a more obviously 'instrumental' form and to lead to the arousal of feelings of guilt. By contrast, in the communities of the 'rough' working class, violence tends to occur to a greater extent in public and to involve, on balance, more pronounced 'expressive' or 'affectual' qualities, that is qualities more closely associated with the arousal of pleasurable feelings. Furthermore, whilst members of the 'respectable' classes, especially 'respectable' males, are allowed, indeed expected, to behave aggressively in specific contexts that are defined as 'legitimate', such as formal sport, members of the 'rough' working class tend either to regard formal sport as too regulated and 'tame',[33] or, when they do take part, they tend, on account of their overly physical, sometimes violent approach, to fall foul of officials and opposing players.[34]

The identities of males from the 'rough' sections of the lower working class thus tend to be based on what are, relative to the standards dominant in Britain today, openly aggressive forms of *macho* masculinity. Many males of this kind also have a high emotional investment in the reputations of their families, their communities and, where they are into 'the football action', their 'ends' as aggressive and tough. This pattern is produced and reproduced, not only by the constituent *internal* elements of 'ordered segmentation' but also – and this is equally crucial – by some of the ways in which their communities are locked into the wider society. For example, lower working-class males are typically denied status, meaning and gratification in the educational and occupational spheres, the major sources of identity, meaning and status available to men higher up the social scale. This denial comes about as a result of a combination of factors. For example, the majority of lower working-class males do not have – nor do they typically prize – the characteristics and values that make for educational and occupational success or for striving in these fields. At the same time, they tend to be systematically discriminated against in the worlds of school and work, in part because they find themselves at the bottom of a hierarchical structure which seems to require a relatively permanent and relatively impoverished 'underclass' as a constituent feature.[35]

Because it is difficult for males from the 'rough' sections of the lower working class to achieve meaning, status and gratification and to form satisfying identities in the fields of school and work, there is a greater tendency for them to rely for these purposes on forms of behaviour that include physical intimidation, fighting, heavy drinking, and exploitative sexual relations. In fact, they tend to have many of the characteristics attributed by Adorno and his colleagues to the 'authoritarian personality'.[36] It is, of course, possible for these *macho* lower-class males to develop forms of relatively high self-esteem on the basis of local and, above all, peer group acknowledgement of their toughness, their prowess as fighters, their courage, their loyalty to the group, their exploits as drinkers, and generally because they handle themselves in a manner that they and their peers consider to be 'streetwise'. At the same time, because they stand at the bottom of the overall social hierarchy and because they experience a pattern of early socialization which – relative to the patterns characteristic of more 'respectable' groups – is conducive to a lower degree of internalization of stable controls on the use of violence, they are more liable to respond aggressively in situations which they perceive as threatening to their self-esteem. The complex requirements of 'street smartness' tend to limit the contexts in which fighting is regarded as appropriate by such groups. However, males of the kind we are describing do tend to rely on physical intimidation and to fight more frequently than males from other groups. On the one hand, they tend rationally to seek out physical confrontations because these are, for them, a source of identity, status, meaning and pleasurable excitement. On the other hand, they tend to respond aggressively in threatening situations because they have learned not to exercise the degree of self-control that is demanded in this regard by the dominant norms of British society.

IX VIOLENT MASCULINITY AND DISORDERLINESS AT FOOTBALL: SOME HISTORICAL EXAMPLES

Because they have relatively few economic and other power resources, and because they tend to experience unfamiliar territories and people as potentially threatening and hostile, the tendency to behave aggressively that is regularly produced within specific sections of lower working-class communities has tended to be expressed, for the most part, within these communities themselves. However, it has also been sporadically expressed outside them, thereby giving rise to 'moral panics' among more established groups. The areas of social life outside lower working-class communities where such aggressiveness has found expression have tended to shift under the influence of changing fashions, for instance from cinemas, to dance halls, to seaside resorts. However, it seems that one relatively permanent context for such behaviour has been provided by Association Football. That is, virtually since its emergence in the late nineteenth century in its modern form, the game has been accompanied by fan disorder, much of it involving physical aggression and violence. The incidence of such disorder seems to have varied over time, depending, for example, upon the changing attraction of the game to the 'rougher' sections of the lower working class, and upon the changing proportion of communities in society at large whose structures approximate to 'ordered segmentation'. Another way of expressing this second point would be to say that the changing rate of fan disorderliness at and in connection with football appears to have depended largely on the degree to which the working class has become 'incorporated' into the mainstream of British social life and hence constrained to adopt, in Elias's use of the term, the more 'civilized' values and modes of behaving characteristic of and demanded by the more 'established' social classes.[37] This raises a number of complex issues which we cannot hope to deal with in a paper of this length. What we can do, however, is cite a few examples of football crowd disorders that were reported before the present period and show how, according to our findings, the football hooliganism problem escalated to the 'crisis' proportions that are widely perceived as existing today.

The following report of a fracas between rival football fans at a railway station appeared in the *Liverpool Echo* in 1899:

> An exciting scene took place at Middlewich Station on Saturday evening, after a match between Nantwich and Crewe for the Cheshire Final. Both parties assembled on opposite platforms waiting for trains. They commenced operations by alternately hooting and cheering, and then one man challenged an antagonist to a fight. Both leaped on the metals and fought desperately until separated by the officials. Then a great number of the Nantwich men ran across the line, storming the platform occupied by the Crewe men. Uninterested passengers bolted right and left. The special then came in and the police guarded them off, many of them carrying away marks that will distinguish them for some time.[38]

Ten years later, in 1909, we are told by the *Glasgow Herald* that, at the Scottish Cup Final between Rangers and Celtic at Hampden Park,

> About six thousand spectators tore up goal-posts, fences and pay-boxes, set fire to them and danced around them in the middle of the pitch. Police, firemen and ambulance men were stoned, fire-engines damaged and hoses slashed. The police, after throwing the stones back at the rioters, finally cleared the ground at seven o'clock, at a cost of fifty four constables injured and the destruction of virtually every street-lamp around Hampden.[39]

Then, in 1920, according to a report in the *Birmingham Daily Post* of the court action taken by a spectator against Birmingham, now Birmingham City FC:

> Plaintiff . . . said he paid 1s to stand to see the match. The affair happened on 'Spion Kop' . . . Immediately after the interval, 'bottles were flying around like hailstones'. Witness tried to get away, but he was struck on the head, and received an injury which necessitated seven stitches. He had seen other disturbances on 'Spion Kop', and on one occasion a week or so before he was injured, he saw men using bottles as

clubs instead of using their fists. The bottles used were half-pint stout bottles.[40]

And, in 1934, a reporter in the *Leicester Mercury*, describing the return of Leicester City fans from a match at Birmingham, wrote:

> Everything had gone smoothly from the time of the departure at New Street and it was feared that something extraordinary had happened to cause the train to pull up . . . only 300 or 400 yards from its destination. After a thorough search of all the coaches, it was found that the communication cord had been pulled . . . [It] was ascertained that the hooligan element sometimes found on the trips had caused not a little damage to the rolling stock, some of it almost new. Windows were smashed, seats cut and torn, and the leather window-straps slashed with knives.[41]

These few examples go some way towards dispelling the mistaken notion that football hooliganism as a social phenomenon is entirely new. However, they do not give an idea of the changing rates of football hooliganism over time. Our finding, based on a detailed analysis of the Football Association's records and an extensive search of newspapers since the 1880s, suggests that, since that period, the rate at which fan disorders have been reported has followed a curvilinear trend. More specifically, the rate was relatively high in the three and a half decades before the First World War; fell, but never even remotely approached zero-point, in the inter-war years; remained low from the end of the Second World War until the late 1950s; then started rising, relatively slowly at first, but more sharply from the mid-1960s, especially from 1966 when the World Cup Finals were staged in England. How can one explain this pattern? Here, sketched in very broad outlines, is the explanation, partly hypothetical, on which we are working.[42]

Before the First World War, British society stood, in Elias's terms, at a somewhat lower stage in its 'civilizing process' than we do today. One of the consequences of this was that social relations then were generally characterized by a higher level of open violence, and this was reflected in the behaviour of football crowds, the social composition of which, ever since the dawn of crowd-drawing professional teams, has been predominantly working class. However, although this process certainly did not start then, and although it has been uneven, characterized by conflict and to some extent contradicted by opposing trends, since the end of the First World War the working class has slowly become more incorporated into mainstream society and accorded more of the rights of citizenship. As this process occurred, so there took place a diffusion of more 'civilized' standards down the social scale, a process that was reflected in the more orderly behaviour of football crowds and that was buttressed, it seems reasonable to hypothesize, by such more fundamental social processes as rising affluence, the growing power of trade unions, and the increasing equality of women.[43] Rising affluence would have contributed to incorporation and had a 'civilizing' effect by, for example, relieving some of the starker forms of domestic pressure and helping to provide alternative avenues for the establishment of satisfying identities. The growing power of trade unions would have had such an effect because it helped to secure improved pay and working conditions, and because it contributed to the increasing institutionalization of industrial conflict, hence in the longer term – though not as part of some simple 'progressive' trend – lessening its violence. And the growing power of women would have been 'civilizing' in its effects because it drew more men into the nuclear family and the home, hence softening the *macho* tendencies that had been more prevalent in former times. At the same time, parental control over the early socialization of children would have been increased, leading it to take place less and less in the context of the street and less and less under the sole or main influence of age peers. The lengthening of the educational process and the formation of youth organizations of various kinds would have worked in the same direction.

However, although this process of incorporation and growing 'civilization' embraced wider and wider sections of the working class, it did not affect all sections to the same extent. More particularly, the groups least affected seem to have been those who remained trapped in poverty at the bottom of the social scale. What appears, in fact, to have happened is that, whilst the 'respectable' sections of the working-class have increased in size, the gap between them and the dwindling lower working class, including the sections who remain 'rough', has widened. Although their numbers may have started to grow again in the course of the current recession,[44] it is these groups of 'rough' working-class people that tend to behave in ways that approximate most closely to the standards generated by what Suttles terms 'ordered segmentation'. Such youths and young men have been drawn increasingly into attending football matches since the 1960s, and it is they who constitute the majority inside the core groups who engage in the most serious forms of football hooliganism. In order to see how and why they have been drawn into the game, it is necessary, briefly, to examine some aspects of its treatment by the mass media.

X   FOOTBALL AND THE MEDIA

During the inter-war years and, in fact, right up to the 1960s, English football crowds tended to be praised by the media for their good

behaviour. More particularly, when incidents of misbehaviour by foreign fans or by fans from the non-English parts of the British Isles were
reported in the press, the reports often included statements of the 'it
couldn't happen here' variety. Take, for example, the following extract
from a report in the *Leicester Mercury* describing disorderly incidents
that occurred at a match in Belfast in 1928:

> . . . the half-time interval in a cup-tie between Celtic and Linfield was
> given to a diversion which introduced the stoning of the musicians in the
> band, and the intervention of the police who used their truncheons to
> keep the more heated rivals in the crowd apart . . .
>
> In many centres of England during the next few weeks the big issues at
> stake in the Cup and the League will unite thousands of people in a single
> thought . . . And happily all these things will be duly settled without a
> single policeman having to raise his truncheon to preserve the peace.[45]

Although the behaviour of English football crowds had grown more
orderly since before the First World War, reports such as this ignored
the disturbances that continued to occur at and in conjunction with
football matches in England throughout the inter-war years. Nevertheless, although they were marginally factually inaccurate in this regard,
by praising the 'typical' English fan they appear to have reinforced the
tendency for crowds to be well behaved and to have drawn 'respectable' people into watching football in greater numbers. In other words,
media treatment and crowd behaviour around this time seem to have
mutually reinforced each other to produce a 'feedback cycle' which had
the effect of leading to a more or less continuous enhancement in the
'respectability' of crowds.[46] In the late 1950s, however, in conjunction
with the 'teddy boy' scare and the more general moral crisis of those
years over working-class youth, the media picked on and amplified the
sort of violent incidents that had always from time to time occurred at
crowded football grounds. It was the preparations for staging the
World Cup in England in 1966, however, that appear to have been of
decisive significance in this regard. This event meant that English
crowds were about to come under the scrutiny of the *international*
media and, in that context, popular newspapers in England began to
focus on football hooliganism as a threat to the country's international
prestige. For example, in November 1965, when a 'dead' hand grenade
was thrown onto the pitch by a Millwall fan during the encounter of his
team with London rivals Brentford, the *Sun* printed the following story
under the headline 'Soccer Marches to War':

> The Football Association have acted to stamp out this increasing mob
> violence within 48 hours of the blackest day in British soccer – the

grenade day that showed that British supporters can rival anything the South Americans can do.

The World Cup is now less than nine months away. That is all the time we have left to try and restore the once good sporting name of this country. Soccer is sick at the moment. Or better, its crowds seem to have contracted some disease that causes them to break out in fury.[47]

Around the time of the 1966 World Cup too, the popular press started sending reporters to matches to report on crowd behaviour and not simply on the game itself.[48] Not surprisingly, these reporters saw incidents since, although by this time they were probably on the increase, they had always tended to occur at least fairly frequently in and around football grounds. What is more, because it tended to sell papers in an industry that was growing more competitive, and because of the increase in the moral and political panic about youth violence which occurred in the mid-1960s, they tended to report such incidents sensationalistically. In that way, football grounds began increasingly to be 'advertised' as places where fighting or 'aggro', and not just football, regularly took place. This drew in young males from the 'rough' sections of the working class, probably in greater numbers than before, adding to the already existing momentum for 'respectable' people to withdraw their support, especially from the goal-end terraces, and contributing to the position that we find ourselves in today: namely a situation where hooligan incidents are larger in scale and a much more regular accompaniment of matches than used to be the case and where the English hooliganism problem has been exported abroad to an extent sufficient to lead the terms 'English football fan' and 'hooligan' to be widely regarded on the Continent as coterminous. The mass media, of course, cannot be said to have *caused* this process but, by initially exaggerating what were usually only minor incidents and by, in effect, 'advertising' football grounds as places where disturbances regularly take place and where local reputations for more than just football are at stake, they can be said, as a kind of self-fulfilling prophecy, to have played an important part in the development of football hooliganism in its distinctively contemporary form.

Once adolescent and young adult males from the 'rough' working class had been attracted to the game in larger numbers, they stayed there, largely because football is, in a number of ways, a highly appropriate context for the sorts of activities that they find meaningful, exciting and enjoyable. At a football match, for example, they are able to act in ways that are frowned upon by officialdom and much of 'respectable' society, and they can do so in a context that provides relative immunity from censure and arrest. The game, too, can generate high levels of excitement and the focus of this excitement is a contest – a 'mock battle' with a ball – between the male representatives of two communities. Though formally controlled, usually less openly violent and, in a sense, more abstract, it is in many ways analogous to the sorts of confrontations which occur between the hooligans themselves. That is, it too is a form of masculinity ritual. Also, to the extent that the away team brings with it large numbers of the supporters, a ready-made group of opponents is provided and, in that context, the rivalries that exist between groups of local 'hard cases' can be at least temporarily submerged in the interests of 'home end' solidarity.

XI CONCLUSION

By way of conclusion, we wish to stress that our argument is not that youths and young men from the lower working class are the *only* football hooligans. Nor is it that all adolescent and young adult males from lower working-class communities use football as a context for fighting. Some fight elsewhere and others fight hardly at all. Our point is rather that youths and young men from the 'rough' sections of the lower working class – we do not regard the concepts 'rough working class' and 'lower working class' as synonymous in any simple sense – seem to be the most central and persistent offenders in the more serious forms of football hooliganism. Nor is it our argument that what we have described as some of the typical attributes and values of football hooligans are specific to these groups or solely generated by 'ordered segmentation'. Quite similar forms of masculinity are evident in the police force and the army, for example, and perhaps in other occupational contexts too.[49]

Finally, it is not our contention that, because hooliganism at football matches can be shown to be deeply rooted in the British past, it has therefore been entirely unchanging in its forms, contents and consequences. Among the factors at work shaping the specific character of the 'football hooligan phenomenon' since the late 1950s have been: the structural changes that have occurred in the 'rough' and 'respectable' sections of the working class, and in the relationships between them; the rise of a specifically teenage leisure market; the increased ability and desire of young fans to travel to away matches on a regular basis; changes in the structure of the game itself; specific attempts by the football authorities to curb hooliganism and, above all, the involvement of central government in this process; changes in the mass media, above all the advent of television and the emergence of the 'tabloid' press with its competition-generated and commercially oriented concept of 'newsworthiness'; and, finally, the recent virtual collapse of the youth labour market. In our view, these features, which are all in some sense at least historically specific, have made a significant contribution to the form, content and extent of football hooliganism since the 1950s. Where we differ from others who have written on the subject is over the extent to which any one or any combination of these features should be given central causal status in explaining the generation of football hooliganism. Our research leads us to believe that the values which underlie hooligan behaviour at football matches and in match-related contexts are relatively persistent, deeply rooted and long-standing features of the communities of specific sections of the working class. It follows, if we are right, that an adequate understanding of football hooliganism requires not only an analysis of social (including 'economic') developments since the Second World War, but, more crucially, a *developmental* account of, firstly, the manner in and degree to which such communities and the values they espouse have been produced and reproduced over a much longer span of time, and, secondly, of the varying extent to which football has formed an arena for the expression of these values.

10

Sport as a Male Preserve: Notes on the Social Sources of Masculine Identity and its Transformations

Eric Dunning

I INTRODUCTION

Few sociologists would disagree that the changing relations between the sexes are one of the most important social issues of our times, though the majority would probably see them as less important than, say, poverty, starvation, unemployment and racial conflict.[1] However, with the sole exception of the threat of nuclear war, which has universal implications and which would, in all probability, be universal in its consequences if the threat became reality, there is a sense in which relations between the sexes are *more* fundamental than these other issues. That is the case because, even though it is mainly middle-class women in the more industrialized countries who have begun to become conscious of male dominance, or patriarchy, as socially problematic and have started to fight against it, there is a sex/gender dimension to all other fundamental social issues such as class and race. However, despite the universality and social significance of gender differentiation and the increasingly problematic character of relations between the sexes in more industrialized societies – something that is especially evident in the break-up and/or transformation of traditional forms of marriage and the family that appears to be currently occurring – such issues cannot be said to have been adequately theorized sociologically as yet.[2] Nor, as part of the overall nexus that is relevant in this connection, has much attention been paid to sport, traditionally one of the major male preserves and hence of potential significance for the

functioning of patriarchal structures. Possible reasons for this twofold
failure of the sociological imagination are not difficult to find.

In recent years, mainly as a result of the feminist challenge, it has
become increasingly clear that sociology arose as a subject shot through
with patriarchal assumptions. Comte, for example, saw women as
'intellectually inferior' to men and believed that the family has to be
based on the dominance of the husband.[3] Not dissimilar assumptions
can be found in Durkheim's work[4] and they continue to pervade more
modern contributions to the subject. The sociology of sport is one of
the least developed areas of sociology[5] but, given the patriarchalism
implicit in the discipline in general, it is hardly surprising that assumptions indicative of an unquestioned male dominance have been widely
incorporated into such contributions as have been made to this field so
far. One of the consequences of this has been that the patriarchal
character of modern sport and the part that it may play in maintaining
male hegemony have been questioned only by a handful of feminist
writers. However, they have tended, for the most part, to focus on such
issues as discrimination against women in sport[6] and, although their
work has helped to bring about a situation where it is possible, none of
them has yet attempted a systematic theorization of the forms of male
dominance that exist in and through sport or of the transformations
that have occurred in that regard. I want to make a *start* in that
direction in this paper. More particularly, using British data, I want to
look at sport as a male preserve and at the part it plays, relative to other
sources, in the production and reproduction of masculine identity.
Before I become more concrete, however, I shall set forth some of the
principal sociological assumptions on which my substantive arguments
are based.

II   THE BALANCE OF POWER BETWEEN THE SEXES: SOME SOCIOLOGICAL ASSUMPTIONS

The first point to make is that, like all other social interdependencies,
the interdependency of men and women is best conceptualized, at least
in the first instance, in terms of the balance of power, or 'power-ratio',
between the parties involved. This constitutes a 'deep structure' within
which the ideologies and values that govern relations between the sexes
are generated and sustained. Although such ideologies and values
constitute an active ingredient in the balance of power between the
sexes – in the sense, for example, that they can play a part in mobilizing
men and women to fight for what they perceive their interests to be – it
is the case that transformations in sexual relations and in the ideologies
and values that govern them are often dependent on prior changes in

the underlying balance of power that are unintended and not embedded in specifically articulated ideologies and values. The second point is that the balance of power between the sexes will tend to veer in favour of men to the extent that violence and fighting are endemic features of social life. That is the case, of course, in warrior societies, but it also tends to hold true in industrial societies where the power of military relative to civilian elites is high. It also tends to be the case in those areas of social structure where social conditions lead to the production and reproduction of fighting gangs. The balance of power between the sexes will also veer in favour of men to the degree that their chances for engaging in unified action are greater than those of women, and to the extent that men monopolize access to and control of the principal institutional determinants of life chances, especially in the economy and the state. Furthermore, the more extreme the forms of male dominance in a society are, the greater will be the tendency for strict segregation between the sexes to prevail. A corollary of these assumptions is that the power chances of men will tend to be reduced and those of women correspondingly increased whenever relations in a society or part of a society become more pacified, when the chances for women to engage in unified action come to approximate or to exceed those of men, and to the degree that the segregation of the sexes begins to break down. A further corollary is that *macho* values will tend to play a more important part in masculine identity under social conditions where fighting is frequent and the balance of power is skewed more heavily in favour of men. Correspondingly, the *macho* tendencies of men will undergo what might be called a shift in a 'civilizing' direction to the extent that social relations are pacified, the power chances of women are greater, and sexual segregation is broken down.

Underlying these assumptions are two ostensible facts: firstly that, although there is a degree of overlap between the sexes in this regard, men tend in general to be bigger and stronger than women and, therefore, better as fighters; and secondly, that pregnancy and the nursing of children tend to incapacitate women, among other ways, as far as fighting is concerned. Of course, modern weapons technology has the potential for offsetting and perhaps for removing altogether the inbuilt fighting advantages of men. Similarly, modern birth-control techniques have reduced the time spent by women in pregnancy and nursing children. In other words, the power chances derived by men from their strength and capacity as fighters tend to vary inversely with technological development – that is, they are greater when technological development is low and vice versa. However, it is reasonable to suppose that the level of state-formation, more especially the degree to which the state is capable of maintaining an effective monopoly on the use of physical force, is probably the most significant influence of all.

This way of approaching the problems of male power and masculine identity derives from the work of Norbert Elias.[7] It is rather different from that of those Marxists who attribute the *macho* complex largely to the demands and constraints of performing manual work.[8] More particularly, whilst such constraints may play a part in sustaining the more extreme forms of *macho* identity, for instance by placing a premium on physical strength, it is difficult to see how they could have generated *on their own* an ethos in which toughness and ability to fight are central and which celebrates fighting as a principal source of meaning and gratification in life. Indeed, it is arguable that such an approach is itself an exemplification of the kinds of patriarchal assumptions that have been implicit in a lot of sociological theorizing so far. That is the case to the extent that the production and reproduction of material life are conceived as located primarily in the economy, and that the significance of the family and relations between the sexes are relegated, at least implicitly, to a subordinate position in this regard.

A point has now been reached at which some of the relationships between sport and patriarchy can be considered. In order to illustrate these relationships, three case studies will, fairly briefly, be discussed. These case studies are: the development of modern 'combat sports'; the emergence and subsequent (relative) decline of the *macho* subculture that traditionally came to be associated mainly with Rugby Union football; and the phenomenon of 'football hooliganism' as it exists in contemporary Britain.

III ASPECTS OF THE DEVELOPMENT OF MODERN COMBAT SPORTS

All sports are inherently competitive and hence conducive to the arousal of aggression. Under specific conditions, such aggression can spill over into forms of open violence that are contrary to the rules. In some sports, however – rugby, soccer, hockey and boxing are examples – violence in the form of a 'play-fight' or 'mock battle' between two individuals or groups is a central and legitimate ingredient. In present-day society, sports of this kind are enclaves for the socially acceptable, ritualized and more or less controlled expression of physical violence. It is solely with such 'combat sports', more particularly those involving a play-fight between two teams, that I shall be concerned in this essay.

The roots of modern combat sports such as soccer, rugby and hockey can be traced directly to a set of locally variable medieval and early modern folk games that went by a variety of names such as football, hurling, knappan and camp ball.[9] They were played according to oral rules through the streets of towns and across country. There were no agents of 'external' control such as referees and linesmen, and sometimes as many as a thousand people took part on either side. Despite the differences between them, one of the central characteristics of such games, relative to modern sports, was the high level of open violence which they involved. The players engaged in the relatively free expression of emotion and exercised only a relatively loose form of self-control. In fact, such games were a kind of ritualized fighting in which groups were able to pit their strength against local rivals whilst, at the same time, generating, in a relatively pleasurable form, excitement akin to that aroused in battle. Games of this type evidently corresponded to the structure of a society where the levels of state-formation and of social development more generally were relatively low, where violence was a more regular and open feature of everyday life than it is today, and where the balance of power between the sexes was skewed more heavily in favour of men. In short, these folk games were expressive of a fairly extreme form of patriarchy. As such, they embodied the expression of *macho* values in a relatively unbridled form.

The first significant developments in the direction of the 'modernization' of such games took place in the nineteenth-century public schools.[10] It was in that context that players began to be subjected to the restraint of written rules, many of them expressly concerned with the elimination or control of the more extreme forms of violence. In other words, the incipient modernization of football and related games involved a complex of changes that made them more 'civilized' than their antecedents had been. The comparative is significant. That is, they did not become 'civilized' in an absolute sense but only more so. They continued to reflect the patriarchal assumptions characteristic of a society still at a relatively early stage in its emergence as an urban-industrial nation-state. This can be seen from the fact that such games were justified ideologically, partly as training grounds for war, partly in terms of their use in the education of military and administrative leaders for Britain's expanding empire, and partly as vehicles for the inculcation and expression of 'manliness'.

A good idea of the norms of manliness involved in the public school games of that stage is given in an account by an Old Rugbeian which appeared in the school magazine in 1860. In it, he contrasted the then current game with the rugby football of his schooldays, some two or three years earlier. The Old Rugbeian wrote:

> You should just have seen the scrummages in the Sixth Match two years ago. . . . Fellows did not care a fig for the ball then except as it gave them a decent pretext for hacking. I remember a scrummage! . . . we'd been

hacking for five minutes already, and hadn't had half enough, in fact, the swells had only just begun to warm to their work, when a bystander . . . informed us that the ball was waiting our convenience on top of the island . . . And then there was Hookey Walker, the swell hack on the Sixth side; my eye! didn't he walk into the School! only shut up ten fellows for the season, and sent half a dozen home for the rest of the half . . . . [M]erely to see him come through a scrummage was a signal for all the ladies to shriek and faint. Bless you, my dear fellow, they enjoy looking on at a scrummage of all things now – more shame to us. And there was none of that underhand shuffling play with the ball then that there is now; no passing it along from one to the other; all was manly and straightforward. Why, to let the ball go after you had once got into a scrummage was considered to be as flagrant a transgression of the rules of football as to take it up when you were off your side. Nor did you see any of that shirking outside scrummages that's always going on nowadays. No one thought you worth your salt if you weren't the colour of your mother earth from head to toe ten minutes after the match had begun. But, dash my buttons! you haven't a chance of getting a decent fall in the present day; and no wonder either when you see young dandies 'got up regardless of expense', mincing across Big Side, and looking just as if their delicate frames wouldn't survive any violent contact with the ball. Hang the young puppies! We shall have fellows playing in dress boots and lavender-coloured kid gloves before long . . . My maxim is hack the ball on when you see it near you, and when you don't, why then hack the fellow next you.[11]

This account gives a good idea of the norm of 'manliness' which governed Rugby football at that stage. It also provides evidence for the contention that the game was being transformed in a 'civilizing' direction. Thus the Old Rugbeian recommended a return to the glories of his schooldays when, he claimed, 'hacking' – kicking opponents on the shins – had occupied a more central place. At the same time, he deplored the advent of 'passing' since, in his opinion, it was leading to the 'emasculation' of the game. The earlier standard he described is reminiscent of ancient Greek boxing and wrestling which, as Elias has shown, were based on a warrior ethos which decreed it to be cowardly to dodge or retreat from an opponent's blows.[12] Since the Old Rugbeian considered it to be 'underhand' and 'unmanly' to feint or pass to a team-mate in order to avoid being hacked, it seems that rugby football was at first based on a similar ethos. The ball was relatively unimportant to the game at that stage. Scrummages were indiscriminate kicking matches in which the 'manly' thing to do was to stand up to an opponent and engage in toe-to-toe hacking. It followed that strength and courage as a 'hack' were the main criteria for establishing a reputation of 'manliness' in the game.

The Old Rugbeian's account also gives an idea of the upper middle- and middle-class male ideal of feminine identity at that stage. Thus, whilst the ideal male is portrayed as swaggering and physically tough, the ideal female – in male eyes – is portrayed as timorous, weak and dependent. This corresponded to the image of masculine and feminine roles embodied in the form of patriarchal nuclear family which was then becoming the norm among the expanding middle classes. It is possible to speculate that, contrary to what is currently a widespread if not the dominant feminist view, this form of family may, in one respect at least, have represented a shift towards the equalization of power chances between the sexes. That is because it tied more males more firmly into the family than had tended to be the case before, thus subjecting them to the possibility of a greater and more regular degree of female influence and control. Also, possibly, working towards an equalization of power chances between the sexes was the overall 'civilizing' transformation that has been depicted here through the medium of sport. It would have had such an effect by placing a complex of internal and external restraints[13] on the expression of aggressiveness by men, for example via the code of 'gentlemanly' behaviour, thus restricting their opportunities for using one of their principal power advantages relative to women – their physical strength and superiority as fighters. This, in its turn, would have increased the chances for women to engage in unified action *on their own*, for instance by organizing marches and demonstrations. It would have had that effect by reducing the likelihood that such demonstrations of nascent female unity and power would be responded to violently by men, in a domestic context by their husbands and fathers, and in the context of demonstrations by the police and general public. More particularly, to the extent that a non-violent response from men to such political acts of women could be expected, the fears of women would have been reduced and their confidence correspondingly enhanced to go ahead with the struggle for what they believed to be their rights. In short, it seems reasonable to hypothesize that the power shift between men and women that first received public expression in the movement of the suffragettes may have been at least partly inherent in the 'civilizing' development that accompanied Britain's emergence as an urban-industrial nation-state.

An implication of the discussion so far is that, despite the fact that it continues to be suffused by patriarchal values and buttressed by predominantly patriarchal structures, modern sport emerged as part of a 'civilizing' transformation one aspect of which was an equalizing shift, however slight, in the balance of power between the sexes. However, this had the consequence of contributing to the development in certain spheres of symbolic expressions of *machismo*. An example is the pattern of socially tolerated taboo-breaking which, in Britain at least, came to be principally, though not solely, associated with the game of Rugby Union football.[14] It is to some salient aspects of this development that I shall now turn.

IV THE RISE AND DECLINE OF A MACHO SUBCULTURE IN RUGBY FOOTBALL

The traditions involved in the *macho* subculture of Rugby Union are enacted after the match either in the clubhouse bar or, if the team has been playing away, on the bus that is carrying the players home. Its central constituents include the male 'striptease', a ritual mocking of the female stripper. The traditional signal for this ritual to begin is a song called 'the Zulu warrior'. Initiation ceremonies are also a customary part of the rugby subculture. In the course of the ceremonies, the initiate is stripped – often forcibly – and his body, especially his genitals, is defiled, perhaps with shoe polish or vaseline. Drinking beer to excess, often accompanied by rituals and races which tend to increase consumption and the speed with which inebriation is reached, also came to be firmly embedded in the rugby club tradition. When drunk, the players sing obscene songs and, if the wives or girlfriends of any of them are present, a song 'Goodnight Ladies' is sung as a signal for them to leave. Events, henceforward, are to be exclusively for males, and any women who choose to stay are regarded as degraded.

These obscene songs have at least two recurrent themes: the mocking on the one hand of women, and on the other of homosexuals. At first sight, these two themes may appear to be unrelated but it is reasonable to hypothesize that both reflect the growing power of women and their increasing threat to the traditional self-image of men. Rugby began to become a game for adults in the 1850s. It was, at first, exclusive to the upper middle and middle classes, a fact which is perhaps significant because the majority of suffragettes came from the same social strata. In other words, it is reasonable to suppose that women at these levels in the social hierarchy were, in that period, increasingly becoming a threat to men and that some of the latter responded by developing rugby football – it was not, of course, the only enclave where this went on – as a male preserve where they could bolster their threatened masculinity and, at the same time, mock, vilify and objectify women, the principal source of the threat. A brief content analysis of a couple of rugby songs will illustrate how that may have been the case.

A principal recurrent aspect of rugby songs consists in the fact that they embody a hostile, brutal but, at the same time, fearful attitude towards women and the sexual act. In the ballad 'Eskimo Nell', for example, even the champion womanizer 'Dead Eye Dick' is unable to provide Nell with sexual satisfaction. This is left to his henchman 'Mexican Pete', who performs the task with his 'six-shooter'. In 'the Engineer's Hymn', the central character, an engineer whose wife 'was never satisfied', had to build a machine in order to fulfil the erotic component of his marital role. The machine succeeded where he had failed but, in the process, his wife was brutally killed. Seldom, if ever, are 'normal' men or women featured in these songs. Superhuman or extra-human powers are required before the 'hero' can satisfy the 'heroine's' voracious sexual appetite. Nothing could be more revealing of the function of these songs in symbolically expressing but also, perhaps, to some extent in symbolically reducing the fear of women who were experienced as powerful and demanding. Such fears are likely to have grown commensurately with the factual increase in women's power.

The second recurrent theme of these obscene songs is the mocking of effeminate and homosexual males. One of the songs traditional in rugby circles has as its chorus:

> For we're all queers together,
> Excuse us while we go upstairs.
> Yes, we're all queers together,
> That's why we go round in pairs.

The function of this chorus appears to be to counter the charge before it is made, and to stress and reinforce masculinity by mocking not only women but also homosexuals. In recent years, as women have grown more powerful and become able to challenge their factual subordination, if not their symbolic objectification, with a slight but nevertheless growing measure of success, less segregated patterns of relations between the sexes have increasingly become the norm. In that situation, men who clung to the old style and continued to enjoy participation in all-male groups must have had doubts cast upon their masculinity. Some may even have begun to doubt it themselves. Doubts of this kind must have been doubly threatening in a social situation such as that of the rugby club where the principal function was the expression of masculinity and the perpetuation of traditional norms in this regard.

British rugby clubs are now no longer such clear-cut male preserves as they used, formerly, to be. The loosening of the structures and ideologies that once held rugby players together in close-knit, all male groups has been a complex process, but just as, if the hypothesis advanced here has any validity, the emancipation of women played an important part in their development, so too has the continuation of this process made a significant contribution to the weakening that has subsequently occurred. A stage has now been reached where women are frequent and, what is more important, *welcome* visitors to rugby clubs. In part, it was financial contingencies, more particularly the use of dances in order to raise funds, that began to bring about this change. But this economic fact reflects wider changes in social structure, particularly in the position of women within that structure.

Dances brought women into the rugby male preserve with official approval. This does not mean that their presence had been entirely disallowed before. On the contrary, they have always been welcome – to make tea, prepare and serve meals, and to admire and cheer on their menfolk. But traditionally their presence was only tolerated if they were content to remain in a subordinate position. The more emancipated women who have now begun to enter clubhouses, however, whether in order to attend dances or simply in order to drink with their men, are increasingly unwilling to accept this. They tend to value independence, to be desirous of equality, and to realize the power which their desirability as mates gives them in relation to men. They are unwilling to accept behaviour which they regard as aggressively intentioned or, alternatively, they use obscenities themselves as a sign of their emancipation.

Since one is dealing here with an activity where women accompany men into a social enclave where the principal activity is male, male dominance remains very definitely involved. Nevertheless, the changes just discussed give an indication of the degree to which male dominance in British society has begun to be challenged and, to a limited degree, eroded. Of course it shows at the same time how far women still have to go in order to achieve anything approximating a measure of full equality with men. For one of the reasons why, in this case, they have to follow the men, is the fact that few comparable leisure activities are available for women. They remain, to a much greater extent than men, locked into domestic and family roles. The lack of leisure facilities for women reflects this fact. So, too, does the fact that it is still difficult for women to enter pubs alone without loss of status or without attracting the unwanted attention of men. This, in its turn, is largely the result of centuries of male dominance and an overall social structure that continues, by and large, to reflect and reinforce that dominance. It also reflects the existence of patterns of socialization which fit women principally for domesticity and the performance of subordinate occupational roles, and which limit their horizons, not only in the occupational sphere, but in the leisure sphere as well.

The changes described here as having occurred in British rugby clubs are, it seems reasonable to hypothesize, symptomatic of the social changes more generally associated with the development of modern sport. There is not sufficient space in this essay for a full discussion of the social roots of these changes. It must be enough simply to say that they occurred as part of the emergence of Britain as an urban-industrial nation-state and that this process involved, among its central, interacting components, the emergence of a social structure characterized by more 'civilized' standards of behaviour and a greater measure of equality between the sexes. There is, however, at least one apparent exception to this generalization: the phenomenon of 'football hooliganism'. That is because it appears to run counter to the hypothesis that 'civilizing' changes have formed part and parcel of the continuing development of Britain as an urban-industrial nation-state. I shall now offer a brief analysis of football hooliganism before developing some concluding remarks.[15]

V   THE SOCIOGENESIS OF FOOTBALL HOOLIGAN VIOLENCE

The most immediately evident characteristics of football hooliganism are fighting and the display of aggression between opposing fan groups. Football hooligan fighting takes a number of different forms and can occur in a variety of different contexts besides the football ground itself. It can, for example, take the form of hand-to-hand fighting between two rival supporters or between two small groups of them. Whatever the scale of the fighting, weapons such as knives are sometimes used in these confrontations, but not invariably. Football hooligan fighting can also take the form of aerial bombardments using as ammunition missiles that range from seemingly innocuous items such as peanuts and paper cups to potentially more dangerous ones such as darts, coins, bricks, slabs of concrete, fireworks, smoke bombs and, as has happened on one or two occasions, petrol bombs.

Missile throwing usually takes place in the context of the football ground itself, though it is not unknown outside it, especially when a heavy police presence prevents the rival fan groups from establishing direct contact. As a consequence of the official policy of segregating rival fans – a policy which was introduced in the late 1960s as a means of combating football hooliganism, though one of its principal effects has been to displace the phenomenon and increase the frequency of its occurrence outside grounds – hand-to-hand fighting is relatively rare on the terraces, though small groups of fans still occasionally succeed, by not wearing identifying favours, in infiltrating the territory of their rivals in order to start a fight. Participating in a successful 'invasion' is a source of great kudos in football hooligan circles. More usually nowadays, however, fighting takes place either before the match, for example in and around city centre pubs, or afterwards when the police are trying to shepherd the away fans to the railway or bus station. It is then that the largest-scale confrontations tend to take place. These often start with a 'run', that is with some 200 or 300 adolescents and young adult males charging down the street searching for a breach in the police defences that will enable them to make contact with the 'enemy'. When they successfully evade police control – what you might call 'hard-core' football hooligans use elaborate strategies in order to achieve this end – what typically takes place is a series of skirmishes, scattered over a fairly large territorial area, each one involving up to, say, 20 or 30 youths. Confrontations also take place when rival fans meet accidentally, as on underground trains and at motorway cafés. In addition, fights sometimes occur *within* particular fan groups, rival participants being drawn, for example, from different local housing estates or different areas of a town. Combined 'fighting crews' are also not unknown. For example, the fans of several different London clubs sometimes congregate at Euston or at one of the other main railway terminals in the capital in order to engage in a united attack on visiting supporters from the north.

During the match, the rival fan groups direct their attention as much or more to one another as they do to the match itself, singing, chanting and gesticulating as expressions of their opposition. Their songs and chants have, as a recurrent theme, challenges to fight and threats of violence. Particular fan groups tend to have their own repertoire of songs and chants but many of these are local variations on a stock of common themes. Central in this connection, as Jacobson has shown,[16] is the fact that their lyrics are punctuated with words like 'hate', 'die', 'fight', 'kick' and 'surrender', all of which convey images of battle and conquest. Here are a couple, cited by Jacobson, from the repertoire of Chelsea fans:

> (Sung to: 'Those were the days my friend')
> We are the Shed,[17] my friends,
> We took the Stretford End.[18]
> We'll sing and dance and do it all again.
> We live the life we choose,
> We fight and never lose.
> For we're the Shed,
> Oh Yes! We are the Shed.

> (Sung to: 'I was born under a wandering star')
> I was born under the Chelsea Shed.
> Boots are made for kicking,

Guns are made to shoot.
Come up to the Chelsea Shed
And we'll all lay in the boot.

Apart from violence, symbolic demasculinization of the rival fans is another recurrent theme of hooligan songs and chants, an example of this being reference to them and/or the team they support as 'poofs' or 'wankers', the latter accompanied by a mass gestural representation of the male masturbatory act. Yet another is degrading the community of the opposing fans, as, for example, with the following song:

(Sung to: 'In my Liverpool home')
In their Highbury slums,
They look in the dustbin for something to eat,
They find a dead cat and they think its a treat,
In their Highbury slums.

As one can see from this description, at least a significant proportion of the football fans who attract the 'hooligan' label appear to be as, or more, interested in fighting as they are in watching football. For them, the match is principally about expressing their *machismo*, either factually by inflicting defeat on the rival fans and making them run away, or symbolically, via the medium of songs and chants.

From this and the earlier discussion, it is clear that a central component of football hooliganism is the expression of a particular masculine identity, what one might call a 'violent masculine style'. The currently available evidence suggests that the majority of hard-core football hooligans come from sections of the socio-economically most deprived levels of the working-class, and it seems reasonable to hypothesize that this violent masculine style is generated by specific structural features of lower working-class communities. Gerald Suttles has coined the term 'ordered segmentation', to describe such communities and, he argues, one of their dominant features is the 'single-sex peer group' or 'streetcorner gang'.[20] Such groups, he suggests, seem 'to develop quite logically out of a heavy emphasis on age-grading, avoidance between the sexes, territorial unity and ethnic solidarity'. However, he documents the occurrence of intra-ethnic conflict between such groups and recognizes elsewhere that ethnic differentiation and solidarity are contingent rather than necessary factors in their formation. That is, age-grading, sexual segregation and territorial identification appear to be the crucial internal structural determinants. In a community where these are central elements of social structure, adolescent males are left largely to their own devices and tend to band into groups determined, on the one hand, by ties of kinship and residential closeness and, on the other, by the threat posed by the development of parallel 'gangs' in adjacent neighbourhoods. Such communities also tend to be internally fragmented. A partial exception, Suttles argues, is provided by an actual or rumoured 'gang' fight, for these can mobilize the allegiance of males throughout a community.

In a later development of this analysis, Suttles introduced the concept of 'the defended neighbourhood', suggesting that the adolescent street groups that grow up in slum communities can be seen as 'vigilante gangs' which develop out of 'the inadequacy of the formal institutions that have authorized responsibility for the protection of property and lives'.[21] This is an interesting idea, in some ways consistent with Elias's theory of 'the civilizing process' with its stress on the part played by developing state control in the emergence of 'more civilized' social standards. That is, following Elias, one would expect to find, even in an urban-industrial nation-state, relatively high levels of overt violence in communities where the state and its agencies have been unable or unwilling to exert effective control. Let me now explore the way in which the structure of such communities leads to the production and reproduction of 'violent masculinity' as one of their dominant characteristics.

To the extent that their internal structures approximate to 'ordered segmentation' and to the extent that they are not subject to effective state control, lower working-class communities tend to generate norms that, relative to those of other social groups, tolerate a high level of violence in social relations. Correlatively, such communities exert comparatively little pressure on their members to exercise self-control over their violent tendencies. Several aspects of their structure tend to work in this direction. Thus, the comparative freedom from adult control experienced by lower working-class children and adolescents means that the latter tend to interact relatively violently and to develop dominance hierarchies of which age and physical strength are central determinants. This pattern is reinforced by the standards characteristic of the dominant adults in communities of this sort. Sexual segregation, the dominance of men over women and the consequent lack of 'softening' female pressure all work in the same direction. Indeed, to the extent that the women in such communities grow up to be relatively violent themselves and to expect violent behaviour from their men, the violent propensities of the latter are compounded. Further reinforcement comes from the frequency of feuds between families, neighbours and, above all, 'streetcorner gangs'. In short, lower working-class communities of this type appear to be characterized by a kind of 'positive feedback cycle' which tends to maximize the resort to violence in virtually all areas of social relations, especially on the part of males.

One of the effects of this cycle is the conferral of prestige on males who can fight. Correlatively, there is a tendency for these males to develop a love of fighting, to see it as a central source of meaning and gratification in life. The central difference in this regard between lower working-class communities and those of their more 'respectable' counterparts in the upper, middle and working classes appears to be that, in the latter, violence in face-to-face relations tends to be normatively condemned whilst, in the former, it tends to be normatively condoned and rewarded. A further difference is the fact that there is a tendency in the 'respectable' classes for violence to be 'pushed behind the scenes' and, when it does occur, for it to take, on balance, a more 'instrumental' form and to lead to the arousal of feelings of guilt. By contrast, in the communities of the 'rough' working class, violence tends to be expressed to a greater extent in public and to take, on balance, an 'expressive' or 'affective' form. As such it tends to be associated to a greater extent with the arousal of pleasurable feelings.

It is reasonable to hypothesize that it is the 'violent masculine style' which is generated in this manner in the 'rough' working class that is principally expressed in football hooligan fighting. That is to say, the currently available evidence suggests that it is youths and young men from this section of the working class who form the hard core of those who most persistently engage in the more violent acts that take place in a football context. Of course, football is not the only venue where this style is expressed. It is, however, in many ways a highly appropriate setting. That is because the football match itself is a play-fight that is centrally about the expression of masculinity, though in a form that is socially approved and controlled. The football team also provides a focus for the identifications of young and young adult males from the working class, and the latter come to see the ground, more particularly, the goal-end terraces, as their own 'turf'. At the same time, football regularly brings into their territory an easily identifiable 'enemy', the supporters of the opposing team, and the latter are seen as 'invaders'. Finally, the large crowd at a football match provides a setting where what are officially perceived to be 'anti-social' acts can be engaged in with relative anonymity and impunity, and the large police presence provides the added excitement of regular brushes with the law. I have now reached a point where I can offer some concluding remarks.

VI CONCLUSION

In this essay, I have suggested that the origins of a number of modern 'combat sports' can be traced to a set of folk games the violence of which is indicative of their rootedness in a society that was more violent and hence more heavily patriarchal than our own. I then traced the incipient modernization of these sports in the public schools, suggesting that the 'civilizing' changes that occurred in that connection were symptomatic of a wider complex of changes, one effect of which was to increase the power of women relative to men. Some men responded to this power shift by establishing rugby clubs – they were not, of course, the only enclaves developed for this purpose – as male preserves where they could symbolically mock, objectify and vilify women who now, more than ever before, represented a threat to their status and self-image. The continuing emancipation of women has now substantially eroded this aspect of the rugby 'subculture'. Finally, I examined the apparent contradiction posed for my thesis by 'football hooliganism' and suggested that one of its central features is a 'violent masculine style' that is structurally produced and reproduced among specific sections of the lower working class. As such, it does not constitute a contradiction of my thesis but is indicative of the unevenness with which the 'civilizing' and state-formation processes have occurred and of the fact that there still exist in present-day Britain areas of social structure that continue to generate *macho* aggressiveness in a more or less extreme form.

A central difference between the *macho* complex expressed in football hooliganism and, more generally, in the violent masculine style of the 'rough' working class, and that expressed in rugby football, consists in the fact that the physical violence and toughness of rugby players tends to be channelled into the socially approved medium of the game, whilst that of the 'rough' working class tends to be a more central life commitment. It is noticeable, furthermore, that, whilst rugby players, when the subculture of their male preserve was at its height, tended to mock, objectify and vilify women *symbolically* through the medium of rituals and songs, women do not figure in the songs and chants of football hooligans at all. This is, perhaps, indicative of the lower power of women in the communities of the lower working class and, consequently, of the fact that they pose a lesser threat to men. Under such conditions, they are *factually* objectified and exploited to a greater degree, and subject much more to the open violence of men.

Probably the main implication of the present analysis is the fact that sport appears to be of only secondary importance with respect to the production and reproduction of masculine identity. Of far greater significance in this regard, it seems, are those features of the wider social structure that affect the relative power chances of the sexes and the degree of sexual segregation that exists within the necessary interdependence of men and women. All that sport appears to do in this connection is to play a secondary and reinforcing role. As such, however, it is nevertheless crucial in sustaining more modified and controlled forms of *macho* aggressiveness in a society where only a few occupational roles, such as those in the military and the police, offer regular opportunities for fighting, and where the whole direction of technological development has been for a long time to reduce the need for physical strength. Of course, to the extent that the socialization of women continues to lead them to be attracted to *macho* men, sports, especially combat sports, will play a part of some significance in perpetuating both the *macho* complex and the dependency of women that flows from that source. It is probably idle to speculate about whether combat sports would continue to exist in a more fully 'civilized' society than our own. One thing, however, is relatively certain in that regard: namely that, even though equalization tends to increase the occurrence of conflict in the short and medium term, such a society would in the longer term have to embody a far higher measure of equality between the sexes, the classes and the 'races' than has so far been achieved.

Notes

PREFACE

1 Norbert Elias, *The Civilizing Process*, Oxford, 1978; *State Formation and Civilization*, Oxford, 1982.

2 For a general characterization of this approach, see Norbert Elias, *What is Sociology?*, London, 1978; see also Johan Goudsblom, *Sociology in the Balance*, Oxford, 1977; and Peter Gleichmann, Johan Goudsblom and Hermann Korte (eds), *Human Figurations*, Amsterdam, 1977.

3 There are one or two notable exceptions. For example, Philip Abrams refers to *The Civilizing Process* as 'the most remarkable recent attempt to contain the social and the individual within a unified scheme of sociological analysis.' See his *Historical Sociology*, Shepton Mallet, 1982, p. 231. See also Zygmunt Bauman, 'The Phenomenon of Norbert Elias', *Sociology*, 13 (1), January, 1979, pp. 117–25. For a critical review of Bauman's article, see Eric Dunning and Stephen Mennell, '"Figurational Sociology": Some Critical Comments on Zygmunt Bauman's "The Phenomenon of Norbert Elias"', *Sociology*, 14 (2), July, 1979, pp. 497–501.

4 See, for example, John W. Loy and Gerald S. Kenyon, *Sport, Culture and Society*, Macmillan, London, 1969, p. 9.

5 As an illustration of this empiricist tendency, it must be enough in the present context to list the titles of the articles published in *The International Review of Sport Sociology*, 1 (17), 1982. They are: 'Factors Affecting Active Participation in Sport by the Working Class'; 'The Social Role of Sports Events in Poland and Hungary'; 'Sport and Youth Culture'; 'The Development of Play and Motoric Behaviour of Children Depending on the Existing Socio-Spatial Conditions in Their Environment'; 'Sports Activity During the Life of Citizens'; 'Sports Clubs and Parents as Socializing Agents in Sport'; 'The Flemish Community and its Sports Journalism'; 'Demystifying Sport Superstition'.

6 Scholars such as Alan Ingham and, although I disagree with many aspects of their approach, John Loy and Gerald Kenyon are prominent among these notable exceptions.

7 See, for example, John Clarke, 'Football and Working Class Fans: Tradition and Change', in Roger Ingham (ed.), *Football Hooliganism*, London, 1978; Ian Taylor, '"Football Mad": a Speculative Sociology of Football Hooliganism', in Eric Dunning (ed.), *The Sociology of Sport: a Selection of Readings*, London, 1971; and 'Soccer Consciousness and Soccer Hooliganism', in Stanley Cohen (ed.), *Images of Deviance*, Harmondsworth, 1971.

8 The neglect of sport may be more common among sociologists of education in Britain than it is in the United States, for there are quite lengthy analyses of sport in Willard Waller, *The Sociology of Teaching*, New York, 1932; and James S. Coleman, *The Adolescent Society*, New York, 1961.

9 Pierre Bourdieu, 'Sport and Social Class', *Social Science Information*, vol. 17, no. 6, 1978.

10 See, for example, Gregory P. Stone, 'American Sports: Play and Display' in Dunning, *The Sociology of Sport*.

11 David Lockwood, 'Race, Conflict and Plural Society', in Sami Zubaida (ed.), *Race and Racialism*, London, 1970, pp. 57–72.

12 In nineteenth-century Britain at least, the conflicts over the attempts to persuade the working class to give up what were perceived as 'barbaric' sports and leisure pursuits and to adopt more 'rational' forms of recreation constituted a social problem of not inconsiderable magnitude.

13 See Emile Durkheim, *The Elementary Forms of the Religious Life*, London, 1976.

14 Such an attempt is made by Robert Coles in his 'Football as a Surrogate Religion', in M. Hill (ed.), *A Sociological Yearbook of Religion in Britain*, no. 3, 1975.

15 For a discussion of sport and the division of labour, see Bero Rigauer, *Sport and Work*, New York, 1981.

16 For a discussion of this issue, see Norbert Elias, 'Problems of Involvement and Detachment', *British Journal of Sociology*, vol. 7, no. 3, 1956, pp. 226–52. See also his *What is Sociology?*

17 Attempts to break out of the common mould in some of these regards can be found in Christopher Rojek, 'Emancipation and Demoralisation: Contrasting Approaches in the Sociology of Leisure', *Leisure Studies*, vol. 2, no. 1, 1983, pp. 83–96; and John D. Ferguson, 'Emotions in Sport Sociology', *International Review of Sport Sociology*, 4 (16), 1981, pp. 15–25.

18 These terms are introduced by Norbert Elias in *What is Sociology?*, pp. 122 ff.

19 It has, of course, also been suggested quite often that sport might form a substitute for delinquency too.

20 Laurence Kitchin, 'The Contenders', *Listener*, 27 October 1966.

21 The idea of 'the detour via detachment' is proposed by Elias in 'Problems of Involvement and Detachment'.
22 See Johan Goudsblom, 'Responses to Norbert Elias's Work in England, Germany, the Netherlands and France', in Gleichmann, Goudsblom and Korte, *Human Figurations*, pp. 37–97.
23 See Ilse Seglow, 'Work at a Research Programme', in Gleichmann, Goudsblom and Korte, *Human Figurations*, pp. 16–21.
24 Goudsblom, 'Responses to Norbert Elias's Work', p. 79.
25 A more complete list of such dualisms would include: involvement versus detachment (value-bias versus value-freedom or ethical neutrality); subjectivity versus objectivity; nominalism versus realism; induction versus deduction; analysis versus synthesis (atomism versus holism); absolution versus relativism; nature versus society; individual versus society; change versus structure (dynamics versus statics); harmony versus conflict; consensus versus force; order versus disorder (structure versus chaos).
26 See, for example, Norbert Elias, 'The Sciences Towards a Theory', in Richard Whitley (ed.), *Social Processes of Scientific Development*, London, 1974, pp. 21–42.
27 For a discussion of 'sport' as a general term and one that refers to activities that are specific to modern societies, see Norbert Elias's essay 'The Genesis of Sport as a Sociological Problem', chapter 3 in this volume.
28 K. R. Popper, *The Poverty of Historicism*, London, 1957.
29 Elias in Whitley, *Social Processes of Scientific Development*, p. 23.
30 Ibid., p. 40.
31 Elias, *What is Sociology?*, p. 112.
32 Ibid.
33 Ibid., pp. 13 ff.
34 Ibid., p. 15.
35 Ibid., pp. 125, 135.
36 The term 'other-directed' is used here in a general sense and not with the specific meaning introduced by David Riesman in *The Lonely Crowd*.
37 Elias, *What is Sociology?*, pp. 74 ff.
38 Ibid., pp. 74, 93.
39 Exceptions in this regard are provided by the work of Immanuel Wallerstein and the 'dependency theory' of André Gunder Frank and others. Their work, however, still tends to be economistic.
40 Elias, *What is Sociology?*, pp. 138–9.
41 The concept of 'interdependency chains' refers to the bonds that exist between human beings linked through a system of functional differentiation. Such bonds can exist between as well as within societies. The concept is similar to the more usual concepts of 'division of labour' and 'role differentiation' but it lacks the economistic connotations of the former and the formalistic emphasis of the latter. It is also used in a non-harmonistic sense and without a connotation of equality, i.e. interdependencies tend to involve a conflictual element and they can vary along a 'symmetry–

asymmetry' continuum. Finally, the term 'chains' carries a connotation of the *constraining* character of social bonds.

42 See Elias, *What is Sociology?*, pp. 63–4 and 99–100 for a discussion of the concept of functional democratization.

43 See, above all, Elias, *The Civilizing Process* and *State Formation and Civilization* for an analysis of 'blind' or 'unplanned' social processes.

44 See Elias, *What is Sociology?*, pp. 156–7, for an explication of this concept. In order to remain strictly true to Elias's formulations, I have had to rely in this discussion to some extent on the original German. See *Was ist Soziologie?*, Munich, 1970, pp. 173–4.

45 *What is Sociology?*, p. 157.

46 *Was ist Soziologie?*, p. 173. The corresponding discussion appears on p. 156 of the English translation.

47 This concept is introduced by Elias in his *Engagement und Distanzierung*, Frankfurt, 1983, pp. 79 ff. An English translation, under the title *Involvement and Detachment*, is scheduled to appear in 1986.

48 C. Wright Mills, *The Sociological Imagination*, Harmondsworth, 1970, pp. 60 ff.

INTRODUCTION

1 Stephen Mennell and Eric Dunning have helped to improve the manuscript, Rudolf Knijff to produce it. I am very grateful to them.

2 Norbert Elias, *The Civilizing Process*, Oxford, 1978.

3 Norbert Elias, *Über die Zeit*, Frankfurt, 1984.

4 A fairly extensive discussion of the problems of involvement and detachment can be found in Norbert Elias, 'Problems of Involvement and Detachment', *British Journal of Sociology*, vol. 7, no. 3, 1956, pp. 226–52. For a longer enquiry, see Norbert Elias, *Engagement und Distanzierung*, Frankfurt, 1983.

5 If one uses the term 'parliament' indiscriminately for medieval and modern representative institutions, and avoids the term 'estate assemblies', one can easily overlook the innovatory change of Parliament in the eighteenth century.

6 J. H. Plumb, *England in the Eighteenth Century*, Harmondsworth, 1950.

7 I apologize for the use of neologisms. But 'industrialization', too, no doubt made people squirm when it was a neologism. What better way is there to facilitate awareness of the fact that the emergence of parliamentary government and of sport in the eighteenth century had the character of a process?

8 Cf P. Corrigan and D. Sayer, *The Great Arch*, Oxford and New York, 1985, pp. 88 ff.

9 Norbert Elias, *The Court Society*, Oxford, 1983.

10 See Norbert Elias, *What is Sociology?*, London, 1978, pp. 158 ff.

11 The imaginary setting of sport as a contest which is, in the last resort, a

game, and as such related to yet different from the real contests and struggles of people's lives, has sometimes given rise to the suggestion that sport is an imitation of real-life struggles. It is not wholly irrelevant that the problem of imitation occurs in this context as it does in that of art.

The oldest and perhaps the most famous discussion about the imitative character of human art is that to be found in Aristotle's *Poetics*. Doubts have been raised about the authenticity of the present text which is, in any case, fragmentary. But what we have is enough to show that Aristotle appears to have been the first to consider the problem of what it is that is being imitated, for instance by a tragedy. 'Tragedy is an imitation not of human beings but of action and life, of happiness and misery.' (John Jones, *On Aristotle and Greek Tragedy*, London, 1962, p. 30). Although the exact meaning of this sentence is not entirely clear, it seems to point in a direction which, I believe, still provides at least part of the answer to the problem of the mimetic character of human leisure pursuits. In his teachings about some of the leisure pursuits of the Athenians, Aristotle employed, and perhaps coined, two of the concepts that are most useful for enquiries into this problem area. I am referring to the concepts of 'mimesis' and 'catharsis'. One cannot be sure of their original meaning. But one can perhaps suggest what they can mean today. 'Mimesis' would gain a clearer meaning if it were not used simply as a more learned expression for 'imitation'. A *Madonna* by Raphael, a *Portrait* by Rembrandt and Van Gogh's *Sunflowers* are not simply imitations of the real thing. What one can say is that elements of the experienced object enter the experience of the same object's representation in a painting. But the experience of the painted object, although in some respects it resembles the experience of the real object, can hardly be called an imitation of the experience of the real-life object. By being painted, the object is transposed into a different setting. The experience of the object, and particularly the complex of feelings associated with it, is, as it were, if one passes from contemplation of the real object to that of the same object as part of a painting, transposed into a different gear. The feeling-aspects of the experience particularly, in that case, undergo a highly characteristic transformation, a *metabasis eis allo genos*. The term 'mimesis' can serve as a conceptual symbol which takes account of that transformation. Used in that sense, it would fill a gap.

Something very similar happens if one compares a real physical contest between human beings with a sports contest. The mimetic character of a sports contest such as a horse race, a boxing match or a football game is due to the fact that aspects of the feeling-experience associated with a real physical struggle enter the feeling-experience of the 'imitated' struggle of a sport. But in the sports experience, the feeling-experience of a real physical struggle is shifted into a different gear. Sport allows people to experience the full excitement of a struggle without its dangers and risks. The element of fear in the excitement, although it does not entirely disappear, is greatly diminished and the pleasure of the battle-excitement is thus greatly enhanced. Hence, if one speaks of the 'mimetic' aspects of sport, one is referring to the fact that it imitates a real-life struggle selectively. The design of a sport-game and the skill of the sportsmen and sportswomen allows the battle-enjoyment to rise without injuries or killings.

It is in this context, too, that Aristotle's concept of 'catharsis' can fill a gap in our conceptual equipment. Sports contests enable people to gain victory over others in a physical struggle without physically hurting them. The resolution of the battle-tension and the exertion through victory can have an exhilarating and purifying effect. One can enjoy the confirmation of one's own worth without bad conscience, a justified accretion of self-love in the certainty that the struggle was fair. In that way, sport provides for self-love without bad conscience.

12 Will Crutchfield, 'To Applaud or Not to Applaud', *International Herald Tribune*, 1–2 June 1985.

13 A variety of examples show that movements tend to be curbed, sometimes refined, in the course of a civilizing spurt. In societies at an earlier stage in a civilizing process, the speech-producing movements tend to be more closely associated with movements of the limbs or other parts of a person. At a later stage in such a process, loud and effusive gestures are usually frowned upon. Speech movements tend to become isolated. In the development of sport, too, one can find examples of this tendency. Earlier forms of what we now call 'boxing', for example in France and Japan, allowed the use of legs as well as arms for weapons. The English form of boxing confined the use of legs to the task of moving the person to and fro. On the other hand, the rules of English soccer prohibited (for all players except the goalkeepers and at 'throw-ins') the use of the arms as means of moving the ball and confined the propelling function to the legs.

Psychologists often investigate the emotions of adult members of their own society as if they had the same character as physiological data which are not much affected by built-in counter-impulses in the form of learned social controls. However, in their primary form, human emotions are closely linked to movements. Babies and small children show that very clearly. It is only gradually that the natural human potential for restraint is activated, and it is only when learned counter-impulses interpose themselves between feeling-impulses and the motor organs that the former assume the character of the emotions that are to be observed in the adult members of societies where a high level of civilizing restraint forms an integral part of the social habitus of most of the adults who are considered to be 'normal'. I doubt whether an adequate theory of emotions is possible as long as psychologists proceed as if their discipline were a natural science. One cannot adequately explore aspects of human beings such as these without a theory of social development in general and, in particular, of civilizing processes.

14 See Eric Dunning and Kenneth Sheard, *Barbarians, Gentlemen and Players: a Sociological Study of the Development of Rugby Football*, Oxford, 1979.

15 A more detailed examination of the balances built into the design of a sport such as soccer is provided in 'Dynamics of Sport Groups with Special Reference to Football', see pp. 208–222.

16 See Elias, *What is Sociology?*, pp. 71 ff.

17 Norbert Elias and John L. Scotson, *The Established and the Outsiders*, London, 1965.

18 Gustave Le Bon, *The Crowd*, New York, 1960 (first published 1895).

19 I am aware of the fact that there are exceptions, of which Julian Huxley's essay, 'The Uniqueness of Man', is well remembered.

1 THE QUEST FOR EXCITEMENT IN LEISURE

1 This is the revised version of a paper, 'The Quest for Excitement in Unexciting Societies', which was delivered at the 1967 Annual Conference of the British Sociological Association in London and originally published in *Sport and Leisure*, no. 2, 1969.

2 See Norbert Elias, *The Civilizing Process*, Oxford, 1978; and *State Formation and Civilization*, Oxford, 1982.

3 This is the preliminary draft from which, after a number of experimental probes, the more precise and comprehensive typology of the 'spare-time spectrum' emerged. See chapter 2 of this volume.

4 The term 'play' can be employed in a variety of senses, and the looseness with which it is often used opens up the way for specific difficulties and misunderstandings. Although we have tried to indicate clearly the sense in which we use the term, it seemed useful to have at one's disposal a more specialized term for the class of spare-time activities to which we refer under 5. The choice of the term 'mimetic' will become clearer in the course of our essay.

5 See Elias, *The Civilizing Process*, for a more extensive treatment of this problem.

6 Jean-Luc Godard, *Le Nouvel Observateur*, 1966. See also *Die Zeit*, 10 March 1967.

7 The concept of 'routinization' used here differs in certain very essential respects from that employed by Joffre Dumazedier in his *Toward a Society of Leisure*, New York and London, 1967, and by Georges Friedmann in his *Industrial Society*, Glencoe, Illinois, 1955. These authors use the term primarily to refer to the way in which mechanization and rationalization lead to monotony and repetitiveness in work tasks which induce feelings of boredom in those who work at them. As it is used here, however, the concept refers to the social and personal control of affects, to the routinization which plays a part in all situations where people have to subordinate momentary feelings and impulses to the set demands made on them

directly or indirectly by the functions which their social position has for others.

8 Norbert Elias, 'Sociology and Psychiatry' in S. H. Ffoulkes (ed.), *Psychiatry in a Changing Society*, London, 1969. See also Norbert Elias, *What is Sociology?*, London, 1978.

9 W. B. Cannon, *The Wisdom of the Body*, London, 1947; see also his *Bodily Changes in Pain, Hunger, Fear, and Rage*, New York, 1929. For further reading see M. L. Reymert (ed.), *Feelings and Emotions: The Moosehart Symposium*, New York, 1950; A. Simon, C. Herbert and R. Strauss, *The Physiology of Emotions*, Springfield, Illinois, 1961; I. J.-Saul, 'Physiological Effects of Emotional Tension', in J. M. Hunt (ed.), *Personality and the Behaviour Disorders*, New York, vol. 1, 1954.

10 See, for example, P. C. Constantinides and N. Carey, 'The Alarm Reaction', in D. K. Candland (ed.), *Emotion: Bodily Change*, New York, 1962.

11 See, for example, K. M. B. Bridges, *The Social and Emotional Development of the Pre-School Child*, London, 1931.

12 For his views on music see, particularly, Aristotle, *Pol.* VII and VIII. With regard to his views on affects in general see *Pol.* I. Psychological (ecstatic) catharsis (purgation) and somatic catharsis resemble each other in some respects and differ in others. Similarities: the throwing out of disturbing matter helps to restore a lost balance. Differences: the ecstatic catharsis produces only temporary restoration and is always accompanied by pleasurable sensations.

13 The extant version of Aristotle's *Poetics* is only a fragment of the original.

14 John Milton, Preface to *Samson Agonistes*, Collected Works, vol. 1, part II, New York, 1931, p. 331.

15 One cannot show here in detail the conditions under which this is likely to happen, though from such premises they are well capable of analysis. It may be enough to say that one of the factors of such a *metabasis eis allo genos*, for such a transition into another class, is the relative lack of autonomy of a mimetic event in relation to events in society at large.

16 Augustine, *Confessions* III. ii. 2

> Rapienbant me spectacula theatrica plena imaginibus miserarium mearum et fomitibus ignis mei. Quid est, quod ibi homo uult dolere cum spectat luctuosa et tragica, quae tamen pati ipse nollet? Et tamen pati uult ex eis dolorem spectator et dolor ipse est uoluptus eius. Quid est nisi miserabilis insania? Nam eo magis eis monetur quisque, quo minus a talibus affectibus sanus est, quamquam, cum ipse patitur, miseria, cum aliis compatitur, misericordia dici solet. Sed qualis tandem misericordia in rebus fictis et scenicis?

The question applies not only to tragedies, but to a wide range of entertainments. To the struggles of gladiators and wild bears in the circuses of Roman towns characteristic of the level of civilization in

Roman society; to boxing matches, all-in wrestling, motor racing, ski-jumping or baseball as well as theatrical performances of all kinds characteristic of the level civilization in advanced twentieth-century societies. It applies, in short, to mimetic performances of all kinds and the whole range of emotions involved in them.

17 *Leisure and Recreation*, New York, 1931, p. 249.

18 'The Play of a Nation', *Scientific Monthly*, XIII, 1921, pp. 351–3.

19 David Kerr, 'The Beatles at Shea Stadium', *Twentieth Century*, Autumn, 1966, p. 48.

20 Review by W. A. Darlington of Strindberg's *The Dance of Death* at the Old Vic with Geraldine McEwan and Sir Laurence Olivier, *Daily Telegraph*, 23 February 1967.

21 See chapter 6 of this volume.

2 LEISURE IN THE SPARE-TIME SPECTRUM

1 An extract from this paper was published in Rolf Abonico and Katarina Pfister-Binz (eds), *Sociology of Sport: Theoretical Foundations and Research Methods*, Basle, 1972.

2 For a discussion of the personal pronouns as a figurational model, see Norbert Elias, *What is Sociology?*, London, 1978, pp. 122 ff.

3 For representative examples of this literature, see Stanley Parker, *The Future of Work and Leisure*, London, 1971; Joffre Dumazedier, *Toward a Society of Leisure*, New York, 1967; and *The Sociology of Leisure*, Amsterdam, 1974; and Alasdair Clayre, *Work and Play*, London, 1974.

4 For the argument that sports are 'unreal', see, for example, Gregory P. Stone, 'American Sports: Play and Dis-Play', *Chicago Review*, vol. 9, no. 3, (Fall 1955), pp. 83–100; reprinted in E. Larrabee and R. Meyersohn (eds), *Mass Leisure*, Glencoe, Illinois, 1958, and in Eric Dunning (ed.), *The Sociology of Sport: a Selection of Readings*, London, 1971. See also Peter McIntosh, *Sport in Society*, London, 1963, pp. 119–20; and Roger Caillois, *Man, Play and Games*, London, 1962, pp. 5–6.

5 Dumazedier and some others have begun to draw such a distinction but a crude 'work–leisure' dichotomy and a tendency to use the terms 'spare time' (free time') and 'leisure' interchangeably continues to be common in writings on the sociology of work where leisure is mentioned.

6 It would be possible to design a corresponding typology of non-spare-time occupations based on the same theoretical frame of reference, and indicating, not only the difference, but also the continuity of the work spectrum and the spare-time spectrum. On one end of the scale are types of work almost wholly devoid of intrinsic and autonomous chances of enjoyable emotional resonance, though people often manage to derive from inherently emotionally dry work routines heteronomously specific forms of pleasurable satisfaction, for instance through gossip companionship, pestering newcomers, pride in the skill with which one performs the routines, competitive victories, and strikes. On the other end of the scale

are types of occupational work with intrinsic chances of a communicable personal emotional resonance as, for instance, teaching or doing research at a university, entering the parliamentary struggle as a Member of Parliament, conducting or playing in a professional orchestra, playing a sport or acting on the stage as a professional, writing novels and other forms of catering professionally for the leisure needs of others.

7   This tendency is, perhaps, most common in the work of Talcott Parsons.

8   Belvoir Street (pronounced *Beaver* Street) is a well-known street in Leicester.

9   See Talcott Parsons, *The Structure of Social Action*, New York, 1949, p. 75.

10   For a discussion of the concept of figurations, see Elias, *What is Sociology?*, pp. 13 ff.

11   See Norbert Elias, *The Civilizing Process*, Oxford, 1978; and Eric Dunning and Kenneth Sheard, *Barbarians, Gentleman and Players: a Sociological Study of the Development of Rugby Football*, Oxford, 1979.

12   William Stephenson, *The Play Theory of Mass Communication*, Chicago, 1967, p. 46.

13   Caillois, *Man, Play and Games*, pp. 5–6.

14   George Homans, for example, argued in his Presidential Address to the American Sociological Association in 1966 that sociology lacks autonomy as a subject and that psychology is the basic social science. A similar point is made by W. G. Runciman in his *Sociology in its Place*, Cambridge, 1970, p. 7.

15   See Elias, *The Civilizing Process*.

16   For a discussion of some of the research findings on extreme isolation, see Peter Watson, *War on the Mind: the Military Uses and Abuses of Psychology*, Harmondsworth, 1978, ch. 13.

17   See the critique of the *homo clausus* concept of human beings and the conceptualization of them as *homines aperti* in Elias, *What is Sociology?*, pp. 119 ff.

18   See chapter 5 of this volume.

3   THE GENESIS OF SPORT AS A SOCIOLOGICAL PROBLEM

1   This essay was previously published in Eric Dunning (ed.), *The Sociology of Sport: a Selection of Readings*, London, 1971. The theoretical framework embodied in it is closely connected with and, in fact, represents an enlargement upon, the theory of civilizing processes set out in Norbert Elias, *The Civilizing Process*, Oxford, 1978; and *State Formation and Civilization*, Oxford, 1982.

2   It is not possible here to enquire in greater detail into the problem why, in contrast to the almost world-wide diffusion and adoption of the 'soccer' type of English football, the diffusion and adoption of the 'rugger' type was far more limited in scope. But it may be worth mentioning that the exploration of problems such as this can provide a good deal of evidence

and can serve as a test case for specific aspects of a sociological theory of sport.

3 Author's translation from Agnes Bain Stiven, *Englands Einfluss auf den deutschen Wortschatz*, Marburg, 1936, p. 72.

4 Prince Puechlser-Muskau, *Briefe eines Verstorbenen*, 9 October 1810.

5 J. G. Kohl, quoted in F. Kluge, *Ethymologisches Wörterbuch*, 17th edn, 1957, article on sport.

6 *Larousse du XIXiéme Siécle*.

7 Norbert Elias, *The Civilizing Process*, Oxford, 1978; and *State Formation and Civilization*, Oxford, 1982.

8 For a discussion of modern professional wrestling as a type of farce, see 'American Sports: Play and Dis-Play' and 'Wrestling: the Great American Passion Play' by Gregory P. Stone, in Eric Dunning (ed.), *The Sociology of Sport: a Selection of Readings*, London, 1971.

9 H. Foerster, *Die Sieger in den Olympischen Spielen*, Zwickau, 1891.

10 Franz Mezoe, *Geschichte der Olympischen Spiele,* Munich, 1030, pp. 100–1; quoted in Ludwig Dress, *Olympia; Gods, Artists and Athletes*, London, 1968, p. 83.

11 Philostratos, *On Gymnastics* (Peri Gymnastike), first half of the third century AD, ch. II.

12 Philostratos mentions that thongs made from pig's hide were forbidden because it was believed that the injuries inflicted by them were too severe. Also that one should not punch with the thumb. It is perhaps worth mentioning these details. One should not think that the customary rules of game-contests in antiquity showed no regard at all for the participants. But rules such as these were simply handed on by oral tradition and thus still left a very wide scope for serious injuries.

13 See Norbert Elias, 'Studies in the Genesis of the Naval Profession', *British Journal of Sociology*, vol. 1, no. 4, December 1950.

14 Philostratos, *On Gymnastics*, ch. 11.

15 Ibid., ch. 43.

16 Dress, *Olympia*, p. 82.

17 Ibid.

18 Ibid., p. 81.

19 For an explanation of this term and for a discussion of problems of 'objectivity' in sociology, see Norbert Elias, 'Problems of Involvement and Detachment', *British Journal of Sociology*, vol. 7, September 1956. See also Norbert Elias, *Involvement and Detachment*, Oxford (forthcoming).

20 One does not need to discuss here the reasons for the wave of secularization which shows itself, among other things, in the transition from the more solemn, more awe-inspiring, and perhaps more expressive representations of gods and heroes in the archaic period – an example is the Medusa from the pediment of the temple of Artemis at Corcyra, 6th century BC – to the idealizing realism of the classical period where gods and heroes are represented as well-proportioned warriors, young or old,

whose bodies speak, though their faces are perhaps a little empty even if, as in the case of the Delphi charioteer, the inlaid eyes and part of the colour have been preserved.

21 The extent to which the characteristics of an earlier stage in the development of state organization, especially in the monopolization and control of physical violence, affects all human relationships, shows itself, among other things, in the frequency with which Greek legends refer to conflicts between father and son. So far as Greek society is concerned, Freud was probably misled in his interpretation of the Oedipus legend or, at least, he saw only one side of the picture, that of a single individual, the son. In the context of Greek society, one cannot help but notice the specific social figuration reflected in this, as in other, related Greek legends. One cannot help questioning the relationship between the son and the father, the young king and the old king, from the father's side as well as from the son's side. From the son's side it may well be, as Freud said, tinged with jealousy over the father's possession of the wife – and, one may add, with fear of the father's physical strength and power. Seen, however, from the father's side, as reflected in Greek legends, the old king's fear and jealousy of the son plays an equal part in the relationship between the two. For, inevitably, the father will grow older and physically weaker, the son, weak as a little child, will grow physically stronger and more vigorous. In ancient times, when the well-being of a whole community, of a clan or a house, was not only factually but – in the imagination of the members of such groups – magically bound up with the health and vigour of the king or the leader, the older man was often ritually killed when he grew older, when his strength and vigour departed, and replaced by one of his sons, the young king. Numerous Greek legends show that the young son, the future heir, had to be hidden from the wrath and persecution of his father while he was still young and that he usually had to be educated by strangers. Thus, 'we know', according to a recent study (Edna H. Hooker, *The Goddess of the Golden Image, in Parthenos and Parthenon, Greece and Rome*, supplement to vol. X, Oxford, 1963, p. 18), 'that royal children in primitive agrarian communities were in constant danger as a potential threat to the king's tenure of his throne or sometimes to a stepmother's ambition for her own sons. Few princes in Greek myth and legend were brought up at home. Some were sent to the Centaur, Cheiron; but most were exposed with tokens of their origin to be reared by strangers'.

King Laius exposed his son Oedipus, fearing that he would be killed by him. Zeus was reared by nurses and brought up in secrecy because his father Kronos felt that he was a menace and tried to kill him. Zeus himself, like Jahwe, was afraid that man would learn to participate in his magical knowledge and violently punished the younger man, Prometheus, who had dared to steal fire from heaven and to give it to people.

It may well be that the escalation of mutual rivalry and jealousy as one ingredient in the complex relationship between father and son, the peculiar process whose reflections we find in Greek and in many other legends, no longer play the part in a society where even male relatives no longer endanger one another's lives, where the state has monopolized the right to use physical violence, that it once played in societies where fathers could kill or expose their children. It would require more figurational investigations of fathers and sons, in order to find out to what extent the son's feeling of rivalry and jealousy of the father, as discovered in his patients by Freud, is at the same time a reaction to the father's feeling of rivalry and jealousy of the son. But if one considers Greek legends, above all the Oedipus legend itself, one can hardly doubt the double-sidedness, the reciprocal feelings of rivalry which play a part in the relationship between father and son. The use made of this legend as a theoretical model seems incomplete as long as the part played by the dynamics of this figuration, by the reciprocity of feelings between a son who, from being weak got stronger, and a father who, from being strong gets weaker, is more fully investigated. In societies where physical strength and power played a much larger part than they do today in the relationships within as well as outside a family, this figuration must have had very great and by no means only unconscious significance. Seen in this context, the Oedipus legend reads like a legend designed to threaten sons that they will be punished by the gods if they kill their fathers. However, the salient point about the legend is probably not, in the first place, the killing of the old king by or in favour of the young king but the breaking of the incest taboo, of the prohibition of the son's intercourse with his mother which, of course, is a much older social prohibition than that against killing the father. In this respect, the Oedipus myth evidently symbolizes a relatively late stage in the development of a society in which, at an earlier stage, neither the killing of the young son nor the killing of the old father was a crime. These legends, thus, can help us to understand a type of human relationship which existed at a stage of social development when the organization which we now call the 'state' was still in its infancy, and when the physical strength of a person, his capacity to ensure his survival through his own fighting power, was a major determinant of all types of human relationships, including that between father and son.

22 Pierre Ducrey, *Le Traitement de Prisonniers de Guerre dans la Grèce antique*, Ecole Francaise d'Athenes, Travaux et Memoires, Fas. XVIII, Paris, 1968, pp. 196 ff.

23 Fr. Schwenn, *Die Menschenopfer bei den Griechen und Romern*, Giessen, 1915.

24 I am quoting these fragments in the translation which Eric A. Havelock has published in his book, *The Liberal Temper in Greek Politics*, New Haven and London, 1964, pp. 127–8. I think his attempt at conveying to a contemporary English-speaking reader the meaning of these fragments, as far as that is possible, succeeds rather well. He also shows, more clearly perhaps than many other writers, that the stress which Plato and Aristotle laid on the central authority of the state as the primary issue of political

problems is often wrongly regarded as characteristic of the ancient Greeks in general, whereas in fact this stress is, at most, characteristic of a late and perhaps only the last phase in the development of the independent Greek city-states. I cannot quite agree, however, with Professor Havelock's interpretation of the teachings of philosophers such as Democritus as 'liberal'. Liberalism as a political philosophy presupposes a very highly developed state organization even though it is aimed at preventing too great an interference of the representatives of the state into the affairs of its individual members. The self-reliance of the individual which Democritus advocates, on the other hand, is characteristic of a stage of development in which an individual and his kin-group cannot yet count on the protection of a reasonably effective and impersonal state organization. It is not really a 'liberal' idea that men have a right and a duty to avenge themselves and to kill their own enemies.

4   AN ESSAY ON SPORT AND VIOLENCE

1 John Stow, *A Survey of London* (1956), first published in 1603 and reprinted in Oxford in 1908.
2 Ibid., pp. 96 ff.
3 Norbert Elias, *State Formation and Civilisation*, Oxford, 1982, pp. 258 ff. 'Feudalization' is an example of a spurt in the opposite direction.
4 Thus Geoffrey Green in his *History of the Football Association* (London, 1953, p. 7) takes the reference to 'the famous game of ball' (*ludum pilae celebrem*) by William Fitzstephen in his panegyric *Descriptio Nobilissimae Civitatis Londinae* (1175, quoted in Stow, *A Survey of London*) as evidence for the fact that football was played by the youth of London in the twelfth century. Though more cautious, Morris Marples in his *A History of Football* (London, 1954, pp. 19–21) concludes that 'there is a good reason to suppose that Fitzstephen is actually describing football.'
5 For an elaboration of this point, see Norbert Elias, *What is Sociology?*, London, 1978, pp. 75–6.
6 Not all games are 'sports' and not all sports are 'games'. The term 'sport-games' refers to those – football, rugby, tennis, cricket, golf, etc. – to which both terms apply.
7 Basketball, which, in its initial form, was invented by Dr James Naismith of Springfield, Massachusetts, is an example of such a game.
8 The point being made here is not weakened by the fact that both 'batsmen' and 'bowlers' in cricket and comparable games alternate defence and attack depending, for example, on the course of the game-contest and the stage in it that has been reached.
9 An example is the change in the 'offside law' introduced in soccer in 1923. For a discussion of this rule change, see chapter 6 of this volume.
10 One often fails to realize how slowly social institutions and the personality structure of individual people have developed to a stage where it is the

norm in all social strata that a grown-up person should be capable of pursuing a specialized activity with single-mindedness and without being distracted from it by other, perhaps momentarily more attractive goals. The fact that the fox-hunting ritual demanded such single-mindedness and the corresponding self-discipline in pursuit of the fox is one example.

I remember another. It may help to increase understanding of the fact that the concentration of attention and conduct on a single goal for hours, days, years on end which – not entirely without a struggle with oneself – can now be regarded in many countries as a normal attainment of persons of all classes, is something which developed slowly in the course of time. It could be taken for granted far less in earlier stages. Thus the disciplinary code approved by the Earl of Leicester for the use of the troops serving under him in the Netherlands in 1585 ordained in art. 48 that soldiers marching in a column along the fields should not start shouting, and presumably disturbing the whole column, if they happened to encounter a hare or any other beast on the way (see C. J. Cruikshank, *Elizabeth's Army*, Oxford, 1966, p. 161). The whole code is instructive. It can serve as a reminder of how few forms of conduct and sentiment which may at present appear to be simply self-evident or rational can be taken for granted.

11   Blaine, *Encyclopaedia of Rural Sports*, London, 1852, p. 89.
12   Quoted in Peter Beckford, *Thoughts on Hare and Foxhunting*, London, 1796, p. 197.
13   Ibid., p. 239.
14   Ibid., p. 166.
15   Ibid., p. 169.
16   Norbert Elias, *The Civilizing Process*, Oxford, 1978, pp. 202 ff.
17   Beckford, *Thoughts on Hare and Foxhunting*, pp. 199 ff. Italics in the original.
18   Ibid., p. 38.
19   Stonehenge, *Manual of Sports*, London, 1856, p. 109.
20   Beckford, *Thoughts on Hare and Foxhunting*, p. 173 (italics added). What Beckford was saying, in other words, was that, if the hounds are trained to kill and like killing, they will in future give good sport. He wished to stress, as one can see, that the pleasure of the battle-excitement and the pleasure of the climax are interdependent.
21   In *Thoughts on Hare and Foxhunting* Beckford underlined the advantages of a peaceful country sport such as fox-hunting by a quotation from a poem: 'No fierce unruly senate threatens here, No axe or scaffold to the view appear. No envy, disappointment and despair.'
22   For observations on the specific type of social control which makes for the development of self-control, see pp. 229 ff of Elias, *State Formation and Civilization*.

5 FOLK FOOTBALL IN MEDIEVAL AND EARLY MODERN BRITAIN

1 Many historians of football treat earlier references to the game as equally reliable. We think that this confidence is not wholly justified and Norbert Elias gives some of our reasons for this scepticism in chapter 4 of this volume. The present chapter was previously published in Eric Dunning (ed.), *The Sociology of Sport: a Selection of Readings*, London, 1971.
2 H. T. Riley (ed.), *Munimenta Gildhallae Londoniensis*, Rolls. Ser., No. 12, London 1859–62, vol. III, appendix ii, extracts from the *Liber Memorandum*, pp. 439–41, Latin and Anglo-French text, with English translation of the Anglo-French.
3 Cal. of Close Rolls, Ed. III (1910), pp. 181–2.
4 J. C. Jeafferson (ed.), *Middlesex County Records*, London 1886–7, p. 97.
5 See a contemporary account published in D. Lysens, *Magna Britannia*, London, 1810; it is also quoted in T. F. T. Dyer, *British Popular Customs*, London, 1900, pp. 70–2.
6 J. F. Earwaker (ed.), *The Court Leet Records of the Manor of Manchester*, London, 1887, p. 248.
7 'The mayor was at the time Andrew Aubrey of the Pepperer's Company, a very wealthy man.' *The Chronicles of London*, Collectanea Adamantea X, Edinburgh, 1885, from 44, Henry III to 17, Edward III, p. 27.
8 Ibid., p. 27.
9 There is every reason to believe that relatively uninstitutionalized forms of football existed side by side with the more ritualized forms in medieval England. In this context, the important thing to grasp is the relatively high level of violence in the latter.
10 See, for example, Robert Redfield who has written, 'Thus we may characterise the folk society as small, isolated, nonliterate and homogeneous, with a strong sense of group solidarity'; 'The Folk Society', *American Journal of Sociology*, no. 52, 1947, pp. 292–308.
11 Ibid.
12 Ibid.
13 C. H. Cooper, *Annals of Cambridge*, Cambridge, 1843, p. 71.
14 O. W. Farrer, *The Marblers of Purbeck*, papers read before the Purbeck Society (1859–60), pp. 192–7.
15 For example, the Manchester decrees promulgated in 1608 and 1609. See p. 194 above.
16 Richard Carew, *A Survey of Cornwall*, London, 1602, pp. 73–5.

6 DYNAMICS OF SPORT GROUPS WITH SPECIAL REFERENCE TO FOOTBALL

1 This chapter first appeared as an article in *British Journal of Sociology*, vol. XVII, no. 4, December 1966, and was reproduced in Eric Dunning (ed.), *The Sociology of Sport: a Selection of Readings*, London, 1971.
2 We are referring here to small group theory in the sense in which this term

is currently used in sociology. We are not referring to other theories of small groups, such as, for example, those concerned with problems of group therapy, although in those cases, too, the figurational approach may be of help.

3 G. Green, *The History of the Football Association*, London, 1953.

4 G. Homans, *Social Behaviour: Its Elementary Forms*, London, 1961, p. 130.

5 R. Dahrendorf, *Class and Class Conflict in Industrial Society*, London, 1959, p. 164.

6 It has been dealt with extensively in Norbert Elias, *The Civilizing Process*, Oxford, 1978, and *State Formation and Civilization*, Oxford, 1982.

7 See chapter 5 of the present volume.

8 For a sociological analysis of the development of football in the public schools, see Eric Dunning and Kenneth Sheard, *Barbarians, Gentlemen and Players*, Oxford, 1979.

9 In order to avoid misunderstanding one has to add that the term 'sociological realism' as used here does not mean what it means if it is applied to Durkheim's theory. Durkheim could not escape from a position where social phenomena appeared as something abstracted and apart from individuals. These abstractions he sometimes reified: he never got beyond a stage where 'society' and 'individuals' appear as separate entities which he tried to bring together again in the end by an almost mystical hypothesis. This criticism is perfectly compatible with the recognition of the intellectual calibre of his work and the scientific advances due to him.

10 There is one characteristic difference between the tension-balance of antagonistic muscles and that of antagonistic players in a game. In the case of muscles, one side relaxes when the other is tensed. In the case of players, the specific character of the tension-balance is due to the fact that both sides are 'tensed'.

7 THE DYNAMICS OF MODERN SPORT

1 This essay was previously published in *Sportwissenschaft*, vol. 9, 1979, 4, under the title 'The Figurational Dynamics of Modern Sport: Notes on the Sociogenesis of Achievement-Striving and the Social Signifiance of Sport'. It is based on the analysis in Eric Dunning and Kenneth Sheard, *Barbarians, Gentlemen and Players*, Oxford, 1979. However the analysis presented here goes beyond that presented there in a number of ways.

2 For a full documentation and analysis of this process, see ibid.

3 *The Civilizing Process*, Oxford, 1978.

4 *What is Sociology?*, London, 1978.

5 That is to say from an evaluation that reflected the interests and values of specific groups in the wider society and that was not worked out autonomously by us specifically for purposes of sociological analysis. See Norbert Elias, 'Problems of Involvement and Detachment', *British Journal of Sociology*, vol. 7, 1956, pp. 226–52.

6 Norbert Elias and Eric Dunning, 'Dynamics of Sport Groups with Special Reference to Football', *British Journal of Sociology*, vol. 17, 1966, p. 79, and chapter 6 of this volume.

7 J. Huizinga, *Homo Ludens: a Study of the Play Element in Culture*, London, 1949.

8 G. P. Stone, 'American Sports: Play and Dis-Play', in Eric Dunning (ed.), *The Sociology of Sport: a Selection of Readings*, London, 1971.

9 B. Rigauer, *Sport und Arbeit*, Frankfurt, 1969.

10 *Homo Ludens*, pp. 223 f.

11 The term 'functional democratization' was, in fact, coined later by Elias to represent more adequately what he had earlier referred to simply as 'growing structural pressure from below'.

12 State-formation, functional democratization and the civilizing process can, I think, also explain this trend more satisfactorily than the hypothesis that a Weberian might develop in this connection, for example that there may be a *Wahlverwandtschaft* or 'elective affinity' between ascetic Protestantism and serious, achievement-oriented forms of sports participation in much the same way that such a relationship was held by Weber to have existed between ascetic Protestantism and the 'spirit of capitalism'. Such an hypothesis is a priori plausible but runs into difficulties such as that posed by the fact that, in England at least, the ascetic Protestants tried to ban sports and pastimes altogether. In any case, Elias's hypothesis is more inclusive and could, potentially at any rate, account sociogenetically for the Protestant ethic. Moreover, with its dissolution and transcendance, firstly, of the dichotomy between 'the material' and 'the ideal', and secondly of that between 'causes' and 'effects' – with its stress on nexuses or constellations of interacting causes and effects, or, more properly, with its concern with the specifically *social*, that is relational dynamics of social figurations. Elias's method does not lead to the insuperable methodological difficulties that Weber's approach entails.

13 A. Trollope, *British Sports and Pastimes*, London, 1868, pp. 6–7.

14 Cf. M. Marples, *A History of Football*, London, 1954.

15 I have called the late nineteenth-century British ruling class the 'public school elite' in order to signify the role of the public schools in unifying its established, landed and ascendant, bourgeois sections.

16 The Corinthians were an amateur team, formed towards the end of the nineteenth century and recruited from the public schools and the Universities of Oxford and Cambridge, who were able for a while to hold their own in competition with the professionals. They were a 'symptomatic exception' to the general trend towards exclusiveness on the part of the public school elite in the sense that they were deliberately formed to combat the growing success of professional teams and to celebrate and sustain the cherished amateur ideal. However, in adopting a non-local, non-institutionally specific pattern of recruitment, they incorporated one of the 'abuses' that were held by the proponents of the amateur ideal, to be destroyed by professionalism. That is, just like the professional teams

which were recruited on a national basis the Corinthians moved away from a pattern of sports representation in which locally and institutionally specific teams, recruited from 'communities' of various kinds, were held to be an essential characteristic of 'true' sport.

17   E. Durkheim, *The Division of Labour in Society*, New York, 1964.
18   *What is Sociology?*, pp. 63 f., 99 f.
19   See chapter 1 of this volume.
20   *The Elementary Forms of the Religious Life*, London, 1976.

8   SOCIAL BONDING AND VIOLENCE IN SPORT

1   This essay was previously published in Jeffrey H. Goldstein (ed.), *Sports Violence*, New York, 1983, under the title 'Social Bonding and Violence in Sport: A Theoretical-Empirical Analysis'. I am grateful to Johan Goudsblom for his helpful comments on an earlier version.
2   H. J. Eysenck and K. D. Nias, *Sex, Violence and the Media*, New York, 1978.
3   P. Marsh, *Aggro: the Illusion of Violence*, London, 1979.
4   A. Yiannakis, T. D. McIntyre, M. J. Melnick, and D. P. Hart (eds), *Sport Sociology: Contemporary Themes*, Dubuque, Iowa, 1976.
5   K. Weis, 'Role Models and the Social Learning of Violent Behaviour Patterns', *Proceedings of the International Congress of Physical Activity Sciences*, Quebec, 1976, pp. 511–24.
6   For this theory, see Norbert Elias, *The Civilizing Process*, Oxford, 1978; and *State Formation and Civilization*, Oxford, 1982.
7   L. Tiger, *Men in Groups*, London, 1969; R. Fox, 'The Inherent Rules of Fighting', in P. Collett (ed.), *Social Rules and Social Behaviour*, Oxford, 1977.
8   P. Marsh, E. Rosser and R. Harré, *The Rules of Disorder*, London, 1978.
9   R. Gardner and K. Heider, *Gardens of War*, Harmondsworth, 1974.
10   G. Owen, *The Description of Pembrokeshire*, in H. Owed (ed.), Cymmrodorion Society Research Series, no. 1, 1892, pp. 270–82. It was originally published in 1603.
11   Ibid.
12   Eric Dunning and Kenneth Sheard, *Barbarians, Gentlemen and Players*, Oxford, 1979.
13   D. Riesman and R. Denney, 'Football in America: a Study in Culture Diffusion', in Eric Dunning (ed.), *The Sociology of Sport: a Selection of Readings*, London, 1971.
14   J. Huizinga, *The Waning of the Middle Ages*, New York, 1924.
15   Marsh *et al.*, *The Rules of Disorder*.
16   Marsh, *Aggro*.
17   E. Bott, *Family and Social Network*, London, 1957; P. Wilmott and M. Young, *Family and Kinship in East London*, London, 1957; H. J. Parker, *View from the Boys*, Newton Abbott, 1974; P. Willis, *Profane Culture*, London, 1978.

9 SPECTATOR VIOLENCE AT FOOTBALL MATCHES

1 This paper is based on the 1984 Edward Glover Lecture given by Eric Dunning at the Royal Free Hospital, London. This series of annual lectures is organized by the Portman Clinic. We are grateful to Ilya Neustadt and Tim Newburn for their critical comments on an earlier draft of the paper.

2 See John Williams, Eric Dunning and Patrick Murphy, *Hooligans Abroad: the Behaviour and Control of English Fans in Continental Europe*, London, 1984; also *The Roots of Football Hooliganism: an Historical and Sociological Study*, London, forthcoming.

3 Paul Harrison, 'Soccer's Tribal Wars', *New Society*, 1974, vol. 29, p. 604.

4 See the discussion in Peter Marsh, Elizabeth Rosser and Rom Harré, *The Rules of Disorder*, London, 1978, pp. 70–2.

5 Simon Jacobson, 'Chelsea Rule – OK', *New Society*, 1975, vol. 31, pp. 780–3.

6 It is perhaps worth pointing out that football match duties provide the police with opportunities both for overtime earnings and for obtaining a welcome relief from normal routines. At football matches, too, not only the hooligans but also the police are provided with opportunities for 'action' in an exciting context. Moreover, on account of the opprobrium which football hooliganism has attracted, it is a context in which the strategies employed by the police seldom draw public criticism.

7 Ian Taylor, 'Football Mad: a Speculative Sociology of Football Hooliganism', in Eric Dunning (ed.), *The Sociology of Sport: a Selection of Readings*, London, 1971, pp. 352–7; see also his 'Soccer Consciousness and Soccer Hooliganism', in Stan Cohen (ed.), *Images of Deviance*, Harmondsworth, 1971, pp. 134–64.

8 John Clarke, 'Football and Working-Class Fans: Tradition and Change', in Roger Ingham (ed.), *Football Hooliganism: the Wider Context*, London, 1978, pp. 37–60.

9 Ibid., p. 51.

10 Stuart Hall, 'The Treatment of "Football Hooliganism" in the Press', in Ingham (ed.), *Football Hooliganism*, pp. 15–36.

11 See Stuart Hall *et al.*, *Policing the Crisis: Mugging, the State, and Law and Order*, London, 1978.

12 Ian Taylor, 'On the Sports Violence Question: Soccer Hooliganism Revisited', in Jennifer Hargreaves (ed.), *Sport, Culture and Ideology*, London, 1982, pp. 152–96; 'Class, Violence and Sport: the Case of Soccer Hooliganism in Britain', in Hart Cantelon and Richard S. Gruneau (eds), *Sport, Culture and the Modern State*, Toronto, 1982, pp. 39–93. David Robins and Philip Cohen recognize the intra-class conflict dimension to the problem when they write: 'The pathos and futility of fighting amongst rival groups of socially dispossessed youth is the best demonstration of the extent of the victory of those who really do hold the class power over them.' See their *Knuckle Sandwich: Growing Up in the Working Class City*, Harmondsworth, 1978, p. 151.

13   See Marsh *et al.*, *The Rules of Disorder*, p. 115 ff.

14   For a more detailed critique of the work of Marsh *et al.*, see Eric Dunning, Patrick Murphy and John Williams, 'Ordered Segmentation and the Sociogenesis of Football Hooligan Violence: a Critique of Marsh's "Ritualized Aggression" Hypothesis and the Outline of a Sociological Alternative', in Alan Tomlinson (ed.), *The Sociological Study of Sport: Configurational and Interpretive Studies*, Brighton, 1981, pp'. 36–52; see also Patrick Murphy and John Williams 'Football Hooliganism: an Illusion of Violence', unpublished paper, University of Leicester, 1980.

15   See Gerald Suttles, *The Social Order of the Slum: Ethnicity and Territory in the Inner City*, Chicago, 1968; and *The Social Construction of Communities*, Chicago, 1972.

16   J. A. Harrington, *Soccer Hooliganism*, Bristol, 1968, p. 25.

17   Eugene Trivizas, 'Offences and Offenders in Football Crowd Disorders', *British Journal of Criminology*, vol. 20, no. 3, 1980, p. 282.

18   Harrison, 'Soccer's Tribal Wars', p. 602.

19   Marsh *et al.*, *The Rules of Disorder*, p. 69.

20   *Oxford Mail*, 9 January 1981.

21   Suttles, *The Social Order of the Slum*, p. 10.

22   Ibid.

23   E. E. Evans-Pritchard, *The Nuer*, Oxford, 1940.

24   Robins and Cohen, *Knuckle Sandwich*, pp. 73 ff.

25   Harrison, 'Soccer's Tribal Wars'.

26   Robins and Cohen, *Knuckle Sandwich*, p. 77.

27   David Robins, *We Hate Humans*, Harmondsworth, 1984, p. 86.

28   Suttles, *The Social Order of the Slum*, p. 169.

29   See, eg., *ibid*, pp. 31–33. See also, Suttles, 1972, pp. 28–9.

30   Suttles, *The Social Order of the Slum*, pp. 176, 181 and 194.

31   The emergence of such a pattern probably depends in large part on the fact that, in common with children generally, lower working-class children have not yet had the chance to develop strong and stable internalized restraints over their emotions and are thus heavily dependent on external controls. Where these are restricted to specific contexts such as the home and discontinuous in their application, there are few checks on the aggressiveness and violence of children's interactions and hence on the emergence of dominance hierarchies of this kind. Such a tendency is liable to be compounded to the extent that violent forms of punishment are used by adults as a means of socialization, and to the extent that children regularly see adults acting aggressively, whether inside or outside the home.

32   Using the term introduced by Norbert Elias, one could say that they have a relatively high 'threshold of repugnance' (*Peinlichkeitsschwelle*) with regard to witnessing and taking part in violent acts. See, *The Civilizing Process*, Oxford, 1978; and *State Formation and Civilization*, Oxford, 1982.

33   See Paul Willis, *Profane Culture*, London, 1978, p. 29.

34   Howard J. Parker, *View from the Boys: a Sociology of Downtown Adolescents*, Newton Abbot, 1974, p. 35.

35 See, for example, Herbert J. Gans; 'Urbanism and Suburbanism as Ways of Life', in R. E. Pahl (ed.), *Readings in Urban Sociology*, pp. 95–118.

36 This may help, in part, to explain the appeal of the National Front and the British Movement to many of the members of such groups.

37 We are using the term 'civilized' here in the technical, relatively detached sense advocated by Norbert Elias. We do not mean to imply by it that members of the working class became somehow 'better' as a result of their incorporation or that their involvement in this process was somehow in their 'true interests' as a class. It is simply that the terms 'civilization' and 'incorporation' seem to us to be relatively object-adequate as means of conceptualizing a social process which, it seems reasonable to hypothesize, factually occurred.

38 *Liverpool Echo*, 1 April 1899.

39 *Glasgow Herald*, 19 April 1909 (paraphrased in John Hutchinson, 'Some Aspects of Football Crowds Before 1914', Proceedings of the Conference of the Society for the Study of Labour History, University of Sussex, 1975, paper no. 13, mimeo).

40 *Birmingham Post*, 14 October 1920.

41 *Leicester Mercury*, 19 March 1934.

42 For a more detailed exposition of our data on these trends, see Eric Dunning, Patrick Murphy and John Williams, *Working-Class Social Bonding and the Sociogenesis of Football Hooliganism*, End-of-Grant Report to the SSRC, 1982. See also our *The Roots of Football Hooliganism*, (forthcoming).

43 Since few historians and even fewer sociologists have studied the inter-war years, this analysis is inevitably highly speculative. It does receive a degree of support, however, from the pioneering work of James E. Cronin. See his *Labour and Society in Britain, 1918–1979*, London, 1984.

44 We do not have the space here to spell out what we take the complex, interactive relationships between poverty, unemployment and 'ordered segmentation' to be. It must be enough to say that part of the relationship, as we see it, consists in the probability that some unemployed youths from 'respectable' working class families will find aspects of the life-styles of their 'rough' counterparts, including taking part in football hooliganism, attractive.

45 *Leicester Mercury*, 10 February 1928.

46 This is to some extent an oversimplification for, as we shall show in *The Roots of Football Hooliganism: an Historical and Sociological Study*, (forthcoming), there was a slight tendency for concern over the behaviour of football crowds to grow as the 1930s came to a close.

47 *Sun*, 8 November 1965.

48 Stan Cohen, 'Campaigning Against Vandalism', in C. Ward (ed.), *Vandalism*, London, 1973, p. 232.

49 For a report on the 'macho' tendencies of the Metropolitan Police, see *Police and People in London*, Policy Studies Institute, London, 1983. The feature of such occupations that appears to be principally responsible for the production and reproduction of these forms of masculine identity

is the fact that, in them, ability to 'handle oneself' is an important occupational requirement.

10   SPORT AS A MALE PRESERVE

1   An earlier version of this paper was given at the Fourth Annual Confer-
    ence of the North American Society for the Sociology of Sport held in St
    Louis, Missouri, in October 1983. My thanks are due to my colleagues
    Clive Ashworth, Pat Murphy, Tim Newburn, Ivan Waddington and John
    Williams from whose critical comments I have benefited greatly.
2   Feminist writers, of course, have made a number of important advances in
    this regard but, on account of the strength of their ideological commit-
    ments, much of what they have written *appears* at least, even to many who
    sympathize with their cause, to be lacking in object-adequacy.
3   See *The Positive Philosophy of Auguste Comte*, translated and condensed
    by Harriet Martineau, London, 1853, pp. 134 ff. To be fair to Comte,
    whilst claiming that women are 'constitutionally in a state of perpetual
    infancy' and 'unfit . . . for the requisite continuousness and intensity of
    mental labour, either from the intrinsic weakness of [their] reason or from
    [their] more lively moral and physical sensibility', he also saw them as
    'spiritually' superior to men and hence as socially more important.
4   See, for example, the discussion in *Suicide*, London, 1952, pp. 384–6.
5   For a discussion of this issue, see Eric Dunning, 'Notes on Some Recent
    Contributions to the Sociology of Sport', *Theory, Culture and Society*,
    vol. 2, no. 1, 1983, pp. 135–42.
6   Exceptions are provided by Boutilier and San Giovanni in their, *The
    Sporting Woman*, Champaign, Illinois, 1983; and Jennifer Hargreaves,
    'Action Replay: Looking at Women in Sport', in Joy Holland (ed.),
    Feminist Action, London, 1984, pp. 125–46.
7   See, above all, *What is Sociology?*, London, 1978; *The Civilizing Process*,
    Oxford, 1978; *State Formation and Civilization*, Oxford, 1982; and *The
    Court Society*, Oxford, 1983.
8   See, for example, the argument put forward by Paul Willis in *Learning to
    Labour*, London, 1977.
9   This analysis is based on that in Eric Dunning and Kenneth Sheard,
    Barbarians, Gentlemen and Players, Oxford, 1979.
10 Ibid.
11 Anon., *The New Rugbeian*, vol. III, 1860; quoted in C. R. Evers, *Rugby*,
    London, 1939, p. 52.
12 Norbert Elias, 'The Genesis of Sport as a Sociological Problem', in E.
    Dunning (ed.), *The Sociology of Sport: a Selection of Readings*, London,
    1971. See also chapter 3 in the present volume.
13 From Elias's standpoint it is strictly speaking wrong to dichotomize 'inter-
    nal' and 'external' restraints. The terms he uses are 'Selbstzwänge' (self-
    constraints) and 'Fremdzwänge' ('other', literally 'stranger', constraints),

and he focuses in his analyses on the changing balance over time between them.

14 See Kenneth Sheard and Eric Dunning, 'The Rugby Football Club as a Type of Male Preserve: Some Sociological Notes', *International Review of Sport Sociology*, 5 (3), 1973, pp. 5–24.

15 The analysis presented here is based on that in, Eric Dunning, Patrick Murphy and John Williams, 'The Social Roots of Football Hooligan Violence', *Leisure Studies*, vol. 1, no. 2, 1982, pp. 139–56; see also 'If You Think You're Hard Enough', *New Society*, 27 August 1981; and *Hooligans Abroad: the Behaviour and Control of English Fans at Football Matches in Continental Europe*, London, 1984. See also chapter 9 in this volume.

16 Simon Jacobson, 'Chelsea Rule – OK', *New Society*, 1975, vol. 31, pp. 780–3.

17 'The Shed' is a stretch of covered terracing at Stamford Bridge, the ground of Chelsea FC.

18 'The Stretford End' is one of the goal-end terraces at Old Trafford, the ground of Manchester United. The 'Stretford-enders' were notorious for their hooligan exploits in the early and mid-1970s.

19 Gerald D. Suttles, *The Social Order of the Slum: Ethnicity and Territory in the Inner City*, Chicago, 1968.

20 Gerald D. Suttles, *The Social Construction of Communities*, Chicago, 1972.

Index